THE NEW CAMBRIDGE SHAKESPEARE

GENERAL EDITOR
Brian Gibbons

ASSOCIATE GENERAL EDITOR
A. R. Braunmuller, *University of California, Los Angeles*

From the publication of the first volumes in 1984 the General Editor of the New Cambridge Shakespeare was Philip Brockbank and the Associate General Editors were Brian Gibbons and Robin Hood. From 1990 to 1994 the General Editor was Brian Gibbons and the Associate General Editors were A. R. Braunmuller and Robin Hood.

THE WINTER'S TALE

The Winter's Tale is one of Shakespeare's most varied, theatrically self-conscious and emotionally wide-ranging plays. This edition provides a newly edited text, a comprehensive introduction that takes into account current critical thinking, and a detailed commentary on the play's language designed to make it easily accessible to contemporary readers. Much of the play's copiousness inheres in its generic intermingling of tragedy, comedy, romance, pastoral and the history play. In addition to dates and sources, the introduction attends to iterative patterns, the nature and cause of Leontes' jealousy, the staging and meaning of the bear episode and the thematic and structural implications of the figure of Time. Special attention is paid to the ending and its tempered happiness. Performance history is integrated throughout the introduction and commentary. Textual analysis, four appendices – including the theatrical practice of doubling and a select chronology of performance history – and a reading list complete the edition.

THE NEW CAMBRIDGE SHAKESPEARE

All's Well That Ends Well, edited by Russell Fraser
Antony and Cleopatra, edited by David Bevington
As You Like It, edited by Michael Hattaway
The Comedy of Errors, edited by T. S. Dorsch
Coriolanus, edited by Lee Bliss
Cymbeline, edited by Martin Butler
Hamlet, edited by Philip Edwards
Julius Caesar, edited by Marvin Spevack
King Edward III, edited by Giorgio Melchiori
The First Part of King Henry IV, edited by Herbert Weil and Judith Weil
The Second Part of King Henry IV, edited by Giorgio Melchiori
King Henry V, edited by Andrew Gurr
The First Part of King Henry VI, edited by Michael Hattaway
The Second Part of King Henry VI, edited by Michael Hattaway
The Third Part of King Henry VI, edited by Michael Hattaway
King Henry VIII, edited by John Margeson
King John, edited by L. A. Beaurline
The Tragedy of King Lear, edited by Jay L. Halio
King Richard II, edited by Andrew Gurr
King Richard III, edited by Janis Lull
Love's Labour's Lost, edited by William C. Carroll
Macbeth, edited by A. R. Braunmuller
Measure for Measure, edited by Brian Gibbons
The Merchant of Venice, edited by M. M. Mahood
The Merry Wives of Windsor, edited by David Crane
A Midsummer Night's Dream, edited by R. A. Foakes
Much Ado About Nothing, edited by F. H. Mares
Othello, edited by Norman Sanders
Pericles, edited by Doreen DelVecchio and Antony Hammond
The Poems, edited by John Roe
Romeo and Juliet, edited by G. Blakemore Evans
The Sonnets, edited by G. Blakemore Evans
The Taming of the Shrew, edited by Ann Thompson
The Tempest, edited by David Lindley
Timon of Athens, edited by Karl Klein
Titus Andronicus, edited by Alan Hughes
Troilus and Cressida, edited by Anthony B. Dawson
Twelfth Night, edited by Elizabeth Story Donno
The Two Gentlemen of Verona, edited by Kurt Schlueter
The Two Noble Kinsmen, edited by Robert Kean Turner and Patricia Tatspaugh
The Winter's Tale, edited by Susan Snyder and Deborah T. Curren-Aquino

THE EARLY QUARTOS
The First Quarto of Hamlet, edited by Kathleen O. Irace
The First Quarto of King Henry V, edited by Andrew Gurr
The First Quarto of King Lear, edited by Jay L. Halio
The First Quarto of King Richard III, edited by Peter Davison
The First Quarto of Othello, edited by Scott McMillin
The First Quarto of Romeo and Juliet, edited by Lukas Erne
The Taming of a Shrew: The 1594 Quarto, edited by Stephen Roy Miller

THE WINTER'S TALE

Edited by

SUSAN SNYDER

AND

DEBORAH T. CURREN-AQUINO

Folger Shakespeare Library

CAMBRIDGE
UNIVERSITY PRESS

CAMBRIDGE UNIVERSITY PRESS
Cambridge, New York, Melbourne, Madrid, Cape Town,
Singapore, São Paulo, Delhi, Tokyo, Mexico City

Cambridge University Press
The Edinburgh Building, Cambridge CB2 8RU, UK

Published in the United States of America by Cambridge University Press, New York

www.cambridge.org
Information on this title: www.cambridge.org/9780521293730

First published 2007
Reprinted 2012

Printed in the United Kingdom at the University Press, Cambridge

A catalogue record for this publication is available from the British Library

ISBN 13 978 0 521 22158 0 Hardback
ISBN 13 978 0 521 29373 0 Paperback

IN MEMORY OF SUSAN SNYDER

AND

WITH GRATITUDE TO ALL FROM WHOM WE HAVE LEARNED ALONG THE WAY

CONTENTS

ILLUSTRATIONS

Illustration 1 by permission of the Walters Art Museum; 2, 5, 12, and 26 by permission of Center Stage and the photographer, Richard Anderson; 3 by permission of the Shenandoah Shakespeare's American Shakespeare Center; 4, 11, 13, 15, 19, and 30 by permission of the Folger Shakespeare Library; 6, 10, and 29 by permission of the Shakespeare Centre Library, Stratford-upon-Avon; 7, 24, and 25 by permission of the Stratford Festival of Canada Archives; 8, 9, 18, 20, 21, and 23 by permission of The Shakespeare Theatre; 14 by permission of the Library of Congress; 16, 22, and 27 by permission of the photographer, Bengt Wanselius; 17 and 28 by permission of the Harvard Theatre Collection.

ACKNOWLEDGEMENTS

Originally this edition of *The Winter's Tale* was to have been edited solely by the eminent Susan Snyder. Serious illness, however, forced her to relinquish that role, but not before she completed the text, textual analysis, and basic draft of the collations. She also left behind a body of notes, which contained insightful observations and probing queries – no surprise to the many students of Shakespeare who have benefited from her splendid scholarship, whether in the classroom, conference lectures, publications, or, as was so often the case, brilliant conversations over tea. I was both honoured and humbled by her recommendation, followed by A. R. Braunmuller's gracious invitation, that I take over the edition. The opportunity to continue where she left off has allowed me to enter into a posthumous collaboration with someone whose ideas – shared generously in the months before she died and through the aforementioned notes – have greatly enhanced my own understanding of Shakespeare's vast romance. The introduction, textual note, textual commentary, supplementary notes, and appendixes fell to me; the collations, in the end, represent a joint venture. The text remains essentially Susan's, with some further stage directions and modifications. On the rare occasion where I have opted for a different emendation, Susan's has been cited in the commentary. Whatever in this edition might be considered most illuminating and truly fine in content and/or expression belongs to Susan and to the series' exemplary associate general editor, A. R. Braunmuller. His sharp eye and cogent criticism – always expressed with unfailing tact, encouragement, and good humour – have saved me from frequent embarrassment. Any errors, omissions, and infelicities of style that remain are my own.

All editions build on those that have come before and this volume is no exception. The commentary attests to my indebtedness to all who have richly dialogued with the play, especially H. H. Furness, J. H. P. Pafford, Ernest Schanzer, Stephen Orgel, Barbara Mowat and Paul Werstine. Since 1995 I have been privileged to assist Barbara and Paul on the New Folger Shakespeare editions and from them I have learned so much. I am also in their debt for the many times in which they directed me to materials that were proving recalcitrant to my own investigative skills, and for so graciously accommodating my deadlines in the midst of their own.

Special thanks to supportive colleagues and friends who, in addition to giving encouragement, have often generously shared ideas, observations, memories of productions seen, research, pre-published material, and actual publications: Peter W. M. Blayney, Joseph Candido, Ralph Cohen, E. Catherine Dunn, Charles Forker, R. C. Hood, Mary Ellen Lamb, Barbara Mowat, Gail Kern Paster, Catherine Shaw, Meredith Skura, Leslie Thomson, Virginia Vaughan, Paul Werstine and Douglas B. Wilson. Two individuals deserving special mention are Robert Turner and Patricia

Parker. Although Turner's wonderful variorum edition was published after the bulk of our own work was completed, both Susan and I benefited enormously from his kind sharing of textual commentary in manuscript form. Parker also shared with me not only crucial essays but also drafts of chapters for a forthcoming book on Shakespeare's language; her fine ear for homonymic patterns and keen insights into the play's emphasis on images of pregnancy and commerce have informed my own thinking in many instances. I would be remiss in not paying tribute to the scholarship and vision of June Schlueter and the late Jim Lusardi who in founding the *Shakespeare Bulletin* allowed me the opportunity to visit in the mind's eye numerous productions of *The Winter's Tale*, details of which have been incorporated throughout this edition.

To be able to work at the Folger Shakespeare Library and have the opportunity to call on the services of its superb staff is a scholar's dream which for me was an everyday reality. The words 'thank you' seem so inadequate when it comes to acknowledging Georgianna Ziegler, the immensely gifted reference librarian, who, on the rare occasion when she does not have an immediate answer to a vexing question, is relentless in finding it and pursuing all possible avenues of research. And then there is the amazing Betsy Walsh, head of reader services, and her terrific staff – especially LuEllen DeHaven, Rosalind Larry, Harold Batie, and Camille Seerattan – who are tirelessly committed to easing the scholar's work. I owe a great debt to Solvei Robertson and Rachel Kunkle, present and former members of the staff of the Academic Programs Division for extensive help with computer disks, pictures, and directory assistance. In an acute hour of need, Solvei, ever thoughtful and resourceful, really came through.

In the summer of 1998 I gave a week-long seminar on the play to the Benedictine Community of the Abbey of Regina Laudis, Bethlehem, CT. Many of my ideas enjoyed vigorous dialogue with the nuns, all of whom shared their enthusiasm for the play and insights born of their contemplative spirit. I am especially grateful to the late Lady Abbess Benedict Duss, Mother Abbess David Serna, Mother Prioress Dolores Hart, Mother Subprioress Maria Immaculata Matarese, and Mother Lucia Kuppens, a fellow Shakespearean whose love for the Bard has not abated in the years since she left academia for the cloister. Gardening with Mother Margaret Georgina Patton, tending sheep with Mother Jadwiga Makarewicz, and working with my many friends from the dairy barn enabled me to live the pastoral richness of the play in ways that I otherwise would never have experienced.

To see *The Winter's Tale* through the choice-making process of rehearsals and the continued fine-tuning of the actual run was my good fortune thanks to Michael Kahn who directed the play for the Shakespeare Theatre in Washington, D.C. in 2002. The opportunity to be present while director and actors wrestled with every word and line helped clarify the play's verbal and visual language in ways that inform both the introduction and textual commentary. I remain enormously appreciative of Michael and the entire company who warmly welcomed an academician into their midst, and to Dawn McAndrews of the theatre's education department for facilitating the arrangement. My conversations with Lise Bruneau (Hermione) and Tana Hicken (Paulina) were particularly helpful.

For the illustrations found in this volume, I am grateful to the following: first and foremost, Jean Miller, former art curator at the Folger whose memory bank of pictures is phenomenal; Julie Ainsworth and Bettina Smith of the Folger's photography department; Liz Stark and Lauren Beyea, public relations associates, the Shakespeare Theatre, Washington, D.C.; Ellen Charendoff, archives assistant, Stratford Festival of Canada Archives; Kate Lau of the Walters Art Museum; Katie Byrnes, company manager, and Richard Anderson, photographer, Center Stage; Helen Hargest and Sylvia Morris, the Shakespeare Centre Library, Stratford-upon-Avon; Lucien Riviere, press office, Royal Shakespeare Theatre; Deona Houff and Brian J. Ososky, marketing and public relations associates, Shenandoah Shakespeare's American Shakespeare Center; Irina Tarsis, curatorial assistant, Harvard Theatre Collection; Ulrika Nilsdotter Geiger, press manager, and Bengt Wanselius, photographer, Royal Dramatic Theatre of Sweden; Jennifer Lam, publicity staff, Brooklyn Academy of Music; and Elizabeth Wehrle, press manager, The Public Theater, New York Shakespeare Festival. My thanks also to Harry Regan for help with computer problems and for putting several photographs into electronic form.

I am deeply indebted to Cambridge University Press: to Brian Gibbons, the general editor for his faith and support from afar; to Sarah Stanton whose encouragement, patience, and consummate courtesy have been a constant blessing; and to the production editor, Alison Powell, and the copy-editor, Susan Beer, for improving every page.

Finally, eternal thanks to my second mother, Philomena Aquino, for her understanding and enthusiastic interest in the project, and to two individuals who have lived it with me on a daily basis and for whom I know these last few years have seemed like a never-ending winter's tale: my dear mother, Adelaide Curren, who never needs to be reminded to awake her faith and whose optimism, insights, and prayerful support are the kind that only a mother can offer; and my wonderful husband John Aquino, whose perceptive eye and ear know no limits, whose energy and tenacity in tracking down leads and rare publications never cease to amaze, and whose generosity of self and time is always demonstrated with infinite good cheer. To him, who forever 'makes a July's day short as December' and whose 'worth and honesty' could well 'be justified by . . . a pair of kings', I can now happily promise evening constitutionals in which the topic of conversation will be something other than *The Winter's Tale*. And last, but never least, to my father, Robert, grace and remembrance always.

Deborah T. Curren-Aquino

ABBREVIATIONS AND CONVENTIONS

Shakespeare's plays, when cited in this edition, are abbreviated in a style modified slightly from that used in the *Harvard Concordance to Shakespeare*. Other editions of Shakespeare are abbreviated under the editor's surname (Orgel, Schanzer) unless they are the work of more than one editor. In such cases, an abbreviated series name is used (Cam., Folger). When more than one edition by the same editor is cited, later editions are discriminated with a raised figure (Collier²). All quotations from Shakespeare, other than those from *The Winter's Tale*, use the lineation of *The Riverside Shakespeare*, under the textual editorship of G. Blakemore Evans.

1. Shakespeare's works

Ado	*Much Ado About Nothing*
Ant.	*Antony and Cleopatra*
AWW	*All's Well That Ends Well*
AYLI	*As You Like It*
Cor.	*Coriolanus*
Cym.	*Cymbeline*
Err.	*The Comedy of Errors*
Ham.	*Hamlet*
1H4	*The First Part of King Henry the Fourth*
2H4	*The Second Part of King Henry the Fourth*
H5	*King Henry the Fifth*
1H6	*The First Part of King Henry the Sixth*
2H6	*The Second Part of King Henry the Sixth*
3H6	*The Third Part of King Henry the Sixth*
H8	*King Henry the Eighth*
JC	*Julius Caesar*
John	*King John*
LLL	*Love's Labour's Lost*
Lear	*King Lear*
Luc.	*The Rape of Lucrece*
Mac.	*Macbeth*
MM	*Measure for Measure*
MND	*A Midsummer Night's Dream*
MV	*The Merchant of Venice*
Oth.	*Othello*
Per.	*Pericles*
PP	*The Passionate Pilgrim*
R2	*Richard the Second*
R3	*Richard the Third*
Rom.	*Romeo and Juliet*
Shr.	*The Taming of the Shrew*

Son.	*The Sonnets*
STM	*Sir Thomas More*
Temp.	*The Tempest*
TGV	*The Two Gentlemen of Verona*
Tim.	*Timon of Athens*
Tit.	*Titus Andronicus*
TN	*Twelfth Night*
TNK	*Two Noble Kinsmen*
Tro.	*Troilus and Cressida*
Ven.	*Venus and Adonis*
Wiv.	*The Merry Wives of Windsor*
WT	*The Winter's Tale*

2. Other works cited and general references

Works mentioned once in the Commentary, the Introduction, and the Appendices appear there with full bibliographical information; others are either cited by the shortened titles below or may be found in the Reading List. References to productions mentioned more than once appear under the director's surname (e.g., Howell, Noble); unless otherwise noted, all references to Kahn are to his 2002 revival. Theatre venues and companies are included below.

Abbott	E. A. Abbott, *A Shakespearian Grammar*, 3rd edn, 1870 (References are to numbered sections)
Adelman	Janet Adelman, *Suffocating Mothers: Fantasies of Maternal Origin in Shakespeare's Plays, Hamlet to the Tempest*, 1991
adj	adjective
adv	adverb
Alexander	*The Winter's Tale* in *William Shakespeare: The Complete Works*, ed. Peter Alexander, 1951
Alfreds	Mike Alfreds, Lyric Theatre, Hammersmith, 1997
Ames	Winthrop Ames, New Theatre, New York, 1910
Anderson	Mary Anderson, Lyceum, London, 1887
Andrews	*The Winter's Tale*, ed. John F. Andrews, Everyman Shakespeare, 1995
Andrews, *World*	John F. Andrews, ed. *William Shakespeare: His World, His Works, His Influence*, 3 vols., 1985
APT	American Players Theatre
Armstrong	Alan Armstrong, review of Syer's 1996 *WT*, *ShakB* 15.2 (1997), 30–32
BAM	Brooklyn Academy of Music
Barkan	Leonard Barkan, '"Living Sculptures": Ovid, Michaelangelo, and *The Winter's Tale*', *ELH* 48 (1981), 639–67
Barnet	Sylvan Barnet, '*The Winter's Tale* on the Stage' (in Kermode, 231–45)
Bartholomeusz	Dennis Bartholomeusz, *The Winter's Tale in Performance in England and America, 1611–1976*, 1982
Bate	Jonathan Bate, *Shakespeare and Ovid*, 1993
BCP	*Book of Common Prayer*

Bedford	Brian Bedford, Stratford Festival of Canada, Ontario, 1998
Belsey	Catherine Belsey, *Shakespeare and the Loss of Eden: The Construction of Family Values in Early Modern Culture*, 1999
Bennett	Kenneth Bennett, 'Reconstructing *The Winter's Tale*', *S. Sur.* 46 (1994), 81–90
Bergman	Ingmar Bergman, Royal Dramatic Theatre of Sweden, Stockholm, 1994 (on tour in the United States at BAM, 1995)
Berry	Ralph Berry, review of Phillips's 1978 *WT*, *SQ* 30 (1979), 168–70
Bethell	*The Winter's Tale*, ed. S. L. Bethell, New Clarendon Shakespeare, 1956
Bethell, *Study*	Samuel L. Bethell, *The Winter's Tale: A Study*, 1947
Bevington	*The Winter's Tale* in *The Complete Works of Shakespeare*, ed. David Bevington, 1980
Bevington, *Action*	David Bevington, *Action Is Eloquence: Shakespeare's Language of Gesture*, 1984
Biggins	Dennis Biggins, '"Exit pursued by a Beare": A Problem in *The Winter's Tale*', *SQ* 13 (1962), 3–13
Bishop	T. G. Bishop, *Shakespeare and the theatre of wonder*, 1996
Bloom	Harold Bloom, ed. *The Winter's Tale: Modern Critical Interpretations*, 1987
Bohnen	James Bohnen, APT, Spring Green, Wisc., 2000
Boorman	*The Winter's Tale*, ed. S. C. Boorman, English Literature Series, 1964
Brissenden	Alan Brissenden, *Shakespeare and the Dance*, 1981
Bristol	Michael D. Bristol, 'In Search of the Bear: Spatiotemporal Form and the Heterogeneity of Economies in *The Winter's Tale*', *SQ* 42 (1991), 145–67
Brook	Peter Brook, Phoenix Theatre, London, 1951
Bullough	Geoffrey Bullough, ed., *Narrative and Dramatic Sources of Shakespeare*, 8 vols., 1957–75 (8:113–233)
Burton	William Burton, Burton's Theatre, New York, 1856
Cahiers E	*Cahiers Elisabethans*
Cam.	*The Winter's Tale* in *The Works of William Shakespeare*, ed. W. G. Clark and W. A. Wright, 9 vols., Cambridge Shakespeare, 1891–3 (vol. 3)
Campbell	Douglas Campbell, Stratford Festival of Canada, Ontario, 1958
Capell	*The Winter's Tale* in *Mr William Shakespeare, his Comedies, Histories and Tragedies*, ed. Edward Capell, 10 vols., 1767–8 (vol. 4)
Capell, *Notes*	*Notes and Various Readings in Shakespeare*, 3 vols., 1779–83
Cavell	Stanley Cavell, 'Recounting Gains, Showing Losses (A Reading of *The Winter's Tale*)', in *Disowning Knowledge in Six Plays of Shakespeare*, 1987
Cercignani	F. Cercignani, *Shakespeare's Works and Elizabethan Pronunciation*, 1981
Chambers	E. K. Chambers, *William Shakespeare: A Study of Facts and Problems*, 2 vols., 1930

Charlton	*The Winter's Tale,* ed. H. B. Charlton, Arden Shakespeare, 1916
Coghill	Nevill Coghill, 'Six Points of Stage-Craft in *The Winter's Tale', S. Sur.* 11 (1958), 31–42
Cohen	Ralph Alan Cohen, Shenandoah Shakespeare's American Shakespeare Center, Blackfriars Theater, Staunton, VA, 2002
Cole	J. W. Cole, *The Life and Theatrical Times of Charles Kean F.S.A.*, 2 vols., 1859
Coleridge	*The Collected Works of Samuel Taylor Coleridge 5: Lectures 1808–19 on Literature,* ed. R. A. Foakes, Bollingen Series 75, 1987, 2 vols. (All references are to Lecture 4 in Coleridge's 1813 Lectures on Shakespeare.)
Collier	*The Winter's Tale* in *The Works of William Shakespeare,* ed. John P. Collier, 8 vols., 1842–4 (vol. 3)
Collier[2]	*The Winter's Tale* in *The Plays of Shakespeare*, ed. John P. Collier, 1853
Companion	*William Shakespeare: A Textual Companion,* Stanley Wells and Gary Taylor, with John Jowett and William Montgomery, *1997*
CompD	*Comparative Drama*
conj.	conjecture, conjectured by
Cowden-Clarke	*The Winter's Tale* in *The Works of William Shakespeare*, ed. Charles and Mary Cowden-Clarke, 3 vols., 1864–9 (vol. 1)
Craig	*Works of Shakespear*e, ed., William J. Craig, 1891
Dash	Irene Dash, 'A Penchant for Perdita on the Eighteenth-Century Stage', in *The Woman's Part: Feminist Criticism of Shakespeare,* ed. Carolyn Ruth Swift Lenz, Gayle Greene, and Carol Thomas Neely, 1980
J. Davis	Joel Davis, 'Paulina's Paint and the Dialectic of Masculine Desire in the *Metamorphoses, Pandosto*, and [*WT*]', *PLL* 39 (2003), 115–43
M. Davis	Montgomery Davis, WSF, 1997
De Grazia	Margreta De Grazia, 'Homonyms Before and After Lexical Standardization', *SJH* 1990, 143–56
Deighton	*The Winter's Tale*, ed. Kenneth Deighton, Deighton's Grey Cover Shakespeare, 1889
Dent	Robert W. Dent, *Shakespeare's Proverbial Language: An Index*, 1981 (references are to proverbs by letter and number)
Dessen	Alan Dessen, 'Massed Entries and Theatrical Options in *WT*,' *MRDE* 8 (1996), 119–27
Dessen-Thomson	Alan Dessen and Leslie Thomson, *A Dictionary of Stage Directions in English Drama, 1580–1642,* 1999
Dolan	*The Winter's Tale*, ed. Frances E. Dolan, Pelican Shakespeare, 1999
Donnellan	Declan Donnellan, Maly Drama Theatre, St Petersburg, 1997 (on tour in Plymouth, England, 1999)
Doran	Gregory Doran, RSC, Stratford-upon-Avon, 1999
Douce	*The Works of William Shakespeare,* ed. Francis Douce, 1807

Douce, *Illustrations*	Francis Douce, *Illustrations of Shakespeare, and of ancient manners with dissertations on the clowns and fools of Shakespeare*, 1807
Draper	R. P. Draper, *The Winter's Tale: Text and Performance*, 1985
Dunlop	Frank Dunlop, Cressida Productions/Warner Bros., 1968 film
Dyce	*The Winter's Tale* in *The Works of William Shakespeare*, ed. Alexander Dyce, 6 vols., 1857 (vol. 3)
Dyce[2]	*The Winter's Tale* in *The Works of William Shakespeare*, ed. Alexander Dyce, 9 vols., 1864–7 (vol. 3)
Dyce[3]	*The Winter's Tale* in *The Works of William Shakespeare*, ed. Alexander Dyce, 9 vols., 1875–6 (vol. 3)
Edelstein	Barry Edelstein, Classic Stage Co., New York, 2003
Eggert	Katherine Eggert, *Showing Like a Queen: Female Authority and Literary Experiment in Spenser, Shakespeare, and Milton*, 2000
ELH	*English Literary History*
ELN	*English Language Notes*
ELR	*English Literary Renaissance*
Enterline	Lynn Enterline, '"You speak a language that I understand not": The Rhetoric of Animation in [*WT*]', *SQ* 48 (1997), 17–44
Erickson	Peter Erickson, 'Patriarchal Structures in *The Winter's Tale*', *PMLA* 97 (1983), 819–29
ES	*English Studies*
Evans	Hugh Evans, OSF, Ashland, Ore., 1965
Ewbank	Inga-Stina Ewbank, 'From Narrative to Dramatic Language: *The Winter's Tale* and Its Source', in *Shakespeare and the Sense of Performance: Essays in the Tradition of Performance Criticism in Honor of Bernard Beckerman*, ed. Marvin Thompson and Ruth Thompson, 1989, pp. 29–47
Ewbank, 'Triumph'	Inga-Stina Ewbank, 'The Triumph of Time in *The Winter's Tale*', *Review of English Literature* 5 (1964), 83–100; rpt. in Hunt, 139–55
Eyre	Ronald Eyre, RSC, Stratford-upon-Avon, 1981
F	*Mr. William Shakespeares Comedies, Histories, and Tragedies*, 1623 (First Folio)
F2	*Mr. William Shakespeares Comedies, Histories, and Tragedies*, 1632 (Second Folio)
F3	*Mr. William Shakespear's Comedies, Histories, and Tragedies*, 1663–4 (Third Folio)
F4	*Mr. William Shakespear's Comedies, Histories, and Tragedies*, 1685 (Fourth Folio)
Faucit	Helena Faucit, Lady Martin, *On Some of Shakespeare's Female Characters*, 5th edition, 1893
Felperin	Howard Felperin, *Shakespearean Romance*, 1972
Felperin, 'Tongue-tied'	Howard Felperin, '"Tongue-tied Our Queen": The Deconstruction of Presence in *The Winter's Tale*', in *Shakespeare and the Question of Theory*, eds. Patricia Parker and Geoffrey Hartman, 1985, pp. 3–18

Fischer	Sandra Fischer, *Econolingua: A Glossary of Coins and Economic Language in Renaissance Drama*, 1985
Folger	*The Winter's Tale*, ed. Barbara Mowat and Paul Werstine, New Folger Library Shakespeare, 1998
Freeman	David Freeman, New Globe, London, 1997
Furness	*The Winter's Tale*, ed. H. H. Furness, The New Variorum Shakespeare, vol. 19, 1898
Gill	*The Winter's Tale*, ed. Roma Gill, Oxford School Shakespeare, 1996
Globe	*The Works of William Shakespeare*, ed. William Clark and W. H. Wright, The Globe Edition, 1864
Golding	Arthur Golding, trans., Ovid's *Metamorphoses*, 1567
Goodland	Katharine Goodland, review of Rowan's 2002 *WT*, *ShakB* 20.3 (2002), 20–1
Gourlay	Patricia Southard Gourlay. '"O My Most Sacred Lady": Female Metaphor in *The Winter's Tale*', *ELR* 5 (1975), 375–95; rpt. in Hunt, 258–79
Granville-Barker	Harley Granville-Barker, Savoy Theatre, London, 1912
Granville-Barker, 'Preface'	Harley Granville-Barker, 'Preface to *The Winter's Tale*', in *Prefaces to Shakespeare*, 1st series, 1927; rpt. in Hunt, 76–81
Greene	Robert Greene, *Pandosto*, 1588
Gurr	Andrew Gurr, 'The Bear, the Statue, and Hysteria in *The Winter's Tale*', *SQ* (1983), 420–25
E. Hall	Edward Hall, Propeller Company, Watermill Theatre (UK) and on tour in the United States, 2005
Hall	Peter Hall, Royal National Theatre, London, 1988
Hands	Terry Hands, RSC, Stratford-upon-Avon, 1986
Hanmer	*The Winter's Tale* in *The Works of Shakespeare*, ed. Thomas Hanmer, 6 vols., 1743–4 (vol. 2)
Happé	Peter Happé, *Notes on The Winter's Tale*, 1969
Heath	Benjamin Heath, *A Revisal of Shakespeare's Text*, 1765
Henley	Samuel Henley (comments in Steevens 1793)
H&S	*Ben Jonson*, edited by C. H. Herford and Percy and Evelyn Simpson, 11 vols., 1925–52 (vols. 2, 7 and 10)
Hinman	*The Norton Facsimile of the First Folio of Shakespeare*, prepared by Carlton Hinman (1968), 2nd edn, 1996 (with new introduction by Peter W. M. Blayney)
Hoeniger	F. David Hoeniger, *Medicine and Shakespeare in Renaissance England*, 1992
Holland	Peter Holland, review of Donnellan's 1999 *WT*, *TLS*, 21 May 1999
Honigmann	E. A. J. Honigmann, 'Re-enter the Stage Direction: Shakespeare and Some Contemporaries', *S. Sur.* 29 (1976), 117–25
Honigmann, 'Stability'	E. A. J. Honigmann, *The Stability of Shakespeare's Text*, 1965
Howard-Hill	T. H. Howard-Hill, *Ralph Crane and Some Shakespeare First Folio Comedies*, 1972
Howard-Hill, 'Editor'	T. H. Howard-Hill, 'Shakespeare's Earliest Editor, Ralph Crane,' *S. Sur.*44 (1991), 113–29

Howell	Jane Howell, BBC-Time Life, 1980 television film
Hudson	*The Winter's Tale* in *The Works of Shakespeare,* ed. H. N. Hudson, 11 vols., 1851–59 (vol. 4)
Hunt	Maurice Hunt, ed. *The Winter's Tale: Critical Essays,* 1995
Hunt, 'Bearing'	Maurice Hunt, '"Bearing Hence": Shakespeare's *The Winter's Tale*', *SEL* 44.2 (2004), 333–43
Hunter	R. G. Hunter, *Shakespeare and the Comedy of Forgiveness,* 1965
Hytner	Nicholas Hytner, Royal National Theatre, London, 2001
Hytner, 'Behold'	Nicholas Hytner, '"Behold the swelling scene": The theatrical consequence of Shakespeare's addiction to truth', *TLS,* 1 November 2002, 20–2
ISJR	*Iowa State Journal of Research*
Jackson	Russell Jackson, 'Shakespeare at Stratford-upon-Avon: Summer and Winter, 2002–2003', *SQ* 54 (2003), 167–85, esp. 174–6
Johnson	*The Winter's Tale* in *The Plays of William Shakespeare*, ed. Samuel Johnson, 8 vols., 1765 (vol. 2)
Joseph	Sister Miriam Joseph, *Shakespeare's Use of the Arts of Language*, 1947
Kahn (1975/76)	Michael Kahn, American Shakespeare Festival, Stratford, CT, 1975 (revived 1976)
Kahn (1987)	Michael Kahn, The Shakespeare Theatre, Washington, DC, 1987
Kahn (2002)	Michael Kahn, The Shakespeare Theatre, Washington, DC, 2002
Kean	Charles Kean, The Princess's Theatre, London, 1856
Keightley	*The Winter's Tale* in *The Plays of William Shakespeare*, ed. Thomas Keightley, 6 vols., 1864 (vol. 2)
Kellner	Leon Kellner, *Restoring Shakespeare: A Critical Analysis of the Misreadings in Shakespeare's Plays*, 1925
Kemble	John Philip Kemble, Drury Lane, London, 1802 (revived 1807 and 1811 at Covent Garden)
Kennedy	Dennis Kennedy, *Looking at Shakespeare: A Visual History of Twentieth-Century Performance*, 1993
Kermode	*The Winter's Tale,* ed. Frank Kermode, Signet Classic Shakespeare, 1988
Kittredge	*The Complete Works of Shakespeare*, ed. George Lyman Kittredge, 1936
Kittredge-Ribner	*The Complete Works of Shakespeare*, revised edn., ed. George Lyman Kittredge and Irving Ribner, 1971
Knight	*The Winter's Tale* in *The Pictorial Edition of the Works of Shakespeare,* ed. Charles Knight, 8 vols., 1839–43 (vol. 2)
Kökeritz	Helge Kökeritz, *Shakespeare's Pronunciation*, 1953
Kretzu	Jon Kretzu, Tygres Heart Shakespeare Company, Portland, OR, 1999
Kulick	Brian Kulick, NYSF, Central Park, New York, 2000
Jewett	Henry Jewett, Repertory Theatre, Boston, MA, 1929

Lamb	Mary Ellen Lamb, 'Engendering the Narrative Act: Old Wives' Tales in *The Winter's Tale, Macbeth*, and *The Tempest*', *Criticism* 40 (1998), 529–53
Lapine	James Lapine, NYSF, Public Theatre, New York, 1989
Lee	*The Winter's Tale* in *The Complete Works of William Shakespeare*, 40 vols., ed. Sidney Lee, University Press Shakespeare, 1907
Levith	Murray Levith, *What's in Shakespeare's Names*, 1978
Lewis	Irene Lewis, Center Stage, Baltimore, MD, 2002
Lithgow	William Lithgow, *The Totall Discourse of the Rare Aduentures and painefull Peregrinations of long nineteene Yeares Trauayles, from Scotland, to the most Famous Kingdomes in Europe, Asia, and Affrica* (1906 edn., Glasgow: J. MacLehose)
Macready	William Macready, Drury Lane, London, 1823; revived Covent Garden (1837); Drury Lane (1843)
Mahood	M. M. Mahood, *Bit Parts in Shakespeare's Plays*, 1992
Mahood, *Wordplay*	M. M. Mahood, *Shakespeare's Wordplay*, 1957
Malone	*The Winter's Tale* in *The Plays and Poems of William Shakespeare*, ed. Edmond Malone, 10 vols., 1790 (vol. 4)
Marrapodi	Michele Marrapodi, '"Of that fatal country": Sicily and the Rhetoric of Topography in *The Winter's Tale*', in *Shakespeare's Italy: Functions of Italian Locations in Renaissance Drama*, ed. Michele Marrapodi, A. J. Hoenselaars, Marcello Cappuzo, and Lino Falzon Santucci, 1993, 213–28
Mason	Monck Mason, *Comments on the Last Edition of Shakespeare's Plays* [the Johnson-Steevens 1778 edn], 1785
Matchett	William Matchett, 'Some Dramatic Techniques in *The Winter's Tale*', *S.Sur.* 22 (1969), 93–108
Maxwell	*The Winter's Tale*, ed. Baldwin Maxwell, in the Pelican *Complete Works of William Shakespeare*, gen. ed. Alfred Harbage, rev. edn, 1969
McDonald	Russ McDonald, 'Poetry and Plot in *The Winter's Tale*', *SQ* 36 (1985), 315–29; rpt. in Hunt, 298–318
McGuire	Philip McGuire, *Shakespeare: The Jacobean Plays*, 1994
Miola	Robert Miola, '"An Alien People Clutching Their Gods"? Shakespeare's Ancient Religions', *S. Sur.* 54 (2001), 31–45
MLR	*Modern Language Review*
Moorman	*The Winter's Tale*, ed. F. W. Moorman, Arden Shakespeare, 1912
Mowat	Barbara A. Mowat, '"What's in a Name": Tragicomedy, Romance, or Late Comedy,' in *A Companion to Shakespeare's Works*, 4 vols., ed. Richard Dutton and Jean Howard, 2004, 4: 129–49
Mowat, 'Rogues'	Barbara A. Mowat, 'Rogues, Shepherds, and the Counterfeit Distressed: Texts and Infracontexts in *The Winter's Tale*', *S. St.* 22 (1994), 58–76
MRDE	*Medieval and Renaissance Drama in England*
Muir and Schoenbaum	*A New Companion to Shakespeare Studies*, ed. Kenneth Muir and S. Schoenbaum, 1971

Mullin-Muriello	Michael Mullin and Karen M. Muriello, comps., *Stratford-upon-Avon: A Catalogue-Index to Productions of the Shakespeare Memorial/Royal Shakespeare Theatre, 1879–1978*, 2 vols., 1980
n	noun
n/nn	note/notes
National	Royal National Theatre, London
NCS	New Cambridge Shakespeare
Neely	Carol Thomas Neely, *Broken Nuptials in Shakespeare's Plays*, 1985
Neilson	*The Winter's Tale* in *The Complete Dramatic and Poetic Works of William Shakespeare*, ed. William A. Neilson, 1906
New Clar	New Clarendon edition
Newcomb	Lori Newcomb, review of Bohnen's 2000 *WT*, *ShakB* 18.4 (2000), 27–8
NJSF	New Jersey Shakespeare Festival
NS	New Shakespeare
Noble	Adrian Noble, RSC, Stratford-upon-Avon, 1992 (on tour in US 1994)
R. Noble	Richmond Noble, *Shakespeare's Biblical Knowledge and Use of the Book of Common Prayer*, 1935
R. Noble, *Song*	Richmond Noble, *Shakespeare's Use of Song with the Text of the Principal Songs*, 1923
Norton	*The Norton Shakespeare Based on the Oxford Edition*, ed. Stephen Greenblatt, Walter Cohen, Jean E. Howard, and Katherine Eisaman Maus, 1997
N&Q	*Notes and Queries*
Nunn	Trevor Nunn, RSC, Stratford-upon-Avon, 1969
Nunn/Barton	Trevor Nunn/John Barton, RSC, Stratford-upon-Avon, 1976
Nuttall	A. D. Nuttall, '*The Winter's Tale*: Ovid Transformed', in *Shakespeare's Ovid: The Metamorphoses in the Plays and Poems*, ed. A. B. Taylor, 2000, 135–49
NYSF	New York Shakespeare Festival
OED	*Oxford English Dictionary*, 2nd edn, 1989
Onions	C. T. Onions, *A Shakespeare Glossary*, 1911, rev. edn, 1953
Orgel	*The Winter's Tale*, ed. Stephen Orgel, Oxford Shakespeare, 1996
Orgel, 'Perspective.'	Stephen Orgel, '*The Winter's Tale:* A Modern Perspective,' in Folger
Orgel, 'Poetics'	Stephen Orgel, 'The Poetics of Incomprehensibility', *SQ* 42 (1991), 431-7
Orgel, 'Ideal'	Stephen Orgel, 'The Pornographic Ideal', in *Imagining Shakespeare: A History of the Texts and Visions*, 2003, 112–44
OSF	Oregon Shakespeare Festival
Overton	Bill Overton, *The Winter's Tale* (The Critics Debate), 1989
Ovid	Ovid, *Metamorphoses*, trans. Arthur Golding, 1567
Oxford	William Shakespeare: *The Complete Works*, ed. Stanley Wells, Gary Taylor, John Jowett, and William Montgomery, 1986

Pafford	*The Winter's Tale*, ed. J. H. P. Pafford, Arden Shakespeare, 1963
Pandosto	Robert Greene, *Pandosto: The Triumph of Time*, 1588 (rpt. in Bullough, 8: 157–99)
PLL	*Papers in Language and Literature*
Partridge	Eric Partridge, *Shakespeare's Bawdy*, rev. edn, 1969
Parker	Patricia Parker, 'Sound Government, Polymorphic Bears: *The Winter's Tale* and Other Metamorphoses of Eye and Ear', in *The Wordsworthian Enlightenment: Romantic Poetry and the Ecology of Reading*, ed. Helen Regueiro Elam and Frances Ferguson, 2005, 172–90
Parker, 'Promissory Economies'	Patricia Parker, 'Temporal Gestation, Legal Contracts, and the Promissory Economies of *The Winter's Tale*', in *Women, Property, and the Letters of the Law in Early Modern England*, ed. Nancy E. Wright, Margaret W. Ferguson, and A. R. Buck, 2004, 26–49.
Parry	*The Winter's Tale*, ed. Christopher Parry, Macmillan Students' Shakespeare, 1982
Paster	Gail Kern Paster, *The Body Embarrassed: Drama and the Disciplines of Shame in Early Modern England*, 1993
PBSA	*Papers of the Bibliographical Society of America*
Phillips	Robin Phillips and Peter Moss, Stratford Festival of Canada, Ontario, 1978
Pierce	*The Winter's Tale*, ed. Frederick Pierce, Yale Shakespeare, 1918
Pitcher	John Pitcher, '"Fronted with the Sight of a Bear": *Cox of Collumpton* and *The Winter's Tale*', *N&Q* 41ns (1994), 47–53
Plutarch	*The Philosophie, commonlie called, The Morals written by the learned Philospher Plutarch* . . . translated out of Greeke into English . . . by Philemon Holland, 1603
PMLA	*Publications of the Modern Language Association*
Pope	*The Winter's Tale* in *The Works of Shakespeare*, ed. Alexander Pope, 6 vols., 1723–5 (vol. 2)
Pope[2]	*The Winter's Tale* in *The Works of Shakespeare*, ed. Alexander Pope, 8 vols., 1728 (vol. 3)
PQ	*Philological Quarterly*
Proudfoot	Richard Proudfoot, 'Verbal Reminiscence and the Two-part Structure of *The Winter's Tale*', *S. Sur.* 29 (1976), 67–78; rpt. in Hunt, 280–97
Pyle	Fitzroy Pyle, '*The Winter's Tale*': *A Commentary on the Structure*, 1969
Ranald	Margaret Loftus Ranald, review of Noble's 1994 *WT*, *ShakB* 12.3 (1994), 13–14
Rann	*The Winter's Tale* in *Dramatic Works of William Shakespeare*, ed. Joseph Rann, 6 vols., 1786–94 (vol. 2)
Ravelhofer	Barbara Ravelhofer, '"Beasts of Recreacion": Henslowe's White Bears', *ELR* 32 (2002), 287–323
RD	*Renaissance Drama*

RDTS	Royal Dramatic Theatre of Sweden
Reed	*The Winter's Tale* in *The Plays of William Shakespeare*, ed. Isaac Reed, 21 vols., 1803 (vol. 9)
Reinhardt	Max Reinhardt, Deutsches Theatre, Berlin, 1906
Richards	Jennifer Richards, 'Social Decorum in *The Winter's Tale*', in *Shakespeare's Late Plays: New Readings*, ed. Jennifer Richards and James Knowles, 1999, pp. 75–91
Ringler	William Ringler, Jr., 'The Number of Actors in Shakespeare's Early Plays', in *The Seventeenth-Century Stage: A Collection of Critical Essays*, ed. G. E. Bentley, 1968, pp. 110–34
Ritson	J. Ritson, *Cursory criticisms on the edition of Shakespeare published by Edmond Malone*, 1792
Riverside	*The Riverside Shakespeare*, textual ed. G. Blakemore Evans, 1974
Rolfe	*The Winter's Tale,* ed. W. J. Rolfe, English Classics, 1879
Rowan	Tom Rowan, Theater Ten Ten at Theater Ten Ten, New York, 2002
Rowe	*The Winter's Tale* in *The Works of Mr William Shakespear,* ed. Nicholas Rowe, 6 vols., 1709 (vol. 2)
Rowe^2	*The Winter's Tale* in *The Works of Mr William Shakespear,* ed. Nicholas Rowe, 2nd edn, 6 vols., c. 1709
Rowe^3	*The Winter's Tale* in *The Works of Mr William Shakespear,* ed. Nicholas Rowe, 8 vols., 1714 (vol. 3)
RSC	Royal Shakespeare Company
Sanders	Wilbur Sanders, *The Winter's Tale* (Twayne's New Critical Introductions to Shakespeare), 1987
SB	*Studies in Bibliography*
Schalkwyk	David Schalkwyk, '"A Lady's 'Verily' Is as Potent as a Lord's": Women, Word, and Witchcraft in *The Winter's Tale*', *ELR* 22 (1992), 242–72
Schanzer	*The Winter's Tale*, ed. Ernest Schanzer, New Penguin Shakespeare, 1969
Schlegel-Tieck	*The Winter's Tale* in *Shakespeares Dramatische Werke,* ed. August Wilhelm Schlegel and Ludwig Tieck, 9 vols., 1825–1833 (vol. 8)
Schmidt	Alexander Schmidt, *Shakespeare Lexicon*, 2 vols., 3rd edn, revised and enlarged by Gregor Sarrazin, 1968
SD	stage direction
SH	speech heading
Shaheen	Naseeb Shaheen, *Biblical References in Shakespeare's Plays*, 1999
ShakB	*Shakespeare Bulletin*
Sh. Theatre	Shakespeare Theatre, Washington, DC
Shurgot, 'Kretzu'	Michael Shurgot, review of Kretzu's 1999 *WT*, *ShakB* 17.3 (1999), 27
Shurgot, 'Whitney'	Michael Shurgot, review of Whitney's 2001 *WT*, *ShakB* 19.4 (2001), 35–6

SJH	*Shakespeare-Jahrbuch* (Bochum)
sig., sigs.	signature(s) (printers' indications of the ordering of pages in early modern books, often more accurate than page numbers)
Siemon	James Edward Siemon, '"But It Appears She Lives": Iteration *in The Winter's Tale*', *PMLA* 89 (1974), 10–16; rpt. in Bloom, 47–58
Sisson	C. J. Sisson, *New Readings in Shakespeare,* 1956
Smallwood	Robert Smallwood, 'Shakespeare at Stratford-upon-Avon, 1992', *SQ* 44 (1993), 343–62
Smallwood, 'Performances'	Robert Smallwood, 'Shakespeare Performances in England,' *S. Sur.* 5 (2000), 244–73
Smallwood, *Players*	*Players of Shakespeare 4: Further Essays in Shakespearian Performance by Players with the Royal Shakespeare Company,* ed. Robert Smallwood, 1998
Smith	Bruce Smith, 'Sermons in Stone: Shakespeare and Renaissance Sculpture', *S.St.* 17 (1985), 1–23
P. Smith	Peter Smith, review of Donnellan's 1999 *WT, Cahiers E* 56 (Oct. 1999), 102–5
SN	*Shakespeare Newsletter*
Snyder	Susan Snyder, 'Mamillius and Gender Polarization in *The Winter's Tale*', *SQ* 50 (1999), 1–8
Snyder, *Journey*	Susan Snyder, *Shakespeare: A Wayward Journey*, 2002 (includes 'Memorial Art in *The Winter's Tale* and Elsewhere: "I will kill thee/And love thee after"' [197–209] and '*The Winter's Tale* Before and After' [221–33])
Sokol	B. J. Sokol, *Art and Illusion in the Winter's Tale,* 1994
Sokol, *Dictionary*	B. J. Sokol and Mary Sokol, *Shakespeare's Legal Language: A Dictionary,* 2000
Sokolov	Stanislav Sokolov, Animated Shakespeare series, *WT* broadcast BBC2, 7 December 1994
Sorrell	Walter Sorrell, 'Shakespeare and the Dance', *SQ* 8 (1957), 367–84
Spevack	Marvin Spevack, *A Complete and Systematic Concordance to the Works of Shakespeare*, 9 vols., 1968–80, vol. 1
SoRA	*Southern Review: An Australian Journal of Literary Studies* (Adelaide)
SQ	*Shakespeare Quarterly*
S. St.	*Shakespeare Studies*
S. Sur.	*Shakespeare Survey*
Stanley	Audrey Stanley, OSF, Ashland, OR, 1975
Staunton	*The Winter's Tale* in *The Plays of Shakespeare,* ed. Howard Staunton, 3 vols., 1858–60 (vol. 3)
Steevens	*The Winter's Tale* in *The Plays of William Shakespeare,* ed. George Steevens and Isaac Reed, 15 vols., 1793 (vol. 7)
subst.	substantively
Syer	Fontaine Syer, OSF, Ashland, OR, 1996
Theobald	*The Winter's Tale* in *The Works of Shakespeare*, ed. Lewis Theobald, 7 vols., 1733 (vol. 3)

Thirlby	Styan Thirlby, unpublished conjectures recorded as manuscript annotations in his copies of contemporary editions (as cited in Turner)
Tilley	M. P. Tilley, *A Dictionary of the Proverbs in England in the Sixteenth and Seventeenth Century*, 1950
Timpane	John Timpane, review of Wentworth's 1996 *WT*, *ShakB* 15.2 (1997), 18–19
TLN	Through line numbering (in Hinman facsimile)
TLS	*Times Literary Supplement*
Traub	Valerie Traub, *Desire and Anxiety: Circulations of Sexuality in Shakespearean Drama*, 1992
Tree	Herbert Beerbohm Tree, His Majesty's Theatre, London, 1906–7
Trewin	J. C. Trewin, *Going to Shakespeare*, 1978
Turner	*The Winter's Tale*, ed. Robert Kean Turner and Virginia Westling Haas, New Variorum Edition of Shakespeare, 2005
UTQ	*University of Toronto Quarterly*
v	verb
Vickers	Brian Vickers, *The Artistry of Shakespeare's Prose*, 1968
Viswanathan	S. Viswanathan, 'Theatricality and Mimesis in *The Winter's Tale*: The Instance of "Taking by the Hand"', in *Shakespeare in India*, ed. S. Nagarajan and S. Viswanathan, 1987, 42–52
Walker	W. S. Walker, *Critical Examination of the Text of Shakespeare*, 3 vols., 1860
Warburton	*The Winter's Tale* in *The Works of Shakspear*, ed. William Warburton, 8 vols., 1747 (vol. 3)
Warchus	Matthew Warchus, RSC, Stratford-upon-Avon, 2002–3
Ward, 'Bedford'	Royal Ward, review of Bedford's 1998 *WT*, *ShakB* 17.2 (1999), 38–40
Ward, 'Davis'	Royal Ward, review of Davis's 1997 *WT*, *ShakB* 15.3 (1997), 27–29
Warren	Roger Warren, *Staging Shakespeare's Late Plays*, 1990
Wells	Stanley Wells, 'Performances in England, 1987–8', *S.Sur.* 42 (1990), 129–48
Wentworth	Scott Wentworth, NJSF, Madison, NJ, 1996
Wexler	Joyce Wexler, 'A Wife Lost and/or Found', *The Upstart Crow* 8 (1988), 106–17
White	*The Winter's Tale* in *The Works of Shakespeare*, ed. Richard Grant White, 12 vols., 1857–66 (vol. 5)
$White^2$	*The Winter's Tale* in *William Shakespeare: Comedies, Histories, Tragedies, and Poems*, ed. Richard Grant White, 3 vols., 1883 (vol.2)
Whitney	Scott Whitney, Harlequin Productions, Olympia, WA, 2001
William	David William, Stratford Festival of Canada, Ontario, Canada, 1986
Williams	Gordon Williams, *A Dictionary of Sexual Language and Imagery in Shakespearean and Stuart Literature*, 3 vols., 1994
H. Williams	Harcourt Williams, Old Vic, London, 1933
D. Wilson	Douglas B. Wilson, 'Euripides' *Alcestis* and the Ending of Shakespeare's *The Winter's Tale*,' *ISJR* 58 (1984), 345–55

Wilson	*The Winter's Tale*, ed. John Dover Wilson and Arthur Quiller-Couch, New Shakespeare, 1931
Wood	Peter Wood, Shakespeare Memorial Theatre, Stratford-upon-Avon, 1960
Wright	George T. Wright, *Shakespeare's Metrical Art*, 1988
WSF	Wisconsin Shakespeare Festival
WVUPP	*West Virginia University Philological Papers*

Unless otherwise noted, all biblical references are keyed to the Geneva version, 1560, and all references to Ovid's *Metamorphoses* are taken from Arthur Golding's 1567 translation. Where titles and excerpts from early modern works appear (e.g., *Pandosto* in Bullough), the original spelling (e.g. u/v, i/j) and punctuation, unless otherwise noted, have been preserved.

INTRODUCTION

> [I] would love to see a rep company do *The Winter's Tale* and *King Lear* together, same actors, same costumes, because I think Shakespeare wrote *The Winter's Tale* to answer *King Lear*'s tragedy with hope. The crucial difference between Leontes and Lear is that Leontes lives to regret and rethink his early selfish definition of love . . . and to accept the miracle of Hermione's revival. The play redefines love as a miracle and a gift, which, once accepted, allows all things, not only reappearances and resurrections, but even total forgiveness.[1]

Love, miracle, gift, resurrection, forgiveness. In three sentences, Jane Smiley, the author of *A Thousand Acres*, the 1991 novel derived from *King Lear*, provides a snapshot of key issues and themes that have dominated the critical and performance afterlife of *The Winter's Tale*, a late play and one of Shakespeare's most theatrically self-conscious and emotionally exhausting. To say that Leontes lives to regret and rethink his earlier selfishness is to address the question of genre and the concept of time that determines in no small measure the narrative and affective contours of each generic type.[2] The proverbial wheel of fortune is allowed in the later text to enter into a new, upward phase, compatible with hope. Leontes has time to get it right – not perfect but certainly better – and to enjoy the fruits of a long and painful journey of self-discovery, something denied Lear. The description of *The Winter's Tale* as the hopeful complement to Shakespeare's great tragedy acknowledges a practice not uncommon among artists, particularly those who leave behind sizeable bodies of work: i.e., the revisiting of themes, situations, and characters explored earlier, the rewrite often appearing more mellow and benign.

The most significant connection between the two dramas, however, may be the one that Smiley only hints at, namely, the sheer 'bigness' of each, or, copiousness.[3] *Lear* features a cosmic storm; *The Winter's Tale* emphasizes that most cosmic of themes, time. In Shakespeare's only tragedy with a fully developed subplot, there are, as critics often point out, two of almost everything,[4] and all expressed in a language

[1] Jane Smiley, 'Taking it all Back', Book World, *Washington Post* (21 June 1998), 8. For a helpful discussion of the kinship between the two plays, see chapters 3 and 4 in David Young, *The Heart's Forest: A Study of Shakespeare's Pastoral Plays*, 1972.

[2] David Scott Kastan provides a thoughtful analysis of the interplay between genre and time in *Shakespeare and the Shapes of Time*, 1982.

[3] The early modern literary ideal of abundance is articulated in Erasmus' *De Copia* (1511), required reading in Elizabethan grammar schools. For a brief but excellent treatment of the topic, see chapter 2, 'Eloquence and Copy', in Madeleine Doran's still indispensable *Endeavours of Art: A Study of Form in Elizabethan Drama*, 1954, esp. 46–52.

[4] E.g., two unfilial daughters, two eyes plucked out, two suitors of Cordelia, two adulterous (in thought, if not in deed) relationships, and two cases of madness (one real, the other feigned).

marked by a preponderance of hyphenated words and the 'out' prefix as though to say that one word alone will not do to express the old king's folly and what he suffers as a consequence. Similarly,[5] *The Winter's Tale* – framed by the words 'vast' (1.1.25) and 'wide gap' (5.3.154), informed by 'a deal of wonder' (5.2.20), and marked by a style given to extensive hyperbole and syntactic amplification – requires a stretching of the imagination. The play's governing aesthetic of multiplicity is evident in the tripartite spatial movement from Sicilia to Bohemia and back to Sicilia, in the temporal passage of sixteen years at the beginning of Act 4, and in the separate plot lines involving the triangle of Leontes, Hermione, and Polixenes, the young love of Perdita and Florizel, and the antics of Autolycus.

The critical commentary that follows is intended to guide the reader through the labyrinthine ways of *The Winter's Tale* without presuming to exhaust the vastness and wonder essential to its 'winter's-taleness'. After an initial focus on genre, title, and iterative patterns, I turn to specific elements such as Leontes' jealousy, the bear episode, the figure of Time, the meaning(s) of Act 5, and the play's sense of an ending. Informing much of the selection of topics is Nevill Coghill's now classic essay defending the play against the charge of 'creaking dramaturgy'.[6] The points Coghill raises are especially useful because they encourage a dovetailing of literary analysis and performance history, thus demonstrating the now widely accepted symbiotic relationship between Shakespeare in the study and Shakespeare on the stage. Sections on the play's date and sources round out the introduction.

Genre and title

[*The Winter's Tale*] is a fairy tale – it is fact. It is romantic – it is realistic. It is tragic – it is comic. It is Christian – it is pagan. It is harsh and crabbed – it is simple and idyllic. It is this – it is that. It is a welter of anachronisms. Its geography is in spots fantastic. It has not only gods, but a bear, a storm, and a yacht, from the machine.[7]

Harold Goddard's description of the play's heterogeneity, cited here, implicitly raises the genre question: What exactly do we call *The Winter's Tale*? Judging from the classification assigned in the First Folio, Shakespeare's contemporaries saw it as a comedy, perhaps primarily because of an ending celebratory of spousal reunion (Leontes and Hermione) and of the pending nuptials of one young couple (Florizel and Perdita) and one not so young (Camillo and Paulina). Some critics continue to favour the rubric of comedy but with various modifiers to indicate a subgenre. The least helpful, though possibly the safest, is something along the lines of 'late comedy', suggesting only a chronological difference from what came before. R. G. Hunter's choice, 'comedy of forgiveness', is more attractive because it recognizes comic conventions but specifies a moral, even spiritual, meaning that distinguishes *The Winter's Tale* from earlier comedies like *The Comedy of Errors*, *The Taming of the Shrew*, and *A Midsummer Night's Dream*. That difference, however, is arguably

[5] Felperin (212) argues for even more amplitude and variety than that found in *Lear*.
[6] See Coghill.
[7] Harold C. Goddard, *The Meaning of Shakespeare*, 2 vols., 1951, 2:263.

one of kind, thereby militating against facile sub-genre status.[8] The story itself is filled with events not typically found in comic works (e.g., the sudden death of a child and the fatal savaging of a man by a bear); likewise, the value system of the first three acts and the fifth extends beyond the social concerns that are the usual purview of comedy to include the ethical and metaphysical assumptions informing tragedy. Such factors, among others, may be responsible for the rivalry between two terms that for over a century have vied for preeminence in the matter of the play's classification: romance and tragicomedy.[9]

ROMANCE, TRAGICOMEDY, TRAGICOMIC ROMANCE

In the late nineteenth century Edward Dowden became the first to classify *The Winter's Tale* and those final plays usually grouped with it (*Pericles*, *Cymbeline*, and *The Tempest*) as romances.[10] What Dowden seems to have had in mind were stories of exotic adventure and travel, shipwrecks, spiritual and/or moral quests, romantic love, reunions of lovers and families long separated, virtue tested and proved triumphant, and nobility hidden and then discovered – all unfolding in a world familiar with supernatural forces, wide-ranging marvels, magic, and enchantment. This romance tradition, primarily available to Shakespeare in narrative form,[11] also included the dramatic as in the medieval saint's play of trial and conversion, a genre replete with one marvel after another.[12] If Shakespeare's final dramas are understood as spiritual journeys ending in self-discovery by the central character,[13] then the saint's play (or miracle play, as it is sometimes called), 'popularly performed late

8 According to the comic *modus operandi*, one does not forgive so much as forget and let bygones be bygones; the Shakespearean comic paradigm is *MND*. In *WT*, the moral imperative is to remember, so as to make forgiveness not only possible but real (see pp. 56, 60–1).

9 In what follows, I draw heavily on the first chapter in Felperin and on the cogent analysis of the naming problem in Mowat.

10 Dowden discerned a common 'romantic incident of lost children recovered by those to whom they are dear', 'romantic' settings of mountains and seas, and perhaps, most important, 'a grave beauty, a sweet serenity, which seem to render the name "comedies" inappropriate' (*Shakspere*, 1877, 55–6).

11 See, e.g., the Greek *Daphnis and Chloe*, classical and medieval versions of the Apollonius of Tyre story, Malory's tales of King Arthur and his knights, Sir Philip Sidney's *Arcadia*, Edmund Spenser's *The Faerie Queene*, and Thomas Lodge's *Rosalynde*.

12 Assuming particular relevance for *Per.* and *WT*, the Digby *Mary Magdalene* (1480–90) features maritime journeys, marital separation, the birth of a baby in the midst of a storm, a wife's apparent death and her miraculous recovery courtesy of Mary's intervention, and a final reunion of husband and wife. Although not extant in English, the saint's play dramatizing the legend of the sixth century cleric Theophilus, a precursor of Faust, may hold analogic value among the intertextual materials surrounding *WT*, especially for the final scene in which a 'statue' comes alive. In Rutebeuf's *Le Miracle de Theophile* (c 1270) – discussed in Robert G. Hunter, *Shakespeare and the Mystery of God's Judgments*, 1976, 20–5 – a statue of the Virgin Mary becomes animated as she takes pity on the repentant sinner praying before her, eventually returning to him in the chapel with the contract she successfully wrestles from Satan. Marina Warner (*Alone of All Her Sex: The Myth and the Cult of the Virgin Mary*, 1976, 323) and Émile Mâle (*The Gothic Image: Religious Art in France in the Thirteenth Century*, 1958, 260) address the popularity of the legend in both literature and the visual arts. See illustration 1, p. 4.

13 Warren, *Staging*, 239. He came to this view as a result of watching the rehearsal process of Peter Hall's 'romance' marathon at The National Theatre in London in 1988.

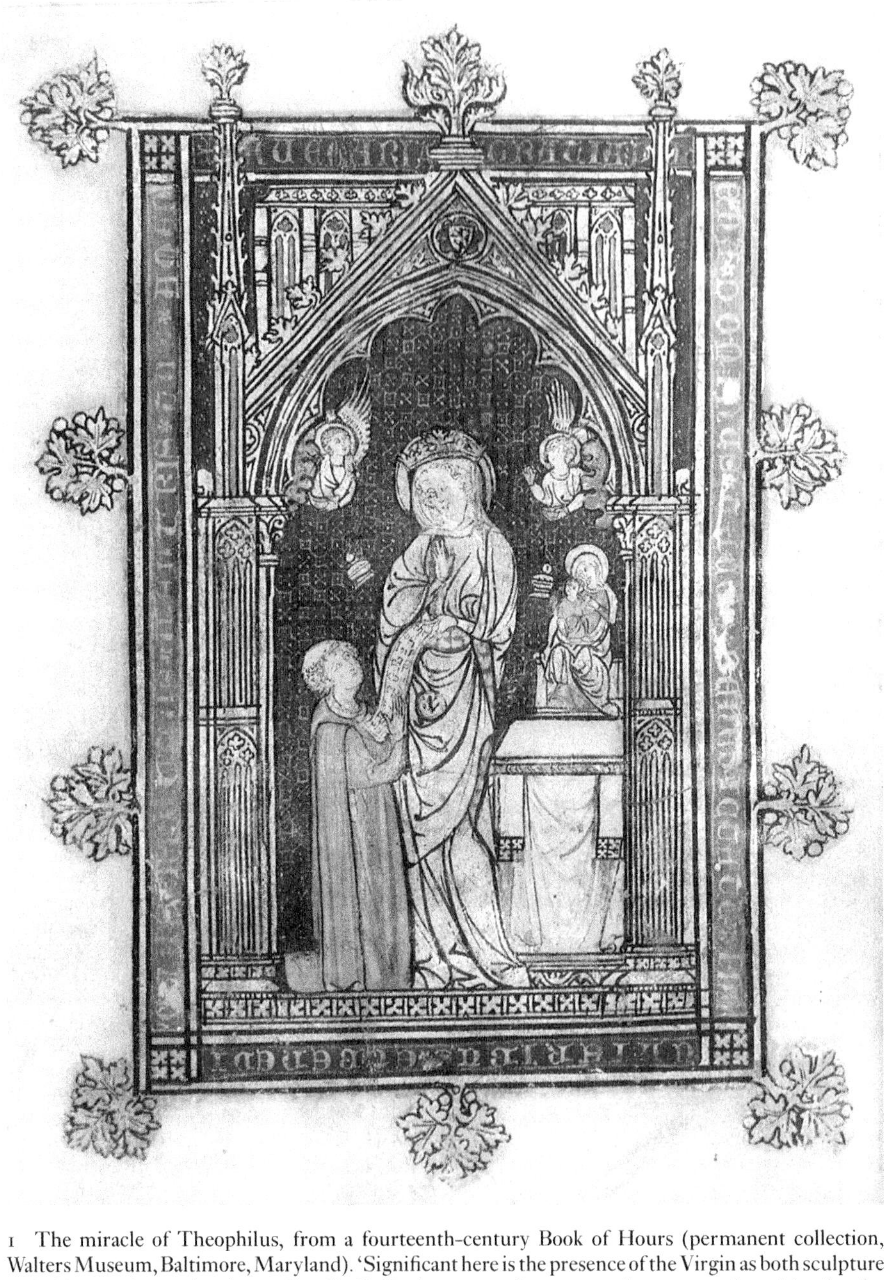

1 The miracle of Theophilus, from a fourteenth-century Book of Hours (permanent collection, Walters Museum, Baltimore, Maryland). 'Significant here is the presence of the Virgin as both sculpture and vision, underscoring the medieval belief in the power of prayer to gain access to the spiritual realm represented by the image' (from the leaflet guide to the exhibit 'Images of Devotion: Personal Piety in Medieval Manuscripts and Ivories', Walters Museum, 1999).

into the sixteenth century above and beyond the biblical mystery cycles' (Felperin, 13), may constitute the most significant influence on *The Winter's Tale* and its companion pieces in the Shakespeare canon.

While Dowden's choice has by and large become the norm, many critics since the early twentieth century have inclined toward 'tragicomedy', a classification well known in Shakespeare's time but not used by the Folio editors. In the preface to *The Faithful Shepherdess* (first performed *c.* 1608), John Fletcher defined the genre as 'want[ing] deaths, which is enough to make it no tragedy, yet brings some near it, which is enough to make it no comedy, which must be a representation of familiar people . . . A god is as lawful in [tragicomedy] as in a tragedy, and mean [i.e. ordinary] people as in a comedy'.[14] But typical of the tragicomedies by Beaumont and Fletcher written in 1608–12, which likely contributed to Shakespeare's foray into the genre, is an absence of the miraculous wonders and transformative journeys (whether actual or figurative) that mark Shakespeare's late plays. Even critics who manifest an affinity for the term assert essential differences between Shakespeare's final creative burst and such works as *The Faithful Shepherdess*, *Philaster*, and *A King and No King*.[15]

The title of the play tilts the debate in favour of 'romance' for, by definition, winter's tales were strange and fanciful oral narratives intended to while away the long, cold hours of the dark nights of winter and, therefore, not meant to be taken seriously or to withstand the rigours of logical interrogation.[16] Mamillius himself specifies a story of 'sprites and goblins' suitable for idle pastime (2.1.25–6). That the play's first reference to such a tale occurs in the domestic company of women (see illustration 2, p. 6) and is put in the mouth of the androgynous Mamillius – still 'unbreeched' (1.2.154) and whose name etymologically denotes 'breasts' – is significant, for this type of narrative in the patriarchal culture of the early modern period was traditionally gendered female.[17] Unlike the more serious and disciplined classical works learned in the grammar schools, where boys began the process of sharply defining their masculine identity, effeminate oral tales were considered trivial and inferior and, therefore, properly left behind in the nursery.[18]

[14] Lying behind Fletcher's definition is Guarini's *Compendio della poesia tragicomica* (1601), which provided the essential criteria: a story in which tragic and comic parts are mixed, with persons of high rank approaching death but ultimately avoiding it, and a 'happy ending' that purges melancholy.

[15] See, for example, Joan Hartwig, *Shakespeare's Tragicomic Vision*, 1972; Robert Henke, *Pastoral Transformation: Italian Tragicomedy and Shakespeare's Late Plays*, 1997; and Lee Bliss, ed. *A King and No King*, 2004.

[16] In an 1813 lecture devoted to *WT* and *Oth.*, Coleridge (in Foakes, 1.551, 555), noted the 'exquisite significance' of Shakespeare's titles (singling out *MND*, *AYLI*, and *WT*). According to a report of the lecture in *The Bristol Gazette* (11 November 1813), *WT*'s title, in the manner of 'a bill of fare before the feast', announces 'a wild story, calculated to interest a circle round a fireside'. Schlegel had also thought that plays like *WT* and *MND* were most appropriately named (*A Course of Lectures on Dramatic Art and Literature by Augustus William Schlegel*, trans. John Black, 2 vols., 1815, 2.181).

[17] As in *Mac.* 3.4.62–5. See Lamb for an excellent discussion of this female gendering and of the male anxiety it prompted. The connection to the female in winter's tales suggests yet another link to 'romance', whose audience was and continues to be typically identified as female.

[18] Erasmus' disdain was common in contemporary childrearing manuals:'A boy (may) learn a pretty story from the ancient poets, or a memorable tale from history, just as readily as the stupid and vulgar ballad, or the old wives' fairy rubbish such as most children are steeped in nowadays by nurses and serving women' (*De pueris instituendis*, in William Harrison Woodward, ed., *Desiderius Erasmus concerning the Aim ad Method of Education*, 1964, 214, as cited in Lamb, 531).

2 2.1.22–32: Mamillius tells his 'winter's tale' in the domestic company of women. Olivia Birkelund (Hermione), James Bonilla (Mamillius), and Diana LaMar (Lady/Emilia), from Irene Lewis's 2002 production for Center Stage, Baltimore, Maryland. Richard Anderson, photographer.

3 2.1.32 SD–60: Leontes invades the female domain that has nurtured Mamillius. Cliff Chamberlain (Leontes), Becky Peters (Hermione), and Kelli Holsopple (Mamillius), from Ralph Cohen's 2002 production for Shenandoah Shakespeare's American Shakespeare Center, Staunton, Virginia. Tommy Thompson, photographer.

But Mamillius' choice of a 'sad' tale as best for winter, like the seasonal reference itself to a barren time of year, complicates the surface meaning of such stories as idle and fanciful, suggesting instead something serious and consequential, i.e., something potentially tragic. Its placement, quickly followed by one of the play's most disturbing moments – the abrupt, violent severing of Mamillius from the comfort of the female domain he has known – reinforces this sense.[19] Certainly the figure of Time confirms a deeper signification of 'tale' (4.1.14) when he says: 'I, that please some, try all – both joy and terror / Of good and bad, that makes and unfolds error' (4.1.1–2); 'error' here implies not just 'a mistake' but 'moral transgression' (*OED* 5). By Act 5, where the words 'wonder', 'marvel', 'admirable', and 'amazement' – along with references to an old tale, i.e. old-fashioned and far-fetched – proliferate,[20] an overlay is in place that encourages an understanding of the title as a fantastic 'old tale' of serious, moral things. The use of the definite article in the play's title furthers the sense that what is being dramatized is not only the quintessential concentration of romantic fancy but also 'the essential story of winter itself'.[21] The 'tale' of the text as we have it need not necessarily correspond to the actual story Mamillius starts to tell about a man who dwelt by a churchyard,[22] but a looser relation is probable: the sad wintry tale of the first part (tragedy) completed by the (overall) joyous spring-like tale of the second (comedy).

The passage perhaps most relevant to the genre question seems unequivocally to identify the play as tragicomedy, although not in the conventional mould of avoiding death. After several acts of jealous rage, vile accusations, a state trial, a blasphemous rejection of Apollo's oracle, and the demise of several characters, the genial and kindly Shepherd who enters at 3.3.57 italicizes the shift from tragedy to comedy. Having discovered an abandoned baby girl, he announces to his son, the Clown, fresh from his own grim discoveries: 'Thou met'st with things dying,

[19] See Paster (Chapter 5, 'Quarreling With The Dug') on the profound effect this moment likely had on early modern male audiences. Directors who have captured the psycho-physiological impact on Mamillius include Noble (who kept the boy onstage as a horrified witness to his mother's plight), Bergman (who positioned him behind a panel, from which he finally emerged visibly weakened and distressed), and Syer (who had him, after everyone else had exited, return to pick up the pieces of the toy he had left on the floor and which Leontes had crushed at 'schoolboy's top' (2.1.103), his sobbing cough prophetic [Armstrong, 30]). See also illustration 3, p. 6.

[20] For 'wonder', see 5.1.132; 5.2.14, 20, 147; and 5.3.22; for 'marvel', 5.1.187 and 5.3.100; for 'admirable', 4.4.200; for 'amazement', 5.3.87; and for 'old tale', 5.2.25, 53; and 5.3.117.

[21] Overton, 70.

[22] Schanzer's view (8–9), a notion anticipated by Goddard who claims that Leontes' entrance at 2.1.32 'turns from narrative into drama the boy's tale of sprites and goblins, the first chapter of which he has already enacted' (262). Of Tom Rowan's decision to open the play with a Mamillius 'in green breeches reading a book', Katharine Goodland writes: 'The unfolding drama becomes an incarnation of Mamillius' imagination as he peruses his storybook. This interpretation solves one of the longstanding cruces of Shakespeare's play: the character so noticeably absent from the text after he dies offstage emerges as the narrative agent, at once the desiring subject and the object of desire, the dreamer and the dream' (*ShakB* 20.3 [2002], 20). Lapine's use of 2.1.22–9 as a prologue to the play served a similar purpose.

4 An emblematic depiction of the play's generic division between tragedy and comedy articulated at 3.3.101–2, 'Thou met'st with things dying, I with things newborn.' From Andrea Alciati, . . . *Emblemata* . . . , 1661 (Folger Shakespeare Library).

I with things newborn' (3.3.101–2).[23] Brian Bedford's staging of the end of 3.3 at Stratford, Ontario in 1998 typifies the generic sea-change as conceived by directors: the clouds lifted and the sun broke through to bathe the stage in a golden light.[24] But just when it seems that the play has declared how it should be called, the Shepherd heralds Fortune's newly benevolent phase as he and his son celebrate not only the baby, but the riches found with her: 'This is fairy gold, boy, and 'twill prove so. . . . Home, home, the next way. We are lucky, boy . . . 'Tis a lucky day, boy, and we'll do good deeds on 't' (3.3.109–10, 120). In an instant, with the reference to fairies and magic, we are brought back to the genre of romance.[25]

[23] C. B. Hardman, 'Theory, Form, and Meaning in Shakespeare's *The Winter's Tale*', *RES* (n.s.) 36. (1985), 229, quotes from Evanthius a passage that became the staple of early modern distincions between comedy and tragedy:'in tragoedia fugienda vita, in comedia capessanda exprimitur' – i.e., 'for tragedy ought to express the abandonment of life, and comedy the commencement of life'. See illustration 4, above.

[24] From Ward, 'Bedford', 40.

[25] As was lyrically suggested in Lewis' production, where, following the post-Act 3 interval, a procession of disparate souls – the actor who doubled the roles of Time and the Shepherd, accompanied by two Bohemian denizens and a tame bear – made its way across the rear of the stage to herald Act 4 (see illustration 5, p. 9); while Time spoke his monologue, the heretofore predatory bear now graciously provided a comfortable bed on which the other two characters reclined to the dulcet tones of a windpipe.

5 The lyrical and metamorphic opening to the second half of Irene Lewis' 2002 production for Center Stage, Baltimore, Maryland. Laurence O'Dwyer (Old Shepherd/Time), David Steinberg (Bohemian servant), and Warren 'Wawa' Snipe (Bear) carrying Karen Hansen (Dorcas). Richard Anderson, photographer.

Rather than restricting the naming question to an 'either/or' solution, Barbara Mowat persuasively argues for an inherited generic DNA that renders both *romance* and *tragicomedy* 'truly useful names for Shakespeare's late plays', especially when taken in combination (Mowat, 138). Looking to such sixteenth-century dramatized romances as *Sir Clyomon and Clamydes*, *Mucedorus*, and *The Rare Triumphs of Love and Fortune*,[26] she detects an earlier tradition of tragicomedy compatible with romance. While Sidney may have had foremost in mind something like *Cambyses* when he coined the phrase 'mongrel tragi-comedy' for plays given to the gross absurdity of mixing tragic and comic elements,[27] works such as the three cited above might also qualify in their to and fro between comic and tragic forces and between the impulses of Eros and Fortune. *The Winter's Tale* explicitly invokes the *Cambyses* model in the Clown's love of 'a ballad but even too well, if it be doleful matter merrily set down, or a very pleasant thing indeed and sung lamentably' (4.4.188–90). In the end, however, by making quests, family reunions, and improbable events central, 'mouldy tales' (Ben Jonson's phrase for old-fashioned, far-fetched stories) project a fundamental 'romance' ethos. The syntax of Mowat's proffered hybrid, *tragicomic romance*, effects a helpful rapprochement between the rival terms and perfectly embraces a play whose very title foregrounds 'romance'.

[26] These plays not only look back to the tradition of narrative classical and chivalric romance but also illustrate the gradual secular transformation of the saint's play (Felperin, 13).

[27] Sir Philip Sidney, *An Apology for Poetry* (1595), ed. Geoffrey Shepherd, 1965, 135.

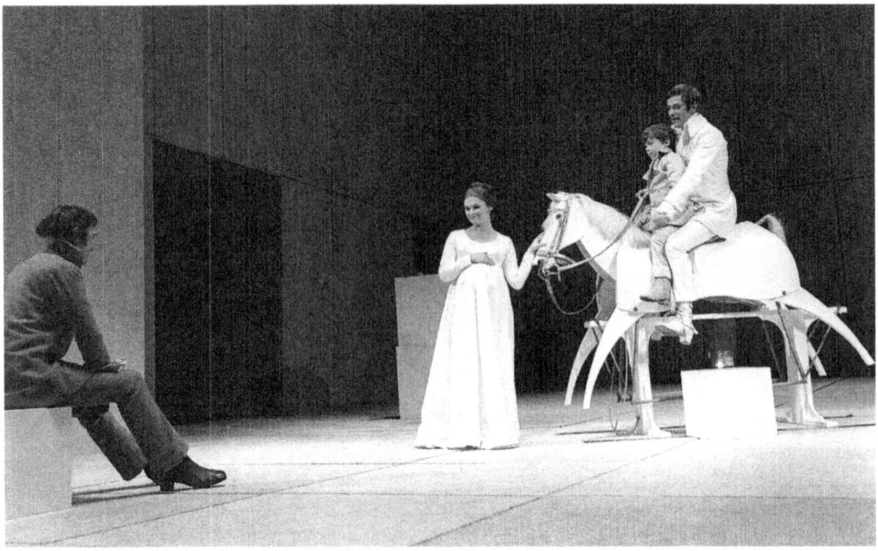

6 Act 1, scene 2 staged in the private, domestic setting of a nursery: Judi Dench (Hermione), Barry Ingham (Leontes), and Jeremy Richardson (Mamillius), from Trevor Nunn's 1969 RSC production, Stratford-upon-Avon. Tom Holte Theatre Photographic Collection, Shakespeare Birthplace Trust.

PASTORAL

Adding to the play's generic copiousness is the infusion of pastoral, a literary tradition bipartite in meaning and often tripartite in design; it is also a genre that easily coexists with both romance (e.g., the classical *Daphnis and Chloe* and Sidney's *Arcadia*) and tragicomedy (e.g. Guarini's *Pastor Fido* and Fletcher's *The Faithful Shepherdess*). At the heart of pastoral, etymologically derived from the Latin word for shepherd (*pastor*), is a basic contrast between the ways and means of the court (or city) and those of the country, with the latter typically idealized. Distinctions are cast in terms of sterility vs. fecundity, sophistication vs. simplicity, and artifice vs. naturalness. The trajectory of pastoral involves a journey from the court to the country (or a similarly remote world like Prospero's island), with movement back to the court either promised (*The Two Gentlemen of Verona*, *As You Like It*, and *The Tempest*) or actualized (*A Midsummer Night's Dream*). The journey to the other world, Northrop Frye's 'green world',[28] proves therapeutic in solving problems, repairing fractured relationships, and clearing true love's obstacle course of all its hurdles. *The Winter's Tale*, after almost three acts in the court of Sicilia and an act-long sojourn in the country setting of Bohemia, follows the spatial dynamic of *A Midsummer Night's Dream*. But in contrast to traditional pastoral, the character most in need of healing, Leontes, never makes the journey to Bohemia; instead, Bohemia comes to him, in the revitalizing presence of Perdita and Florizel (see 5.1.122 SD n.

[28] Frye, 'The Mythos of Spring: Comedy', in his *The Anatomy of Criticism* (1957), rpt. 1971, 163–86, esp. 181–6.

7 Act 1, scene 2 staged with festive formality: Brian Bedford (Leontes), Margot Dionne (Hermione), and Ted Follows (Polixenes), with members of the Festival Company, from Robin Phillips and Peter Moss' 1978 production for the Stratford Festival of Canada. Daphne Dare with Michael Maher, designers; Robert C. Ragsdale, photographer.

and 150–1) and in the welcome arrivals of Polixenes, Camillo, and Perdita's foster family (as reported in 5.2).

On the surface, *The Winter's Tale*'s two worlds are sharply distinguished. Each has its presiding deity: the god Apollo in Sicilia and the goddess Nature in Bohemia. Sicilia is peopled with royals, nobles, gentlemen, servants and ladies-in-waiting, a judicial officer and one lone jailer; Bohemia, though having a court with a king and a prince, is dominated by a human landscape of shepherds. The prince himself is more at home in the country, where he has fallen in love with a presumed shepherd's daughter and is comfortable in pastoral attire (4.4.1–52). Even court personnel in Bohemia seem in short supply, the only active courtier being Camillo, who seems to have replaced Archidamus of 1.1; the sole other character with court connections is one who has given up 'three-pile' velvet for both the tattered garb of a rogue and the apparel of a pedlar who 'haunts wakes [i.e. rural feasts], fairs, and bear-baitings' (4.3.91–2).

The major event in the Sicilia of the first three acts is a trial dealing with the charge of marital infidelity; in Bohemia, its counterpart is a holiday festival that does double duty as an engagement party. Whereas scenes in Sicilia tend to favour the interiority of palace rooms, a prison, and a court session,[29] the Bohemian sequence (with the

[29] The trial episode (3.2) may be in question because of Hermione's line about being brought forth in the 'open air' (see 3.2.104 n.), but most directors prefer the interior of a judicial chamber. Performance examples of Sicilia's interiority include illustrations 6, 7, and 8, on pp. 10, 11 and 12.

8 2.3.26–39: Paulina's initial confrontation with the Lords. Stephen Patrick Martin (Second Lord), Ralph Cosham (Antigonus), John Lescault (First Lord), and Tana Hicken (Paulina), from Michael Kahn's 2002 production for The Shakespeare Theatre, Washington, DC. Richard Termine, photographer. At 'That presses him from sleep' (2.3.39), Paulina seen through a scrim moved across a platform and through a hidden door into the wings, from which she entered at Leontes' query, 'What noise there, ho?' (39), the centre stage, previously darkened at 26, now in full light.

possible exception of 4.2) unfolds in the open space of a coastal shore (3.3), a country road (4.3), and the grounds of the Shepherd's cottage (4.4).[30] Adrian Noble's use of a huge gauze box remains one of the more unusual theatrical strategies for defining this spatial separation of two worlds and underscoring the claustrophobia of Leontes' court. Quickly flown in and out during the scenes in Sicilia, the box 'creat[ed] a sense of psychological or emotional isolation' that was completely absent from the Bohemia phase of the action (Smallwood, 'Shakespeare 1992', 349). The sounds of Sicilia and Bohemia are also dissimilar. While the text never calls for music in Leontes' court of the first three acts, Bohemia is awash in required songs and dances that help create a felt atmospheric contrast (see illustrations 11 and 12, p. 15, and also Appendix C, p. 270). This is not to say that Sicilia does not have its

[30] While perhaps not beginning outside the cottage, the sheepshearing festival and its aftermath clearly move there at some point (see headnote to 4.4 and 4.4.183–4 n.). Eyre's choice of an indoor setting for the scene is a notable departure from performance custom. For stagings of some of Bohemia's exterior scenes, see illustrations 9 and 10 on pp. 13 and 14.

9 3.3.26–35: Antigonus' dream on the coast of Bohemia. Ralph Cosham (Antigonus) and Lise Bruneau (Hermione), from Michael Kahn's 2002 production for The Shakespeare Theatre, Washington DC. Richard Termine, photographer. The 'ghost' of Hermione, as often happens in modern productions, spoke the lines.

10 The entrance of Richard McCabe's Autolycus into the open space of Bohemia (4.3), from Adrian Noble's 1992 RSC production, Stratford-upon-Avon. Malcolm Davies Collection, Shakespeare Birthplace Trust. The 'fantastical, unnaturalistic' entrance was designed not only to make the contrast between Sicilia and Bohemia as sharp as possible but also to make it immediately felt as such (McCabe, in Smallwood, *Players*, 63).

11 A satyrs' masque, from *The Plays of Shakespeare*, edited by George Steevens, 1793 (Folger Shakespeare Library).

12 In Irene Lewis' 2002 production for Center Stage, Baltimore, Maryland, the ritual dance by Warren 'Wawa' Snipe served as a substitute for the dance of the twelve satyrs (4.4.322 SD). Richard Anderson, photographer.

13 Time points to the twenty-fourth hour on a clock, from Giuseppi Maria Mitelli, *Le Ventiquattr' hore dell'humana felicita* . . . , 1675. The iconic image illustrates how time is measured in Sicilia. (Folger Shakespeare Library).

own sound-scape, but as rendered in performance it inclines toward the piercing, harsh, and ominous.[31] Even time passes differently. Measured in Sicilia by a clock's minutes and hours (1.2.43, 286, 287) and in days (1.2.446, 2.3.197), weeks (1.2.39), and months (1.2.41, 101), time in Bohemia is cyclic and seasonal: nature provides the calendar as in Perdita's litany of flowers (4.4.74–129) (see illustrations 13, above, and 14, p. 17).[32]

[31] As in Bedford's calibrated orchestration of sound at Stratford, Ontario in 1998: shouting matches of increasing volume and pitch, heavy prison doors clanging shut, a wailing baby, and ear-shattering thunderclaps (see Ward, 'Bedford', 39).

[32] In contrast to Bohemia's more leisurely pace as befits a holiday festival, the tempo in Sicilia is driven by speed: characters escape 'tonight' (1.2.431), 'tak[ing] the urgent hour' (1.2.460) and 'scour [ing] . . . on their way' (2.1.35); are hastily imprisoned and give birth prematurely; become seriously ill almost over

14 Time as experienced in Bohemia: cyclic (the serpent), seasonal (the four figures), and diurnal (the sun dial). From Moralia Horatiana, 1656 (engraving from 1607) (1963 facsimile edition, The Library of Congress, Washington, DC).

Polixenes' allusions to a shepherd's note and 'twinned lambs' (1.2.1–2, 66), idyllic images appropriately assigned to the king of Bohemia, not only sum up the difference between the two kingdoms[33] but also highlight pastoral variation. By reversing

night; and are repeatedly ordered to carry out tasks 'straight' or 'presently' (i.e., immediately). The pattern is especially pronounced in the final thirteen lines of Act 2, scene 3: e.g., 'An hour since' (194), 'Hasting' (196), 'their speed' (196), 'Twenty-three days' (197), 'tis good speed' (198), and 'suddenly' (199).

[33] Adelman distinguishes (220–2) male pastoral – static and nostalgic in Sicilia – from female – creative and full of hope in Bohemia. More often than not, when nature's imagery fleetingly appears in Leontes' court, a sordidness attaches to it: e.g. the king's fishing metaphors, which are tainted by his fears of cuckoldry (1.2.185–205); and the lone 'tuft of pines' used for spying (2.1.34–35), a purpose very different from that to which Bohemian hedges are put (4.3.5 and 4.4.782).

15 Mount Etna, from Gabriel Rollenhagen, *Nucleus emblematum selectissimorum . . .* , 1611 (Folger Shakespeare Library).

the geographical settings of Greene's *Pandosto*, where Leontes' counterpart presides over cold and wintry Bohemia and Polixenes' over warm and bucolic Sicilia, Shakespeare 'rejects the convention of the latter as only an Arcadian country, the stereotyped and monothematic island which Greene inherited from the pastoral tradition' dating back to the poetry of Theocritus. Instead, the playwright creates a Sicilia 'overloaded with ambiguous, contrasting and polysemous connotations' appropriate to a world of suspicion, jealousy, and volcanic outbursts (Marrapodi, 214).[34] Ultimately, with the 'statue scene', Shakespeare restores Sicilia to its Arcadian roots in art and reconciles it with the pastoral ideal of resolved problems and harmonized relationships.

It is Bohemia, however, that constitutes the major departure from convention, for while filling the spatial function of pastoral as being the world of country, Bohemia cannot be simplified as only that. It has its own court (4.2) and its country space has different degrees of 'civilization' – moving from a wild, deserted, barren coast where predatory animals have been spotted and a violent storm brews (3.3) to something out of time with the actual figure of Time presiding (4.1) to a country highway where robbers and rogues abound (4.3) to a well-structured and organized sheep-shearing feast with its own hierarchical protocol and codes of decorum and hospitality (4.4).

[34] See illustration 15, above. William Burton (New York, 1856) became the first director to set Act 1 clearly in Sicily, 'a cut-out of Mount Etna visible in the background' (Bartholomeusz, 104).

The country road where the Shepherd's son is waylaid by Autolycus is not quite as threatening as the coast but neither is it as safe and civilized as the settings of Act 4, scenes 2 and 4. Even in the protective environment of the sheepshearing festival a con-man triumphs, and while Perdita may correspond to the pristine idealized shepherdess of convention,[35] Mopsa and Dorcas' heritage derives from a coarse, lusty vintage inclusive of menacing satyrs (see 4.4.322 SD n.).

Unlike the perfect idyll where shepherds pass the day piping, meditating, engaging in singing contests, and conversing with the beloved, Bohemia knows such urban pastimes as bearbaitings (4.3.92), the vices of gambling and petty theft (4.3.25–7), and the punishments of stocks, 'gallows and knock . . . beating and hanging' (4.3.22, 27–8). With the mention of 'gallows' and 'hanging', we are into a world in which mortality is not contemplated with stylized detachment.[36] Instead, the play's last individual death, on the coast of Bohemia, occurs to the accompaniment of a raging storm and is particularly gruesome. Even the Shepherd's feeling of betrayal and his lament for what he foresees as his miserable end (4.4.432–42) registers palpable pain, his mind focused on the emotional reality of death.

What finally, and perhaps most importantly, signifies Bohemia as a different kind of pastoral world is its commercial image, introduced in Polixenes' tribute to a savvy Camillo who has 'made . . . businesses [that only he] can sufficiently manage', a service from which the king hopes to continue to 'profit' (4.2.11–12, 16). Although an economic lexis of 'loss . . . and gain, and pay and owe, and debt and repay' operates throughout the play,[37] it is particularly strong in Bohemia (especially at the sheepshearing festival).[38] A monetary rather than barter economy (4.3.31–3; 4.4.575–94), class consciousness (4.4.156–7, 412, and 684–703), and social mobility, whether defined as up for the 'wealthy arrivistes'[39] among the shepherds – a demographic surprising to Polixenes' court (4.2.31–41) – or as down for Autolycus (4.3.13–14), inscribe Bohemia as a socio-economic, materialist world inhabited by usurers (4.4.251–2), shopkeepers (4.4.654), and lawyers (4.4.203), and where even shepherds have servants (4.4.183–209). As the action prepares to move back to the formal court setting of Sicilia, we are reminded in Autolycus' pretence of urinary need (4.4.782)[40] that in the country (as well as at court) social status and decorum are

[35] The text indicates a young woman of mesmerizing beauty and grace (4.4.1–5, 78, 109–10, 135–46, 156–9, 178) but also one having sexual desires and given to earthy outspokenness (4.4.83, 99–103, 130–2). In a departure from earlier depictions of Perdita as a pastoral princess, Granville-Barker sought a natural, unpoetical country girl obviously brought up by shepherds, a choice that received mixed reviews (see Bartholomeusz, 157–8).

[36] For Richard McCabe (Autolycus in Noble), 4.3.28 offered 'a glimpse of vulnerability in [his] character's otherwise impervious, jocund outer shell'; the ugly, purple bruise revealed on the line suggested that Autolycus 'had once narrowly escaped a lynching, the memory and scar of which will always haunt him' (Smallwood, *Players*, 64).

[37] Cavell, 200; see also Fischer, Parker ('Promissory Economies'), and Bristol (esp. 162–6).

[38] E.g. 'purse', 'money', 'compter' (i.e. counter), 'pennyworth', 'marted', 'coin', 'purchase', 'cheat', 'custom', 'exchange', 'traffic', 'tradesmen', and 'business'. Even songs become powerful sales devices, as in the chant at 4.4.213–24 that 'speaks over four centuries to our own consumer-conscious society, advis[ing] all to "Come buy"' (McCabe, in Smallwood, *Players*, 65); see also 4.4.304–5 n.

[39] Bristol, 163; see also 4.3.31–3 n.

[40] The passage functions as 'a perlocutionary demonstration of rank' (Paster, 27).

pervasive concerns. Bohemia thus emerges as perhaps the richest, most complex, and most diverse pastoral world in Shakespeare.

HISTORY

No one would ever argue that *The Winter's Tale* is a history play, certainly not in the sense that *Henry VIII* is, despite its strong 'romance' affinity with other late plays, or even in the way *Cymbeline* can claim to be, with its underlying political and military conflict between Britain and Rome and its Holinshed-derived names and royal lineage. But current critical thinking has moved discussion of *The Winter's Tale* beyond the more traditional emphasis on romance, tragicomedy, and pastoral to demonstrate that it is neither ahistorical nor apolitical.[41] Viewed from this perspective, the play registers a 'radical political openness' as it 'teeters in the gap between the ideology of absolutism and anti-absolutist elements incompletely contained'.[42] For some critics, the play is 'deeply implicated' in the political discourse surrounding tensions between England and Scotland in 1604–10 and James I's proposal to unify the two countries (the Sicilia-Bohemia polarization reflecting contemporary political oppositions);[43] for others, it either mirrors in the stage family of King Leontes the royal family of James I (the first time such a domestic unit existed at court since the death of Henry VIII in 1547),[44] or remembers and refigures the dead Elizabeth in the 'statue' of Hermione, de-eroticized and consequently no longer a threat, either sexual or political, to masculine rule.[45]

The thematic and plot-driven concern with succession and an underlying interrogation of monarchical power are perhaps the clearest links between *The Winter's Tale* and the history play as Shakespeare defined it.[46] From the opening scene touting young Mamillius' promise through both Leontes' obsession with the purity of his blood line and the oracle's prophecy to the emphatic remembrance of the oracle and the recovery of Perdita in Act 5, the issue of succession and the related fear of a wife's infidelity (especially strong in a patriarchal society) reverberate.[47]

41 This new trend is fundamentally different in scope and intent from the 'old' historicism that viewed the play as political allegory (see, e.g., Horace Walpole and Glynn Wickham, who, respectively, found links with Henry VIII, and with Mary Stuart and James I). For helpful overviews of criticism, see Pafford (xxxvii–xliv), Draper (7–9), and the introduction in Hunt.

42 William Morse, 'Metacriticism and Materiality: The Case of Shakespeare's *The Winter's Tale*', *English Literary History* 58 (1991), 283–304. Similarly, Simon Palfrey argues that the play belongs to a 'politically restless genre' that offers 'a robust and often irreverent challenge to providentialist or conservative teleologies' (*Late Shakespeare: A New World of Words* [1997], 230).

43 Donna Hamilton, '*The Winter's Tale* and the Language of Union, 1604–1610', *Shakespeare Studies* 21 (1993), 228–52.

44 David Bergeron, *Shakespeare's Romances and the Royal family*, 1985, 157–78.

45 Katherine Eggert, *Showing Like a Queen: Female Authority and Literary Experiment in Spenser, Shakespeare, and Milton*, 2000, chapter 5.

46 Recent studies of these two related issues include Stuart Kurland's examination of royal prerogative and the dynamic between a king and his courtly counsel ('"We Need No More of Your Advice": Political Realism in *The Winter's Tale*', *Studies in English Literature 1500–1900* 31 [1991], 365–86) and Constance Jordan's focus on Leontes' tyranny in relation to contemporary thoughts on monarchical authority and the need for a king to trust and love his people (*Shakespeare's Monarchies: Ruler and Subject in the Romances*, 1997, chapter 4).

47 Phyllis Rackin examines the paradox of women who ostensibly have no voice within the patriarchal historiography of the early modern era but who nonetheless manage, by their very presence as 'keepers

Even in Bohemia, Polixenes, like the anxious Henry IV, worries about the fitness of his son to succeed him and the choice of a suitable mate to carry on the dynasty (4.2.21–38; 4.4.397–400). When the play ends, Leontes seems to have found an heir in Perdita, but in the play's patriarchal world, it is Florizel, the future husband of Perdita and the direct heir of Polixenes, who becomes the real successor to Leontes: the king, once both fathers are dead, of Sicilia and Bohemia. Although the play's performance history tends to showcase the reunited married couple as the closing image – Hermione and Leontes are often the last to exit – the final visual effect in two recent revivals tapped into the succession theme: in Bedford, the audience was left with the image of Perdita and Florizel all alone on stage, 'kissing in a pool of golden light'; in Bohnen, with the sight of Perdita returning to the stage after everyone else had departed to retrieve a bouquet, at which point her eyes met those of the ghostly Mamillius.[48]

Just as important in connecting the play to the genre of history is the issue of royal authority. Unlike Hal, who is a monarch in training, Leontes already wears the crown, but as Shakespeare shows in all of his history plays, especially *Richard II*, the education of a king is a lifelong process, and the chief lesson to be mastered is the ability to wield power without abusing it. One of those rare rulers uniformly blessed with wise and good counsellors – there is not one 'yes' man in the group, each defending Hermione to Leontes' face[49] – the deluded king is incapable of heeding their wisdom because he has become what he vigorously protests: a tyrant.[50] When Paulina indirectly labels him as such (2.3.115), his words both prove her point and reveal his need to deny it:

On your allegiance,
Out of the chamber with her! Were I a tyrant,
Where were her life? She durst not call me so
If she did know me one. (2.3.120–3)

That the charge is particularly abhorrent to Leontes is evident by the way he brings it up at the opening of the court session which, he claims, will clear him 'of being tyrannous, since we so openly / Proceed in justice' (3.2.5–6). The trial, however, does just the opposite, and the charge is repeated, first with more damning authority when the oracle's message is read, exonerating everyone but Leontes, who

of the unwritten and unknowable truth' of biological legitimacy, to subvert the patriarchal historical record (*Stages of History: Shakespeare's English Chronicles* [1990], 146 ff.).

[48] See Ward, 'Bedford' (40) and Newcomb (27–8). Besides celebrating the triumph of young love, Bedford's choice anticipated the union of two rival kingdoms; Bohnen's, on the other hand, looked both to the past in its remembrance of a lost brother and to the continuity of Leontes' line: Perdita, not Florizel, is the real replacement for Mamillius; as such, she might recall the dead Elizabeth, who in becoming queen followed (one step removed) a brother who died young.

[49] That they are rhetorically ineffective points to the limits placed on counsel in a court – like that of James I – ruled by an absolutist king.

[50] Shakespeare may have switched the realms of Sicilia and Bohemia as he found them in his source, in part, because of the contemporary association of tyranny with Sicilia: 'The tyrannies which were used in Sicilia were in times past so famous, that they grew unto this Proverbe, Invidia Siculi non invenire tyranni, tormentum majus [i.e., the envious pine at others' success; no greater punishment than envy was devised by Sicilian tyrants]' (William Lithgow, *The Totall Discourse of the Rare Aduentures and painefull Peregrinations of long nineteene Yeares Trauayles* . . . [1632], as cited in Marrapodi, 216).

is declared a 'jealous tyrant' (3.2.131), and then in Paulina's no-holds-barred triple iteration (3.2.172, 176, 204). Only when Leontes ceases his tyrannical behaviour does he become open to good counsel, thereby permitting Paulina to assume the role of effective counsellor that she will play for the next sixteen years. Appropriately, 'tyrant' (along with its variants 'tyrannous' and 'tyranny') never appears again. When the action returns to Leontes' court in 5.1, in an almost throw-away line the king gives a clue as to his criteria for the ideal monarch. Upon hearing mention of Libya, he recalls its ruler, 'the warlike Smalus, / That noble honoured lord, [who] is feared *and* loved' (5.1.156–7, italics mine). A king who inspires respect, awe, and love is one who would seem to have learned the distinction James I drew in his accession speech to Parliament (19 March 1603) between a righteous king and a tyrant:

> That whereas the proud and ambitious tyrant does think his kingdom and people are only ordained for satisfaction of his desires and unreasonable appetites, the righteous and just king does by the contrary acknowledge himself to be ordained for the procuring of the wealth and prosperity of his people, and that his greatest and principal worldly felicity must consist in their prosperity; if you be rich I cannot be poor, if you be happy I cannot but be fortunate: and I protest that your welfare shall ever be my greatest care and contentment . . . [51]

While not a history play per se, *The Winter's Tale* is, as Stephen Orgel reminds us, 'deeply informed by the political and legal history of Jacobean England': the questions it raises concerning monarchical rights and duties, protocol, available sanctions when dealing with a criminal king, and the 'relation between royal authority and the will of the people' were issues 'being actively debated' in the early years of King James I's reign, and 'the play's focus on the king is certainly a reflection of the world of contemporary politics' (Orgel, 'Perspective', 258). In mixing things up generically, *The Winter's Tale* exemplifies what Polonius would recognize as 'tragical-comical-historical-pastoral'.

Iterative patterns in *The Winter's Tale*: sameness with a difference

Holding the play together is an elaborate network of illuminating parallels and contrasts that encourage the reader/spectator to remain fluidly engaged in remembering, redefining, and reassessing the past as it bears on the present and future.[52] Both Sicilia and Bohemia are home to kings capable of volcanic outbursts, to harsh fathers, to spies, to the pragmatically faithful Camillo, to paragons of maligned female beauty and virtue, and to love that is threatened and tested – Leontes fails his test as husband, while Florizel passes his as wooer. Leontes' vulgar imaginings of Hermione and Polixenes engaged in lustful activities have their more natural and primal counterpart in the bawdy behaviour of Mopsa and Dorcas and in the dance of the satyrs. A courtier has his shoulder torn out by a bear at the end of the tragic first half (3.3.87), and a rogue fabricates a shoulder injury early in the comic second

[51] *The Political Works of James I* (1616), ed. Charles Howard McIlwain (1918; rpt. New York: Russell & Russell, 1965), 279.

[52] Siemon and Proudfoot deal extensively with the play's many iterations.

half (4.3.67–8). The innocent but disastrously misinterpreted hand-holding of Act 1 gives way first to a handfasting in Act 4 that anticipates the nuptial bliss of young lovers (a moment cut short by a king's sudden rage) and then to the exquisitely delicate taking of hands in Act 5, where the gesture becomes emblematic of a spousal bond restored.[53] Rough seas deliver Perdita to Bohemia (3.3.1–6) and back again to Sicilia (5.2.100–2).

Such parallels are generally marked by differences indicative of the movement from tragedy to comedy. For example, when violence erupts in Bohemia, its force is limited, as seen in the angry Polixenes who, in one breath, threatens death (4.4.400–2) and disfigurement (405–6) but almost in the next rescinds the first sentence (4.4.412–14) and offers a way of escaping the second (admittedly with a chilling caveat) (4.4.414–21). The vile name-calling of Hermione and the injuries done her when reworked with respect to Perdita are confined to a father's brief curse (4.4.438) – nothing like those directed by Lear at his daughters – and to three royal insults, tame by comparison to Leontes': 'sheep-hook' (4.4.400), 'fresh piece / Of excellent witchcraft' (4.4.402–3), and 'enchantment' (4.4.414), the last two revealing an implicit receptivity to the young girl's physical charms. As Proudfoot notes (283), Perdita's acceptance of a part to be played 'in Camillo's comedy of disguises' (4.4.626–7) recalls Hermione's 'theatrical image of her plight' (3.2.33–5), the parallel serving to 'pinpoint . . . the contrast between their roles and the actions they are engaged in'. In short, the cloud that develops at 4.4.397 begins to break up around 4.4.461 and disappears by 4.4.514. Comic conventions – particularly a pragmatic adviser and the security of enough time to get out of a difficult situation – are in play so as to contain anger, dismay, and discomfort, all painfully real but none allowed their full tragic scope as in earlier acts.

Further connecting the play's two halves are reverberating themes: time and memory, hospitality,[54] deceptive appearances,[55] waiting,[56] and the nature vs. art

[53] For a detailed study of the play's iterative hand imagery, see Viswanathan. Examples of the taking, giving, kissing, or holding of hands as in a dance include 1.1.25; 1.2.102, 107 SD, 114, 125, 442; 4.4.167 SD, 342, 346–7, 363, 370, 530; 5.2.119, 134; 5.3.46, 89, 107, and 144.

[54] Examples include Sicilia's entertaining of Bohemia in Act 1; the welcoming of guests to the sheepshearing festival in 4.4; Leontes' reception of Perdita and Florizel in 5.1 and his reported greeting of others in 5.2; and finally, Paulina's hosting of the royal party who honours her 'poor house' by their visit (5.2.88, 5.3.2–8). The overall movement is from hospitality understood in terms of reciprocity (see Marcel Mauss, *The Gift: Forms and Functions of Exchange in Archaic Societies*, trans. Ian Cunnison, 1925) to a sense of gift-giving as purely selfless, i.e. non-reciprocable (see Jacques Derrida, *Given Time: 1. Counterfeit Money*, trans. Peggy Kamuf, 1992, and *The Gift of Death*, trans. David Wills, 1995). For an extensive discussion of the hospitality theme as grounded in *WT*'s social time, see Bristol.

[55] Among them Leontes' misreading of gestures (1.2), a faint that appears fatal (3.2), a supposed victim of foul play (4.3), a purported shepherdess among a proliferation of disguises (4.4), and a 'statue' that comes alive (5.3).

[56] Whether (fruitlessly) for Mamillius to grow up, for Polixenes to change his mind about prolonging his holiday, for the return of the emissaries from Apollo's temple and the reading of the god's oracle, for Time to unfold error and restore that which was lost, and for a statue to move. Waiting is imaged in pregnancy (Hermione's, possibly Dorcas', and the usurer's wife of Autolycus' ballad), in wrinkles (5.3.28), in the painful remembrance of 'three crabbed months' when the desired hand of the beloved was withheld (1.2.101), and in the flowers that bloom only in season.

debate.[57] To these may be added a homophonic matrix linking bearing, birth, and bears,[58] and an elaborately sustained metatheatrical motif.[59]

Leontes' jealousy in criticism and performance

Just 107 lines into his onstage life, the king of Sicilia registers physical distress and unambiguous suspicions indicating that all is not well among the seemingly amicable trio of husband, wife, and longtime friend of the former:

> Too hot, too hot!
> To mingle friendship far is mingling bloods.
> I have *tremor cordis* on me: my heart dances,
> But not for joy, not joy. (1.2.107–10)

Before departing the scene, Leontes will have engaged in tortured asides and exchanges that often seem more like 'convulsed, explosive monologues' than conversations,[60] his agitation noted by Polixenes and Hermione as early as 1.2.145–6. Fractured in syntax, frequently shifting in address, elliptical, and repetitious, the king's language resists clear explication,[61] and in that mirrors a mind increasingly unstable and a temper of escalating violence (e.g. 1.2.121–6, 136–45, 178–205, 214–16, and 281–93).[62] Even the qualitative sound is harsh and cacophonous, abrupt plosives and sinister sounding sibilants assaulting the ear.[63]

To explain an all-consuming jealousy that 'erupts . . . unheralded like a scream . . . unexpected . . . no one before or afterwards see[ing] any evidence of its cause',[64] critics have thought in terms of Oedipal anxieties and repressed homoerotic desires;[65] of culturally constructed gender systems and patriarchal fears of a woman's subversive power;[66] and of Bakhtin's theory of social time, according to which Leontes'

[57] The debate, which looms so large in Acts 4 and 5, is introduced perhaps as early as 1.1.19 in the use of the verb 'trained' (Bate, 237). See also Barkan, who makes the principle of verisimilitude central to his study of *WT*.

[58] The seminal work in this area is Stephen Booth's 'Exit, Pursued by a Gentleman Born', *Shakespeare's Art from a Comparative Perspective, Proceedings: Comparative Literature Symposium*, Texas Tech. Univ., ed. Wendell M. Aycock, 12 (1981), 51–66; see also De Grazia, Hunt, and Parker.

[59] Andrews (238) compiles an impressive list of theatrical metaphors, situations, and pretences. The metatheatrical motif was especially prominent in Bergman's conception of *WT* as the dramatic entertainment for a child's birthday celebration; the opening of the play proper featured children wearing the masks of comedy and tragedy (see illustration 16, p. 25).).

[60] The director Adrian Noble's description as quoted in the foreword to Andrews, xiv.

[61] On 'linguistic opacity' as a basic feature of the play's style, see Orgel, 'Poetics'.

[62] Coleridge was the first to offer a detailed validation of the emotional/psychological realism of Leontes' jealous rage ('Notes on [*WT*]', in Foakes, 1.551–2).

[63] McDonald's observation in 'Poetry and Plot' (in Hunt, 300); the essay is an excellent analysis of the ways in which language dovetails with structural and thematic patterns informing the play. Many directors translate Leontes' verbal violence into physical action: e.g. being rough with Mamillius (in Donnellan), striking/bullying Camillo (in Syer), and attempting to rape one of Hermione's ladies (in Bergman).

[64] Noble (in Andrews, xiv). Approaching the issue from the perspective of the study rather than the stage, Bethell (*Study*, 78) and Pafford (lxxi–lxxii) offer similar assessments.

[65] See, e.g., Murray M. Schwartz, 'Leontes' Jealousy in [*WT*]', *American Imago* 30.3 (1973), 250–73; C. L. Barber and Richard Wheeler, *The Whole Journey: Shakespeare's Power of Development*, 1986, 328–34; Kay Stockholder (*Dream Works: Lovers and Families in Shakespeare's Plays*, 1987, 184–96; and Adelman.

[66] See Erickson, Schalkwyk, and Marilyn Williamson, 'The Romances: Patriarchy, Pure and Simple', in *The Patriarchy of Shakespeare's Comedies*, 1986, 111–23.

16 The masks of tragedy and comedy at the beginning of Ingmar Bergman's 1994 production for the Royal Dramatic Theatre of Sweden, Stockholm. Bengt Wanselius, photographer. The masks introduced the play's metatheatrical motif.

jealousy 'is a type of spatiotemporal derangement of the ethos of gift, hospitality, and expenditure, mandated by the observances of the Winter Festival or Christmastide' (Bristol, 154). Cultural materialists look to the foundation of the nuclear family and the attention paid in the early modern period to 'marital jealousy as one of the central dangers of love' (Belsey, 104).

Others have sought clues earlier than 'Too hot, too hot' that would make Leontes' suspicions appear more credible. Coghill (31–3), for example, calls attention to the terseness of Leontes' persuasion (1.2.29–30) and to the provocative implications of a visiting king who elaborately emphasizes his nine-month stay while standing in close proximity to a visibly pregnant Hermione (1.2.1–7).[67] Coleridge (1.551) argued for 'At my request he would not' (1.2.86) as the first sign of something being amiss, a line that Macready reportedly said 'suspiciously' (Bartholomeusz, 66), and the actor in Bedford 'stonily' (Ward, 'Bedford', 39).[68] Since 1929 the theatrical potential of 1.2.82–5 has been widely recognized. The ethically charged 'offences', 'sinned', 'fault', and 'slipped' can assume equivocal meaning if these are the only words overheard by a Leontes who, coming forward from behind at 1.2.82 (see Supplementary note to 1.2.33, p. 251), incorrectly assumes the antecedents of 'we' and the thrice repeated 'us' to be Hermione and Polixenes.[69] In William, for instance, a shaft of light caught the actor's face as he clearly misinterpreted what was nothing more than 'relaxed familiarity. . . . the damage was done: the jealousy struck here, and "Too hot", twenty-five lines later was the first expression of it' (Warren, 99).[70]

While some actors play Leontes' jealousy as a passion that comes over him without warning,[71] others convey from his first appearance a smouldering jealousy rooted in marital tensions prior to the onset of dramatic action.[72] Such was Kean's choice in 1856, a major innovation in the scene's performance history:

> [At] the opening of the scene . . . Hermione is seated at the foot of the couch of Leontes, in earnest conversation with Polixenes their guest, who bends forward to address her. Leontes anxiously watches them, as if his mind were already disturbed by the suspicion of undue intimacy; and when they descend to the front, after the conclusion of the banquet, his manner of soliciting his friend to remain, and his demeanour in their subsequent dialogue, was at intervals cold though courteous, studied but not warm, diplomatic more than affectionate, an effort of the tongue rather than a desire of the heart'.
>
> (from Cole's *Life of Kean*, as quoted in Bartholomeusz, 87)

Likewise, John Gielgud (in Brook), 'dressed in hectic red', fixed his dark and brooding gaze on Hermione and Polixenes from the beginning, never preoccupying

67 Wilson (131) and Matchett (esp. 96) concur, the latter offering a detailed reading of Polixenes' procreative puns. Draper (15), however, as a 'matter of practical theatre', thinks it 'absurd' that the audience would grasp a Leontes 'already distorting what he hears'. See also 1.2.3 n.

68 '[F]rom now on words that have borne only one – and that an essentially innocent – meaning, take on a jealous ambiguity' (Draper, 15–16). See collation for 1.2.86.

69 Wilson's stage direction to this effect followed by a year Henry Jewett's introduction of such business into theatrical practice (Boston, 1929), 'both scholar and actor [obviously] influenced . . . by the realistic assumptions of the time about the actor's art' (Bartholomeusz, 167).

70 For additional textual clues, see notes to 1.2.20, 90–5, and 107 SD. Kahn used Polixenes 'tomorrow' (10) to prompt a gasp of disappointment by Hermione, which led to a visibly puzzled Leontes turning abruptly toward her.

71 For J. C. Trewin, Eric Porter's Leontes (in Wood) was 'lividly a man in whom jealousy could flare without preparation: he could have been a Celt' (*Shakespeare on the English Stage, 1900–1964: A Survey of Productions Illustrated from the Raymond Mander and Joe Mitchenson Theatre Collection*, 1964, 246). Judith Flanders in her review of Hytner's production described Alex Jennings' 'sudden, roaring paranoia' as 'mak[ing] the maggots crawling in his soul shockingly visible' (*TLS*, June 8, 2001).

72 See, e.g., Berry's review of Phillips (169); Kahn, having explored homoerotic implications in 1975/6 and 1987, was more interested by 2002 in probing the state of a marriage that was not new, finding evidence of something strained in the gap of years between offspring. In her illuminating study of family values in the early modern era, Belsey (108) demonstrates how the period 'brings emotion inside marriage, and . . . sees emotion as unstable, unpredictable, arbitrary. Leontes finds it – to the infection of his brains and the hardening of his supposedly cuckolded brows'.

17 Act 1, scene 2: John Gielgud as Leontes, from Peter Brook's 1951 production, The Phoenix Theatre, London. Angus McBean, photographer (Harvard Theatre Collection).

himself with other business (Bartholomeusz, 170) (see illustration 17, p. 27). Before the opening dialogue between Camillo and Archidamus, Christopher Plummer's Leontes (in Campbell) was heard to say, 'We shall ride to Delphos and / Then Apollo shall our menial be'; the interpolation was clearly meant to show a king already 'charmed [possessed?] by the dark god' who presided over the decadent revel serving as backdrop for 1.2 (Bartholomeusz, 185). More subtly, Philip Goodwin's Leontes (in Kahn) appeared moody and absorbed in his own thoughts when first seen at a piano where he played sombrely, oblivious to all about him.[73] Occasionally, directors and actors have intended an ostensibly pleasant and warm demeanour to function as a mask not removed till 'Too hot, too hot'.[74]

Beginning with Nunn's revival in 1969, lighting techniques have often been used to heighten Leontes' delusional condition, apparently with the intention of making it, if not psychologically credible, at least theatrically convincing.[75] Choosing to 'bypass . . . questions of how and when Leontes' jealousy arises by having [the audience] experience it as Leontes himself does', Nunn illuminated Hermione and Polixenes with strobe lighting during Leontes' asides; as a result, the couple's physical proximity resembled an embrace and their gestures appeared to enact the king's fantasy of 'paddling palms and pinching fingers' (Draper, 57–8). In the 1976 Barton–Nunn collaboration, Leontes' asides were also specially lit; this time, however, the focus was on the king rather than on those he watched, who remained in near-darkness. Across the Atlantic, more than twenty-five years later, the audience's distance from Leontes and his sickness collapsed again in Syer's use of 'a sultry red light' and 'a projected backdrop of jungle vegetation', against which Hermione and Polixenes at centre stage 'wordlessly enacted the scene of seduction imagined by Leontes, who stood downstage facing the audience': The audience 'saw what his mind saw and felt his shock and revulsion' (Armstrong, 30).

The Syer example demonstrates how stage business carries the greatest potential for encouraging Leontes to misread what is nothing more than the social behaviour of a good hostess, who might playfully nudge Polixenes into dancing (as in Doran)[76] or laughingly try to teach him how to play the piano (as in Kahn; see illustration 18, p. 29).[77] Of course, the more physical the contact and rapport between queen and

73 The piano as a symbol of artistic temperament was crucial to Goodwin's interpretation of the role.

74 Such was Tim Pigott-Smith's approach, given Hall's directorial reading of Leontes' jealousy as preexistent to the opening scene (Warren, 104). According to one review of Eyre's revival, Patrick Stewart's geniality seemed 'desperately willed' (*TLS*, 10 July 1981, 782), providing 'a brilliantly executed study in barely controlled hysteria' (Draper, 59).

75 Sound effects have also been employed to the same end: e.g., Doran used a whispering sound over the tannoy system at the beginning of what was a crowded, formal court scene: the hissing, however, came not from all the extras on the stage – rather 'it seemed, from inside Leontes' own head, from his as-yet-subconscious fear that Sicilia might be a "so-forth" [1.2.215]' (Smallwood, 'Performances', 263).

76 See Smallwood, 'Performances', 263.

77 Although there is never any doubt in *Pandosto* that Bellaria is innocent of her husband's reckless charge of adultery, Greene details a daily 'honest familiarity' conducive to misinterpretation (see *Pandosto* in Bullough, 158).

18 1.2.110–25: Seated at the piano where Leontes had sat moments before, Lise Bruneau's Hermione and Brent Harris' Polixenes physically took over Leontes' space; Bruneau's playful coaxing of Harris' fingers over the keyboard literalized such phrases as 'paddling palms', 'pinching fingers', and 'virginalling/Upon his palm'. From Michael Kahn's 2002 production for The Shakespeare Theatre, Washington, DC. Richard Termine, photographer.

guest, the more understandable is Leontes' dismay at feeling like an outsider. The problem, though, with a sensually flirtatious Hermione and a bold, even brazen, Polixenes[78] is, as noted above, that too much credence may accrue to Leontes' suspicions, thereby calling into question 'the linchpin of the plot': Hermione's innocence, Felperin's provocative deconstruction of the inciting action notwithstanding.[79]

No matter how performed so as to justify Leontes' paroxysms and no matter what critical lens used to probe the cause of his suspicions, perhaps the best we can do is to take Quiller-Couch's 'piece of impossible improbability' (Wilson, xvi) as a classic example of the conventional *donné* that requires no exposition and demands audience acceptance in order to get on with the story. In this regard, we might take a cue from what Camillo says in the following exchange with Polixenes, whose question concerning the cause of Leontes' baseless accusations casts him temporarily in the role of surrogate for the reader/spectator:

POLIXENES How should this grow?
CAMILLO I know not; but I am sure 'tis safer to
Avoid what's grown than question how 'tis born.
(1.2.426–8)

Even before this moment, Camillo advises against trying to explain what is irrational when he speaks of Leontes' 'diseased opinion' (1.2.294), 'sickness' (1.2.379, and 'folly' (1.2.424), which one 'may as well / Forbid the sea for to obey the moon / As or by oath remove or counsel shake' (1.2.421–3). Whereas in *Othello* the playwright explores how a decent mind can be corrupted, how someone not innately jealous can be made so, in the late romance 'the focus is not on the genesis and growth of . . . jealousy but on its effects and repercussions' (McGuire, 163). The play is, after all, a winter's tale, and Leontes' jealousy, surprising and seismic, taps into its strangeness. As the 'agent to bring an evil force rapidly into play' (Pafford, lxxi–ii), Leontes, not Othello, epitomizes Emilia's dictum that 'jealious souls . . . are not ever jealious for the cause, / But jealious for they're jealious. It is a monster / Begot upon itself, born on itself' (*Othello* 3.4.159–62).

'Exit pursued by a bear'

Shakespeare's notorious stage direction occasioned little or no editorial/critical treatment before the twentieth century, as attested by the contrasting coverage in the variorum editions of Furness (1898) and Turner (2005).[80] Francis Gentleman's comment in Bell's 1774 acting text (which drops all reference to the bear) hints at

[78] I have in mind a Polixenes patting Hermione's stomach (Howell); a queen attired in a décolleté maternity gown and receptive to her guest's hugs and love-sick looks (Hands); and the sight of Bohemia, during the 'Affection' speech, 'sitting in [Leontes'] chair . . . Hermione draped over him, laughing and holding his shoulders' (Shurgot, 'Kretzu', 27).

[79] 'Linchpin of the plot' is M. Beard's phrase in her joint review of Alfred and Freeman (*TLS* 20 June 20 1997). Orgel's description of Felperin's essay 'Tongue-Tied' as 'brilliantly mischievous' (22) is apt.

[80] Furness has nothing on the bear; Turner, on the other hand, devotes four pages to it, with only one nineteenth-century comment.

a reason for the early uninterest: 'Shakespeare had here introduced a bear – a most fit actor for pantomimes or puppet-shows; but blushing criticism has excluded the rough gentleman.' The implication is that in its association with low comedy, the bear (as portrayed by an actor) is best passed over in silence. From the 1930s on, however, scholarship reveals a dual interest in how the episode was originally staged and in what meaning it has beyond the theatrical value of spectacle.

Beginning with W. J. Lawrence in 1935 and continuing through Turner, a consensus has developed backing a human actor in the role when first performed;[81] critics holding this view cite the 'beares skyne' in Henslowe's inventory of stage properties at the Rose Theatre and 'man for bear' implications in other plays from the period.[82] They point to the 'bear rampant [as] of all beasts the most easily personated by a man';[83] and, while conceding the widespread popularity of bearbaiting on Bankside, they argue that bears for baiting were not all that tame, and even less likely is a bear trained to the point where it could be trusted to wait backstage, enter on cue, and rush at Antigonus without mauling him. Recently, Teresa Gaines and Barbara Ravelhofer have cogently reopened the debate in favour of a real bear, specifically one of the two polar cubs captured during an Arctic expedition, presented to James I in 1609, and kept, not among the King's beasts in the Tower, but in Henslowe's menagerie in the Bear Garden.[84] Gaines thinks that the cubs, by virtue of their age, would have posed little danger to those onstage or off; Ravelhoffer discusses bearbaiting as a 'showpiece of controlled violence' (288) and addresses other more creative ways of employing bears to demonstrate the 'performing' animal's amenability to training and discipline (309–15). As evidence of a penchant for bears in the years usually assigned to *The Winter's Tale*, 1610–11 (Pafford, 69), proponents point to the bear-drawn chariot in Jonson's *Masque of Oberon* (1611) and to the revision of *Mucedorus* (1610) that replaced the original use of a bear's head with business involving the whole creature. Despite Turner's blunt dismissal (274) of the 'real bear' thesis as 'ridiculous', it would appear that the issue remains open.[85]

Even more a matter for debate is the meaning of the bear. Unrequired by the plot – Antigonus could have conveniently perished with the offstage mariners – and

[81] Lawrence, *Those Nut-Cracking Elizabethans*, 1935, 12. Besides Turner, others include Coghill (34), Biggins (3), Pitcher (47), and Orgel (155–6).

[82] See Pitcher's discussion of *Cox of Collumpton* (1600) (esp. p. 50). George Reynolds, who backs a real bear in *WT*, nevertheless offers several citations in support of the claim that 'man for bear' was the norm on the early modern stage ('*Mucedorus*, Most Popular Elizabethan Play?', in *Studies in The English Renaissance Drama*, ed. Josephine Bennett, Oscar Coghill, and Vernon Hall, Jr, 1959, 248–68, esp. 259–60).

[83] G. B. Harrison, ed., *The Winter's Tale* (Penguin, 1947), 132.

[84] Grant, 'Polar performances: The King's bear cubs on the Jacobean stage', *TLS* 14 June 2002, 14–15; and Ravelhofer, '"Beasts of Recreacion": Henslowe's White Bears', *ELR* 32 (2002), 287–323, esp. 307, 314, and 318. The idea of a real bear seems to have originated in 1905 (see Turner, 274) and picked up support in Quiller-Couch, who thought that one from a nearby bear-pit was used to 'make a popular hit' (Wilson, xx). Ravelhofer provides a brief overview of the debate and is especially illuminating on the 'place of the bear in Stuart urban culture' (287).

[85] Not just as evidenced by Gaines and Ravelhofer, but also by the changing view of Gurr, who in 1983 had declared for 'a man in a bearskin' (424) but by 1992 had switched to the 'real' bear side (see *The Shakespearean Stage 1574–1642*, 3rd edn, 200).

absent from *Pandosto*, the episode appears designed to convey multiple meanings. On a very basic level, the animal can be seen as a land-version of the savage nature that destroys the mariners on the seas. The Clown's account supports this in paralleling the shipwreck and the bear's ravening Antigonus. On a deeper level, the choice of a bear carries generic, symbolic, and/or anthropological significance. If, as Louise Clubb contends, the animal traditionally thought of as unformed at birth and licked into shape (see Tilley, S284) is seen as 'both more and less terrible' than other wild beasts – savage and yet tamable – then the bear in the scene of generic transition (3.3) becomes the 'tragicomic beast par excellence', ensuring 'the tempering of pain or laughter'.[86] Symbolically, the bear may function as 'an emblem of divine retribution' (Biggins, 13), a view that lies behind the performance choice of doubling the animal with Time, who 'makes and unfolds error' (4.1.2).[87] As a symbol of ferocity and cruel authority, a common association in contemporaneous texts,[88] the wild animal preying on a courtier may further represent the deranged king who had brutalized his court (Biggins, 13; Ravelhofer, 307)[89] – something actually seen in Michael Bogdanov's 1990 revival for the English Shakespeare Company.[90] If the episode is read in light of Ovid's myth of Callisto, one of Diana's nymphs ultimately transformed into a bear, the predatory beast may figure Hermione,[91] as was the case in Freeman's production at the Globe (1997).[92] Understood within the context of European folklore, the animal evokes the 'carnivalesqe' or 'Candlemas' bear who indicates the end of the Christmas holiday season and the beginning of the agricultural work year; as a 'figure of boundaries and of transformations', it thus becomes a 'significant marker of spatiotemporal form' (Bristol, 158–62, esp. 161, 159).

While realistic treatments of the bear have been memorable in the play's performance history,[93] the more noteworthy depictions since the 1960s have tended

86 Louise G. Clubb, 'The Tragicomic Bear', *Comparative Literature Studies* 9 (1972), 17–30. Coghill describes the ursine dispatch of Antigonus as a 'dramaturgical hinge' (34–5).

87 As in Barton–Nunn, Kahn (1975/6), and Syer. Of the Barton–Nunn doubling, Robert Speaight described 'exit, pursued by a bear' as becoming 'exit, summoned by Time', who appeared 'for all the world like a Jacobean policeman' (SQ 28 [1977], 189).

88 See, e.g., Edward Topsell, *The Historie of Foure-Footed Beastes* (1607), 43; also Prov. 28.15: 'As a roaring lion, and a ranging bear; so is a wicked ruler over the poor people'.

89 Detecting a bear/Leontes link in 1.2.155–6 and 2.3.90–2, Hunt marshals numerous examples of wordplay on 'bear' to underscore a 'bearish' Leontes in the first three acts who in 'devour[ing his surrogate] Antigonus', destroys the vices he had unleashed within himself, thereby making possible the happy ending (Hunt, 'Bearing', 335).

90 Pitcher (47) reports a clawed Leontes, with 'a mitt of skin for his hand and arm, . . . [who] towered over Antigonus and tore at him'. Ten years later, to the same end but less violently, Kulick had Leontes drape a bearskin over his shoulder and stalk his prey.

91 See Bate (224–7, esp. 226–7) and Parker ('Polymorphic Bears' 187–9).

92 Where Hermione rose from a supine position in the discovery place, painted her face white, and donned white claws before chasing after Antigonus (see Paul Nelson, *ShakB* 16.1 [1998], 5–9). While she didn't double as the bear, the queen in Noble played a diversionary role that caused the bear to move from the baby toward Antigonus (see Smallwood, 350).

93 Kean's bear, e.g., was praised as 'a masterpiece of the zoological art' (*The Times*, 1 May 1856, quoted in Bartholomeusz, 91), and reviews of the Granville-Barker and Brook revivals singled out convincingly predatory bears. More recent treatments in the same vein can be found in Bedford and Lewis.

toward the stylized, suggestive, or symbolic: e.g. a huge constructed bear supported by an actor in eight-inch boots who appeared in strobe lighting (Nunn), a looming bear-shadow seen in a flash of lightning (Eyre), a screech and growl heard in the dark and morphing into the Shepherd's cry (Lapine), a large cloth painting of a bear into which Antigonus exited (Whitney), and the use of a bear's head or a bear mask (Kahn, Cohen). Some of the more unusual stagings (besides the doubling with Hermione and Leontes) include a large polar bear rug that rose like a giant to consume a shocked Antigonus (Hands) and the fallen canopy of Leontes' palace that gradually took the shape of a bear as it engulfed the fleeing courtier (Doran). Illustrating the fruitful collaboration of scholarship and performance, several directors have utilized set design, properties, and costumes to weave the iterative wordplay on 'bear' into a running visual motif.[94]

'Exit pursued by a bear' will always challenge a director's creativity not because Antigonus' violent departure from the action can be played as either terrifying or hilarious but because its 'double-take' (Gurr, 423) or 'atmospherically ticklish' (Biggins, 6) quality allows it to be played and perceived as both/and: 'a frisson of horror instantly succeeded by a shout of laughter' (Coghill, 35).[95] The Clown's later narrative (3.3.81–96) alternates with hysterical speed between the fate of the mariners and the gruesome end of Antigonus; often delivered in hyper-kinetic fashion, it retrospectively diminishes the horror and enhances the comic-grotesque. By contrast, Antigonus' dream of the ghostly Hermione shortly before his exit contextualizes the moment as serious.[96] This ambiguity of tone makes the episode 'the dramatic equivalent of the narrative distancing effected by the archaic manner of "an old tale" . . . What such a scene, and the whole play, demands is a . . . flexible response . . . a condition of mind in which the audience can be aware of different, and even contradictory, levels of meaning, just as a child can respond to a story by seeming to immerse himself completely in its imaginative world and yet remain easily aware that it is only a story' (Draper, 11). Almost a century of commentary and staging demonstrates that the bear, complex and ambiguous, cannot be dismissed as either 'charming divertissement' or an 'instance of bad taste' (Bristol, 159).

[94] Examples include the constellation of 'Ursa major' reflected on a cyclorama before the play began (Ward, 'Davis', 27), the ever-present polar bear rug that began to shrink after devouring Antigonus in Hands (Nicholas Shrimpton, *S. Sur.* 40 [1988], 178), the teddy bear held by Mamillius in Kretzu, and Leontes' hat made of bear fur in Howell along with what struck one reviewer as the increasing amount of fur on his costumes the more paranoid the king became (G. M. Pearce, *Cahiers E* 20 [1981], 98). See also Bartholomeusz (222) on the pervasive bear imagery in Barton-Nunn. More recently, there was the transformed bear in Lewis (see p. 8n.25) who, with a rose in his mouth, bade a friendly farewell during the curtain call.

[95] Warren (*Staging*, 128) recalls Hall's view that the episode should be 'grotesque and take the breath away' and that 'we should not look at it for too long' (presumably to preclude any inclination to laugh). Reviews of Brook, Nunn, and Phillips suggest a terrifying bear, while those of Evans and Davis point to an indisputably comic one. Productions deliberately intending a mixed response include Wentworth (see Timpane, 18) and Bohnen, in which the aural approach involved an animal growl, a human scream, and then the bear's stomach-clearing belch (Newcomb, 28).

[96] For Shakespeare's early audiences, contemporary accounts of actual bear killings might have encouraged a response more akin to the terrified shudder than the uneasy giggle; for one such incident, see Hunt, 'Bearing', 345 n.23.

The figure of Time

A sense of time – the 'two hours' traffic of the stage' – is obviously important to all drama, but *The Winter's Tale* is acutely, perhaps even peculiarly, time-sensitive since Shakespeare incarnates the temporal principle in an actor assuming the choric role of Time.[97] While unnecessary to the mechanics of plot (in this he is similar to the bear), the speaker who opens Act 4 is, like the playwright, protean, sharing a bit of himself with almost every character and informing every scene.[98] He may introduce himself as though this is his first coming, but we have met him before in different guises.

Archidamus, for example, who appears only in the first scene and who could therefore play any number of parts thereafter, prefigures Time in his brief exchange with Camillo.[99] As the first to mention Mamillius and the boy's promise, Archidamus alludes to something that can be realized only in the course of time. By speaking of a potential visit from Leontes to Polixenes in the context of competitive hospitality, he connects the future to the present, and his assertion that he speaks 'in the freedom of my knowledge' and 'as my understanding instructs me' (1.1.10, 16–17) fits Time's omniscience and capacity for revealing truth in good course. When coupled with the earlier reference to Mamillius' youth, Archidamus' insight into the desire of old men trying to escape death for as long as possible captures in small the whole life cycle.[100]

Time's talk of news being 'brought forth' (4.1.27) recalls one of the first images to greet the audience: a visibly pregnant woman (see 1.2.0 SD n.), perhaps the most graphic sign of the waiting endemic to the temporal process. Time also says that he has spoken of Polixenes' son, whom he names in 4.1.22. If Time has reported this son previously, he has done so either in a speech not now recorded or, as is more likely, that has been spoken through others: Hermione who, as a mother, is the first

[97] Various incarnations include Kean's spectacular tableau with Time (as Cronos) surmounting the globe (Cole, 2.172) – traces of which can be found in Hall (Warren, 129); a blond maiden (in Reinhardt; cited in Kennedy, 60–1); 'an octogenarian with little make-up and no paraphernalia other than an hour-glass' (Munich, 1959; cited in Ewbank, 'Triumph', in Hunt, 154–5 n.); an elegant old woman clad in black and holding an old-fashioned alarm clock (in Bergman); a drunkard (in Freeman); and a dapper gentleman with a pocket-watch who, at 4.1.4, turned his back toward the audience to reveal emblematic wings (in Kulick).

[98] Possibly the reason for Barry Edelstein's decision to have 'the entire company come . . . on stage [in 4.1], each with a ticking metronome, to tell sixteen years in passing' (Nina da Vinci Nichols, 'New York Performances', *SN* 52.4 [Winter 2002/03], 115).

[99] Ewbank observes that the opening scene of exposition 'places the play in a perspective of naturally ripening time, opening backwards as well as forwards' ('Triumph', in Hunt, 140); see also Draper (12), who finds a similar fusion of past, present, and future in 5.2. Mullin-Muriello records a doubling of Archidamus and Time at Stratford-upon-Avon in 1942, and the SQ bibliography for 1997 cites one in Vancouver, BC.

[100] Camillo, too, speaks for Time as he 'describes the span of the relations between the Kings of Sicilia and of Bohemia: from an indicative past [1.1.19] . . . to a present consequent upon that past [1.1.19–21] . . . to a desired (but soon to be threatened) future [1.1.27]'' (Ewbank, in Hunt, 140–1). The courtiers' shared banter on crutches (1.1.34–40) might also trigger in the mind's eye the image of Time specified in *Much Ado About Nothing* (2.1.358) and found in the iconography of the period (see illustration 19, p. 35).

19 The Triumph of Time, from Francesco Petrarca, *Opera*, 1508 (Folger Shakespeare Library). In the early modern period Time was typically depicted as an old man, usually winged and sometimes on crutches. Missing from this illustration is another emblem, the scythe.

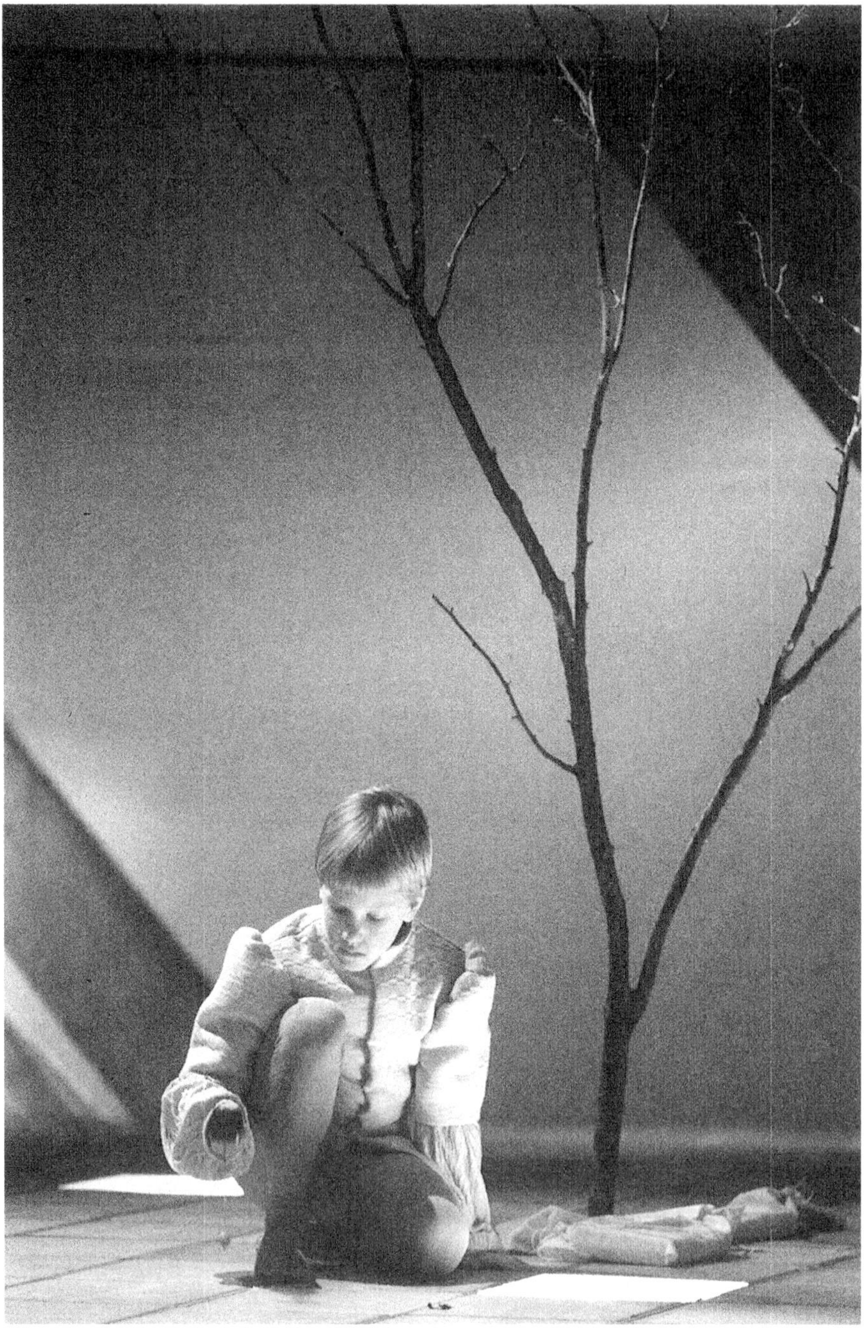

20 Roberto Conte (Mamillius), from Michael Kahn's 1987 production for The Shakespeare Theatre, Washington, DC. Joan Marcus, photographer. As though to say the 'tale' being told is the boy's, many productions open with an image of Mamillius.

to bring up Bohemia's son (1.2.34); Leontes who asks about the as yet unnamed boy in a context that pairs him with young Mamillius (1.2.161–3); and Polixenes who refers to the son who 'makes a July's day short as December' (1.2.167). Mamillius himself provides an especially intriguing link to Time, as emphasized in recent productions where the play opens not with the exchange between two courtiers but with the boy, either silent (see illustration 20, p. 36) or speaking some of Time's lines (as in Hytner). Although on the surface it appeared that Noble chose not to include Time as a character, reducing him instead to a message that arrived by way of a red balloon (in 4.2), the production's opening image of the boy turning a snow globe implied a fusion of the two figures in the director's mind.[101] In Rowan, the doubling was explicit: the boy seen opening and reading a book as the play began reappeared as a ghost to open Act 4. Commenting on the appropriateness of embodying Time in Mamillius, Goodland (20) quotes the director: 'Time, for a family that has lost a child, is forever after measured by that moment.'[102] In such stagings, Mamillius clearly appropriates Time's function as chorus and teller of the 'tale' (4.1.14).

The oracle of Apollo, like Time, is cryptic and all-knowing; and as the action shifts to Bohemia, an animal appears whose hibernating habits make it one of the most time-sensitive of creatures.[103] Even the Shepherd's first wish that youth would 'sleep out' (3.3.59) the intervening years between childhood and adulthood looks ahead to Time's desire to give his scene 'such growing / As you had slept between' (4.1.16–17). By Act 4, scene 1, then, the enigmatic Time proves to be no newcomer to the stage after all.[104]

Subsequent scenes will continue to make the character's presence felt: in other images of pregnancy (4.4.236–9 n. and 260–1 n.), in references to the Shepherd's dead wife (4.4.55–62) and father (4.4.434–6), and in Perdita's litany of flowers, each of which has its season. Draper notes (13) how the Shepherd, described as 'stand[ing] by like a weather-bitten conduit of many kings' reigns' (5.2.48–9), seems to span the whole range of time. As the action draws to a close, Paulina controls the final revelation, announcing the ripeness of all in her laconic ''Tis Time' (5.3.99), and Hermione, as a 'statue' showing sixteen years of wrinkles, once again illustrates Time

[101] As the boy turned the globe and peered into it, the Sicilian court, frozen in place behind him within a floor-to-ceiling gauze box, came to life. The box flew out, the boy joined the group, and the audience was left to wonder 'Was it his birthday party. . . . and was the whole story really going to be just his dream?' (Smallwood, 349).

[102] Similarly, but with a different choice of property, Kretzu had Mamillius pick up a clock, wind it, and set it down again before stepping into the masked ball revealed behind him as the curtain rose; he too would deliver Time's monologue (Shurgot, Kretzu review, 27).

[103] Bartholomeusz (222) thinks the merging of the bear with Time in the Barton-Nunn revival crystalized Time as the central principle of the production.

[104] Because Kahn wanted Time to double in the minor parts that advance the story, the actor also appeared as the jailer (2.2), a doctor reporting on Mamillius' physical condition (2.3), the voice of the oracle and the messenger who later delivered the news of Mamillius' death (3.2), and a gentleman (5.2). In addition to Time/Bear, Time/Archidamus, and Time/Mamillius, doublings include the Shepherd (in Lewis), the Clown (in Kulick), Antigonus (in Beerbohm-Tree, Eyre, and Doran), and Perdita (as well as Mamillius in E. Hall); see also table in Appendix B.

as process, thereby becoming the key recipient of Time's 'mak[ing] and unfold[ing] error' (4.1.2).[105]

Just as Time has surrogates throughout the play, his monologue serves as a lexical repository of words heard before and yet to come,[106] and like the play itself, it is divided into two halves. The first fifteen lines introduce Time as an abstract principle and the second fifteen summarize what has happened during the sixteen-year gap between what Bristol calls (154–8, 162–7) the play's two solstitial seasons of Christmas and mid-summer. The events and circumstances reported (see 4.1.17 n., 23 n.), however, do not occur in a vacuum but are set within the context of the first part of the speech: 'Far from having abandoned time-thinking, Shakespeare presses home the fact that the "wide gap" of dramatically "untried growth" is part of the universal process of time . . . Rather than being timeless, *The Winter's Tale* is thus set in a context of *all* time' (Ewbank, 'Triumph', in Hunt, 145). In the tradition of the emblem-book, the character and the monologue serve, respectively, as picture and explication of the 'motto' that articulates the shift from tragedy to comedy: 'Thou met'st with things dying, I with things newborn' (3.3.101–2).

While the play's performance history reflects some unease with the figure who opens Act 4 in rhymed couplets, rarely since Charles Kean's spectacular restoration of Time in 1856 has the character been omitted.[107] Productions since the mid-twentieth century, in fact, show an increasingly ubiquitous Time and thus underscore the character's importance as the begetter of all the dramatic agents and the overarching teller of the tale. Douglas Campbell seems to have been the pioneer in this regard, opening his 1958 *Winter's Tale* at Stratford, Ontario with Time as prologue; the figure then wandered in and out of the action before finally bidding the audience farewell as, all alone on a darkening stage, he closed the book he had opened so much earlier (Bartholomeusz, 188). Many revivals have followed suit with intriguing variations.

Nunn, for example, used the same transparent box that held Da Vinci's Renaissance man whirling about to the accompaniment of the first few lines from 4.1 not only to open the production but also to enclose the jealous king, the figure of Time (in his Folio place), and the statue of Hermione, thus making clear Time's power to overthrow and to make things new. Eyre chose to follow a courtly dance with an elaborate 'Twelfth Night Pageant of Time', the character at the stroke of midnight seeming 'to part his own loins to reveal a playful Mamillius . . . [who] represent[ed]

[105] Lise Bruneau (Hermione in both Syer and Kahn) described the character's seclusion as a 'hibernation' (from a conversation with the actress).

[106] Examples include 'if' (which looks back to the note of contingency in the opening line and in the Oracle's message), 'gap' (which echoes strategically in 5.3.153–5), 'grace' (most associated with Hermione), 'glistering' (a variation on Leontes' 'glister' at 3.2.167), '(self)-born' and 'brought forth' (see p. 24 in this introduction), 'tale', 'growth' (and its variants 'growing' and 'grown'), 'wondering', 'try'/'untried', and, perhaps most significant, 'time' itself.

[107] As it was in Kemble, Macready, and Ames. Warchus' loosing of a hawk (see 4.4.15 n) immediately before the intermission, to mark the passage of sixteen years, stands out as a rare example of the complete omission of 4.1 in modern productions (see Jackson, 175).

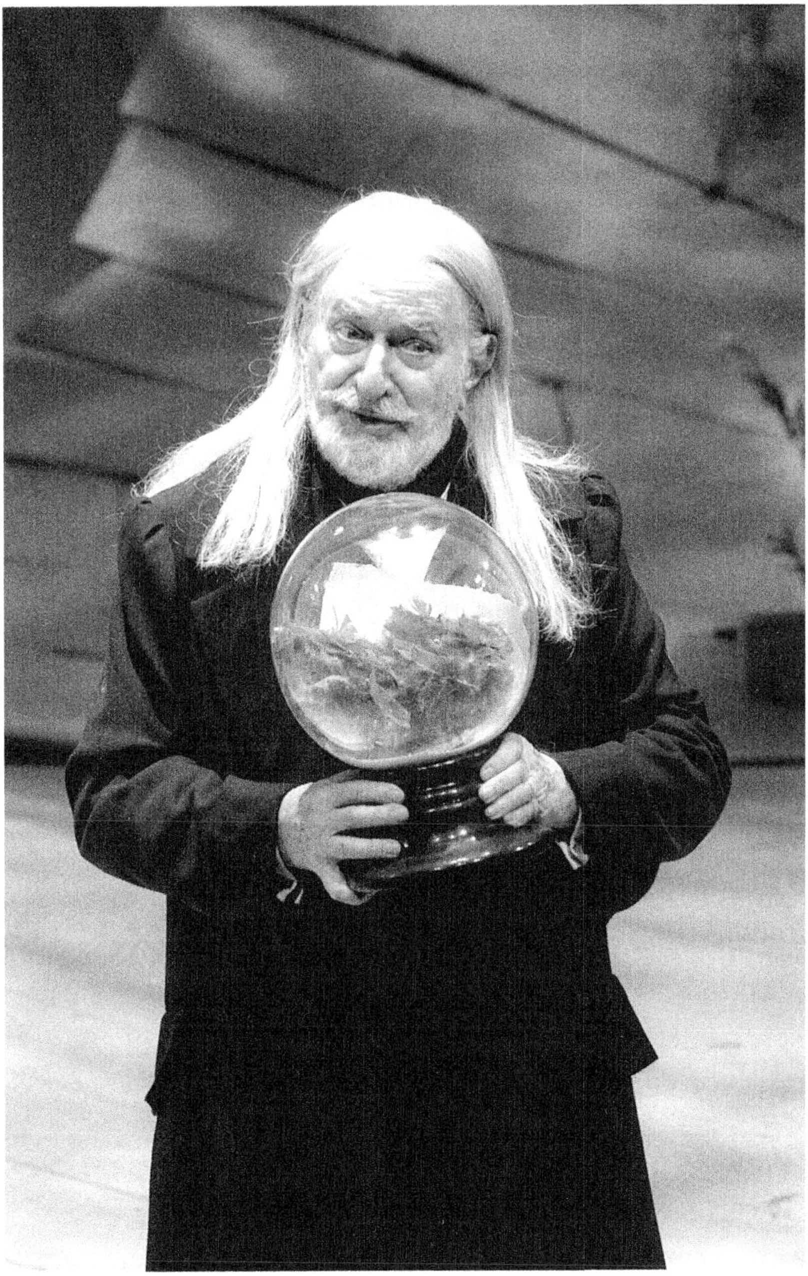

21 Act 4, scene 1: Emery Battis as Time, from Michael Kahn's 2002 production for The Shakespeare Theatre, Washington, DC. Richard Termine, photographer. At 4.1.16, instead of an hour glass, Battis turned his chief prop, a snow globe, from the side depicting a miniature set of Sicilia to that showing Bohemia.

Truth', first concealed and then revealed by Time (Draper, 52–3).[108] Donnellan began with an old woman sweeping the stage; she would return to do the same before and after the interval, the difference being that as the second half began she shed her peasant look to reveal a beautiful young woman, a fitting harbinger of the romantic love that would bloom in Bohemia; one more appearance would come at the end as she escorted a ghostly Mamillius offstage. Capturing time-as-process, this shape-changing Time also caught the play's Ovidian penchant for metamorphosis (see Sources, p. 70).[109]

For almost fifty years in both scholarship and performance Time has been recognized as something other than a seemingly disruptive presence in Act 4. What critics have long perceived – the character as thematic matrix and structural unifying force – directors have creatively implemented. As Coghill writes (36), to dispense with Time would be a 'loss to the theme and quality of the play . . . for Time is absolutely central to both and if he were not a character in the play, it would be necessary to invent him'.

Act 5 and the triumphs of Time

Passing hurriedly in Sicilia, leisurely in Bohemia, and abstractly in the 'gap' of sixteen years, Time makes and unfolds, destroys and creates, and ultimately 're-creates'. That re-creation, the triumph of Act 5, is a triple miracle of rebirth: the first is Leontes' moral growth and the second is Hermione's willingness to 'be stone no more' (5.3.99), the second made possible in no small measure by the first. Both king and queen have shut themselves up for sixteen years: Leontes in a palace that has become a penitential cloister; Hermione in an enclosure affording security and time to heal. Both have waited for the fulfillment of the oracle, one in sorrowful expiation (5.1.1–6) and the other in hopeful patience (5.3.125–8).[110] Central to each one's hiatus from the dramatic action is Paulina, as facilitator of moral reclamation for Leontes and as nurturer of physical and emotional health for Hermione (presumably the purpose of those 'twice or thrice a day' visits to a 'removed house' [5.2.90–1]). As the queen steps down from the pedestal that symbolizes her life of stone-like seclusion, extending her hand to her long-estranged

108 Less grandiose but to the same end, William, who covered the entire stage in white gauze to suggest 'all time frozen in eternity', used the amplified voice of Time to deliver part of the title page of *Pandosto* as the words first heard by the audience: 'Although by the means of sinister fortune truth may be concealed, yet by Time, it is most manifestly revealed'. The effect was to place the whole action, not just the second half, 'within the larger perspective of the workings of Time, imaged in a cool and abstract way' (Warren, 95).

109 In Kahn (see illustration 21, p. 39), Emery Battis at the beginning of Act 1 turned a snow globe to bring the characters behind him to life; reappearing in 4.1, he turned the property so that the miniature replica of wintry Sicilia gave way to that of springtime Bohemia; at the end of 5.3 as he ushered all the characters off, the colour of his coat had changed from black to white.

110 The difference derives in part from the way in which each relates to Apollo's message: the oracle's contingent 'if' (3.2.133) informs Leontes' waiting, whereas Paulina's more optimistic 'till' (5.1.40) governs Hermione's.

husband, who poignantly senses bodily warmth as he takes that hand (5.3.107–9), both Hermione and Leontes embrace once again a world of flux and uncertainty. In doing so, two individuals risk beginning anew as a couple, thus collaborating in Time's third miracle, perhaps its most amazing triumph: the rebirth of a marriage.

'SIR, YOU HAVE DONE ENOUGH': HOW CHANGED IS LEONTES?

[F]rom the text it is difficult to see that [Leontes] is changed; there is no evidence that he has, like Wolsey, come to know himself and to be aware of his littleness and still less of its blessedness. Anyone who has come to have a sense of his sin and to be sorry for it must be said to have grown to some extent. Leontes had no choice; he was bludgeoned to his senses and to sorrow, but he is not shown as achieving humility, and his 'growth' seems to be what may be described as an unavoidable minimum in the circumstances. (Pafford, lxxiii)[111]

I feel whatever he might say about his shame and the goodness of the blessed Gods, he's basically the same man with whom we started the play. People don't change that much. The spirit is still there. What is quite frightening about [*WT*] is that right until the end you occasionally see little flashes of the person you saw right at the beginning.[112]

From both an editor and an actor comes essentially the same answer: there is little or no change in the king of Sicilia by the end of the play. Pafford, however, offers a convenient disclaimer when he states that 'as a stage figure, [Leontes] must be accepted . . . at least as a reformed and contrite man' (lxxiii). What I wish to argue here is not that Leontes becomes a moral paragon (he does not) or that he becomes worthy of Hermione (he never could) but rather – in the midst of a growing chorus of those who reject the notion of meaningful change[113] – to make a case for reclamation that is not only visible but that also goes beyond the facile reformation required for the conventional happy ending in comedy. Tragicomic pastoral romance, at least in Shakespeare's hands, demands more than the equivalent of Claudio's one night's penance in *Much Ado*. Fast and easy 'comic' conversion does occur in *The Winter's Tale* but at the halfway point when the rage that emerged instantaneously disappears just as quickly (3.2.150–4). The remaining acts reveal that the conversion has in a word 'taken'.[114] We receive that information indirectly through the testimony of the unimpeachable Time (4.1.17–19) and the credible Camillo, adviser to kings (4.2.5–7; 4.4.492, 527–34); with the return of the action to Leontes' court in 5.1, we witness it directly.

[111] In a footnote, Pafford cites the following as examples of Leontes' lack of spiritual growth: 'a true penitent for wife-murder should not say that if he remarried he would murder his wife if Hermione's ghost appeared, or tell Florizel that his mother was obviously a faithful wife – a stock phrase, but one which should not so readily have come to Leontes. Worst of all is his desire for Perdita'.

[112] Patrick Stewart, Leontes in Eyre's 1981 RSC revival, as quoted in Judith Cook, *Shakespeare's Players*, 1983, 120.

[113] E.g. Traub, Schalkwyk, Eggert, and J. Davis. A welcome exception is James A. Knapp, 'Visual and Ethical Truth in [*WT*]', *SQ* 55 (2004), 253–78.

[114] Snyder and I read Leontes' penitential years differently; like Sokol (78), she sees them as essentially 'nonprogressive' (see her essay 'Memorial Art', in *Journey*, 204–5, 207–8).

The courtiers' proposal that Leontes end his long night of 'saint-like sorrow' (5.1.2) implies that mourning and penance have become a way of life;[115] i.e. they have become habitual, which understood in the context of Aristotelian ethics, suggests character formation, specifically the regimen by which one becomes a good person through daily practice and discipline.[116] As the religious diction of the scene's opening lines makes clear, Leontes' fidelity to the penitential promise he made at the end of the trial episode deserves the highest praise:

> No fault could you make
> Which you have not redeemed; indeed, paid down
> More penitence than done trespass. At the last,
> Do as the heavens have done, forget your evil;
> With them, forgive yourself. (5.1.2–6)

What adds to the power of these words is the ethical colouring of the speaker, for if one can judge someone, at least in part, by the company he/she keeps, Leontes' choice has been impeccable, and, if transformation is to happen, imperative.[117] There has, of course, been Paulina, whose name signifies conversion both sudden and permanent (see List of Characters, p. 80). The voice of conscience and the keeper of Hermione's memory and honour (5.1.50–1), her function from Act 3, scene 2 to the time Leontes says 'O peace, Paulina' (5.3.135) is that of guide, confessor, and even therapist (Hall's view as recorded in Warren, 124, 139–41). But also by the king's side for sixteen years have been two men who were deeply affected by their direct experience of the divine (3.1); once merely emissaries, Cleomenes and Dion now appear as trusted confidants and counsellors (see 5.1.0 SD CLEOMENES, DION n.). That the advice to put away sackcloth and ashes in favour of remarriage and procreation (5.1.24–34) comes from them suggests that by the highest standards of this world, Leontes has evidently repented enough and that one might even be excused for thinking that the gods concur.

Unlike the earlier Leontes, the later version (silent for almost thirty lines [5.1.21–48]) listens to counsel, in this instance, two arguments, both of which are good. They operate, however, within contrasting contexts: the immanent (remarry for the good of the kingdom [5.1.24–34]) versus the transcendent (heed the 'tenor' of Apollo's oracle [5.1.37–8]). Leontes' inclination to reject the former even before Paulina

[115] Productions make this clear through mourning drapery and black or grey costumes (see Headnote to 5.1), props such as Hermione's tomb and/or prominent pictorial representations (as in William, Syer, and Hytner), and stage business: e.g., Bergman opened the scene with a self-flagellating Leontes in sackcloth, surrounded by a group of nuns chanting a lamentation hymn; after completing his act of mortification, Leontes donned a friar's black penitential gown (see illustration 22, p. 43). See also 5.1.0 SD n.

[116] *Nichomachean Ethics*, Book 2, 'Moral Goodness' , trans. J.A.K. Thomson, Penguin Classics, rev. ed. 1976, rpt. 1987.

[117] What makes Leontes' conversation partners in 5.1 even more noteworthy is the absence of such characters from the primary source, without whom there is no moral support team either to reinforce the king's penitential resolve or to praise it.

22 Act 5, scene 1: The penitent Leontes as seen in the female monastic setting Bergman used to open 5.1. Börje Ahistedt (Leontes), Bibi Andersson (Paulina), and Gerd Hagman (Abbess), from Ingmar Bergman's 1994 production for the Royal Dramatic Theatre of Sweden, Stockholm. Bengt Wanselius, photographer.

reminds him of the latter speaks to an interior change; his response is worth quoting in full because it is easy to use it to criticize the king:

> Whilst I *remember*
> Her and her *virtues*, I *cannot forget*
> My *blemishes* in them, and so still think of
> The *wrong I did myself*: which was so much
> That heirless it hath made my kingdom, and
> Destroyed the *sweet'st companion* that ere man
> Bred his hopes out of, true.
> (5.1.6–12, *italics* mine)

While some detect a trace of the selfish Leontes in 'so still think of / The wrong I did myself' (Pafford, lxxiii n.), it is possible to read the line as indicating self-recognition. Leontes rightly puts the onus of the wrongs perpetrated against both kingdom and wife on himself; he acknowledges his own moral defects ('blemishes') which stand out all the more because of Hermione's virtues; he articulates the truth of her fidelity and, by extension, the legitimacy of both Mamillius and Perdita (see 5.1.12 n.). Most important, however, is the way the passage begins and ends with an acute remembrance of what has been lost, a woman of virtue and the 'sweet'st companion'. The latter comment, when coupled with 'bred' and 'hopes', further implies a changed perception of Hermione's sexuality, once considered threatening but now sweet and honourable.[118]

If there is any danger that the penitence is becoming routine and the king is simply going through the motions of a 'performed . . . saint-like sorrow', Paulina, like Lear's Fool, is always there with just the right abrasive phrase to rub salt into monarchical folly. 'She you killed', a dramatically efficient indicator of her sixteen-year regimen, strikes the king 'sorely', and 'is as bitter / Upon [her] tongue as in [his] thought' (5.1.15, 18–19). His entire reply, especially the request that 'she say so but seldom' (20) might suggest that he would like to mute the horror of his earlier actions, but the speech is 'of a chastened and at least partly healed man', whose sober and quietly expressed admission of wrong, in sharp contrast to his earlier 'hysterical self-laceration' – a sign in itself of Paulina's successful ministry – 'has earned [him] . . . the right to use understatement . . ., at the furthest remove from the hyperboles which expressed his distortion of the truth. He is well on the way to complete recovery' (Warren, 139).

For Leontes, the pain of remembered sorrow is never-ending, always front and centre in his consciousness, and so unlike Shakespeare's narrative source where there is nothing comparable to the first 177 lines of Act 5.[119] What Shakespeare

[118] The conclusions drawn throughout this section as they relate to Leontes' growing awareness of Hermione's womanliness as something good and desirable, though arrived at independently, are compatible with Neely's analysis (205) of the king's new apprehension of Hermione as 'peerless [5.1.56], 'sexual' [54], and human [59–60]'.

[119] The only information related by the narrator about the king long absent from the story reveals a man in whom lust, envy, and cruelty are very much on display (see *Pandosto*, in Bullough, 192–3).

23 Act 5, scene 1: Perdita and Florizel at Leontes' court. Mireille Enos (Perdita), Jeremiah Wiggins (Florizel), and Philip Goodwin (Leontes), from Michael Kahn's 2002 production for The Shakespeare Theatre, Washington, DC. Richard Termine, photographer. Florizel and Perdita were costumed so as to recall Polixenes and Hermione from 1.2 and positioned at the same piano where the other two had sat earlier (see illustration 18).

dramatizes in the opening sequence of the scene is nothing less than a test that Leontes passes, resisting the easy proposal offered by the courtiers in favour of the hard course of action advocated by Paulina. The interlocutory function of 'bit players' like Cleomenes and Dion seems at least in part to drive home the moral and spiritual resolve of a king committed to the will of the gods, a far cry from his earlier blasphemy, 'There is no truth at all i'th'oracle. . . . this is mere falsehood' (3.2.138–9). As Mahood observes (*Bit Parts*, 80), the faith of the two courtiers in this scene 'is less entire than that of the arch-sinner, and the effect of this is to throw Leontes' steadfastness into high relief. Only the man who has felt the full power of the god trusts unwaveringly to the oracle.'

Sixteen years of penance and remorse, however, while reforming Leontes, have not exactly renewed him. Sin would appear to have been purged but the purification brings no joy. If the seemingly endless cycle of potentially numbing sameness is to stop so that Leontes and his kingdom can move on, an outside force is needed. That jumpstart comes with the arrival of Perdita and Florizel, who bring the natural vitality of youth and the pastoral world to a court grown aged and cheerless. Leontes, once again cast in the role of host, recognizes the impact of the moment:

'Welcome hither, / As is the spring to th'earth' (5.1.150–1).[120] For the first time in the play, the king of Sicilia, as though going through a thaw of his own, speaks pastoral's language of rebirth, his lyrical appreciation of natural forces replacing the negatively tarnished images of cattle, angling, and ponds in his earlier discourse (e.g. 1.2.122–4, 178–9, and 193). While the comment concerning the marital fidelity of Florizel's mother (5.1.123–5) might suggest an old and unsettling preoccupation, it functions primarily as a way of bringing to the king's mind his long-estranged boyhood friend, now before him in the person of Florizel. (Even Pafford, who is critical of so much of Leontes' dialogue, concedes these lines as nothing more than a stock compliment.) The resemblance is such that joy and anguish fuse as the king moves from a momentary recollection of youthful exuberance, even abandon,

> Your father's image is so hit in you,
> His very air, that I should call you brother,
> As I did him, and speak of something wildly
> By us performed before[,] (5.1.126–9)[121]

to what is never far from the surface, namely, the keen awareness of his folly, which destroyed so many relationships:

> O, alas!
> I lost a couple that 'twixt heaven and earth
> Might thus have stood, begetting wonder, as
> You, gracious couple, do; and then I lost –
> All mine own folly – the society,
> Amity too, of your brave father . . .
> (5.1.130–5)

Memories of those actually and seemingly lost forever along with awareness of his own culpability in those losses colour every moment for Leontes. That they do so even at times of ineffable joy (e.g., 5.1.147–8, 169–77; 5.2.43–7, 73–5; 5.3.32–4, 37, 39–40, 147–9) contributes to an image of reformation that makes him more sympathetic as he moves toward the blessings awaiting him.[122]

One passage in particular casts Leontes' moral recovery in the guise of a vitality long dormant. After learning that Florizel has not been fully honest about his situation and that he and the 'goddess' (5.1.130) accompanying him are not married, Leontes expresses an interest in Perdita that strikes Paulina as inappropriate (a) because his look shows an eye too youthful, and (b) because his dead queen 'was more worth such gazes / Than what [Leontes] look[s] on now' (5.1.222–6). These five

120 In Campbell, Leontes' words described the impact of Florizel and Perdita's arrival with exactness, their exuberant, bright greens and pinks appearing in sharp contrast to the blacks, greys, brown and scarlet of the Sicilian court (Bartholomeusz, 187–8). At the exact moment of the couple's arrival on stage, Stewart's bed-ridden Leontes in Eyre rose; in Doran, Sher's king, formerly on the floor engrossed in a book, literally fell over in shock at what he saw before him.

121 The passage recalls Hermione's request that Polixenes share stories of youthful escapades (1.2.59–61).

122 Among those who remain unsympathetic are Bristol (p. 166) and Felix Schelling, *Elizabethan drama, 1556–1642*, 2 vols., 1908, 2:201–2.

lines are all that remain from several pages in *Pandosto* detailing the king's protracted lust, which leads him to imprison Dorastus/Florizel, proposition Fawnia/Perdita, and, when that fails, threaten to rape her (see Bullough, 193–8). Not only does Shakespeare reduce the incest motif, he changes the whole tenor of the king's seeming interest in Perdita: first, by couching it in the subjunctive; second, by placing it within the context of Florizel's request that Leontes remember his own youth and wooing days (5.1.217–20); and third, by following it with a quick rejoinder to Paulina, 'I thought of her [Hermione] / Even in these looks I made' (see 5.1.226–7n). The attraction then, part of the rejuvenating process reflective of the king's moral recovery, is healthy rather than incestuous, a difference further clarified by the promise to enable rather than derail (as in the source) Florizel's cause (5.1.226–31).[123] What begins as 'jesting' (Andrews, 212), 'amiable banter' (Schanzer, 228), or 'mere civility' (Ranald, 14) becomes in the

> collation of [Leontes'] thoughts . . . Shakespeare's transformation of the 'unlawful lust' of his source into a kind of regenerative innocence . . . The love that stirs in Leontes for his daughter is not antithetical to, but continuous with, his love for her mother . . . And as that great creative continuity puts roots down into Leontes' soul, he finds that he is . . . nothing but a 'friend' to Florizel's 'desires'.[124]

Leontes exits the scene with purposeful energy and enthusiasm, his sentences volitional in thrust, and clear, direct, and confident in the predication of intent:

> I will to your father;
> Your honour not o'erthrown by your desires,
> I am friend to them and you; upon which errand
> I now go toward him. Therefore follow me,
> And mark what way I make. Come, good my lord.
> (5.1.228–32)

Emotionally, behaviourly, and morally, the Leontes who enters the chapel in Act 5, scene 3 is neither the arrogant king of the first three acts nor the broken man who closes Act 3, scene 2 (see illustration 24, p. 48); humbled and full of gratitude (5.2.45–7, 120; 5.3.1–2), and with the emotional floodgates open (5.2.38–47), he is ready for Paulina's *coup de grâce*, the statue as shock therapy (Warren, 148).

HERMIONE'S RESURRECTION: REAL OR FEIGNED?

Physically absent from the stage since her faint in the trial scene but not forgotten, Hermione returns to the action at the end of Act 5. Throughout the play she is a woman who waits: first, as visibly pregnant; then, as in a state of hibernation from the world of Sicilia; finally, as a statue awaiting animation. But is she or is she not an

[123] Productions, of course, can treat 5.1.222–6 so as to make both the on- and offstage audiences feel uncomfortable, as in Donnellan where Leontes violently reached out for Perdita. Although Kahn alleviated tension by keeping Leontes by Paulina's side and a good distance from Perdita, the young woman, jumping up from her seat at the piano and shooting a disapproving look at the king, clearly heard the lines as a threat.

[124] Sanders, 109; Mahood (*Wordplay*, 160) holds a similar view.

24 Act 3, scene 2: Paulina's castigation of Leontes in the trial scene. Brian Bedford (Leontes), Martha Henry (Paulina), Rod Beattie, Peter Hutt, and Gregory Wanless (Lords), and James McGee (Attendant), from Robin Phillips and Peter Moss' 1978 production for the Stratford Festival of Canada. Daphne Dare with Michael Maher, designers; Robert C. Ragsdale, photographer.

exquisitely carved piece of stone? Shakespeare seems to want it both ways: as marvel and as something that can be explained in human terms. Beginning at 3.2.169, everyone, onstage and off, is led to accept Paulina's news of Hermione's death (3.2.198) as fact. Paulina's hysterical grief and her daring Leontes to view the dead body of his queen (3.2.200–4) – something he himself wishes to do (3.2.231–2) and evidently does (5.3.139–40) – give credence to the announcement,[125] as do the appearance of Hermione's ghost to Antigonus in a dream and Leontes' later claim that he has 'said many / A prayer upon [Hermione's] grave' (5.3.140–1). The final scene itself, with its central property of Hermione's 'statue', which Paulina promises to animate, suggests that what is to happen is nothing short of a miracle, a resurrection from the dead. The entire atmosphere proclaims wonder: the chapel, the sounds of gentle music, the religiously sonorous 'Behold' (5.3.20), the reverential silence of the spectators, and both Paulina's command to 'awake your faith' (5.3.94–5) and

[125] See Kaara L. Peterson, 'Shakespearean Revivifications: Early Modern Undead', *S. St* 32 (2004), 240–66, esp. 251–2. Faucit provides an inventory of how Paulina's stratagem may have been carried out, complete with an empty coffin to be entombed (382–3).

her chant-like invocation (5.3.99–103).[126] Then, just when awe is at its most intense, Shakespeare undercuts the wonder with Hermione's statement that she never really died (5.3.125–8). When read in light of Paulina's proposed scenario by which she would select a new wife for Leontes (5.1.76–81, 82–4)[127] – along with reports of her private visits to a 'remov'd house' (5.2.90–1) and her protestations not to touch the freshly painted statue – Hermione's startling revelation becomes the new truth: '[She] is not a Lazarus, come from the dead . . . that she is *believed* dead is one of those errors which Time makes and unfolds' (Coghill, 40).

As an elaborate ruse by Paulina, Shakespeare's surrogate, the statue business would on the surface seem to rob the moment of mystery. But Shakespeare teases the reader and spectator by abruptly cutting off any explication (5.3.128–30), and by intimating that the logistics of Hermione's well-kept seclusion may be amazing in their own right, straining credulity 'like an old tale' to be 'hooted at' (5.3.117, 116). What the characters and the audience are being told, then, is to savour the moment in all its wonder and amazement. Whether to believe in Hermione's resurrection, which takes up far more playtime than the few statements to its contrary, is perhaps best answered by Draper (72): We 'believe and disbelieve simultaneously, yielding to the theatrical experience . . . and yet [knowing] that what [we] witness is "romance"', that this is not real.

HERMIONE: 'O, SHE'S WARM!'

No matter one's ultimate position on the 'resurrection' versus 'restoration' scenario, for Hermione, like Leontes, there is a triumph of time. If not physically stone, she has, like him, been stone emotionally, the rhythms of life she once knew and enjoyed frozen. Coghill, who emphatically opts for restoration over resurrection, nevertheless concludes that the play ends in a miracle, but one limited to Leontes; the miracle, however, is broader than that, extending to the queen as well.[128] It is the miracle of her becoming warm again.

Hermione's descent from wherever her 'statue' is positioned is dramatically constructed so as to constitute a choice.[129] Before she shakes off her numbness (5.3.102), the long-absent queen, who can see (5.3.67) and hear (as she will the music and Paulina's incantation), has had time to take in the husband she last heard angrily blaspheming Apollo but who now appears humble, reverential, and overcome with unspeakable emotion (5.3.49–50). Although informed by Victorian sensibilities,

[126] In Phillips (see illustration 25, p. 50) and Howell, the darkness, lit only by candles, evoked an aura of religious mystery; in Lewis, as the statue came up through a trap, a scrim depicting a rose and leafed branches came down simultaneously from the ceiling, with falling confetti punctuating the moment (see illustration 26, p. 50); and in Whitney, Hermione's descent from a pedestal inside a curtained metal cylinder suggested movement 'from one realm of existence into another; from perhaps . . . death into life . . . from dream into miracle' (Shurgot, 'Whitney', 36).

[127] These lines constituted for Faucit (382) the 'first hint . . . that Hermione is still alive'.

[128] For Coghill (40), the play is 'about a crisis in the life of Leontes, not of Hermione, and her restoration to him . . . is something which happens not to her, but to him. He had thought her dead by his own hand . . . and [his finding] her unexpectedly alive . . . is the miracle'. My disagreement with Coghill has to do with his focus on Leontes at the expense of Hermione.

[129] Contrary to Bristol's claim ('Spatiotemporal form', as revised in *Big-Time Shakespeare*, 1996, 173).

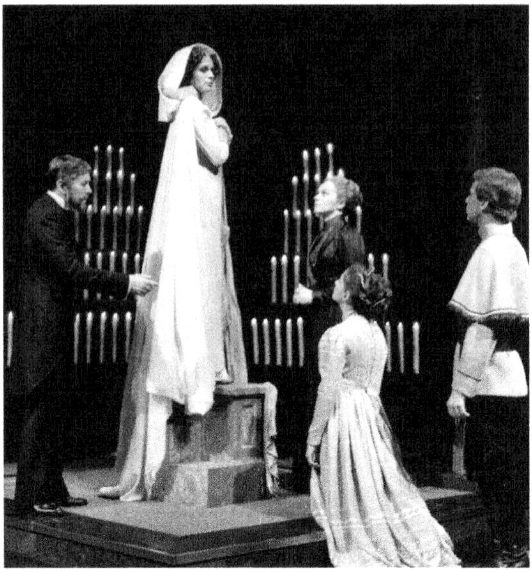

25 Act 5, scene 3 (statue scene): Brian Bedford (Leontes), Margot Dionne (Hermione), Martha Henry (Paulina), Marti Maraden (Perdita), and Stuart Arnott (Florizel), from Robin Phillips and Peter Moss' 1978 production for the Stratford Festival of Canada. Daphne Dare with Michael Maher, designers; Robert C. Ragsdale, photographer.

26 Act 5, scene 3 (statue scene): Caitlin O'Connell (Paulina), Olivia Birkelund (Hermione), Jon DeVries (Leontes), and Tina Jones (Perdita), from Irene Lewis' 2002 production for Center Stage, Baltimore, Maryland. Richard Anderson, photographer. Birkelund's Hermione ascended through a trap behind a scrim bearing the image of a rose.

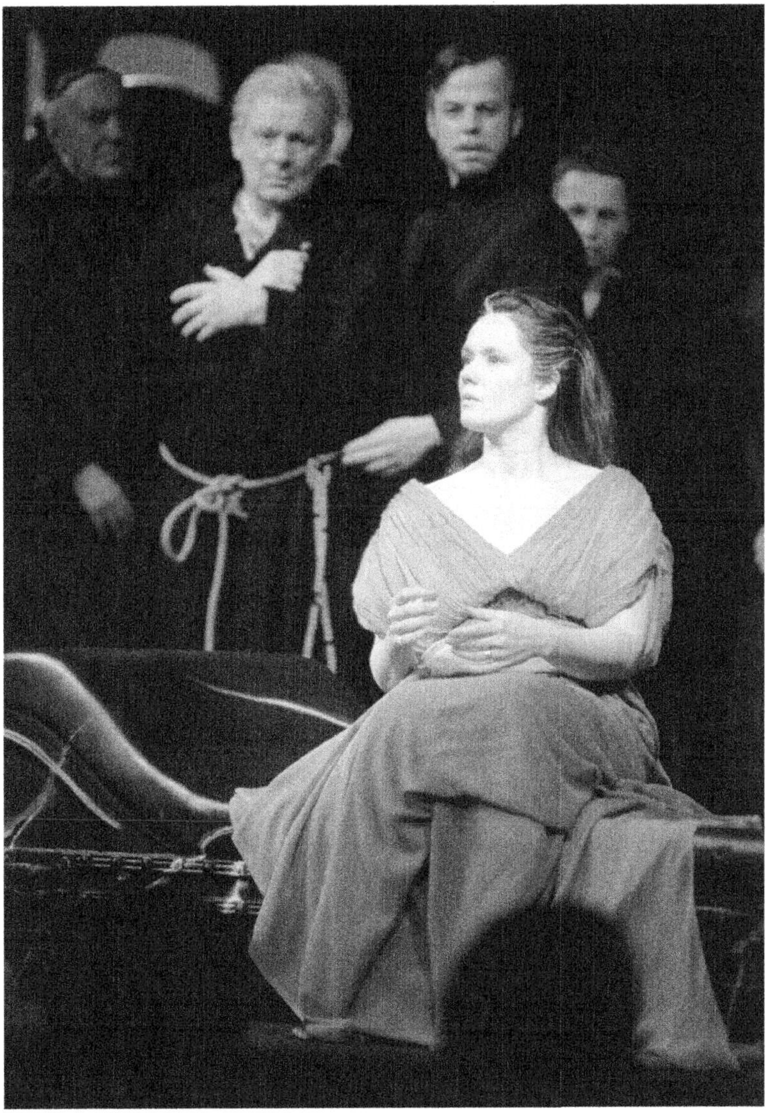

27 Act 5, scene 3 (statue scene): Pernilla August (Hermione), Börje Ahistedt (Leontes), and Krister Henriksson (Polixenes), from Ingmar Bergman's 1994 production for Royal Dramatic Theatre of Sweden, Stockholm. Bengt Wanselius, photographer. Having been carried in by several monks and then placed 'effigy-like' on a chaise that functioned as a tomb, Hermione moved her fingers at 'be stone no more' (5.3.99) and then slowly sat up.

Helena Faucit's recounting of what went through her mind when Hermione hears Leontes' voice clarifies what is obvious to an actor but not necessarily to a reader; that is, the character as statue thinks and feels:

Her heart hitherto . . . full only of her lost children, [Hermione] finds herself forgetting all but the tones of the voice, once so loved, now broken with the accents of repentance and woe-stricken desolation . . . her heart . . . begins to throb again, as she listens to the outpourings of a devotion she had believed to be extinct . . . Paulina had, it seemed to me, besought Hermione to play the part of her own statue, in order that she might hear herself apostrophised, and be a silent witness of the remorse and unabated love of Leontes before her existence became known to him, and so be moved to that forgiveness, which, without such proof, she might possibly be slow to yield (Faucit, 386).[130]

Specifically, Hermione hears the king remember their courtship in a way vastly different from his recollection in Act 1; she hears him find in her older appearance the young woman he fell in love with, remembering even the way she stood (while earlier actresses had stood gracefully or imposingly, Mrs Kean evidently took her cue from 5.3.34–6 to make 'maiden bashfulness' the key [Cole, 2, 178]); and like Paulina and the audience, she may also detect what has been apparent since the middle of Act 5, scene 1, a sensate Leontes, who becomes increasingly receptive to signs of life in a 'statue': wrinkles (5.3.28), breath and blood circulation (5.3.62–5, 78), and 'motion' in the eye (5.3.67). Marjorie Garber observes a 'rite of passage' moment here: 'as [Leontes] progresses through a sequence of comparisons and contrasts, his faith is awakened'.[131] So much so that he is determined to kiss the statue, a rapturous response that 'signals Paulina [his readiness] for reunion with the woman Hermione' (Neely, 206).

With Leontes' specific request that the statue 'speak . . . hear . . . [and] move' (5.3.91–4), Paulina, recognizing that ''tis time' for her Prospero-like control over others to end, exhorts the figure to 'be stone no more'. Even though it is inconceivable that she would urge the woman 'whose memory' Paulina has held in honour to return to a man whose moral rectitude cannot be avouched (5.3.88–9; see also 5.1.79–81), Hermione does not move for the longest while. By not stirring until after Paulina's eighth command (5.3.99–103), the queen, now in control of her re-entry into the world, makes everyone, Paulina included, wait in tense anticipation for what *she* deems the right moment. The waiting is thus theatrically charged with a deliberative force that, especially if she moves at the word 'redeemed' (as Bruneau did in Kahn), registers moral, even spiritual, choice (see 5.3.99–103 n).

Choosing to move, however, is not the queen's only volitional act, though it is the one that makes all else possible. For Paulina to say to Leontes, 'Nay present your hand. / When she was young, you wooed her; now, in age, / Is she become the suitor?' (5.3.107–9), Hermione presumably is seen extending her own hand,[132] something that Paulina has said she can make the statue do (5.3.89) but which she has

[130] While Faucit's recollection supports my argument, I in no way intend that it be interpreted as prescriptive; the sound of Leontes' voice could well evoke an unsympathetic response.

[131] Garber, *Coming of Age in Shakespeare*, 1981, 180.

[132] As in most productions, although Bergman had Hermione, after sitting up, remain seated, completely still until Leontes touched her. See illustration 27, p. 51.

not specified in her incantation. Like her emphatically delayed descent, Hermione's first gesture immediately following her initial movement is also freely chosen. This taking of hands, 'the gesture of relationship',[133] resonates with memory: the recent handfasting of Perdita and Florizel, the more distant giving of Hermione's hand to Polixenes (1.2.107), and the long ago betrothal of Hermione and Leontes (1.2.100–4). But the gesture not only recalls past moments – all of which unfortunately carry an association with something negative (i.e., interruption, misreading, or sour recollection) – it also functions as a sign of harmony restored (Bevington, *Action*, 141), explicitly 'mak[ing] the marriage a true re-marriage'.[134] The illocutionary force of Leontes' exclaimed, almost exhaled, 'O, she's warm' (5.3.109) says as much. Rhapsodizing the intimate sense of touch, the expression yields what one critic dares to call 'the most important discovery in [*WT*] – the discovery of warmth' (Sanders, 118).[135] So distasteful to Leontes in 1.2.107 ('Too hot, too hot!'), bodily warmth is now felt as something good and, in the context of an art perceived as 'lawful as eating' (5.3.111), deemed natural and desirable; the perlocutionary effect on Hermione is that both the exclamation and the perception precipitate a further intimacy, her embrace of Leontes.[136]

A perfect example of how 'action is eloquence', the gesture is noted twice: first in terms of what she does – Polixenes' 'She embraces him' (5.3.111); and then in terms of how – Camillo's 'She hangs about his neck' (5.3.112). What the pragmatic counsellor to kings and young lovers describes is an embrace usually performed as indicative of a desire not to let go,[137] a choice that finds support in the lack of dialogue by either husband or wife as others demand to hear Hermione's voice and have their curiosity satisfied. The connectedness, in fact, is so intense that Paulina must urge Hermione to turn away from Leontes and toward her kneeling daughter, to whom she has thus far made no overture. The sequence is significant: upon her re-entry into the world, Hermione emerges first as wife; only when the marital bond is restored does she then act as mother.[138]

133 The phrase is Ann Pasternak Slater's (*Shakespeare the Director*, 1982, 52).

134 Viswanathan, 50. Neely (207) emphasizes Hermione's autonomy in the gesture (the queen does the proposing) and Leontes' 'abandonment of [his] possessiveness'.

135 Sanders, who lingers over this moment (117–8), notes the iteration of 'warm' in the final scene, here at 5.3.109 and earlier at 5.3.35 and 66. The only other use of 'warm' in the text occurs as a variant at 3.3.71–2: the Shepherd's 'they were warmer that got this than the poor thing is here', an earthy appreciation of sexual relations as healthy and natural that accompanies the play's shift from tragedy to comedy.

136 On the illocutionary and perlocutionary force of words, see J. L. Austin's seminal study of speech acts, *How to Do Things with Words*, 1965, esp. 99–103.

137 E.g. Macready (as described in Faucit, 389–90), Howell, and more recently, Kahn, Cohen, and Lewis. Those, however, who prefer to 'keep [spousal] forgiveness in question' advocate either a 'perfunctory' embrace (Wexler, 116) or no embrace at all, the latter obviously requiring the cutting of lines (as seen in Phillips and Hall, respectively). Of the 'reserved' accord between Hermione and Leontes in Phillips, Berry (169) writes, 'She has yet to forgive him from her heart'. For contrasting stage images, see illustrations 28 and 29, pp. 54 and 55.

138 A priority emphasized in Bohnen (see Newcombe, 28). In readings different from that offered above, Traub (45–7) and Eggert (163–5) emphasize a de-eroticized Hermione whose return is nothing more than wish-fulfilment for Leontes: a wife, whose sexuality no longer poses a threat since she has been chastened figuratively through stone. This, however, is to minimize, if not ignore, the power of Leontes' exclamation and the emphasis throughout 5.3 on the living femaleness of the

28 Act 5, Scene 3: The Leontes–Hermione reunion. John Gielgud (Leontes) and Diana Wynyard (Hermione), from Peter Brook's 1951 production, The Phoenix Theatre, London. Angus McBean, photographer (Harvard Theatre Collection).

But how is the queen's silence toward Leontes to be interpreted? She speaks not a single word to him, her eight-line speech directed first to the gods and then solely to Perdita. The silence is intriguingly open to interpretation: perhaps an acknowledgement of 'the problems raised by her voice in the first three acts' when all of her responses were so terribly misread by Leontes (Enterline, 41–2), or an indicator of female suppression (Schalkwyk, 264–70) and 'a submissiveness most unlike her previous animation' (Traub, 230), or a sign of either her withholding forgiveness or of a reconciliation only tentative at best.[139] Silence, however, can be interpreted positively, as signifying, among other things, a deeply felt happiness and relief like that of Virgilia's when Coriolanus returns from battle, a response that earns her an epithet especially apt for Hermione in her moment of marital reunion: 'My gracious silence' (*Cor.* 2.1.175). At such a time, silence, having its own eloquence,

statue (her lips, eyes, posture, colour, and breath); see Bishop on the link between female eroticism and theatricality in the statue scene (168, 173–5). Snyder's view of Leontes' desire to monumentalize Hermione runs parallel to Traub's but ultimately reaches a different conclusion: by beseeching Paulina to animate the statue (5.3.91–4) and finding such animation 'lawful as eating' (5.3.111), Leontes finally breaks free from his earlier 'necrophilic need for immobile perfection' and embraces the 'realm of change', imperfection, and 'quotidian relationship' ('Memorial Art', in *Journey*, 205–6).

[139] See Wexler, 116: 'How can a woman forgive her husband for causing the death of their son and ordering the murder of their daughter? The play expresses both the wish for forgiveness and the impossibility of receiving it . . . only God could forgive Leontes – no wife could'; and Bristol ('Spatiotemporal Form' as revised in *Big-Time Shakespeare*,174): 'To describe [Hermione's embrace of Leontes] as a reconciliation . . . is simply a form of wishful thinking'.

29 Act 5, scene 3: The Leontes–Hermione reunion. Douglas Hodge (Leontes) and Anastasia Hille (Hermione), from Matthew Warchus's 2002 RSC production for the Roundhouse Theatre, London. Malcolm Davies Collection, Shakespeare Birthplace Trust.

may be the only language possible;[140] the third gentleman's account of the meeting between Leontes and Polixenes as a 'sight which was to be seen, cannot be spoken of' (5.2.37–8), and Paulina's approval of the onlookers' silence, especially Leontes', at 5.3.21–2, further contextualize this subsequent silence as good and proper. Besides, the silence does not exist in a vacuum; it is permeated with the emotional value of the three gestures noted: the giving of the hand, the taking of it, and the embrace, gestures that bookend the play, reminding us of another '[shaking of] hands as over a vast, and embrac[ing] as it were from the ends of opposed winds' (1.1.25–6).

'To put the question as crudely as possible', Bristol asks (166), 'why does Hermione agree to take Leontes back and why on earth would she want him?' Life – and the tabloid news that invites us to become voyeurs – is filled with stories that ask similar questions. The point is, as set up in the text, she does, and one reason might be the change she directly witnesses in Leontes. Turner says it well: Hermione remained sequestered 'so that which was lost could be found, not only Perdita but Leontes as well, whose regeneration is a major part of the triumph of time' (Variorum, commentary for 5.3.125–8). In his discussion of the 'logic' of deaths in plays like *The Winter's Tale* and *Much Ado*, Robert Bennett contends that 'rebirth is contingent upon actions that signal a spiritual growth or correction. In Shakespeare, . . . the return from supposed death is never an action that a character

[140] See Inga-Stina Ewbank, 'Shakespeare's Poetry', in Muir and Schoenbaum, 104; also John Russell Brown, *Shakespeare's Plays in Performance*, 1967, 43: 'Silence is often used by Shakespeare to accentuate a reaction that can only be expressed physically . . . Joy [may be] expressed by an inarticulate response, identified in the comments of bystanders'.

takes at an arbitrary time but is one made natural by an action taken by another that signals the time is right'.[141] In *The Winter's Tale*, both Paulina, Time's human surrogate, and the long-lost Perdita, who seeks blessing from a statue and permission to kiss its hand (5.3.44–6), give that signal. But it remains for someone else to precipitate Hermione's return: namely, Leontes, whom the queen sees before her as both penitent and husband, the latter receptive to a womanliness no longer cursed but celebrated. By her proffered hand, Hermione signals forgiveness; by Leontes' taking her hand and entering into the embrace that she initiates, he signals acceptance of that forgiveness so as to make possible reconciliation.

As early as Act 2, scene 1, lines 99–100 Hermione tells Leontes that his offence is so great that a facile '[I] did mistake' will not make things right again. After the king's abrupt turn from blasphemous rejection of the oracle to a plea for Apollo's pardon, Paulina echoes Hermione's sentiment, if not her style, as she angrily declaims a hyperbolic regimen of penance (3.2.207–11). Sixteen years of remorseful remembrance may provide Leontes with a 'recreation' (3.2.237) that is 're-creating', but as his courtiers observe, he has yet to forgive himself (5.1.6). For such forgiveness to occur, Shakespeare seems to say, the king must directly confront the ones sinned against. In the penultimate scene we are to understand he does so with Perdita, Polixenes, and Camillo; the reported reunion with Perdita, in particular, carries with it the implication of divine pardon. But for the process to be complete Leontes needs the forgiveness of the Other (the woman most grievously offended) before he can receive forgiveness from the self. That seems to be the meaning behind Hermione's extended hand and poignant embrace. Perhaps more than anything else, what distinguishes *The Winter's Tale* as tragicomic romance from comedies like *The Two Gentlemen of Verona, Much Ado About Nothing, All's Well That Ends Well*, and *Measure for Measure* is that the whole process – confession, contrition, atonement, the giving and accepting of forgiveness – instead of being short circuited, plays out in the fullness of time, so brilliantly imaged in Hermione's sixteen years of wrinkles: 'Wrinkles are the anti-romantic attribute of mature life: if Hermione is to be restored to Leontes with any significance to that restoration, she must return at time's full cost, her loss made calculable and conscious. The wrinkles are signs that suffering really *means*.'[142] They are also signs that forgiveness, if it is to *mean*, requires time.

PATRIARCHY: RESTORED AND REFORMED

That *The Winter's Tale* ends with patriarchy intact – Leontes has the last word and exits the play issuing orders – is obvious. Given when the play was written and the royal patronage of Shakespeare's dramatic company, how could it be otherwise? Hermione herself says as much when, in the few words allotted to her

141 *Romance and Reformation: The Erasmian Spirit of Shakespeare's 'Measure for Measure'*, 2000, 147.

142 Rosalie Colie, *Shakespeare's Living Art*, 1974, 282. Colie's observation provides an eloquent rebuttal to Bristol's thesis that the play's 'spatio-temporal economy' precludes the achievement of forgiveness in the fullness of time. While not espousing Hunter's strictly theological/allegorical reading, I have drawn much from his probing study of forgiveness in the play (185–203).

in 5.3, she asks Perdita 'how [she] found / [Her] *father's court*' (5.3.124–5, *italics* mine); the linkage of the implied 'lost' and explicit 'found' echoes the key terms in the oracle's prophecy (3.2.133–4), itself patriarchal, as does Paulina's preceding 'Our Perdita is found' (5.3.121). Such collaboration with Apollo renders the women 'good patriarchalists all along' (Adelman, 234). To read the king's imperative mode as silencing female voice ('O peace, Paulina' [5.3.135] and 'Look upon my brother' [5.3.147]); to see the king as essentially unchanged because of his determination to learn female secrets in post-play revelations; and to regard Hermione's return as a victory of male wish-fulfilment are arguments that have been cogently made in recent years.[143] But the triumphs of Time suggested in the preceding pages allow a perception of the final scene as rehearsing a new, more inclusive patriarchal structure (at least by early modern standards), one in which the female presence emerges as strong, vibrant, assertive, and perhaps, most important, desirable.[144]

No other Shakespearean romance emphasizes the woman's part so much as *The Winter's Tale* does; in this it is similar to *King John*, the history play in which women are insistently and unusually prominent. But unlike *John*, in which the women disappear halfway through the play, *The Winter's Tale* never loses the female presence. Act 4 has Perdita (and by implication Hermione), while Act 5 unites the major female characters in a triad whose power is both visual and vocal. As the play draws to a close, the possessive pronouns used by Paulina and Hermione respecting Perdita – 'Our', 'my', and 'mine own' – convey a sense of female solidarity, as does the mother-daughter narrative that 'opens up a space for the female narrative . . . thus far suppressed [in Shakespeare]' (Adelman, 234). The female enclosure of Paulina's 'removed house', into which men are invited (a sharp contrast to their invasion of such space in 2.1), holds one woman who commands attention as the object gazed upon and another who orchestrates the gaze. But, as we have seen, even the woman viewed is able to gaze back with 'motion' in her eye and to exercise her will – her 'self' – in deciding exactly when she will 'descend' and 'be stone no more'. Hermione's final declaration of agency (5.3.125–8) is followed by further female assertiveness, Paulina's determining what questions will be answered and when (5.3.129–31). Moreover, with one exception – the commitment to get Paulina an 'honourable husband' (5.3.143) – half of the king's final speech focuses on her as an equal or a superior: she has entered into a mutual agreement by which each would select the other's mate (5.3.138); she is responsible for the restoration of Hermione (5.3.138); she possesses a level of awareness greater than his own (5.3.139–40); and she is the one who will 'lead [all] from hence' (5.3.151–2). The man who earlier had refused to listen to the woman's view and who had called this particular woman – the end of a line of scolding females inclusive of Adriana, Kate, and Beatrice – 'mankind

143 For the first, see Eggert and Schalkwyk; for the second, J. Davis; and for the third, Traub.

144 See Gourlay, Dash, Neely, and Adelman. Even Lamb (536–7), who claims that male anxiety about women's influence remains unresolved in the final scene, locates something redemptive in Leontes' willing immersion in Paulina's winter's tale (5.3.116–17).

witch' and 'Dame Partlet' (2.3.67, 75) has grown dependent on the 'unruly' woman's positive force and is unwilling to lose it from his immediate circle:

[In *WT*] the restoration of social order is effected not by a husband or well-meaning friend as in previous shrew plays but by the ungovernable lady herself . . . At the close of the play, it is Leontes, not the woman who has berated him, who grows in understanding, while the scold is finally rewarded with a husband . . . not for her acquired docility, but unremitting outspokenness . . . It is now the shrew who educates those around her, while her refusal to conform to the dictates of her society contributes to the welfare of the community as a whole. Where the overbearing woman of folk tale is forced to acknowledge her failings, and defer to the opposite sex, Paulina scolds the representative of the patriarchy into repentance, and induces his renunciation of a mistaken stance.[145]

As *The Winter's Tale* ends, a man may speak the final words, but it is a woman who acts: as leader, director, and chief dispenser of information. The result is a twist on the patriarchally inspired adage 'Fatti maschii parole femine' ('Deeds are for men, words for women').

But even if, as some contend, the ending constitutes a male victory in that female words, secrets, and narratives are appropriated by men, such possessiveness in itself need not be construed as entirely negative since the potential is there to yield a more inclusive, liberating, and benign order: patriarchy reformed, or, to use Bill Overton's term, 'tamed' (85).[146] A single word and one passage are illustrative. Just as the first word in a play can be significant – e.g., 'Who's' (*Hamlet*), 'Tush' (*Othello*), 'When' (*Macbeth*), and 'If' (*The Winter's Tale*, see 1.1.1 n.) – so too can the last. Functioning as an adverb drawn into what is more of a request, perhaps even a plea ('Hastily lead away', 5.3.155), than an order, 'away' loses its earlier exclusionary and harshly imperative force;[147] agency is now imparted to someone else and the speaker relegated to object ('us' being implied). For the first time, the King includes himself in a communal, almost democratic, enterprise that will allow each member to 'leisurely . . . demand and answer to his part / Performed in' the 'gap' that has separated them (5.3.152–4).

The passage in which Leontes abruptly couples Paulina and Camillo (5.3.132–46), rather than revealing disturbing traces of the earlier unyielding autocrat (Schalkwyk, 268–9),[148] likewise points to the king's successful completion of his own monarchical education (see pp. 21–2 in this introduction), for underlying the suddenly imposed

[145] Scragg, *Shakespeare's Mouldy Tales: Recurrent Plot Motifs in Shakespearian Drama*, 1992, 94–6.

[146] Adelman specifies the return of masculine authority as 'grounded in a benignly generative maternal presence' (194). See also Peter Erickson: '[*WT*] concentrates on reforming patriarchy and assimilating women with a boundless capacity to forgive into the revised image of benign patriarchy' ('Adrienne Rich's Re-Vision of Shakespeare', in Marianne Novy, ed., *Women's Re-Visions of Shakespeare: On the Responses of Dickinson, Woolf, Rich, H.D., George Eliot, and Others*, 1990, 187).

[147] Compare 2.1.60, 103; and 2.3.42, 132, where, as Bishop perceptively notes (130), the word reveals Leontes' compulsion 'to banish the whole world and leave him in the company only of his own fantasies'. I am indebted to Bishop for calling my attention to the iterative value of the word.

[148] McGuire, who discusses the segment at some length (172–4), notes how silent assent to the proposed marriage has solidified into stage tradition and speculates on the implications of unconventional choices: e.g., Camillo's refusing to extend his hand to Paulina and, if he does assent, the theatrical options open to her: willingly offering her own hand, reluctantly permitting him to take her hand, or boldly refusing his hand.

marital arrangement is a sensitivity to the needs and desires of his subjects.[149] Leontes hears the loneliness in Paulina's lament for Antigonus (5.3.130–5) and is reminded of their mutual agreement by which she would select his spouse and he hers (5.3.136–7). He then indicates an awareness of the potential groom's (heretofore unknown) thoughts on the matter: 'I'll not seek far – / For him I partly know his mind – to find thee / An honourable husband' (5.3.141–3). Taking his role of matchmaker seriously, Leontes seeks to match honour with honour (see 5.3.144 n.).[150] Patriarchal authority, then, is asserted but not with the voice of a tyrant; rather, in a way analogous to James I's imaging of himself, Leontes can be seen acting in the role of paterfamilias, benignly knowing and doing what's best for his people,[151] finding, as James said in his accession speech, 'felicity . . . in their prosperity' and 'protest[ing] that [their] welfare shall ever be [his] greatest care and contentment'.

The Winter's Tale's sense of an ending: happiness qualified

For all the euphoria of multiple reunions, 'conflicts ostensibly resolved' may 'still lurk in the background' (Traub, 230).[152] In other words, an ending does not necessarily mean closure.[153] As the characters exit, they plan to tell their individual stories and to demand answers, some of which may never prove fully satisfactory, if the position articulated in Leontes' 'I . . . have in vain said many /A prayer upon her grave' (5.3.139–41) is any measure of the persuasive storytelling that will be required. Is the king who had encouraged Paulina's tirade:

> A thousand knees,
> Ten thousand years together, naked, fasting,
> Upon a barren mountain, and still winter
> In storm perpetual, could not move the gods
> To look that way thou wert . . .
> (3.2.207–11)

[149] The passage also speaks to Leontes' personal transformation, specifically his recovery of the waggish nature that Hermione was once sure of (1.2.64–5) and which Leontes himself confirms at 5.1.127–9. Happy to be a married man again, he is almost Benedick-like in wanting others to share the same joy; compare (*Ado*, 5.4.122–4). But having been on the receiving end of Paulina's tongue-lashing for so many years, he may also reveal a look of mischief in knowing what's in store for Camillo. The return of the wag bodes well for Leontes' emotional health, the re-marriage, and the kingdom at large.

[150] Perhaps Shakespeare is offering a final exoneration of Camillo, whose failure to defend Hermione more boldly in 1.2 might still rankle. Schalkwyk's contrasting view (268–9) of Leontes and the matchmaking business is based on a different interpretation of 5.3.144–6 – i.e. Paulina, not Camillo, is the one being justified.

[151] See Jonathan Goldberg, 'Fatherly Authority: The Politics of Stuart Family Images', in *Rewriting the Renaissance*, ed. Margaret W. Fergusson *et al.*, 1986, 3–32; also McGuire, 173:'The counsellors' betrothal, if it occurs, redeems kingly authority by making it . . . an instrument through which "great creating nature" works.' Although often understood as 'must', Leontes' 'shouldst' in 5.3.136 may indicate 'subjective' rather than 'absolute obligation', i.e. as 'ought to' (Schmidt).

[152] In Warchus (see illustration 29, p. 55), 'a sense of awkwardness [was conveyed] . . . as though there [remains] a good deal of unfinished business to be settled among the two kings and the queen' (Jackson, 176); see also Hytner, 'Behold', 21–2. In Lewis, where the embrace had been especially warm, an implicit tension underscored the final exit: after Florizel left by himself, Hermione and Perdita departed together, followed by Polixenes, and then a solitary Leontes.

[153] Palfrey, 230.

forgetting the need for such a regime? How could the prayers he said be 'in vain' given the heinousness of his sins, their consequences in some cases irreversible?[154] Will the women need to remind him that those very prayers helped effect the interior changes that enabled Hermione to return as wife? To the extent that Leontes may still not fully 'get it', his reformation remains a work in progress, a phrase applicable to the play's ending as a whole. What I have proposed is Leontes' moral trajectory, not his canonization; re-marriage as a beginning, not an end; patriarchy as potentially reformed, not permanently disabled; and forgiveness, as an ongoing process, not a *fait accompli*. Tentativeness and liminality do not erase the 'exultation' partaken by the play's 'precious winners all', but they do qualify it.

There is, however, another, and perhaps more powerful, qualifier: Shakespeare's insistence that both characters and audiences 'remember it all',[155] both the good and the bad, the gains and the losses. It is this comprehensive memory bank, particularly in terms of its painful holdings, that requires a 'no' answer to Kenneth Bennett's question about the play's concluding joys, '[I]s it happiness unalloyed?' (85). Time, precious time, is never to be recovered, as evidenced by the sixteen years etched so permanently on a still beautiful but now visibly wrinkled Hermione and by a daughter all grown up, neither parent part of that process. Polixenes' simple use of the word 'brother' as he tries to alleviate Leontes' pain (5.3.53–6) reminds us of just how strong that friendship had been and of all those years when no such direct address was possible. But most moving are the irrevocable losses of those who have died. Twice in the final act Paulina refers warmly to Antigonus (5.1.42–4; 5.3.132–5), the second time revealing a side not seen before, as she laments a lost husband (evidently worth lamenting in her eyes). Even more painful, however, is the loss of the promising and innocent Mamillius, whose memory Shakespeare invokes in Act 5 (see 5.1.115–22, 130–3, 173, and 175–7). Seven lines before the final stage exit, when Leontes introduces Hermione to her future son-in-law, there may also be an implicit remembrance of the Mamillius that might have been.[156]

[154] A question that may have been behind the conclusion to E. Hall's innovative and well-received all male production in 2005, perhaps the darkest on record. This was a *Winter's Tale* without any sense of reconciliation, each character turning away from Leontes until only the figure of Mamillius remained in his presence; and when the son abruptly blew out a candle, he seemed to suggest that the play was not only his nightmare – he had literally hovered over the entire action – but also one that Leontes was doomed to live again and again, always seeking and never finding forgiveness.

[155] The phrase belongs to the late Lady Abbess Benedict Duss, O.S.B., Abbey of Regina Laudis, Bethlehem, CT. It was her advice to the actress Patricia Neal as she began work on her autobiography *As I Am*, after a long period of much personal and physical loss. Throughout this introduction, especially in dealing with the topics of forgiveness and remembrance, I have frequently drawn on insights gleaned while giving a seminar on *WT* to the abbatial community.

[156] As a way of encouraging audiences 'to celebrate what has been repaired while not forgetting the facts of loss' (Timpane, 19), some productions bring the boy and/or Antigonus back as ghosts (or as statues flanking Hermione's [in Syer]) to witness the reunions from which they are physically excluded, occasionally offering benediction to the living. See p. 21 in this introduction for one example; others include the productions of Lapine, Wentworth, Davis, Kretzu, and Donnellan. The last is particularly surprising because of the bleakness and violence that were its hallmarks (see Stephen Phillips' account in *ShakB* 18.1[2000], 31, and reviews by P. Smith and Holland).

The memories that pervade Act 5 are especially poignant because they are infused with a sense of having been pondered; they register not only painful loss but also keen awareness of responsibility for that which is no more (see pp. 44–6). In her two references to the dead Antigonus, Paulina, though not overtly casting blame on the king, indirectly reminds him and us of the primary cause of her grief. But perhaps the most significant passage in this regard is Leontes' 'What! Look upon my brother. Both your pardons, / That e'er I put between your holy looks / My ill suspicion' (5.3.147–9). Apparently detecting unease in Hermione and Polixenes,[157] Leontes, briefly but compellingly, faces his original sin of misjudgment brought on by paranoid jealousy and, in the midst of others, formally asks pardon of the two innocents he had wrongfully accused so long ago.[158] Otherwise gratuitous,[159] the king's recollection is perhaps Shakespeare's way of saying 'forgive, but never forget', lest the sinner commit or allow the same offence again. Even one of the play's final words, 'dissevered', so harsh in meaning and sound, reminds us, in the midst of what is essentially a happy context, of the fractured relations that have held our attention for so long and the one man responsible for them. Juxtaposed with the exuberance of 'Hastily lead away', the tragic-sounding 'dissevered' strikes a discordant note yielding not indeterminacy but a further layering of the conventional 'happy ending' appropriate for this complex play.

If *Hamlet* and *Lear* are, as R. A. Foakes argues, plays with unique cultural sonorities that speak to different eras,[160] then perhaps *The Winter's Tale* is especially suited to a period of intense fragmentation, global violence, culture wars, and ideological debates intransigently pitting science against art, and scepticism against faith. It is, after all, a play that accepts imperfections and change (Hermione's wrinkles) as part of life,[161] treats forgiveness and reconciliation as ongoing imperatives, harmonizes polarities, and demands its characters and audiences to account for their parts, to awaken their faith, and to 'resonantly remember'.[162] Beginning with the contingency of 'if' and ending with the discordance of 'dissevered' echoing in the ear,

157 In performance, it is usually Leontes who initiates the repairing of the breach, but Cohen effectively chose to have Hermione whisper something in the king's ear at 5.3.146 while nodding in the direction of Polixenes, apparently urging her husband to take this final step toward full reconciliation. While Leontes as initiator suggests a welcome sensitivity to the discomfort of others, Cohen's choice has the advantage of showing the king listening to and heeding the woman's voice, a definite change from the man who had scorned female speech with the dismissive 'women say so – / That will say anything' (1.2.129–30).

158 Eggert (164), who sees no sign of redemptive remembrance in the lines, claims that 'nothing alters in [Leontes'] personality as his wife rejoins him; instead, there is something passingly chilling in [his] final speech, which returns the play to its initial situation of Leontes' ordering his wife to make contact with Polixenes'. But it is precisely this similarity to the beginning (especially if the blocking at 1.2.27 is repeated here) that bespeaks difference.

159 In that the passage interrupts the logical flow of Leontes' final speech and delays the imminent exit already anticipated at 5.3.146.

160 Foakes, *Hamlet versus Lear: Cultural Politics and Shakespeare's Art*, 1993.

161 See Snyder, 'Memorial Art', in *Journey*, 205–6.

162 The phrase comes from Eva Hoffman, 'Let Memory Speak', *New York Times* Book Review, 23 January 1994, 5.

Shakespeare's bittersweet tale of winter may be the miracle play for the twenty-first century.

Date

One of Shakespeare's late plays, *The Winter's Tale*, first published in the 1623 Folio, is usually dated 1610–11, most editors placing it after *Pericles* and *Cymbeline* and before *The Tempest*, the three dramatic works with which it is canonically linked in terms of subject matter and a late verbal style.[163] Dating the play benefits greatly from Simon Forman's eyewitness account of a performance at the Globe on 15 May 1611 (see Appendix A), a date that serves as a *terminus ad quem* (but see 'Revision Theory' below). A *terminus a quo* is harder to specify.[164]

In the servant's report that three of the newly arrived countrymen 'call[ing] themselves saltiers' had recently danced at court (4.4.306–12, 317–18), critics, beginning with A. H. Thorndike,[165] have found a plausible allusion to the satyrs' dance in Jonson's *Masque of Oberon*, performed for King James on 1 January 1611. Those who find the dance in Act 4 integral to *The Winter's Tale* rely heavily on this allusion,[166] which points to a date early in 1611, or a compositional process that might have begun late in 1610 but which was not completed until early in the following year. But since both the dance and the passage introducing it form a self-contained sequence, it is possible that the play was completed earlier, the dance and preceding lines added later (*Companion*, 601). Perhaps pushing composition back further in 1610 was the catalytic effect of a revival of the anonymous *Mucedorus* by Shakespeare's company on 18 February 1610, along with a new edition of the old-fashioned romance (having an expanded bear episode) the same year.[167] The Oxford editors, arguing on stylistic grounds, reverse the usual *Cymbeline* (1609–10)/*Winter's Tale*

[163] On the shared subject matter, see, p. 3. As to style, the following features are commonly listed as indicative of *WT*'s lateness in the canon: dense, tortured syntax, often the result of extensive interruption of thought and/or convoluted periodicity; flexible and embedded use of rhetorical schemes (especially of repetition); and frequent ellipsis. Metrical features include a preponderance of weak, light, and double endings and a favouring of run-on lines, elision, mid-line beginnings and endings of speeches, and floating caesurae (instead of the usual medial position in the early plays).

[164] Glynne Wickham's thesis that *WT* was occasioned by the investiture of Prince Henry as Prince of Wales in 1610 has received little support ('Shakespeare's Investiture Play: The Occasion and Subject of [*WT*]', *TLS*, 18 December 1969, 1456).

[165] Thorndike, 'Influence of the Court-Masques on the Drama, 1608–15', *PMLA* 15 (1901), 114–20.

[166] E.g., Sorrell, 380; and Pafford, xxii.

[167] *Mucedorus* was first published in 1598, with a second edition in 1606. Numerous reprintings occurred after the 1610 edition, the first of which was 1611, its title page – like that of the preceding edition – referring to a court performance on Shrove Sunday, which E. K. Chambers originally documented as 3 February 1611 (*The Elizabethan Stage*, 4 vols., 1923, 4.36). A date in early February of that year would suggest that *WT* followed soon after the performances of both the Jonson masque and *Mucedorus*, and thus only a few months before the 11 May date provided by Forman, except that Chambers, after inspecting plague records, changed the date of performance to 18 February 1610 (*Shakespeare*, 2.489). See also Roslyn Knutson, *The Repertory of Shakespeare's Company 1594–1613*, 1991, 138, 197.

chronology[168] and propose 1609 for the latter (*Companion*, 131).[169] Sometime in that year, the King's Men began to use Blackfriars, a private theatre with an appeal to courtly tastes and, on account of such indoor features as candlelight in contrast to the natural lighting of the Globe, a greater capacity for maximizing the impact of theatrical marvels like the statue scene; such a venue makes possible a date before the end of 1609 or early in 1610.[170] Without definitive evidence, the best estimate for dating the play is sometime between 1609 and the first few months of 1611, with a shrinking consensus still favouring the latter end of that time frame, i.e. 1610–11.

REVISION THEORY

Further complicating the issue of compositional date is a theory first broached by J. E. Bullard and W. M. Fox in 1952, later supported by David Bergeron, and most recently expanded and cogently argued by Susan Snyder.[171] Briefly summarized, the theory holds that sometime after Forman saw the play in May 1611 and before a known court performance in November of that year or another one recorded between December 1612 and February 1613, Shakespeare rewrote the ending so as to subordinate the father-daughter reunion (presumably the original finale) to the spectacular return of a wife/mother long thought to be dead.[172] Evidence marshalled in favour of the revision claim includes (1) Shakespeare's striking departure in the play as we have it from the conclusion of his primary source (to whose narrative he

[168] Critics and editors often point to Boccaccio's *Decameron* (Day 2, Tale 9), a probable source for *Cym.*, as lying behind a single passage in *WT* (4.4.745–51), thus making *WT* the later play; but such intertextuality does not necessarily argue priority.

[169] Maxwell also places the text in the 1609–10 period but after *Cym.* Although it is possible that Shakespeare decided to rework and develop further narrative strains introduced in *Per.* before turning his attention to the matter of Britain and Rome, it is just as easy to argue that some time might pass between similar works, so as not to appear to be repeating himself too obviously. A somewhat different intervening work might also enhance the creative process, especially one (like *Cym.*) which includes the restoration of a daughter to her father and a death/resurrection motif involving the heroine, but which, unlike *Per.*, has as a major part of its plot a strained marital relationship caused by a husband's unfounded jealousy.

[170] The publication of the Sonnets in the 1609 Quarto might also have bearing on the dating issue. Generally thought to have been written in the 1590s (though there is some hint of (re)writing post-1600; see Colin Burrow ed., *The Complete Sonnets and Poems* [Oxford Shakespeare, 2002]), their appearance in print might have made them fresh again for the author. If Shakespeare did turn to *WT* with the Sonnets – and their seasonal imagery, thematic emphasis on time and art, and central relationship involving two men and a woman – newly reborn in his consciousness, it becomes intriguing to think that he created not just *a* dramatized sonnet sequence but *the* dramatization of his own unique contribution to the sonnet genre.

[171] Bullard and Fox, Letter in *TLS*, 14 March 1952, 189; Bergeron, 'The Restoration of Hermione', in *Shakespeare's Romances Reconsidered*, ed. Carol McGinnis Kay and Henry E. Jacobs, 1978, 125–33; and Snyder,' [*WT*] Before and After', in *Journey*, 221–33.

[172] The first recorded court performance was on 5 November 1611; the second was part of the nuptial festivities surrounding the marriage of Princess Elizabeth to the Elector Palatine on 14 February 1613. *WT* appears on a list of fourteen plays presented by Shakespeare's company as part of the entertainments held beginning in late December 1612 and extending into February (see Chambers, 2.343). If revision did occur, Greg inclines toward the nuptial occasion as the precipitating cause (W. W. Greg, *The Shakespeare First Folio*, 1955, 417). Bergeron (126–9) makes a case for Anthony Munday's civic pageant *Chruso-thriambos: The Triumphes of Golde* (staged in the streets of London on 29 October 1611) as the impetus. See also Supplementary note to 5.3.99–103.

is otherwise generally faithful) in which Hermione's counterpart remains dead;[173] (2) Forman's contemporary account of the performance he attended which makes no mention of an animated statue;[174] (3) the failure of the oracle to prepare us for Hermione's return;[175] (4) the ghost-like appearance of Hermione in Antigonus' narrated dream;[176] (5) the bear incident and the satyrs' dance, possibly later additions since neither is necessary to the plot;[177] (6) the awkwardness of Act 5, scene 2 with its multiple narrators of events not dramatized but which have been elaborately prepared for in the audience's mind;[178] and (7) the dramatic short shrift given to the Shepherd, Clown, and Autolycus, all of whom, especially the last, are major players in Act 4 and might therefore be expected have a significant function when they reappear in Sicilia.[179] For Snyder, who rightly observes that '[w]e can never know for sure whether the last scene of [*WT*] was added after first composition . . . and the original ending recast' (*Journey*, 230), it is not one thing alone that makes revision likely but a combination of all of the above.

As compelling as the revision theory may be, however, there are enough hints before the penultimate scene that, when combined, make a case for the opposite

173 The absence of a restored wife/mother in Greene's *Pandosto* notwithstanding, it is possible that Shakespeare found the seeds of Hermione's restoration in two passages from his source, each detailing a separate death-like trance of Bellaria (see Bullough, 166, 167).

174 Eyewitness accounts, however, are not always complete or precisely accurate, and can reflect the interests/biases/tastes of the viewer. The reliability of Forman, an astrologer and charlatan doctor, is, as many have noted, particularly suspect. But as Snyder observes, the first two-thirds of his notes provide both an accurate and a detailed summary of the plot, making it odd for him to exclude something so momentous as a statue come to life; Snyder also argues that the part of the summary dealing with the Leontes-Perdita reunion reads 'as if Forman saw it rather than heard it recounted [as in 5.2]' (*Journey*, 225).

175 See Turner, 240. It has become a commonplace in *WT* criticism that nowhere else in the canon does the playwright leave the audience in the dark about the restoration of one thought to be dead, but there is one case that bears some similarity to the surprise revealed at the end of *WT*: namely, the discovery in *Err.* that the Abbess of Act 5 is the long-lost wife of Egeon and mother of the Antipholi brothers.

176 Kermode conjectured (88) the possibility of revision specifically in light of Antigonus' dream of Hermione, but see 3.3.15–18 n. D. Wilson argues (350) that the passage 'foreshadows a train of ghostly images' in 5.1, which in turn prepare us for Hermione's restoration.

177 As with the statue, Forman records nothing of the bear and the satyrs. If these two episodes represent later additions to a play already completed, such interpolation does not prove revision of the ending but 'point[s] . . . in a similar direction' (Snyder, *Journey*, 230).

178 The narrated reunions of 5.2 can, of course, be justified on dramatic grounds as a way of preventing Hermione's return from becoming anticlimactic. Perhaps Shakespeare did not want to repeat himself, having emphasized a father-daughter reunion in *Per.*, and having provided the potentially comic, almost never-ending, proliferation of discoveries in the final scene of *Cym.* (assuming, of course, its priority).

179 Citing Sir Arthur Quiller-Couch ('Shakespeare's Later Workmanship: [*WT*]', *North American Review*, May 1906, 757) and Overton (74), Snyder pays special attention to this point; she contends that, were the narrated material in 5.2 enacted, Autolycus would have bridged the hierarchical gap between royals and peasants, while the Shepherd and Clown would have enjoyed their moment in the spotlight as dispensers of information to which they alone are privy: 'Without [the scene depicting the actual reunion between Leontes and Perdita], none of them is really necessary' (*Journey*, 222). That may be so but there is enough material for them in 5.2 as it stands to afford each of them an adequate swan song, something that many productions have demonstrated.

conclusion.[180] To take the trial scene first, the dramatic focus on an isolated Hermione – standing alone in her defence, all eyes fixed on her, and all ears attentive to her testimony – prefigures the queen as a statue, a similarity not lost on critics and directors (see Appendix C, p. 272). Paulina's 'if you can bring / Tincture of luster in her lip, her eye, / Heat outwardly or breath within' (3.2.201–3) bears a striking correspondence to the emphasis on the statue's lips, eyes, warmth, and seeming breath (5.3.64–8, 78). The rebirth/resurrection motif that runs throughout the play in the underlying myth of Proserpina (see 'Sources', p. 70) is especially pronounced in Act 4, scene 4: e.g., Perdita's litany of flowers (4.4.73–85, 103–8, 113–27), specifically the marigold 'that goes to bed wi'th'sun, / And with him rises' (4.4.105–6). The motif is also present in the biblical name of Dorcas (see List of Characters and Appendix B, p. 264), in the Shepherd's lively remembrance of his dead wife and Perdita's second mother (4.4.55–64), and in Autolycus' comic prognostication of the fate awaiting a certain Shepherd's son who 'shall be flayed alive . . . then stand till he be three-quarters and a dram dead; then recovered again with aqua vitae or some other hot infusion' (4.4.745–8). In light of what happens in the 'statue' scene, at least two passages become more nuanced when read retrospectively: the debate on art vs. nature (4.4.85–103), particularly Polixenes' claim that 'the art itself is nature' (4.4.97); and the allusion to the Ovidian tale of Deucalion and Pyrrha (4.4.411), which involves stones taking on human life. In Act 5, scene 1, besides the frequency with which Hermione is the subject of the discourse (6–17, 30, 34–5, 50, 53–67, 74, 78–80, 83, 95–103, 224–7), several lines either link her with an art form ('picture' [5.1.74] and 'verse' [5.1.101]) or describe her as worthy of admiring 'gazes' (5.1.225). Within the space of eighteen lines, Shakespeare also has a character refer twice to the dead coming back to life (5.1.42–3 and 57–60). Even the emphasis on verisimilitude, so prominent in the praise of Giulio Romano's style (5.2.83–7) and of the statue itself (5.3), is present much earlier: in Paulina's description of the infant Perdita as the 'copy of the father' (2.3.97–107), the terms she uses 'are similar to those in which the work of art is praised, but [as with the statue] the triumph of verisimilitude is that of "good goddess nature"' (Barkan, 663).

So extensive are these hints that revision would have required not only creating a new scene (5.2) to replace the original conclusion but also considerable tinkering with earlier scenes, particularly Act 5, scene 1, which, in a hypothetical first version, would not have needed so much emphasis on Hermione and the topic of remarriage. Siemon (50–52) relates the statue sequence to a continuous 'insistence upon the unreliability of appearance' from Hermione's first entrance until her descent from the pedestal and to an iterative 'pattern of loss and recovery' requiring both her

[180] Bullough (132) makes the unsupported claim that 'from the moment when Paulina brought news of Hermione's supposed death . . . [it is obvious] the intention was to bring her back'. Modern productions have, on occasion, foreshadowed the statue episode: e.g., Hall introduced statues into the first scene (Wells, 143), whereas Donnellan waited until 5.2 to have a character feign the pose of a Greek statue (see 5.2.104 SD n.). While not making use of a statue motif, Warchus' decision to open his production with a dumb show involving the disappearance of a lady from a casket and her sudden reentry through the audience (Jackson, 175) is in the same anticipatory vein.

death and return. Since the restoration of those thought dead is a feature found in *The Winter's Tale*'s companionate romances, it seems more likely that Shakespeare would have envisioned such a plot element as part of his reworking of *Pandosto*. Whether or not Shakespeare had worked out from the beginning the statue scenario as the vehicle for restoring Hermione, the living statue in the final scene marks 'the culmination of statue allusions and actual statue scenes . . . throughout Shakespeare's earlier plays' (Smith, 'Sermons', 18).

Sources

ROBERT GREENE'S *PANDOSTO*

Although a strong tradition of native romance literature, both narrative and dramatic, lies behind *The Winter's Tale* (see pp. 3–5 in this introduction), the primary source is Robert Greene's *Pandosto, The Triumph of Time*, a popular work first published in 1588; subsequent editions appeared in 1592, 1595, 1607, and frequently thereafter. Geoffrey Bullough convincingly claims that Shakespeare used one of the first three editions since the wording of the oracle in the 1607 and later texts read 'The King shall *die* without an heir', not 'live', the verbal choice in both the play and the pre-1607 editions (my *italics*, Bullough, 118). Shakespeare took from *Pandosto* its basic narrative line, major characters (whose names he changed), and, not infrequently, specific diction, phrasing, and imagery.[181] But as always with Shakespeare, it is the differences – those of omission, addition, and variation – that hold the most interest (many of which are cited in the headnotes to scenes and in the glosses).

Shakespeare's keen sense of what is required when moving from narrative to drama is clear in moments both large – like Leontes' sudden explosion of jealousy, something that develops over time in *Pandosto* (see 'Leontes' jealousy', pp. 24–30), and small – such as the exchange in which Leontes reveals his suspicions to Camillo and urges him to poison Polixenes. In the source, after reporting the king's desire to have his boyhood friend killed and the promise of reward to Franion (i.e. Camillo) for carrying it out, the narrator relates how the cupbearer tries to dissuade his master, moving from a religious argument that such a deed would be an 'offence . . . to the gods' to a political one: the murder of Egistus would have a devastating effect not only on international relations but also on Pandosto's 'owne subjectes [who] would repine at such trecherous crueltie' (*Pandosto*, in Bullough, 159–60). In *The Winter's Tale*, after allowing a suspenseful buildup in which Leontes hints at what troubles him and Camillo grows increasingly uneasy (1.2.212–75), Shakespeare has the loyal counsellor respond not with logic and political strategy but with shock and disbelief as he protests Hermione's innocence (1.2.276–81, 318–20). Camillo urges the King to be 'cured' of his 'diseased' and 'most dangerous' opinion (1.2.293–5) and finally

[181] In addition to the oracular message, the official indictment and much of Hermione's own defence are among the passages that follow closely the language in *Pandosto*.

declares his love, only to be rudely cut off (1.2.321). The result is an interpersonal dynamic charged with affective and theatrical vitality.[182]

The most revealing differences, however, are those affecting the macrostructure of *The Winter's Tale*, the chief ones being the reversed locales (Leontes' counterpart presides over Bohemia, while Polixenes' rules Sicilia), the introduction of new characters, and the radical overhaul of the ending. Regarding the first, as Michele Marrapodi observes, Shakespeare deliberately exploits the 'pliable, polyvalent iconography of Sicilia', which included not only the conventional model of Arcadia but also the 'mythological country of classical literature' that was home to monsters, giants, tyrannous kings, and malignant gods: 'an insidious and ambiguous isle, surrounded by strong winds and threatening currents and often shaken by earthquakes and volcanic eruptions' (Marrapodi, 214–15).[183] A region thought to be peopled by those 'full of envy . . ., suspicious and dangerous in conversation, being lightly given to anger and offences, and ready to take revenge of any injury committed',[184] would certainly be an appropriate habitat for a king given to paranoid jealousy and unmitigated rage. Home to Mount Etna, Sicilia, however, was not only linked with destruction but also with fertility, thus making it equally suitable for the final scene of rebirth and renewal. As George Sandys describes Etna:

> The lower parts are luxuriously fruitfull, the middle wooddy, the vpper rocky, steepe, and almost couered with snow: yet smoking in the midst like many conioyning chimnies, & vomiting intermitted flames, though not but by night to be discerned; as if heate and cold had left their contentions, and imbraced one another.[185]

That a mother and daughter should lose and find each other in Sicilia is especially fitting when one considers the myth of Ceres and Proserpina (see pp. 70–1), which informs *The Winter's Tale* but not *Pandosto*.[186]

Among the characters introduced by Shakespeare are Paulina, Autolycus, Clown, Antigonus, and Time, two of whom are given a substantial portion of the play's

182 Much earlier in his career, Shakespeare had done something similar in *King John*. Just as Leontes' indirection in the first part of the exchange recalls the John-Hubert temptation scene (*John* 3.3.19–66), so the injection of the personal and affective in the next phase echoes similar changes introduced into the Hubert-Arthur 'blinding' episode (4.1) vis-à-vis its counterpart in the presumed source, *The Troublesome Raigne of Iohn, King of England*. For another example of Shakespeare's stylistic reworking of Greene for dramatic effect, see 4.2.33 n.

183 Here and elsewhere I am greatly indebted to Marrapodi, especially for calling my attention to the relevant works of Lithgow and George Sandys.

184 Lithgow, 339; see also, p. 21n.50 in this introduction. Shakespeare's *Much Ado*, an earlier play dealing with unfounded jealousy, violent male temperament, machismo attitudes, and a mock death and 'resurrection', is also set in Sicilia.

185 *A Relation of a Iourney begun An. Dom. 1610 . Fovre Bookes. Containing a description of the Turkish Empire, of Egypt, of the Holy Land, of the Remote parts of Italy, and Ilands adioyning* (1615) (cited in Marrapodi, 215).

186 Finally, on the assumption that *Cym.* was written before *WT*, the patrilineal heritage of Posthumus Leonatus – son of Sicilius Leonatus – may have subconsciously influenced the creative process.

text.[187] In her function as moral adviser, Paulina is essential to the king's interior change, a development missing from the source; and as the temperamental foil to Hermione, she allows Shakespeare to split the proverbial good woman into two, one patient in adversity, the other expressing 'the angry, active side of the female response to Leontes' outrage'.[188] While both Autolycus and Clown inject humour and comic business into a plot that originally had little of either, it is the singing itinerant pedlar, with his inventory of ballads and tricks, who is essential to the Dionysiac spirit that sets Bohemia apart from the Apollonian world of Sicilia. With the figure of Antigonus, Shakespeare adds to the marriage theme of *The Winter's Tale*, showing a second couple whose marital bond is severed, this one permanently. Antigonus also functions as a scapegoat for Leontes' sins, and, together with Paulina and Camillo, enters into human collaboration with something larger to yield the restorations that conclude the play.

The nature of this larger force relates directly to the last of the major new characters introduced by Shakespeare, a figure who does more than personify the subtitle of the narrative source (see illustration 30, p. 69):

> The *Pandosto* story itself fails to work out its motto – *Temporis filia veritas* – for it puts all the emphasis on fortune, with her wheel, as the ruling agent of human affairs. Shakespeare, on the other hand, makes the Triumph of Time into a controlling theme of his tale; and in doing so he transforms what the conventional motto suggests – a simple victory of Time, the Father of Truth – into a dramatic exploration of the manifold meanings of Time.
>
> (Ewbank, 'Triumph', in Hunt, 140)

Shakespeare's Mariner presciently hints at some of these 'manifold meanings' that distinguish Greene's Time, which is 'wanton' and 'dall[ying]' (*Pandosto*, in Bullough, 173),[189] from Shakespeare's, which has the telic design of Fate, the moral rigour of Justice, and the regenerative mercy of Providence. Unlike *Pandosto*'s 'shipmen', who suffer no punishment for their part in casting a baby to the elements, *The Winter's Tale*'s doomed Mariner speaks of a retributive power at work in the storm that brings the ship to Bohemia (3.3.3–6). His fear is repeated as judgment by the Third Gentleman in Act 5 who moralizes the separate fates of Antigonus and the mariners, 'wracked the same instant of their master's death, . . . so that all the instruments which aided to expose the child were even then lost when it was found' (5.2.59–62). Likewise the name 'Perdita', which Hermione commands Antigonus to call the infant, suggests human divining of the oracle's reference to

[187] According to Spevack's *Concordance*, Paulina has the second highest percentage of lines (9.8%) after Leontes (20.3%), and the third highest percentage of words (9.6%) following Leontes (19.8%) and Autolycus (9.7%).

[188] Peter B. Erickson, 'Patriarchal Structures in *The Winter's Tale*', *PMLA*, 97 (1982), 819–29.

[189] Where Shakespeare, for instance, has Antigonus, inspired by a dream, deposit the infant in Bohemia, Greene shows the baby arriving on the shores of Egistus' kingdom purely by chance (*Pandosto*, Bullough, 167, 173). Likewise, the Prince and Fawnia are fortuitously shipwrecked on the coast of Pandosto's Bohemia. There is no plan as outlined by Camillo for the couple's flight since Camillo's counterpart, Franion, disappears from the story once he helps Egistus escape Pandosto's rage.

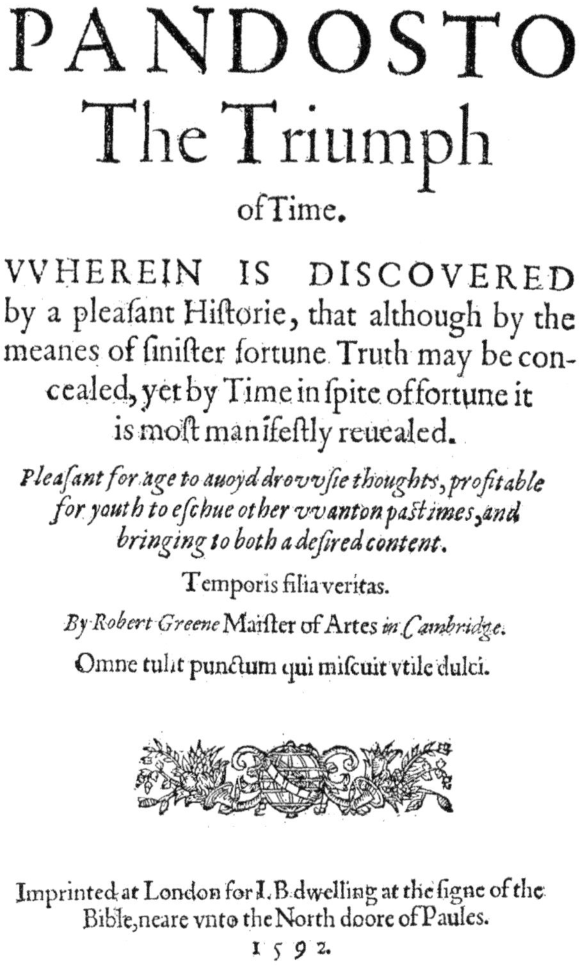
PANDOSTO
The Triumph
of Time.

VVHEREIN IS DISCOVERED
by a pleaſant Hiſtorie, that although by the
meanes of ſiniſter fortune Truth may be concealed, yet by Time in ſpite of fortune it
is moſt manifeſtly reuealed.

*Pleaſant for age to auoyd drovvſie thoughts, profitable
for youth to eſchue other vvanton paſtimes, and
bringing to both a deſired content.*

Temporis filia veritas.

By Robert Greene Maiſter of Artes *in Cambridge.*

Omne tulit punctum qui miſcuit vtile dulci.

Imprinted at London for I. B. dwelling at the ſigne of the
Bible, neare vnto the North doore of Paules.
1592.

30 Title page of Robert Greene's *Pandosto* (1592 edition) (Folger Shakespeare Library).

'that which is lost'. By contrast, the etymology of 'Fawnia', the name chosen by the baby's foster parents in *Pandosto*, evokes not the divine but the pastoral; attractive, even appropriate, the image of a young doe is nowhere as profoundly symbolic as 'Perdita'. In short, the genial figure of 4.1 gives voice to Time as rhetor: his argument (4.1.29), the deliberate rather than random use of human instruments to resolve conflicts and thus ensure an ending of unfolded error, wonder, and multiple resonances.

This new ending is the most defining change Shakespeare makes in refashioning *Pandosto*. He rejects Greene's decisions to have Bellaria, Hermione's counterpart, remain dead, and Pandosto, after being reunited with his grown daughter and attending her nuptials, kill himself – his unassuaged guilt over past offences compounded by his recent incestuous attraction to Fawnia.[190] Instead, Shakespeare shows a repentant and changed Leontes, minimizes the threat of incest, restores Hermione, and foregoes the king's suicide (see pp. 41–9). Such deliberate choices yield a conclusion markedly different in tone from the 'Tragicall stratageme' Greene chose 'to close up the Comedie' (*Pandosto*, in Bullough, 199).

OVID'S *METAMORPHOSES*

To create a play rich with metamorphic change,[191] Shakespeare turned to Ovid's *Metamorphoses*, as found in Arthur Golding's 1567 translation,[192] specifically the myths relating to Autolycus (Book 11; see List of Characters), Callisto (Book 2; see p. 32 in this introduction), Deucalion (Book 1), Proserpina (Book 5), Pygmalion (Book 10), and Orpheus and Eurydice (Book 10) – the last four closely entwined in *The Winter's Tale*.[193]

Although mentioned explicitly only once (4.4.116–18), the myth of Proserpina's abduction from earth to the underworld and her divinely ordered return to earth for six months of the year served Shakespeare well in both its mother-daughter dynamic of loss and recovery and its Sicilian setting from which Proserpina is taken and to which she is ultimately restored.[194] There is also the myth's intrinsic connection to seasonal change, a motif that pervades the whole play but is especially pronounced in its second half where the youth, beauty, and freshness of a Perdita immersed in floral imagery reincarnates Proserpina as the embodiment of spring: '[F]or the Renaissance, the fundamental myth of spring's return was that of Proserpina', and

190 Ambiguity of syntax may even imply Fawnia's death, for after Pandosto's suicide, 'Dorastus taking his leave of his father, went with his wife and the dead corps into Bohemia, where after they were sumptuouslie intoombed, Dorastus ended his daies in contented quiet' (*Pandosto*, in Bullough, 199).

191 Examples forming an iterative pattern conducive to the play's mythic quality include a con man, nominally linked to the god Mercury, who is the master of disguise; a princess appearing as a shepherdess 'prank'd up' to be the goddess 'Flora' (4.4.10, 2), a prince (himself disguised as a country swain) who woos (4.4.25–31) in the imagery of Arachne's tapestry (*Metamorphoses*, Book 6), and, most important, an apparently dead queen who returns as a 'statue' brought to life. To such characters may be added the songs, imagery, and dialogue that imaginatively transport us through all the seasons in Act 4, from spring (4.3.1–3; 4.4.3) to winter (4.4.79) to autumn (4.4.79–81) to middle summer (4.4.107) and back to spring (4.4.113–27). Even the flowers have 'metamorphic power' as 'daffodils . . . charm the wild winds of March' (4.4.118–20) (Bate, 231).

192 Plutarch's *Lives* is the other major work from antiquity to have clearly influenced *WT* (see List of Characters).

193 In addition to Barkan, my discussion of Ovid's influence on *WT* has benefited from the work of Bate (esp. 219–39), Enterline, Nuttall and Parker, who, in addition to the *Metamorphoses* also notes the influence of Ovid's *Fasti* for its treatment of the Callisto and Ceres-Proserpina myths ('Polymorphic Bears', 187, 188).

194 As Neely (197) and Enterline (43) note, the myth may also be implicated in the actual statue scenario; Shakespeare would have read in Golding's translation how the devastated Ceres, upon hearing of her daughter's abduction, stood 'starke as stone . . . And long she was like one that in another worlde had beene' (5.509–11).

since *The Winter's Tale* 'locates itself within the economy of the seasons, the tale of winter cannot avoid gesturing towards the eventual return of spring. The unstated alternative title of the play may therefore be said to be "Waiting for Proserpina"' (Bate, 219, 220).

When Shakespeare turns to his final scene, the myth of Proserpina and 'great creating Nature' recedes to make way for two others: that of a restored wife in the tale of Orpheus and Eurydice (see 5.3.106–7 n. and 114–15 n.),[195] and, most important, the myth of 'great creating [Art]' in the story of the misogynist sculptor Pygmalion, whose kiss and touch, as blessed by an approving Venus, animate his marble creation of ideal womanliness.[196] With its emphasis on the capacity of art to surpass nature and its urging of the imagination and the senses to bring art to life, the story would readily appeal to a playwright dramatizing the 'nature vs. art' debate and crafting his own 'statue' scene, especially since Ovid yokes the myth of animated stone to human love. But where Pygmalion's creation is one of idealized perfection, Shakespeare's wrinkled 'statue' is humanly imperfect. In the depetrification of a Hermione who is not really a statue and of an emotionally ossified Leontes who softens at the sensation of warmth, Shakespeare translates Ovidian 'metamorphosis into metaphor' (Bate, 236), a translation heralded at 5.2.76–7: 'Who was most marble there changed colour'.

The Ovidian preoccupation with 'life harden[ing] into stone or stones soften[ing] into life' is not limited to the final scenes of *The Winter's Tale*, for Polixenes' allusion to the myth of Deucalion and Pyrrha (4.4.411), who repeopled the world by turning stones into human flesh and bone, speaks to the same 'elemental tensions' present throughout the play 'between death and life, expressed as between hardness and softness' (Barkan, 641, 661). The allusion assumes special significance for the final scene of *The Winter's Tale* when one recalls that Deucalion was the son of Prometheus, the first sculptor to have breathed life into statues.

Each of the major Ovidian myths discussed has undercurrents which, though not played up by Shakespeare, can affect how we read their presence in the play: Proserpina will always return in the spring but she will always have to be elsewhere for half of the year; her story is also inclusive of her mother Ceres' desire for revenge. Eurydice's restoration to Orpheus is painfully brief, and Pygmalion's story is framed at one end by an account of prostitutes turned into stone and at the other by the incestuous relations of the progeny produced through the sculptor's union with the ivory maiden. Even the tale of Deucalion ends, as Barkan perceives (643–4), 'with a reminder that the stone remains within us': 'Hence comes the

[195] The other great story from antiquity involving the restoration of a dead wife to her husband is that of Alcestis, which Shakespeare would have known through Chaucer's *The Legend of Good Women*, Gower's *Confessio Amantis*, and George Pettie's *Pallace of Pleasure*. There were also several Latin translations of Euripides' *Alcestis* printed before 1611, one of which, George Buchanan's 1539 translation, was 'for the common practice of performance in the schools'; in arguing for Euripides' play as a source for the 'statue' scene, D. Wilson (345) speculates that Shakespeare 'might just possibly have seen such a production'.

[196] For other influences on the statue's animation in *WT*, see Supplementary Note to 5.3.103.

hardness of our race and our endurance of toil; and we give proof from what origin we are sprung.'[197] Whether read benignly as metamorphosing classical myth into something lighthearted (Nuttall) or more darkly as shadowed by complex meanings related to the female voice (Enterline), *The Winter's Tale* emerges as perhaps the most Ovidian of Shakespeare's plays.

[197] *Metamorphoses* (1.414–15), trans. Frank Justus Miller, Loeb Classical Library, 2 vols., 1966.

TEXTUAL NOTE

This edition of *The Winter's Tale* is based on the text that appeared in the First Folio of 1623, the earliest printed version of the play and the one from which all subsequent editions derive. It is generally agreed that the text – exceptionally clean, with full and accurate act and scene divisions,[1] and posing few textual difficulties – was transcribed by Ralph Crane, a professional scrivener who worked for Shakespeare's company, the King's Men, starting in 1619, three years after Shakespeare's death. Crane is also thought to have prepared the printer's copy for other Folio texts, among them *The Tempest*, *The Two Gentlemen of Verona*, *The Merry Wives of Windsor*, and *Measure for Measure*.[2] The provenance of the transcript itself is a matter of conjecture;[3] the paucity of stage directions, along with Crane's penchant for massed entries at the beginning of a scene, makes it unlikely that Crane worked from the play's promptbook. More probable is an authorial manuscript, either Shakespeare's foul papers or a clean transcript of them. For more on Crane's scribal habits and the narrative of the text's origins, see Textual Analysis (pages 256–61). Passages possibly indicative of revision (e.g., 4.4.306–22) are addressed in the introduction (pp. 63–6) and in the Commentary.

Throughout this edition spelling, punctuation, and capitalisation have been modernized.[4] For example, since F spells both 'then' and 'than' as 'then', we have silently emended the spelling to 'than' when the modern sense requires it; where, however, F's spelling might be semantically unclear, we have collated the change in spelling (e.g., 2.1.136 and 160). Crane's liberal use of the colon has been extensively curtailed in favour of the period, semicolon, dash, or exclamation mark, given the particular syntactic construction (e.g. 'best!' and 'Go;' [3.1.15, 21] and Paulina's eight separate commands in 5.3.99–103). Likewise, the frequent presence of parentheses has

[1] Some early editors, however, left Time's speech unnumbered, with the result that their 4.1, 4.2, and 4.3 correspond to F's and this edition's 4.2, 4.3, and 4.4.

[2] See Howard-Hill. Arguments for a Crane transcript as the copy behind F's *Othello* and *Cymbeline* are found in E. A. J. Honigmann, *The Texts of Othello and Shakespearean Revision* (1996) and in Martin Butler, ed., NCS *Cymbeline* (2005); Honigmann also includes *2 Henry IV* as another possibility (pp. 165–8). According to Howard-Hill ('Editor', 74), Crane's role in supplying F copy may be so extensive that the scribe 'must be seen as one of the crucial figures in the preparation of the Folio – and, almost certainly, as part-author of many lines that have passed into literary history as quintessential Shakespeare'.

[3] As Wells and Taylor observe, 'Obscurity of origin is an effect of Crane's habit of imposing his personal characteristics on the manuscripts that he transcribed' (*Companion*, p. 601).

[4] Early modern 'i/j', 'u/v', and the 'long s' [ſ] have been silently normalized in the text but not, with respect to 'i/j' and 'u/v', in titles of early modern works or in quoted passages from them (e.g., all quotations from Greene's *Pandosto* are taken directly from Bullough, without any alteration of spelling or punctuation).

generally been replaced by dashes or commas. Where appropriate, quotation marks have been inserted, and where there is no intervening stage direction, the double dash is used to indicate a shift of address within a speech. Both punctuation forms are collated (see below). When words concluding in 'ed' receive an accentuation not found in modern speech but required to maintain the meter, the ending is marked with a grave accent (e.g., crabbèd, enclosèd, condemnèd, and blessèd). Speech headings have been expanded and rendered consistent (e.g., F's *Antig.* and *Ant.* appear as ANTIGONUS throughout; similarly with *Paul.* and *Pau.* as PAULINA; and *Aut.* and *Autol.* as AUTOLYCUS).

In conformity with the practice of the series, the collation appears at the foot of the text and records only substantive departures from Folio as they apply to wording, punctuation, stage directions, speech headings, and lineation. In the format of the collation, the authority for this edition's reading follows immediately after the quotation from the text, with other readings arranged chronologically. The form 'This edn' is used for innovations of our own, but when the variant has been introduced by an earlier editor or conjectured by a textual commentator, those authorities are cited in abbreviated forms, e.g., Rowe and conj. Thirlby, respectively. *Subst.* stands for substantively and indicates that only the relevant elements have been transcribed. (See pp. xv–xxviii for an explanation of the abbreviations used in this edition and a full list of the editions and commentaries cited.)

With respect to quotation marks, the collation typically records the first authority from the eighteenth century to italicize rather than enclose passages in quotation marks, italics being the convention at the time; the collation in such instances reads, for example, *Johnson* (*subst.*) or *Capell (subst.)*; we have not sought out the first editor who happened to use the modern convention. When the nature of an utterance is clearly exclamatory, emendations of F's question mark to an exclamation point have not generally been collated; on occasion, such instances are recorded as a way of reminding the reader of how pervasive the practice was to use the question mark to register both interrogation and exclamation. When, however, the exclamatory nature of the passage is open to interpretation, we have collated the change, sometimes addressing it in the Commentary as well (e.g., Leontes' 'Good Queen!' [2.3.58] and Paulina's 'not women!' [5.1.109]). The rearrangement of a pentameter shared by two or more characters and printed as prose in F has been collated and discussed in the Commentary only when controversial in the play's textual scholarship; in such cases, other editorial choices are sometimes cited so as to allow the reader the opportunity to entertain reasonable alternatives (e.g., 1.2.45, 227, 338–9; 2.1.3–4).[5] As has been customary in editions of Shakespeare since the eighteenth century, white space is used to suggest linked lines.

[5] Wright (Appendix C, p. 295) counts 330 shared lines; together with short lines not readily linked (58), they constitute 18.41 % of the play's verse lines. The other main deviation from the pentameter norm is the hexameter: 63 cases or one every 32 lines (Wright, Appendix B, p. 293).

With few exceptions, F's stage directions are rarely descriptive, the majority consisting of generic entrance and exit cues.[6] In an attempt to help the reader imagine the play as performed, we have frequently modified, repositioned, or added to F's stage directions (e.g., 4.4.397), always enclosing the emendation in square brackets to alert the reader to editorial intervention. Every effort has been made to register the first suggestion of an added stage direction but, given the proliferation of single volume texts since the end of the nineteenth century, some may have been anticipated by editors not acknowledged in the collation. Where some stage business is obviously intended in the text but its exact nature is unclear, we have not, in general, imposed a stage direction; instead, we have often used the Commentary to provide possibilities to help readers reach their own judgments about what is happening on stage (e.g., the business between Leontes and Antigonus at 2.1.153 and between Hermione and Leontes at 5.3.107–9). On occasion, when the gesture implicit in the text may be literal or figurative – e.g., the Lords' kneeling at 2.3.152 – we have again avoided interpolation but have by way of the Commentary alerted the reader to the possibility of consequent stage business – i.e., in the example cited, if the characters do actually kneel, when do they rise? In such instances, we frequently draw on choices culled from the play's performance history. When we do introduce a stage direction, we try to place it where the stipulated business seems (at least to us) most likely, and always with an eye to the theatrical implications of the emendation (e.g., 5.3.44 and 48). Crane's massed entries have been emended to register only those characters whose presence is required at the beginning of a scene; separate entrances are provided for other characters who subsequently become part of the scene's action, with the corresponding stage direction provided immediately before the character's verbal and/or physical participation (see, for example, Paulina's entrance at 2.3.26).[7]

Scene headnotes contain information concerning such issues as location (if that is not clear from the dialogue), the passage or non-passage of time, and the scene's relation to Shakespeare's source; sometimes performance choices are cited so as to enhance the reader's staging of the scene in his/her mind's eye.

Unless otherwise noted, all quotations from other Shakespearean plays are taken from the Riverside edition. The *OED* has served as the overall lexical guide, and where a word has undergone semantic change since Shakespeare's time, the difference is noted in the Commentary.

6 The eight stage directions carrying some descriptive sense are as follows: 'Enter . . . Hermione (as to her Triall) . . .' (TLN 1174–5; 3.2.10); 'Exit pursued by a Beare' (TLN 1500; 3.3.57); 'Enter Time, the Chorus' (TLN 1579; 4.1.0); 'Enter Autolicus singing' (TLN 1668; 4.3.0); 'Heere a Daunce of Shepheards and Shephearddesses' (TLN 1988–9; 4.4.167); 'Enter Autolicus singing' (TLN 2043; 4.4.212); 'Heere a Dance of twelue Satyres' (TLN 2164; 4.4.322); and 'Enter . . . Hermione (like a Statue:) . . .' (TLN 3185; 5.3.20).

7 In two instances (4.3. and 5.2), the entries are consistent with modern editorial principles.

The Winter's Tale

LIST OF CHARACTERS

LEONTES, *King of Sicilia*
HERMIONE, *Queen to Leontes*
MAMILLIUS, *young Prince of Sicilia*
PERDITA, *daughter to Leontes and Hermione*

CAMILLO, ANTIGONUS, CLEOMENES, DION } *Four Lords of Sicilia*

PAULINA, *wife to Antigonus*
EMILIA, *a lady-in-waiting to Hermione*

POLIXENES, *King of Bohemia*
FLORIZEL, *Prince of Bohemia*
ARCHIDAMUS, *a Lord of Bohemia*

SHEPHERD, *reputed father of Perdita*
CLOWN, *his son*
[MOPSA], [DORCAS] } *Shepherdesses*

AUTOLYCUS, *a rogue*

[*A* Mariner]
[*A* Jailer]

Other Lords, [Ladies,] Gentlemen, [Officers,] and Servants
Shepherds and Shepherdesses

[Satyrs *for a dance*]

[Time, *as Chorus*]

Notes
WT is one of seven plays in F to include a list of characters titled 'Names of the Actors'; the list appears at the end of the text and is followed by 'Finis'. The scribe Ralph Crane, who almost certainly wrote the text supplied to the printers, may also have provided the descriptions of the roles given above, with the exceptions of the Shepherd who is listed as 'Old Shepherd', and Emilia who appears simply as 'a lady'. (For more on the list as it appears in F, see 'Textual Analysis', p. 259.) Throughout F Autolycus is spelled Autolicus, and Cleomenes is Cleomines; Florizel appears (with one exception, see 4.4.1. SH n.) as Florizell; Mamillius, though spelled Mamillus in the list, is Mamillius in stage directions

and dialogue. F's list has been expanded to include additions (which appear in brackets) by Rowe and subsequent editors. As Pafford notes (163), many of the names – Leontes, Camillo, Antigonus, Cleomenes, Dion, Archidamus, Autolycus, Hermione, and Aemylia – are found in Plutarch's *Lives of the Noble Grecians and Romanes* (most of the names drawn from the *Lives* of Camillus, Agis, and Cleomenes). While Shakespeare had used Plutarch (in Sir Thomas North's 1579 translation [and later edns]) earlier in his career, it was very much on his mind in the years immediately leading up to *WT* (see *Ant.*, *Cor.*, and *Tim.*, usually dated 1607–8). Plutarch also includes the names Polyxemus and Paulinus.

LEONTES Pandosto in Robert Greene's novel of the same name. Echoing in Shakespeare's mind may have been the city Leontium mentioned in Plutarch's 'Life of Cleomenes', and from *Cymbeline* (assuming the usual chronology that places it before *WT*) the name Posthumus Leonatus for the husband who falsely accuses his wife of infidelity, wishes her dead, repents his error, and finally is reunited with her. The name links the King to Leo, the lion, 'the central zodiacal sign of summer, identified with the sun as its planet' (Bristol, 156).

HERMIONE Bellaria in *Pandosto*. The name 'Hermione' had been used for a male character – the lover of the heroine – in *The Rare Triumphs of Love and Fortune*, acted at court in 1581–2 and printed in 1589. Etymologically, the name suggests a link to the Greek god Hermes (Mercury in Roman mythology), the messenger of the gods known for eloquence (see Autolycus below for other traits). Murray Levith reports that Ruskin noted the meaning 'pillar-like', appropriate for the character in the final scene (Levith, 109). In classical myth Hermione, the daughter of King Menelaus of Sparta and Helen, is promised to Orestes, married to Neoptolemus, and, after the slaying of her husband by Orestes (recovered from his earlier bout of madness as a result of killing his mother Clytemnestra), finally wedded to her former betrothed (separation from whom she had bitterly lamented). Citing Ovid's *Heroides* (*Ep.*8), Bullough (124) notes that 'the double pathos of wife without husband and daughter without mother [Helen having eloped with Paris] may have appealed to Shakespeare, but his Hermione, unlike Ovid's, does not seek relief in copious tears'.

MAMILLIUS Garinter in *Pandosto*. The name comes from the Latin word for 'breast' and may owe something to the title of Greene's *Mamillia* (1583).

PERDITA Fawnia in *Pandosto*. The name means 'she who is lost'; like the names Marina (*Per.*) and Miranda (*Temp.*), its meaning is underscored in the text (3.3.31–3; see also 3.2.133 and 5.1.40).

CAMILLO Franion in *Pandosto*. Camillo is the courtier trusted by Leontes to hear his innermost thoughts as well as 'chamber counsels' (1.2.233–4); he is also referred to as a 'cupbearer' (1.2.310) assigned to Polixenes during that king's stay in Sicilia (the Latin *camella* is a diminutive of *camera* for 'goblet'; Levith [109], however, proposes 'camilla'= 'attendant'). 'The Patrician name continued as a surname and Christian name in Italy and several books by authors named Camillus were printed before 1611' (Pafford, 163 n.4).

ANTIGONUS. No counterpart in *Pandosto*. Although the name probably derives from Plutarch's 'Life of Cleomenes', it is possible that the eponymous figure of Sophocles' *Antigone* (a Latin translation of which was published in England in 1581) is implicit; in sacrificing her life in defence of the ties of humanity and kinship against the cruelty of tyrannical power, she both parallels and contrasts with Antigonus. Antigonus/Antigone comes from two Greek words meaning 'against generation, against childbearing' (De Grazia, 145).

PAULINA No counterpart in *Pandosto*. The feminine version of 'Paul', the name evokes the epistle writer and martyr St Paul who zealously converted the Gentiles and whose epistolary voice is chastening. Levith thinks the Latin word 'paulus' = 'small' may suggest that Paulina is of short stature (109).

EMILIA No counterpart in *Pandosto*. The name appears with some frequency in Shakespeare: as the name of the Abbess and long-lost wife of Egeon *(Err.)*, of the wife of Iago and lady-in-waiting to Desdemona (*Oth.*), and (post-dating *WT*) of the beloved of both Palamon and Arcite in *TNK*. Mahood suggests identifying Emilia with the second lady in 2.1 who sounds 'a little older and more staid' (9).

POLIXENES Egistus in *Pandosto*. The name has been associated with Polus, the North Star (Bristol, 156), and with the Greek 'polyxenos', which means 'hospitable and much visited' (Levith, 109).

FLORIZEL Dorastus in *Pandosto*. Florizel, in wooing Perdita, assumes the name of 'Doricles' (see 4.4.146n.), which Shakespeare may have found in Virgil's *Aeneid*, 5. 620. In the Spanish romance *Amadis de Grecia*, a continuation of *Amadis de Gaule*, Don Florisel, a prince in the guise of a shepherd, woos a lovely shepherdess, who is unaware of her real identity as a princess. The name has 'floral' overtones and furthers the image of Florizel as a 'prince of romance' (Draper, 27).

CLOWN No counterpart in *Pandosto*. The designation 'probably means both that the role was played by the theatrical company's [low] comic actor and that the character is to be viewed as a rustic simpleton' (Folger, 243).

DORCAS Levith links the name to 'dorkas' = 'roe or gazelle' (110), but there is also a biblical connection having implications for the 'statue' scene. In Acts 9. 36–41 a resurrection story is told of a good and holy woman named Tabitha, 'which by interpretation is called Dorcas', who becomes sick and dies; the apostle Peter is summoned and he raises her from the dead. Orgel calls her a 'prototype of Hermione' (171).

MOPSA Charles Boyce (*Shakespeare A To Z*, 1990, 442) points out that the name 'was conventionally rustic, used for peasant women in several sixteenth-century romantic works', most notably Sidney's *Arcadia*. In *Pandosto*, Mopsa is the name of the Shepherd's wife, the foster-mother of Fawnia (= Perdita).

AUTOLYCUS Shares some similarities with Capnio, the old and 'wylie' court servant of Dorastus in *Pandosto*. Autolycus (the name means 'the wolf himself') tells the audience he received his name because he was 'littered under Mercury' (4.3.24–5), who in Roman mythology is, among other things, the cunning god of theft, commerce, and gain. Ovid describes Autolycus, the son of Mercury and Chione, as being very much his father's son: 'Awtolychus . . . proved a wily pie [magpie], / And such a fellow as in theft and filching had no peer. / . . . he could men's eyes so blear [deceive] / As for to make the black things white, and white things black . . .' (*Metamorphoses*, 11. 360–63, spelling modernized). Since Mercury is identified with the Greek god Hermes (see Hermione above), there may be a subtextual link between Autolycus and the Queen potentially exploited by doubling (see Appendix B, p. 265 n. 8). The name Autolycus also appears in Plutarch's *Life of Lucullus*.

SATYRS Twelve countrymen – three carters, three shepherds, three neatherds, and three swineherds – who make 'themselves all men of hair' (4.4.306–8).

TIME Although *Pandosto* offers no counterpart, its elaborate subtitle probably lies behind Shakespeare's allegorical figure who appears only in 4.1: 'Pandosto. The Triumph of Time. Wherein is discovered . . . that although by the means of sinister fortune Truth may be concealed, yet by Time . . . it is most manifestly revealed. . . . *Temporis filia veritas* [Truth is the daughter of Time]' (see illustration 30, p. 69).

THE WINTER'S TALE

1.1 *Enter* CAMILLO *and* ARCHIDAMUS

ARCHIDAMUS If you shall chance, Camillo, to visit Bohemia on the like occasion whereon my services are now on foot, you shall see, as I have said, great difference betwixt our Bohemia and your Sicilia.

CAMILLO I think this coming summer the King of Sicilia means to pay Bohemia the visitation which he justly owes him.

ARCHIDAMUS Wherein our entertainment shall shame us; we will be justified in our loves; for indeed –

1.1] F (*Actus Primus. Scœna Prima.*) 7 us;] F (vs:); us, *Theobald*

Act 1, Scene 1

The expository dialogue of Camillo and Archidamus derives from passing references in Greene's *Pandosto* to the promise of young Garinter (Mamillius) and to the shared youth and continuing friendship of the kings of Sicilia and Bohemia. Although F makes no mention of the scene's location, early editors often specified an antechamber in Leontes' palace. As suggested by the prose format, the polite conversation between the courtiers (called 'two chit-chatters' by Coleridge [in Foakes, 1.551]) is private, relaxed, and casually repetitive ("as I have said" [3]). Archidamus appears only here; Camillo apparently takes over his position and function when he journeys to Bohemia with Polixenes. In the Globe Theatre where we know the play was performed (and presumably at Blackfriars), Archidamus and Camillo probably entered the stage area from one rear door and exited through the opposite. (See Supplementary note, p. 251.)

1 **If . . . chance** The scene begins and ends in the subjunctive mood of speculation and contingency, an appropriate prelude to the world of 'ifs,' 'doubts,' and 'dreams' imagined by Leontes in subsequent scenes. Shakespeare's only other play to begin with 'If' is *TN*.

2 **on foot** employed. Archidamus refers to his role in facilitating the present visit of Polixenes, or perhaps in planning the reciprocal one that Leontes contemplates (5–6).

3–4 **great . . . Sicilia** Several commentators see here a pointer to Sicilian courtly elegance as opposed to the simpler life in Bohemia, expanded in Archidamus' following two speeches and eventually structuring the larger tonal contrast of court scenes in Acts 1–3 with the pastoral sequence in Act 4.

5 **this . . . summer** The first reference to the play's pervasive concern with time is natural and seasonal ('Bohemian' time), yet delineated with precision ('this coming'), typical of the way time is measured in Sicilia. The mention of a forthcoming summer here, Mamillius' later assertion that a 'sad tale's best for winter' (2.1.25), and the suggestion of a 'Candlemas bear' in 3.3 (Bristol, 158–62) indicate the dramatic action begins in winter, often visually emphasized in productions through an arctic white scene design (Nunn), a Lapland motif of reindeer hunts on hangings and Eskimo costumes (Barton-Nunn), fur-trimmed coats, hats, and muffs (Howell), a Christmas tree (Bergman), or falling snow (Sokolov, Kahn).

6 **Bohemia** Polixenes, the King of Bohemia.

6 **justly** duly, reciprocally.

7–8 **Wherein . . . loves** i.e. in the planned return visit, the hospitable provision (see *OED* entertainment 11b) will embarrass the Bohemian hosts in its deficiency, but they will be absolved by their good will. F's punctuation connects 'Wherein . . . us' grammatically with Camillo's previous 'visitation'. Theobald's emendation links the phrase instead with 'will be justified', making the speech flow more gracefully; but Archidamus' next speech is also marked by abrupt shifts and new beginnings, a pattern typical of *WT*'s rhythmic temper.

8 **justified** absolved, excused; 'a glance at the

CAMILLO Beseech you –

ARCHIDAMUS Verily I speak it in the freedom of my knowledge. We cannot with such magnificence – in so rare – I know not what to say. We will give you sleepy drinks that your senses, unintelligent of our insufficience, may, though they cannot praise us, as little accuse us.

CAMILLO You pay a great deal too dear for what's given freely.

ARCHIDAMUS Believe me, I speak as my understanding instructs me, and as mine honesty puts it to utterance.

CAMILLO Sicilia cannot show himself over-kind to Bohemia: They were trained together in their childhoods; and there rooted betwixt them then such an affection which cannot choose but branch now. Since their more mature dignities and royal necessities made separation of their society, their encounters, though not personal, hath been royally attorneyed with interchange of gifts, letters, loving embassies, that they have seemed to be together though absent, shook hands as over a vast, and embraced as it were from the ends of opposed winds. The heavens continue their loves.

9 Beseech] F (*'Beseech*) 16 Believe] F (*'Beleeue*) 23 hath] F; have F2

doctrine of salvation by faith rather than by good works' (Schanzer). The word frames the play; in 5.3.145, however, the meaning relates more to vindication and the validation of worth.

10 Verily A mild oath meaning 'truly'.

10 in the freedom of enabled or privileged by.

12 sleepy soporific.

12 that so that.

13 unintelligent unaware.

15 freely (1) of one's own accord, willingly, unreservedly; and possibly (2) gratis, i.e., without expecting anything in return.

18 over-kind too kind, kind enough.

19 trained (1) 'instructed', and also (2) 'disciplined' like plants, in a particular direction; the second meaning governs the following choice of 'rooted' (19) and 'branch' (21). Like the syntax of 1–4 and 11–14, the imagery from this point to the end of the scene becomes expansive, fitting the play's temporal and spatial dynamic.

21 branch (1) proliferate, but also (2) diverge from a central beginning (anticipating the following reference to the kings' physical separation in adulthood).

21–2 mature dignities and royal necessities 'positions and duties that come with maturity and kingship' (Folger).

22 society companionship, company.

23 hath have (see Abbott 334).

23 royally attorneyed carried out by proxy on a grand scale (an example of Shakespeare's legal terminology; see Sokol, *Dictionary*, 16).

24 embassies messages; see *John* 1.1.6, 'Silence, good mother, hear the embassy.'

25 vast great distance or boundless expanse. Only in Shakespeare's late plays is the word used as a noun: see *Per.* 3.1.1 ('The god of this great vast, rebuke these surges') and *Temp.* 1.2.327 ('Shall, for that vast of night that they may work').

26 ends . . . winds opposite points on the compass, conceived as sources of the different winds. Renaissance cartography often imaged the four 'corners' of the earth as winds blown by cherubic figures.

26–7 The heavens continue i.e. 'May the heavens continue', the optative subjunctive.

ARCHIDAMUS I think there is not in the world either malice or matter to alter it. You have an unspeakable comfort of your young prince Mamillius. It is a gentleman of the greatest promise that ever came into my note.

CAMILLO I very well agree with you in the hopes of him. It is a gallant child, one that indeed physics the subject, makes old hearts fresh. They that went on crutches ere he was born desire yet their life to see him a man.

ARCHIDAMUS Would they else be content to die?

CAMILLO Yes, if there were no other excuse why they should desire to live.

ARCHIDAMUS If the King had no son, they would desire to live on crutches till he had one. *Exeunt*

1.2 *Enter* LEONTES, HERMIONE, MAMILLIUS, POLIXENES, CAMILLO

POLIXENES Nine changes of the wat'ry star hath been
The shepherd's note since we have left our throne

1.2] F *(Scæna Secunda.)* **0** SD] F; *Enter . . . Camillo following Capell; Enter . . . and Attendants Theobald (* with no exit at the end of 1.1*)*

28 malice or matter ill will (hatred) or cause (reason). See Supplementary note (p. 251).

29 unspeakable inexpressibly great, beyond words.

29–30 of your . . . Mamillius in your . . . Mamillius. (See Supplementary note, p. 251.)

31 note observation (as in 1.2.2).

33 gallant excellent (a general term of praise).

33 physics . . . subject is wholesome to the people. This phrase and the emphasis on patriarchal succession (33–40) support recent scholars' focus on the play's political dimension (see Introduction, pp. 20–2).

36–40 Would . . . one The language moves from polite discourse to friendly joking: Even if there were no heir, those on crutches would come up with an excuse to live.

Act 1, Scene 2

After the prose of the two courtiers' off-duty small talk in 1.1, the shift to verse on the introduction of royalty transforms F's undefined space into something slightly more formal, though not a full public court scene, the frequent addition (following Theobald) of 'attendants' to the entrance direction notwithstanding; see Supplementary note, p. 251.

0 SD HERMIONE Showing Hermione as obviously pregnant is a 'directorial decision' (Barnet, 233), one supported, however, by textual implication. In the next scene, which follows close upon the hasty departure of the anxious Polixenes and Camillo, Hermione's attending ladies report that the queen 'rounds apace' and is 'spread of late into a goodly bulk' (2.1.16, 19–20); she also gives birth to a strong, healthy baby a short time after (within twenty-three days to be exact, 2.1.182–7, 2.3.192–8).

0 CAMILLO Named in Crane's typical massed entry, Camillo should perhaps not enter until he is needed at 207, since he has just exited at the end of the previous scene (Ringler, 114n.). Wells and Taylor (*Companion*, 601) argue that since Camillo later knows about the difficulty in persuading Polixenes to stay on, he must have been on stage for some of the early action. Leontes later in the present scene must believe Camillo to be within earshot when he summons him. An entrance 'following' (as in Capell) is attractive in that it gives the actor time to exit and then reappear behind the entering royal party.

1–2 Nine . . . note The shepherd has observed nine changes of the moon ('the wat'ry star'), i.e., the passage of nine months. The moon is 'wat'ry' because it governs the tides; see *Ham.* 1.1.118–19, 'and the moist star / Upon whose influence Neptune's empire stands'.

Without a burden. Time as long again
Would be filled up, my brother, with our thanks,
And yet we should, for perpetuity,
Go hence in debt. And therefore, like a cipher,
Yet standing in rich place, I multiply
With one 'we thank you' many thousands more
That go before it.

LEONTES Stay your thanks a while,
And pay them when you part.

POLIXENES Sir, that's tomorrow.
I am questioned by my fears of what may chance
Or breed upon our absence, that may blow
No sneaping winds at home, to make us say,
'This is put forth too truly.' Besides, I have stayed
To tire your royalty.

LEONTES We are tougher, brother,
Than you can put us to't.

POLIXENES No longer stay.

LEONTES One sennight longer.

8 'we . . . you'] *Pope (subst.)*; we . . . you F 14 'This . . . truly'] *Theobald*; This . . . truly F

3 **Without . . . burden** With nothing to fill it, therefore, empty. In conjunction with the preceding temporal reference to nine months and subsequent words like 'filled up' (4), 'perpetuity' (5), and 'multiply' (7), 'burden' (*OED n* 4: that which is borne in the womb) participates in a 'language of fertility' (Barnet, 223) that may provide further support for a visibly pregnant Hermione and incrementally contribute to Leontes' impending rage. In Syer, Polixenes addressed his 'pregnant opening sentence' to Hermione, not Leontes (see Armstrong, 30).

3–6 **Time . . . debt** I could occupy another nine months with thanking you and still depart forever in your debt.

6–7 **like . . . place** like a zero, which generates value not from its own worth but from its placement after a number.

9 **Stay** Hold back. Leontes echoes the proverbial idea of withholding thanks until one has left (Tilley P83); see *Temp.* 3.3.39, 'Praise in departing', which Prospero utters as an aside, knowing in advance what he plans for Alonso *et al.* If, as some actors (e.g. Gielgud) have suggested, Leontes enters the dramatic action already troubled by jealous suspicions, then what appears to be proverbial banter may assume a more ironic, even sinister, connotation.

11 **questioned** agitated, disturbed. Folger's paraphrase of 'I am questioned' = 'I am tormented' draws upon a legal meaning of the noun 'question', i.e. 'the application of torture as part of a judicial examination' (*OED n* 2). Camillo's precise noting of this 'material' concern (1.2.212–13) has been used to argue for his onstage presence this early in the scene.

12–14 **that . . . truly** that may as yet arouse (*OED* blow *v* 18) no publicly reproving (*OED* sneap *v* 2) winds at home to persuade me that my anxiety was well grounded; or, with 'winds' as subject, that no reproving winds have yet made known (*OED* blow *v* 11: 'utter'; 13: 'proclaim'; 27: 'expose, betray'). 'Sneaping', when used of the wind, may also mean biting, nipping, checking the growth of (*OED* gives line 13 as an example of the adjective). Some editors have followed Johnson in reading 'that may blow' as a wish, usually altering the preceding comma to a semicolon or period.

16 **Than . . . to't** Than to be pushed beyond our powers by you.

POLIXENES Very sooth, tomorrow.
LEONTES We'll part the time between's then: and in that
I'll no gainsaying.
POLIXENES Press me not, beseech you, so.
There is no tongue that moves, none, none i'th' world,
So soon as yours could win me. So it should now,
Were there necessity in your request, although
'Twere needful I denied it. My affairs
Do even drag me homeward, which to hinder
Were, in your love, a whip to me, my stay
To you a charge and trouble. To save both,
Farewell, our brother.
LEONTES Tongue-tied our queen? Speak you.
HERMIONE I had thought, sir, to have held my peace until
You had drawn oaths from him not to stay. You, sir,
Charge him too coldly. Tell him you are sure
All in Bohemia's well; this satisfaction
The bygone day proclaimed – say this to him,
He's beat from his best ward.
LEONTES Well said, Hermione.
HERMIONE To tell he longs to see his son were strong.
But let him say so then, and let him go;
But let him swear so, and he shall not stay;

32 bygone day] Rowe[2]; by-gone-day F 32 proclaimed – say] *Orgel;* proclaym'd, say F

17 **Very sooth** Indeed.

18 **between's** between us.

19 **I'll . . . gainsaying** I won't accept any contradiction, or more colloquially, I won't take 'no' for an answer.

20 **tongue . . . moves** voice that persuades. In Henry Jewett's 1929 production in Boston, Polixenes delivered this line and the next to Hermione (Bartholomeusz, 166).

21 **could** that could.

25 **Were . . . me** Would be a punishment to me, even though it arose from your love for me (or my love for you).

26 **charge** (1) burden, or, more specifically (2) expense.

30 **Charge** Urge, press (1.2.19), exhort (*OED v* 14).

31 **satisfaction** reassuring information, which has apparently arrived in the recent past, perhaps as recently as yesterday ('the bygone day').

33 **ward** defensive position in epée and other single sword-fight. Hermione indirectly presents Leontes' pressing hospitality as a one-on-one competition between him and Polixenes, thereby building on the motif of rivalry introduced so harmlessly in 1.1, and underscoring the personal nature of the conflict here and to come.

33 **Well . . . Hermione** Collier[2] directs that Leontes draw apart after this reply, since he is apparently unaware as late as 85 that Polixenes has been persuaded to stay. (See Supplementary note, p. 251).

34 **tell** say. Here and in 36 Hermione calls attention to the difference between 'saying' and 'swearing' (Pafford).

34 **strong** i.e. as an argument.

35 **But** Only.

We'll thwack him hence with distaffs.
[*To Polixenes*] Yet of your royal presence I'll adventure
The borrow of a week. When at Bohemia
You take my lord, I'll give him my commission
To let him there a month behind the gest
Prefixed for's parting – yet, good deed, Leontes,
I love thee not a jar o'th'clock behind
What lady she her lord. – You'll stay?

POLIXENES No, madam.

HERMIONE Nay, but you will?

POLIXENES I may not, verily.

HERMIONE Verily?
You put me off with limber vows; but I,
Though you would seek t'unsphere the stars with oaths,
Should yet say, 'Sir, no going.' Verily,
You shall not go – a lady's 'verily' 's
As potent as a lord's. Will you go yet?
Force me to keep you as a prisoner,
Not like a guest. So you shall pay your fees

37 We'll] F (Wee'l) 38 SD] *Rowe; not in* F 42 parting–] *Orgel;* parting: F 44 lord.–] *Oxford;* Lord. F 45 Nay ... Verily] *Orgel; as three lines* ... will? / ... verely. / Verily F*; as two lines* ... verily. / Verily *Collier* 45 Verily?] F; Verily! *Capell* 48 'Sir ... going'] *Theobald (subst.);* Sir ... going F 49 go–] *Orgel;* go; F 49 'verily'] *Theobald (subst.);* verely F 49 's] *Staunton;* 'is F 52 guest.] F (Guest:); guest? *Rowe*

37 In view of the promised action with the distaff (an instrument used in spinning, and hence symbolic of women's domain), Hermione's 'We' apparently signifies wives and mothers in general rather than herself and Leontes in particular. Significantly, it is a woman in her role as mother who brings up the existence of Polixenes' son. In Kahn, Hermione playfully wielded the bow of Mamillius' violin as if it were a sword or fencing instrument.

38 **adventure** venture, risk.

40 **take** receive.

41 **let him** Malone suggests either 'let' = retard (i.e. Leontes' departure) or 'let him' = hinder himself. For the objective pronoun as reflexive, see Abbott 223.

41 **behind** after.

41 **gest** a stage of a royal progress, thus a planned stay of a particular length.

42 **good deed** indeed.

43 **jar** tick.

44 **What lady she** Whatever lady. For the extra pronoun to add emphasis, Lee compares 'God he knows' (*R3* 3.1.10 and 26).

45 **verily** Here and in 48, 49, and 54, Shakespeare may have been remembering the expression 'verely, verely' that echoes throughout John's gospel (Shaheen, 721).

46 **limber** limp, feeble.

47 Even if you should use vows forceful enough to dislodge the stars from their fixed spheres.

48–50 Schalkwyk views the exchange between Hermione and Polixenes as a microcosm of *WT*'s exploration of 'the radical instability, for patriarchy, of [the female] word' (246). Informing both Sicilian and Bohemian society is the recognition that legitimacy of the bloodline, so crucial to patriarchal authority, depended on the woman's word concerning paternity–a word, however, considered less trustworthy than man's because 'women ... will say anything' (1.2.129–30).

52–3 **So ... depart** Prisoners were charged for their board and lodging while incarcerated and required to pay a fee when discharged.

When you depart, and save your thanks. How say you?
My prisoner? or my guest? By your dread 'verily',
One of them you shall be.

POLIXENES Your guest, then, madam.
To be your prisoner should import offending,
Which is for me less easy to commit
Than you to punish.

HERMIONE Not your jailer, then,
But your kind hostess. Come, I'll question you
Of my lord's tricks and yours when you were boys.
You were pretty lordings then?

POLIXENES We were, fair queen,
Two lads that thought there was no more behind
But such a day tomorrow as today,
And to be boy eternal.

HERMIONE Was not my lord
The verier wag o'th'two?

POLIXENES We were as twinned lambs that did frisk i'th'sun
And bleat the one at th'other. What we changed
Was innocence for innocence; we knew not
The doctrine of ill-doing, nor dreamed
That any did. Had we pursued that life
And our weak spirits ne'er been higher reared
With stronger blood, we should have answered heaven

54 'verily'] *Theobald (subst.)*; Verely F 64 And . . . lord] *Cam.; as two lines* . . . eternal. / Was . . . F; *as two lines* . . . eternal. / Was . . . two? *Malone* 66 twinned] *Rowe (subst.)*; twyn'd F

56 **import offending** indicate that I had committed an offence.

61 **pretty lordings** bonny (*OED adj* 4a) little lords; in light of 60 and 65, 'pretty' perhaps also means 'artful, clever, roguish' (*OED adj* 2b).

62 **behind** yet to come.

65 **wag** mischievous boy. At the previous mention of 'boy eternal', Philip Goodwin's Leontes, who had moved upstage to play with Mamillius, took the newly opened gift box that had held a toy top and, placing it over his head, chased his son offstage, much to the amusement of Hermione and Polixenes (Kahn).

66 **twinned lambs** The complete implication of the children in each other is intensified by F's spelling *twyn'd* (a variant of 'twined' = entwined, interwoven, *OED* twine v^1 1b, c, d and twined *adj*). Photographs of Henry Kolker (Leontes) and Charles Balsar (Polixenes) from Winthrop Ames's 1910 New York production reveal the two kings, with their mustaches, neatly trimmed black Italianate beards, dark hair, and ermine costumes, as 'mirror images of each other' (Bartholomeusz, 136).

67 **changed** exchanged.

71–2 **And our . . . blood** And had our vital powers (weak because of our youth) never been strengthened by maturing passions.

Boldly, 'not guilty', the imposition cleared
Hereditary ours.

HERMIONE By this we gather
You have tripped since.

POLIXENES O my most sacred lady,
Temptations have since then been born to's: for
In those unfledged days was my wife a girl;
Your precious self had then not crossed the eyes
Of my young playfellow.

HERMIONE Grace to boot!
Of this make no conclusion, lest you say
Your queen and I are devils. Yet go on –
Th'offences we have made you do we'll answer,
If you first sinned with us, and that with us
You did continue fault, and that you slipped not
With any but with us.

LEONTES Is he won yet?

HERMIONE He'll stay, my lord.

LEONTES At my request he would not.
Hermione, my dearest, thou never spok'st
To better purpose.

73 'not guilty'] *Pope (subst.)*; not guilty F 79 boot!] *Capell (after Johnson)*; boot: F 85 won] F *(woon)* 86 At . . . not] F; *as aside Capell, Wilson*

73–4 the imposition . . . ours (1) setting aside the original sin perpetrated by Adam and Eve in the Garden of Eden and inherited, according to Christian belief, by all their descendants (nominative absolute construction expressing a condition, Abbott 377); (2) original sin being not imputed to us. The ambiguity ('innocent except for' or 'innocent even of') is functional. Polixenes' first meaning accords with adult doctrinal orthodoxy and his second with childhood innocence as he nostalgically conceives it to have been experienced by himself and Leontes. See Gen. 3, Isa. 53:6, and Rom. 5:12–21.

75 tripped sinned, possibly with the more specific meaning of stumbling or falling sexually (Williams, 314).

77 unfledged The pastoral imagery introduced by Polixenes continues with this avian metaphor referring to the period before a young unfeathered bird is strong enough to fly on its own; compare 'lambs' (66).

79 Grace to boot Capell's paraphrase 'Grace befriend us!' (*Notes*, 2. 162) has been followed in sense by most editors. Compare *R3* 5.3.301, 'St. George to boot.' Also possible is 'You do us grace in addition,' which perhaps accords better with the playful irony of what follows. Hall understood the colloquialism as 'Thanks very much' (Warren, 97).

80 Of . . . conclusion Don't draw any conclusion from this premise (for if you follow that train of thought you'll be calling us 'devils' [81] next).

82–5 If Leontes has left Hermione and Polixenes talking by themselves (see 33n.), he might rejoin them at this point to have his suspicions awakened by the allusion to 'offences' committed between them. See Introduction, p. 26.

82 answer answer for.

83–4 that . . . that if . . . if (*OED* that *conj.* 8).

86 At . . . not Coleridge (in Foakes, 1.551) saw here 'the first working of' the jealous fit. While the line can certainly be delivered lightheartedly, actors often put Coleridge's theory into practice; Jeremy Kemp (in Howell), e.g., in his close-up evinced surprise, with a flicker of doubt hinting at something more ominous. See Collation.

HERMIONE Never?
LEONTES Never but once.
HERMIONE What, have I twice said well? When was't before?
I prithee tell me; cram's with praise, and make's
As fat as tame things. One good deed dying tongueless
Slaughters a thousand waiting upon that.
Our praises are our wages. You may ride's
With one soft kiss a thousand furlongs ere
With spur we heat an acre. But to th'goal:
My last good deed was to entreat his stay.
What was my first? It has an elder sister,
Or I mistake you – O, would her name were Grace!
But once before I spoke to th'purpose? When?
Nay, let me have't, I long.
LEONTES Why, that was when
Three crabbèd months had soured themselves to death
Ere I could make thee open thy white hand
And clap thyself my love; then didst thou utter,
'I am yours for ever.'
HERMIONE 'Tis grace indeed.
Why, lo you now, I have spoke to th'purpose twice:
The one for ever earned a royal husband,
Th'other, for some while a friend.

98 you –] *Orgel;* you: F 98 Grace!] *Theobald;* Grace. F 103 And] F2; A F 104 'I . . . ever'] *Theobald (subst.);* I . . . ever F

90–5 Overton notes (57–8) how Hermione's 'innocently suggestive language' here ('cram's', 'make's', 'ride's', 'kiss,' 'spur,' and 'heat') may register subliminally with the audience as background for Leontes' sudden jealousy; an actor may see the words having a similar effect on Leontes himself.

91 tame things (1) household pets, indulged with extra food, or (2) poultry and other domesticated creatures, overfed to fatten them for better eating.

91–2 One . . . that Failure to speak well of a good action cuts off a thousand others that might otherwise follow it.

94 furlongs furrow-lengths, each one-eighth of a mile (see 'acre', 95).

95 heat traverse at full speed.

95 acre furlong.

98 Grace The primary meaning behind the pun on the female name is the theological virtue of (1) being sanctified by divine favour, or (2) being granted an excellence or power by God.

99 But Only.

101 crabbed frustrating, provoking; of the nature of the crab-apple (hence 'soured themselves to death').

102–3 open . . . love Leontes recalls, not just Hermione's consent to marry him, but the formal joining of hands that sealed their betrothal: *OED* clap *v* 7a, 'to strike (hands) reciprocally in token of a bargain'. See 4.4.363 n.

104 'Tis grace indeed Hermione is perhaps playing lightheartedly on 'grace', converting what is apparently the theological virtue (98) to one more social and secular, meaning something like the courtesy or graciousness of a favour conferred.

[*She gives her hand to Polixenes*]

LEONTES [*Aside*] Too hot, too hot!
To mingle friendship far is mingling bloods.
I have *tremor cordis* on me: my heart dances,
But not for joy, not joy. This entertainment
May a free face put on: derive a liberty
From heartiness, from bounty, fertile bosom,
And well become the agent; 't may, I grant.
But to be paddling palms and pinching fingers,
As now they are, and making practised smiles
As in a looking-glass, and then to sigh, as 'twere
The mort o'th'deer – oh, that is entertainment
My bosom likes not, nor my brows. Mamillius,
Art thou my boy?

107 SD 1] *Capell (subst.); not in* F **107** SD 2] *Rowe; not in* F **107** hot!] F *(* hot: *)*

107 SD Leontes' reference to 'paddling palms' and 'pinching fingers' (114–5) justifies the gesture proposed by Capell, and this is the logical time for it. The impact of Hermione's joining hands with Polixenes is presumably increased for Leontes by the recollection just before (102–4) of his and Hermione's joining hands in betrothal. Helena Faucit (in Macready's 1837 production) initiated the practice of giving one hand to Leontes on 'husband' (106) and the other to Polixenes on 'friend' (107); 'when Leontes dropped her hand, she moved away with Polixenes letting her hand remain in his' (Bartholomeusz, 75).

108–18 Nunn's use of special lighting effects to isolate Leontes and emphasize his deluded interpretation of the actions of Hermione and Polixenes has become the norm in staging Leontes' asides. While 'Too hot, too hot!' (107) is 'the first overt textual marker' of Leontes' jealousy (Armstrong, 30), earlier visual and subtle verbal clues are available to the actor (see notes to 20, 82–5, 86, and 90–5; and Introduction, pp. 24–6).

108 To . . . bloods If F's spelling *farre* denotes the comparative form, the meaning is something like 'if they push friendship any farther, they'll be mingling bloods', i.e. bodily fluids in sexual intercourse.

109 ***tremor cordis*** 'panting and trembling of the heart' (Philip Barrough, *The Method of Physick*, 7th ed., 1634, 92); the cause could be strong emotion, especially anger.

110 not . . . joy Leontes alludes to an expression that was both proverbial (Dent H331.1, 'To have one's heart dance [leap] for joy') and biblical (Ps.28:8, BCP, 'Therefore my heart danceth for joy'), but contradicts the cause.

110, 117 entertainment The word encapsulates the ambiguity that troubles Leontes in the actions he witnesses: its primary meaning here, reception of and provision for a guest (*OED* 11), is complicated by suggestions of taking a person into one's service (*OED* 2a), and amusement or diversion (*OED* 8a), with the added element of playing a part, disguising.

111 May . . . on May assume an honourable aspect. For the rational observation here and in 112–3, compare *Oth.* 3.3.183–86, ''Tis not to make me jealious / To say my wife is fair, feeds well, loves company, / Is free of speech, sings, plays, and dances well; / Where virtue is, these are more virtuous'.

112 heartiness cordiality.

112 fertile bosom generous feelings.

113 become befit, suit, adorn.

113 agent doer.

114 paddling . . . fingers In both other Shakespearean instances of *paddle* ('finger amorously'), a biased onlooker uses the term to interpret behaviour negatively: Iago describing Desdemona's interchange of courtesies with Cassio (*Oth.* 2.1.253–54, 'Didst thou not see her paddle with the palm of his hand?'); Hamlet denigrating Claudius' lovemaking with Gertrude (*Ham.* 3.4.185, 'Or paddling in your neck with his damn'd fingers'). What is essentially one continuous action (see 124 n.) becomes in Leontes' tortured mind two emphatically separate gestures ('paddling' and 'pinching'), thereby intensifying his fury.

117 mort . . . deer either (1) the signal blown on a hunting horn when the deer has been killed, or (2) the animal's dying sigh. In the first sense, Leontes may refer ironically to the ringing obviousness of their lovesickness, but *AYLI* 2.1.36–8 suggests that the stricken deer's sighs could be similarly forceful: 'The wretched animal heav'd forth such groans / That their discharge did stretch his leathern coat / Almost to bursting.'

118 brows forehead (where the cuckold's horns would grow).

MAMILLIUS Ay, my good lord.

LEONTES I'fecks,
Why, that's my bawcock: what? hast smutched thy nose?
They say it is a copy out of mine. Come, captain,
We must be neat – not neat, but cleanly, captain.
And yet the steer, the heifer, and the calf
Are all called neat. – Still virginalling
Upon his palm? – How now, you wanton calf,
Art thou my calf?

MAMILLIUS Yes, if you will, my lord.

LEONTES Thou want'st a rough pash and the shoots that I have
To be full like me. Yet they say we are
Almost as like as eggs – women say so,
That will say anything. But were they false
As o'er-dyed blacks, as wind, as waters, false
As dice are to be wished by one that fixes
No bourn 'twixt his and mine, yet were it true

123 heifer] F3 (*Heyfer*); Heycfer F 124–5 neat. – . . . palm? –] *Riverside (after Pafford subst.; as aside Capell)*; Neat. . . . Palme? F

119–36 As Snyder argues, 'Although Leontes doesn't take formal possession of Mamillius until Act 2, he starts enlisting him on his side as soon as his sexual suspicions are awakened . . . The coopting move is apparent not only in the dialogue . . . but visually, as a new stage grouping is inaugurated: the initial configuration of the court scene, three adults conversing with each other and a child on the margins, shifts to two and two. Leontes places himself with the boy, whose sex and appearance mirror his, and apart from the heterosexual pair of Hermione and Polixenes, withdrawing from the adult conversation to commune with his son' (Snyder, 6).

119 I'fecks In faith.

120 bawcock fine fellow (Fr. *beau coq*).

120 smutched . . . nose Stage business may be implied here; actors frequently choose to wipe some dirt from Mamillius' nose; as a sign of his increasing instability, Mandy Patinkin's Leontes (in Lapine) did so with considerable roughness.

122 not . . . cleanly Leontes rejects 'neat' (tidy) because it also means 'horned cattle'.

124 virginalling playing with the fingers as on the virginals, an early keyboard instrument possibly deriving its name from the fact that female performers played it; see Son. 128.

125 wanton Probably 'frisky, frolicsome,' rather than the more pejorative senses applied to children, 'naughty', or 'spoiled'. Compare *1H4* 4.1.103, 'Wanton as youthful goats.'

127 pash head.

127 shoots either (1) beard (that makes his face 'rough' and differentiates the mature man from the boy), or (2) horns, continuing Leontes' obsession with cattle and cuckolding (see also 145).

128 full entirely.

129 as . . . eggs For the proverbial likeness of eggs, see Dent E66.

130–1 false . . . blacks Black dye might create falsehood either (1) by concealing the true color ('o'er' understood as 'on top of') – thus, in relation to mourning wear (actually called 'blacks,' *OED n* 5a, b), implying grief that goes no deeper than surface display – or (2) by too plentiful an application ('o'er' understood as 'excessively'), which, since black dye contained vitriol, would rot the fabric.

131 as . . . waters Wind and water were proverbially false; see Tilley W412 and W86, as well as *Oth.* 5.2.134, 'She was false as water'. In Gen. 49.4 it is said to Reuben for defiling his father's bed, 'Thou wast light [i.e. false] as water' (Shaheen, 723).

133 bourn boundary.

To say this boy were like me. Come, sir page,
Look on me with your welkin eye. Sweet villain,
Most dear'st, my collop! Can thy dam, may't be –
Affection! thy intention stabs the centre.
Thou dost make possible things not so held,
Communicat'st with dreams – how can this be?
With what's unreal thou coactive art
And fellow'st nothing. Then 'tis very credent
Thou mayst co-join with something, and thou dost,
And that beyond commission, and I find it,

136 be –] *Rowe;* be F 137 Affection!] *Steevens (* Imagination! *Rowe);* Affection? F 140 unreal thou] *Staunton;* vnreall: thou F

135 welkin sky-blue; or, as Orgel suggests, heavenly (bright, shining).

135 villain used affectionately, with no opprobrium, as in *Err.* 1.2.19, *TN* 2.5.13, and *Tro.* 3.2.33.

136 collop a piece of meat, here a jocular equivalent to 'flesh of my flesh'.

136–45 Can . . . brows This contorted passage is perhaps not meant to carry a clear meaning; Orgel argues that for the 1611 audience obscurity itself would have been the principal message and acceptable as such ('Poetics', 433–7). While a single coherent interpretation remains (perhaps designedly) elusive, it seems likely that audiences might register not only confusion but also some notion of what is being confused, i.e. Leontes buffeted between certainty of Hermione's betrayal and awareness of his own derangement as muddling his thoughts and emotions. When coherent meaning is sought, problems centre on the meaning and grammatical function of 'affection' (see 137n).

136 dam female parent of animals; in reference to human mothers, usually a term of contempt (*OED n*[2] 2, 3); see 2.3.94, and, for semantic amelioration, 3.2.195.

137 affection With no punctuation after 'be' (136), F makes 'affection' the object of 'may't be'; editors who punctuate after 'be', usually a question mark, take it as a vocative, addressed in what follows. It seems likely that 'affection' means 'passion', but whose? If understood as Hermione's lust, 'affection' makes possible things not so held – her normally impossible adultery; if taken to mean Leontes' jealous fantasy, 'affection' propels him to conceive the inconceivable (again, Hermione's adultery). 'Affection' as jealousy makes better sense of 139–41, fastening on dreams and unrealities; but then 'suddenly, (by a wonderful but natural turn in so sick a mind as this speaker's) out of these reflections . . . matter is drawn by him to give his madness sanction; by saying – that since nothings were a foundation for it, somethings might be, and were' (Capell, *Notes* 2.163).

137 intention 'intensity' of passion, which stabs one at the center of his being, or which cuts through pretence to the core of truth; possibly we should read it, David Ward suggests, as 'intensification' in the medical sense, Leontes diagnosing the disabling emotional pathology which wounds his very soul ('Affection, Intention, and Dreams in [*WT*]', *MLR* 82 [1987], 549–50).

140–1 With . . . nothing In not requiring anything substantial to work on, affection can make something of nothing. Since the two clauses seem parallel in meaning as well as form, editors have generally removed F's colon after *vnreall.*

140 coactive acting in concert (in contrast to 'compulsory', its usual meaning in the early modern period) (Orgel). Compare *Tro.* 5.2.118, 'But if I tell how these two did co-act'.

141 fellow'st share or be a partner in, be associated with (*OED* fellow *v* 2a).

141 credent credible.

143 Capell guessed that this was a first try, abandoned in favour of 144; his suggestion has not gained much attention from editors, although it fits the nature of the line which goes nowhere syntactically, can easily be excised, and is succeeded by one beginning exactly the same way.

143 commission what is authorized.

And that to the infection of my brains
And hardening of my brows.

POLIXENES What means Sicilia?

HERMIONE He something seems unsettled.

POLIXENES How, my lord?

LEONTES What cheer? How is't with you, best brother?

HERMIONE You look
As if you held a brow of much distraction.
Are you moved, my lord?

LEONTES No, in good earnest.
How sometimes nature will betray its folly,
Its tenderness, and make itself a pastime
To harder bosoms! Looking on the lines
Of my boy's face, methoughts I did recoil
Twenty-three years, and saw myself unbreeched
In my green velvet coat, my dagger muzzled
Lest it should bite its master, and so prove,
As ornaments oft do's, too dangerous.
How like, methought, I then was to this kernel,
This squash, this gentleman. Mine honest friend,
Will you take eggs for money?

147 SH LEONTES] F; *as continuation of Polixenes' speech Hanmer* 147–8 You look / . . . distraction.] *Theobald; as one line* F 157 do's] F; do *Rowe*

145 hardening . . . brows another reference to Leontes' fear of the cuckold's horns.

145–6 Polixenes' question and Hermione's observation imply some overt manifestation of Leontes' increasing agitation, possibly something more than troubled facial expressions. In Donnellan, Leontes' rough treatment of Mamillius, culminating in a physical attack on the boy, provoked Polixenes' 'What means Sicilia?' and alarmed Hermione and the rest of the court: 'Domestic violence was never far away' in a production that brutally emphasized the behaviour of harsh fathers (Stephen J. Phillips, *ShakB* 18.1[2000]:31).

146 something somewhat.

147 Some editors have reassigned this speech to Polixenes, on the assumption that it arises naturally from his and Hermione's observation that the King looks upset (see 145–6 n.). But F's assignment is appropriate if we see Leontes as seeking to recover his jovial pose as host.

149 moved perturbed.

150 nature natural paternal affection.

151–2 a pastime . . . bosoms a laughingstock to those who are less sentimental.

152 lines lineaments.

153 recoil go back (mentally).

155 coat the skirt or petticoat worn by boys when they were 'unbreeched' (154), not yet in adult male clothes. 'Breeching' was a rite of passage that usually occurred before the age of seven (Snyder, 3–4).

155 muzzled kept in its sheath.

157 do's Rowe's emendation (see Collation) is not necessary if F *do's* is read as a contraction of 'do us'. If 'us' is the object of 'too dangerous', 'to' would be understood; if F *'s* functions in a way parallel to 'bite its master' (156), 'to' is not needed. Alternatively, 'do's' may represent 'does' – a singular verb for a plural subject ('ornaments'), as often in F.

159 squash unripe peapod; the young 'boy' Cesario is said to be 'as a squash is before 'tis a peascod' (*TN* 1.5.157–8).

MAMILLIUS No, my lord, I'll fight.
LEONTES You will! Why, happy man be's dole. My brother,
Are you so fond of your young prince as we
Do seem to be of ours?
POLIXENES If at home, sir.
He's all my exercise, my mirth, my matter;
Now my sworn friend and then mine enemy;
My parasite, my soldier, statesman, all.
He makes a July's day short as December,
And with his varying childness cures in me
Thoughts that would thick my blood.
LEONTES So stands this squire
Officed with me. We two will walk, my lord,
And leave you to your graver steps. Hermione,
How thou lov'st us show in our brother's welcome;
Let what is dear in Sicily be cheap.
Next to thyself and my young rover, he's
Apparent to my heart.
HERMIONE If you would seek us,
We are yours i'th'garden – shall's attend you there?
LEONTES To your own bents dispose you; you'll be found
Be you beneath the sky. [*Aside*] I am angling now,

161 will!] *Rowe;* will: F; will? *Capell* 161 dole.] F; dole! *Hanmer* 176 garden–] *Orgel;* garden: F 178 SD] *Rowe (subst., after* 180*); not in* F

160 **Will . . . money** 'If ordered to stand, will you deliver without resistance?' (Rann). To take eggs for money (Dent E90), glossed by *OED* (egg *n* 4) as 'to be put off with something worthless', seems here to have the related meaning 'to refuse ignobly to meet a challenge'.

161 **happy . . . dole** proverbial (Dent M158), meaning 'may his fortune be that of a happy man'.

163 **seem** 'Seem' could have no implication of deceit, hence Leontes' use of the word to stress his own awareness of his displayed fondness for his son.

164 **exercise** habitual employment.

164 **matter** business. 'Mirth and matter were often opposed to indicate the whole range of human concerns' (Folger).

166 **parasite** hanger-on, flatterer.

168 **childness** childish humour.

169 **Thoughts . . . blood** Melancholy was thought to generate gloom and anger by making the blood thick and heavy, preventing the free flow that gives access to human emotions and enables laughter; compare *John* 3.3.42–6, 'Or if that surly spirit, melancholy, / Had bak'd thy blood and made it heavy, thick, / Which else runs tickling up and down the veins, / Making that idiot, laughter, keep men's eyes'.

169–70 **So . . . me** This young fellow fills the same office with me. 'Squire' reinforces the notion of 'officed', giving Mamillius a quasi-formal status as attendant on and apprentice to his father.

171 **graver** more dignified (because grown-up).

174 **rover** Furness notes that Cotgrave defines *ribleur* as 'a disorderly rover, jetter, swaggerer', a sense for 'rover' more in line with Leontes' joking address to his son as 'captain' (121) and 'sweet villain' (135) than the broader meaning of 'one who runs about'.

175 **Apparent** Closest (as in 'heir apparent'); Wilson sees an ironic overtone of 'claimant', i.e. to Hermione.

176 **shall's** shall we (see Abbott 215).

176 **attend** await.

178 **angling** using guile to entrap, as a fisher uses bait and hook (*OED* angle v^1 2).

Though you perceive me not how I give line.
Go to, go to!
How she holds up the neb, the bill to him!
And arms her with the boldness of a wife
To her allowing husband.
[*Exeunt Polixenes and Hermione*]
Gone already!
Inch-thick, knee-deep, o'er head and ears a forked one!
[*To Mamillius*] Go play, boy, play: thy mother plays, and I
Play too, but so disgraced a part, whose issue
Will hiss me to my grave. Contempt and clamour
Will be my knell. Go play, boy, play. – There have been,
Or I am much deceived, cuckolds ere now,
And many a man there is, even at this present,
Now, while I speak this, holds his wife by th' arm,

180 to!] *Capell;* to. F 181 neb, . . . him!] *Capell;* Neb? . . . him? F; neb, . . . him, *Bevington (with! after* husband *in* 183*)* 183 SD] *Rowe (subst., after* 182*); not in* F 183 already! . . . one!] *Hudson (after Rowe for* already*);* already, . . . one. F 185 SD] *Orgel; not in* F 188 play. –] *Folger;* play, F

179 **give line** allow you full play, like a fish on a line; the expression was proverbial (Dent L304.1), analogous to the modern saying about giving someone enough rope with which to hang himself.

181 **neb** bird's bill, hence mouth or face.

182–3 **arms . . . husband** (1) Fortifies herself to be brazen in her infidelities with the complaisance of her husband; or, perhaps, (2) takes her lover's arm with all the confidence a wife properly evinces to her approving husband. Turner cites in support of the second reading *TNK* 5.3.135, 'Arm your prize', i.e. take your prize (Emily) by the arm; 1.2.191 might also support this reading.

183 **Gone already** It is logical to place the exit of Hermione and Polixenes at this point, as Leontes concludes his observation of them. But his exclamation here is less likely to refer to their departure than to himself, 'gone' in the sense of 'ruined', as in *MM* 5.1.300 and *MV* 3.5.18; the nature of his ruin is elucidated by his following announcement (184) of himself as thoroughly cuckolded.

184 The evidence is solid (as an 'inch-thick' board), plentiful ('knee-deep'), and total ('o'er head and ears') that I am a 'forked one', a horned cuckold (or that Hermione is a double-dealer). Like his earlier twist on a proverbial/biblical expression (109–10), Leontes again would have surprised the play's original audience with his substitution of a cuckold for a lover, the proverb being 'Over head and ears in love' (Dent H268).

185–7 **Go play . . . grave** Leontes moves quickly from child's play (Mamillius) to sexual sport and deception (Hermione) to having an alien role thrust on him, being forced to act the awkward and shaming part of wittol which finally will provoke onlookers to hiss him in contempt. The suggestion of an actor playing a part has led some editors to gloss 'issue' as including an actor's exit from the stage, the other meanings being 'offspring' and 'outcome' (Wilson, Kermode, and Folger); *OED*, however, records no theatrical usage.

187 **Contempt and clamour** Schanzer detects a hendiadys: 'an outcry of contempt'.

188 **my knell** the sounds marking my death (literally, the tolling of the bell, as in Son. 71:2–3).

188 **Go play, boy, play** Whether Mamillius exits (to return at 205), moves to another part of the stage, or remains by his father's side is a directorial choice.

190–204 Wilson specifically suggests a 'side-glance at the audience' for 'even . . . speak this' (190–91), 'think it' (200), 'know't' (202), and 'many thousand on's' (204), a practice frequently adopted in performance, often to laughter. Antony Sher's Leontes (Doran) 'was right downstage in intimate, rather waggish conversation with the audience as he selected candidates in the front rows for those cuckolds, "ere now" and for "Sir Smile" . . .' (Smallwood, 'Performances', 263).

That little thinks she has been sluiced in's absence
And his pond fished by his next neighbor, by
Sir Smile, his neighbor – nay, there's comfort in't,
Whiles other men have gates, and those gates opened,
As mine, against their will. Should all despair
That have revolted wives, the tenth of mankind
Would hang themselves. Physic for't there's none:
It is a bawdy planet, that will strike
Where 'tis predominant; and 'tis powerful, think it,
From east, west, north, and south; be it concluded,
No barricado for a belly. Know't,
It will let in and out the enemy
With bag and baggage: many thousand on's
Have the disease and feel't not. – How now, boy?

MAMILLIUS I am like you, they say.

LEONTES Why, that's some comfort.
What, Camillo there?

CAMILLO [*Coming forward*] Ay, my good lord.

LEONTES Go play, Mamillius; thou'rt an honest man.

[*Exit Mamillius*]

205 not. –] *Oxford; not in* F **206** you, they] F2*;* you F **207** What . . . lord] *Dyce* [2]*; as two lines* . . . there? / I *(* Ay) . . . F **207** SD] *Schanzer (subst.); not in* F **208** SD] *Rowe; not in* F

192 sluiced washed through (with semen).

193 pond fished In sexual slang, 'fish-pond' is the vagina (Williams, *fish*).

194 Sir Smile i.e. 'Mr. Affability, a neighbour pretending to be a man's best friend while charming his wife to bed' (Andrews). Smiling frequently has negative connotations in Shakespeare's plays, concealing villainy (*Ham.* 1.5.106–8, *MV* 1.3.100), enmity (*2H4* Ind. 9–10), tyranny (*Tit.* 2.3.267), and conspiracy (*JC* 2.1.81–2).

197 revolted rebel. The metaphor progresses from wife as land trespassed upon to wife as garrison of a city that treacherously opens its protective gates (195) to the besieger. For 'gates' as vagina, see numerous references in Williams, especially Dekker, *Westward Ho* 5.4.117–18 and Sharpham, *Cupid's Whirligig* 1.4.24, where wives are compared to towns under siege (ultimately a variation of Petrarch's besieged castle).

199–200 It . . . predominant Venus ('It'), the planet governing lust, will 'strike', assert its malign influence, when ascending toward the zenith.

200 think it believe it (Orgel).

202 No . . . belly No fortification [can] block access to a woman's private parts.

204 bag and baggage (1) 'with all one's belongings', i.e. completely; and (2) slang for scrotum and contents (Partridge); Williams cites Middleton, *The World Tost at Tennis*, 609–10: 'a parson's daughter with a soldier between her legs, bag and baggage'.

204 on's of us.

206 I . . . say F2's emendation is widely accepted. Collier proposed the alternative 'like you, you say', and Pafford thought omission of a repeated word a much more likely error; but he nevertheless adopts F2's reading, and indeed it is hard to see how Leontes could find 'comfort' in his own assertion, as opposed to the views of others.

207 SD See 1.2.0 SD n.

Camillo, this great sir will yet stay longer.

CAMILLO You had much ado to make his anchor hold:
When you cast out, it still came home.

LEONTES Didst note it?

CAMILLO He would not stay at your petitions, made
His business more material.

LEONTES Didst perceive it?
[*Aside*] They're here with me already; whisp'ring, rounding,
'Sicilia is a – so forth.' 'Tis far gone,
When I shall gust it last. – How came't, Camillo,
That he did stay?

CAMILLO At the good Queen's entreaty.

LEONTES At the Queen's be't; 'good' should be pertinent,
But so it is, it is not. Was this taken
By any understanding pate but thine?
For thy conceit is soaking, will draw in
More than the common blocks. Not noted, is't,
But of the finer natures? By some severals
Of headpiece extraordinary? Lower messes
Perchance are to this business purblind? Say.

214 SD] *Hanmer; not in* F 215 'Sicilia . . . forth'] *Capell (subst.);* Sicilia . . . forth F 215 a–] *Hanmer;* a F 216 last. –] *Oxford;* last. F 218 'good'] *Hudson;* good F

211 still came home always came back (i.e. would not take hold).

211–16 Leontes' sense of powerlessness, manifested previously when Hermione's pleas persuaded Polixenes to stay while Leontes' did not (86), now resurfaces in paranoid suspicions that others have witnessed Polixenes' contemptuous treatment of him.

213 more material more pertinent.

214 They're . . . already (Imagined) onlookers are already aware of my situation.

214 rounding talking privately.

215 so forth a substitute for what he cannot bring himself to say, 'cuckold' (perhaps, as Delius suggests, he pantomimes horns or something else).

215–16 'Tis . . . last 'The cuckold is the last that knows of it' (Tilley C877; compare Marston, *The Malcontent*, 1.3.97–101, 'A cuckold . . . must be the last must know it' [ed. G. K. Hunter, 1975]).

216 gust taste; thus, know of.

219 so it is as things are.

219 taken 'noted' (222), perceived, observed.

221–2 thy . . . blocks The comparison, only half-stated, is between an apprehension ('conceit') like a sponge that absorbs new information easily, and those like 'blocks', the wooden molds used by hatmakers, that because of their hardness do so only slowly and with difficulty – are blockheads, in short.

223 severals individuals.

224 headpiece brains, intellect. A cuckold's horns may also be implicated.

224 Lower messes Inferior ranks; a 'mess' was a company of people who ate together, hence of the same rank or social class. Those of lesser status would be presumed to have less penetration.

225 purblind (1) dim-sighted, or (2) totally blind. The first may better accord with Leontes' fear that even inferior onlookers may soon perceive his shame.

CAMILLO Business, my lord? I think most understand
Bohemia stays here longer.
LEONTES Ha?
CAMILLO Stays here longer.
LEONTES Ay, but why?
CAMILLO To satisfy your highness, and the entreaties
Of our most gracious mistress.
LEONTES Satisfy?
Th'entreaties of your mistress? Satisfy?
Let that suffice. I have trusted thee, Camillo,
With all the nearest things to my heart, as well
My chamber-counsels, wherein, priestlike, thou
Hast cleansed my bosom; ay, from thee departed
Thy penitent reformed. But we have been
Deceived in thy integrity, deceived
In that which seems so.
CAMILLO Be it forbid, my lord!
LEONTES To bide upon't: thou art not honest; or,
If thou inclin'st that way, thou art a coward,
Which hoxes honesty behind, restraining
From course required; or else thou must be counted
A servant grafted in my serious trust,
And therein negligent; or else a fool

227 Bohemia . . . Stays here longer.] *Steevens; as three lines* . . . longer. / Ha? / . . . longer. F*; as two lines inclusive of* 228 . . . longer. / Ha? . . . why? *Folger* **238** lord!] *Hanmer;* lord. F

230, 231 Satisfy Leontes wrests Camillo's innocent meaning, 'grant Hermione's request', into a sexual one, 'fulfill her carnal desires'.

234 chamber-counsels confidential communications (words, 'counsels', shared in a private room, a 'chamber').

234–5 priestlike . . . bosom like a priest you have heard my confession and absolved me of my sins, fears. Since Protestants 'emphatically denied the priest any sacramental function in Penance', these lines image Leontes's spiritual drama (otherwise presided over by Apollo) in 'pointedly Catholic terms' (Miola, 41).

236 we Leontes' 'I' (232) used in recalling his past trust of Camillo shifts to the royal 'we' to register his sense of betrayal by his counsellor's present reticence.

239–46 Like the fractured syntax in 1.2.137–45, the series of hypotheticals here reflects Leontes' disturbed mental state, one given over to relentless speculations and imaginings.

239 bide dwell.

241–2 hoxes . . . required hamstrings ('hoxes') honesty, preventing it from moving forward on the necessary ('required') course; the metaphor 'alludes to the practice of deliberately laming cattle by cutting the great tendon behind the knee in the hind legs' (Orgel). 'Behind' may be a redundant intensive (redundant because hoxing necessarily happens from behind) to emphasize cowardice (240).

243–4 grafted . . . negligent artificially joined ('grafted') to my interests ('trust') and consequently 'negligent'; 'grafted' is usually glossed simply as 'firmly implanted', but Shakespeare's uses of *graft* / *graff* often have a negative cast, implying a forced or unnatural union that yields inferior fruit (*AYLI* 3.2.117, *2H6* 3.2.214, *R3* 3.7.127, *Luc.* 1062).

That seest a game played home, the rich stake drawn,
And tak'st it all for jest.

CAMILLO My gracious lord,
I may be negligent, foolish, and fearful;
In every one of these, no man is free,
But that his negligence, his folly, fear,
Among the infinite doings of the world
Sometime puts forth. In your affairs, my lord,
If ever I were wilful-negligent,
It was my folly; if industriously
I played the fool, it was my negligence,
Not weighing well the end; if ever fearful
To do a thing where I the issue doubted,
Whereof the execution did cry out
Against the non-performance, 'twas a fear
Which oft infects the wisest. These, my lord,
Are such allowed infirmities that honesty
Is never free of. But beseech your grace
Be plainer with me, let me know my trespass
By its own visage; if I then deny it,
'Tis none of mine.

LEONTES Ha'not you seen, Camillo
(But that's past doubt – you have, or your eye-glass
Is thicker than a cuckold's horn) or heard
(For to a vision so apparent, rumor

251 forth. In] *Theobald;* forth in F

245 played . . . drawn played to the conclusion ('home'), the money wagered ('stake') awarded ('drawn') to the winner.

248–9 no . . . that no one is so guiltless as to preclude. The construction in 249 appears to be Abbott's '"But" signifying prevention' (122).

251 puts forth appears.

253 industriously intentionally.

255 weighing . . . end carefully considering the result.

257–8 the execution . . . non-performance i.e. the later carrying out of an action by me or someone else caused condemnation of the original failure to act.

260 allowed permissible.

262–3 let . . . visage Camillo craves directness, desiring a specific name ('visage') for the offence ('trespass') of which he is accused.

265 eye-glass probably the crystalline humour (an earlier term for the crystalline lens) of the eye, described by Andre du Laurens as 'the steele-glasse of the minde, by which it looketh upon the formes and faces of things', and likened to spectacles for its magnifying quality (*A Discourse of the Preservation of the Sight*, 1599, G1–G1v).

266 thicker . . . horn more dense or opaque than the horns that grow on the cuckold's head, with (as Folger suggests) possible wordplay on the thin horn used as a transparent protective covering (of the alphabet, for instance, which, for schoolboys, was printed on a leaf of paper and mounted on a tablet of wood).

267 to . . . apparent in regard to a thing so clearly seen.

Cannot be mute) or thought (for cogitation
Resides not in that man that does not think)
My wife is slippery? If thou wilt confess –
Or else be impudently negative,
To have nor eyes, nor ears, nor thought – then say
My wife's a hobby-horse, deserves a name
As rank as any flax-wench that puts to
Before her troth-plight. Say't, and justify't.

CAMILLO I would not be a stander-by to hear
My sovereign mistress clouded so without
My present vengeance taken. 'Shrew my heart,
You never spoke what did become you less
Than this, which to reiterate were sin
As deep as that, though true.

LEONTES Is whispering nothing?
Is leaning cheek to cheek? Is meeting noses?
Kissing with inside lip? Stopping the career
Of laughter with a sigh, a note infallible
Of breaking honesty? Horsing foot on foot?

270 confess–] *Pierce (subst.)*; confess, F **272** thought–] *Pierce (subst.)*; Thought, F **273** hobby-horse] *Rowe*[3]; Holy-Horse F

268–9 cogitation . . . think Leontes' mind apparently races ahead of his words. 'My wife is slippery' is the object of 'thought' (268); 'think', as Malone saw, anticipates the conclusion. Hermione similarly anticipates an object at 3.2.48–9. 'My wife is slippery' is also the delayed object of 'seen' (264) and 'heard' (266).

270 slippery unchaste.

273 hobby-horse whore. 'The riding metaphor combines with that of the morris, notorious for licentious behaviour' (Williams). F's error probably arose because the compositor misread *hobby* as *holly*, Ralph Crane's usual spelling for *holy*, and regularized accordingly (Howard-Hill, 132).

274 flax-wench If the term has any specific import beyond 'working girl', it may be appropriate here because 'flax' (a fine, light-coloured textile fiber) was proverbially easy to ignite.

274–5 puts . . . troth-plight goes to work (sexually) before the formal betrothal that would sanction such a union in society's eyes. On early modern customs and rituals governing betrothal and marriage, see Victoria Hayne, 'Performing Social Practice: The Example of *Measure for Measure*', *SQ* 44 (1993):1–29.

275 Say't . . . justify't Say it and swear it as true. Leontes demands that Camillo not only castigate Hermione in words but forcefully assert the accusations as facts, possibly even corroborating and verifying them (*OED* justify *v* 5, 6, and 7).

278 present immediate.

278 'Shrew my heart 'Beshrew me', or 'Beshrew my heart' ('hand', etc.) is a frequent oath in Shakespeare, often followed by 'but' or 'if' to introduce the thing sworn to; here *but* is understood.

280–1 sin . . . true The usual gloss, that suspecting Hermione of adultery is as sinful as the adultery itself would be had it actually happened, makes little sense, since the suspicion if proved true would cease to be sinful. Perhaps Camillo means to liken suspicion and adultery as wrong but then distinguish what is real, the suspicion, from what is not, the adultery.

283 career (1) course (*OED n* 3); and, more specifically, (2) a horse's short gallop at full speed (*OED n* 2).

285 honesty chastity. Wilson compares 'breaking honesty' with *OED* break *v* 15d, 'To break matrimony', commit adultery.

285 Horsing . . . foot Mounting one's foot on the other's; *to horse* could also mean 'to cover a mare' (*OED* horse *v* 6).

Skulking in corners? Wishing clocks more swift?
Hours minutes? Noon midnight? and all eyes
Blind with the pin and web but theirs, theirs only,
That would unseen be wicked? Is this nothing?
Why then the world and all that's in't is nothing,
The covering sky is nothing, Bohemia nothing,
My wife is nothing, nor nothing have these nothings,
If this be nothing.

CAMILLO Good my lord, be cured
Of this diseased opinion, and betimes,
For 'tis most dangerous.

LEONTES Say it be, 'tis true.

CAMILLO No, no, my lord.

LEONTES It is. You lie, you lie!
I say thou liest, Camillo, and I hate thee,
Pronounce thee a gross lout, a mindless slave,
Or else a hovering temporizer that
Canst with thine eyes at once see good and evil,
Inclining to them both. Were my wife's liver
Infected as her life, she would not live
The running of one glass.

CAMILLO Who does infect her?

LEONTES Why, he that wears her like her medal, hanging
About his neck, Bohemia, who, if I
Had servants true about me that bare eyes
To see alike mine honour as their profits,
Their own particular thrifts, they would do that
Which should undo more doing. Ay, and thou
His cupbearer, whom I from meaner form

296 is. You . . . lie!] *Bevington;* is: you . . . lye: F

288 pin and web cataract.

292 nothing have . . . nothings these nothings are empty and meaningless. Given the early modern homonymic connection between 'nothing' and 'noting', Shakespeare's audience might have also understood *nothings* as 'observations'.

294 betimes soon; before it is too late.

299 temporizer a vacillating opportunist (Orgel).

301 liver the seat of the passions in early modern physiology.

303 running . . . glass passing of one hour.

304 her medal a medal of her, portraying her (objective genitive, Abbott 218).

305 who understood as 'whom', object of 'they would do that (to)' at 308 (Abbott 274).

306 bare bore.

308 thrifts advantages.

309 doing i.e. sexual intercourse.

310 cupbearer the court attendant with the task of serving wine. Shakespeare apparently borrowed the term from his source where Franion is twice mentioned as cupbearer to Pandosto.

310–11 from . . . benched from a subservient position have elevated to one of authority. Grounding the general meaning of 'form' = (1) state or (2) rank, is *form* as a kind of bench (*OED*

Have benched and reared to worship, who mayst see
Plainly as heaven sees earth and earth sees heaven
How I am galled, mightst bespice a cup,
To give mine enemy a lasting wink,
Which draught to me were cordial.

CAMILLO Sir, my lord,
I could do this, and that with no rash potion,
But with a ling'ring dram that should not work
Maliciously, like poison. But I cannot
Believe this crack to be in my dread mistress,
So sovereignly being honourable.
I have loved thee –

LEONTES Make that thy question, and go rot!
Dost think I am so muddy, so unsettled,
To appoint myself in this vexation? Sully
The purity and whiteness of my sheets –
Which to preserve is sleep, which being spotted
Is goads, thorns, nettles, tails of wasps –
Give scandal to the blood o'th'prince, my son
(Who I do think is mine and love as mine),

320–1 honourable. / . . . thee – LEONTES . . . rot!] *Steevens; as three lines* Honourable.*)* / . . . thee, / . . . rot: F; *as two lines* honourable . . . thee – / LEONTES . . . rot! *Folger* **321** thee–] *Hanmer (subst.)*; thee, F **323–4** Sully . . . sheets] *Theobald; as one line* F

n 17) and, perhaps by extension, a grade in school (*OED n* 6b); 'bench' is a magistrate's seat (*OED n* 2). An academic starting point for his courtly career fits Camillo, who is valued as 'clerk-like experienced' (387); 'reared' carries on the idea of training a young person. Given the time invested in 'rear[ing him] to worship' (i.e. to a place of honour), Camillo has far-ranging responsibilities that go beyond serving wine (see 234–5 and 321 nn.).

314 give . . . wink put my enemy to sleep forever. In Tree's 1906 production, thunder, usually not heard until the end of 3.2, sounded distantly here.

315 Leontes would find such a drink ('draught') soothing ('cordial').

316 rash fast-acting.

318 Maliciously Violently, with obvious malignant effect, perhaps with a suggestion of the legal sense of wrongful intention as well: the victim's condition as produced by some ill-wisher rather than originating in himself (see 1.1.28 n.).

319 crack flaw (and, perhaps, in a bawdy sense, 'rupture of chastity; whether directly or by indirection, the vulva' (Partridge).

319 dread revered.

320 Who is so supremely honourable.

321 I . . . thee Theobald reassigned this half-line to Leontes, and perhaps Camillo's 'thee' (which lacks the respect a subject owes to the monarch) supports his case. But Kent, outraged at Lear's mistreatment of Cordelia (*Lear* 1.1.156–80), uses 'thou' to his sovereign in a similar situation. Camillo may be speaking in his 'special role as the King's intimate and confessor' (232–6), a position that 'sufficiently justifies its use' (Schanzer).

321 Make . . . rot Leontes' anger perhaps responds to Camillo's unwonted familiarity (see preceding n.), as well as his hesitation. The referent of 'that' may be this protested love of Camillo's, which is seen as only something to talk about rather than act on, or perhaps Hermione's guilt which Camillo doubts. In any case, Camillo is condemned – by his uninstrumental love, his indecision, or his recalcitrance – to rot with inaction.

322 muddy muddled.

323 appoint myself set myself up, possibly in the legal sense of nominating or arraigning.

Without ripe moving to't? Would I do this?
Could man so blench?

CAMILLO I must believe you, sir.
I do, and will fetch off Bohemia for't –
Provided that when he's removed your highness
Will take again your queen as yours at first,
Even for your son's sake, and thereby for sealing
The injury of tongues in courts and kingdoms
Known and allied to yours.

LEONTES Thou dost advise me
Even so as I mine own course have set down.
I'll give no blemish to her honour, none.

CAMILLO My lord,
Go then, and with a countenance as clear
As friendship wears at feasts, keep with Bohemia
And with your queen. I am his cupbearer;
If from me he have wholesome beverage,
Account me not your servant.

LEONTES This is all.
Do't, and thou hast the one half of my heart;
Do't not, thou splitt'st thine own.

CAMILLO I'll do't, my lord.

331 for't–] *Orgel;* for't: F 334 for sealing] F; for-sealing *Cam. conj. (anon.);* forestalling *Wilson (Kellner conj.)* 338–9 I'll . . . lord, / Go] *Folger; as three lines* . . . none. / . . . Lord, / Goe . . . F; *as two lines* none. / My . . . clear *Oxford*

329 **Without . . . to't** If not prompted by fully considered ('ripe') reasons for it.

330 **blench** turn aside; i.e. from constancy to a loved one, as in *Tro.* 2.2.68 and *Son.* 110.7.

331 **fetch off** make away with, make an end of. Pafford suggests an equivocation on 'fetch off' as 'rescue', the first meaning directed at Leontes' understanding and the second indicating his own secret intention to save Polixenes. Schanzer finds a parallel ambiguity in 'removed' (332).

334–5 **thereby . . . tongues** by that means to silence injurious talk. This is the closest Camillo comes to his counterpart's political argument in *Pandosto* (see Bullough, 159–60). To correct the slightly redundant construction, some editors have glossed 'thereby' as 'in addition', but *OED* has no citations for this sense after 1500 and Shakespeare elsewhere uses *thereby* to mean 'by that'. Cam.'s conjectured *forsealing* is not in *OED*, but is a possible coinage with existing senses of *for-*, either 'silencing in advance' or 'sealing off'.

336–8 In the source, Pandosto 'intend[s] also as soon as Egistus was dead, to give his wife a sop of the same sawce, and so be rid of those which were the cause of his restles sorrow' (*Pandosto*, Bullough, 160). Shakespeare has Leontes call for Hermione's death *after* Camillo and Polixenes have fled, a difference that Schanzer sees as making him more sympathetic than his counterpart in Greene.

338 **My lord** The two extrametrical syllables, which occupy a separate line in F (both preceding and following lines are complete without them), may indicate a pause. Orgel's suggestion that the compositor was trying to fill space is unconvincing in view of his failure a few lines below to give the usual separate line to Polixenes' entrance. Turner thinks the phrase was probably an authorial or scribal addition.

340 **keep** continue.

LEONTES I will seem friendly, as thou hast advised me. *Exit*
CAMILLO O miserable lady! But for me,
What case stand I in? I must be the poisoner
Of good Polixenes, and my ground to do't
Is the obedience to a master, one
Who, in rebellion with himself, will have
All that are his so too. To do this deed,
Promotion follows. If I could find example
Of thousands that had struck anointed kings
And flourished after, I'd not do't. But since
Nor brass, nor stone, nor parchment bears not one,
Let villany itself forswear't. I must
Forsake the court: to do't or no is certain
To me a break-neck.

Enter POLIXENES

Happy star reign now!
Here comes Bohemia.
POLIXENES [*aside*] This is strange; methinks
My favor here begins to warp. Not speak? –
Good day, Camillo.
CAMILLO Hail, most royal sir.
POLIXENES What is the news i'th'court?
CAMILLO None rare, my lord.

347 lady!] *Pope;* lady. F 359 SD] *Oxford; after* Bohemia F 359 now!] *Theobald;* now, F 360 SD] *Oxford; not in* F 361 speak?–] *Capell;* speak? F

347 **for** as for.

349 **ground . . . do't** reason for doing it.

351–2 **Who . . . too** Who, being in conflict with his true nature, wishes to have all his followers similarly violate their natures, or their respect for anointed sovereignty.

351 **with** against.

353–5 **If . . . do't** The invocation against regicide would have had a special appropriateness at the first recorded court performance on 5 November 1611, anniversary of the 1605 'Gunpowder Plot' by dissidents to blow up King James, his family, and the Parliament.

358–9 **to do't . . . break-neck** to obey and kill Polixenes or to disobey and spare him, either way surely means my destruction.

359 **Happy . . . now** Camillo's exclamation either (1) invokes the luck he needs in this dangerous situation, or (2) praises the good fortune of Polixenes' opportune appearance.

361 **warp** Although *OED* cites this line for 'warp' = shrivel, shrink (*v* 15b), two other meanings seem preferable: (1) become bent or uneven as the result of contraction (*OED v* 14 a, b; see *AYLI* 3.3.87–9, 'then one of you will prove a shrunk panel, and like green timber warp, warp') and (2) swerve, go astray (*OED v* 19a).

363 **None rare** Nothing extraordinary.

POLIXENES The King hath on him such a countenance
As he had lost some province, and a region
Loved as he loves himself. Even now I met him
With customary compliment, when he,
Wafting his eyes to th'contrary and falling
A lip of much contempt, speeds from me and
So leaves me to consider what is breeding
That changes thus his manners.

CAMILLO I dare not know, my lord.

POLIXENES How, dare not? do not? do you know and dare not?
Be intelligent to me, 'tis thereabouts;
For to yourself what you do know you must,
And cannot say you dare not. Good Camillo,
Your changed complexions are to me a mirror,
Which shows me mine changed too; for I must be
A party in this alteration, finding
Myself thus altered with't.

CAMILLO There is a sickness
Which puts some of us in distemper, but
I cannot name the disease, and it is caught
Of you, that yet are well.

POLIXENES How caught of me?
Make me not sighted like the basilisk.
I have looked on thousands who have sped the better

371 That . . . lord | *Oxford; as two lines* . . . manners. / I . . . F 382 Of . . . me | *Steevens; as two lines* . . . well. / How . . . F

365–6 lost . . . himself Since Leontes thinks of his wife in terms of land that has been trespassed (see 197 n.), Polixenes' words may carry, as Andrews suggests, an ironic allusion to Eph. 5.28: 'So ought men to love their wives as their own bodies. He that loveth his wife loveth himself.'

368–9 falling / A lip letting his lip droop.

370 breeding developing.

372–3 What do you mean by 'dare not'? Do you mean that you don't know? Or do you mean you know and don't dare tell me? Explain to me ('Be intelligent to me'), it's something like that. Capell and some later editors joined the second 'dare not' with 'Be intelligent to me', but the punctuation (supported rhetorically by the line's chiasmic construction–specifically, antimetabole) makes good sense without emendation.

374–5 For . . . not For you must acknowledge knowing what you know and can't say you dare not know it; i.e. you can't disclaim knowing what you know.

376 complexions looks, demeanour; possibly, as Moorman thinks, the plural refers to Leontes' as well as Camillo's.

377–8 be . . . in partake of.

380 distemper acute mental distress, associated with a disturbance in the bodily 'humours' (*OED n*[1] 4); see 2.3.38 n.

383 Don't make me out to have a gaze like that of the basilisk (a fabulous serpent whose fatal look was proverbial); see Dent B99.

384 sped fared, gotten along.

By my regard, but killed none so. Camillo,
As you are certainly a gentleman, thereto
Clerk-like experienced, which no less adorns
Our gentry than our parents' noble names,
In whose success we are gentle, I beseech you,
If you know aught which does behove my knowledge
Thereof to be informed, imprison't not
In ignorant concealment.

CAMILLO I may not answer.

POLIXENES A sickness caught of me, and yet I well?
I must be answered. Dost thou hear, Camillo,
I conjure thee by all the parts of man
Which honour does acknowledge, whereof the least
Is not this suit of mine, that thou declare
What incidency thou dost guess of harm
Is creeping toward me; how far off, how near,
Which way to be prevented, if to be;
If not, how best to bear it.

CAMILLO Sir, I will tell you,
Since I am charged in honour, and by him
That I think honourable; therefore mark my counsel,
Which must be e'en as swiftly followed as
I mean to utter it; or both yourself and me
Cry lost, and so good night.

POLIXENES On, good Camillo.

CAMILLO I am appointed him to murder you.

386 **thereto** besides.

387 **Clerk-like experienced** Trained as a scholar (*OED* experience *v* 3a).

388 **gentry** either (1) high position or (2) persons born to such position. If the first, Polixenes presents Camillo's learning as an alternative basis for his high rank, in place of noble birth. See next n.

389 **In . . . gentle** In succession from whom we are noble. Polixenes uses the royal plural; Camillo's parents may have been honourable (473) but certainly not royal. The careful affirmation of Camillo's status as 'gentleman' along with his scholarly credentials (385–7), followed by an appeal to obligations recognized among honourable men (395–7), suggests that Camillo's high position was achieved by merit rather than through his lesser, though respectable, birth. For discussion of how young gentlemen in Shakespeare's time sought social advancement through means other than inherited estates, see Lawrence Stone, *The Crisis of the Aristocracy, 1588–1641*, abridged ed. (1967), 183–232, 258–60.

392 **ignorant concealment** concealment that keeps me ignorant; for the transferred epithet, compare *Temp.* 5.1.67, where 'ignorant fumes' means 'fumes that render them uncomprehending'.

395 **conjure** charge (perhaps with a hint of magic).

395 **parts** obligations, duties.

398 **incidency** event likely to happen.

405–6 **both . . . night** declare us lost, and farewell forever.

407 **him** the man.

POLIXENES By whom, Camillo?
CAMILLO By the King.
POLIXENES For what?
CAMILLO He thinks, nay, with all confidence he swears,
As he had seen't, or been an instrument
To vice you to't, that you have touched his queen
Forbiddenly.
POLIXENES O then my best blood turn
To an infected jelly, and my name
Be yoked with his that did betray the best!
Turn then my freshest reputation to
A savour that may strike the dullest nostril
Where I arrive, and my approach be shunned,
Nay, hated too, worse than the great'st infection
That e'er was heard or read.
CAMILLO Swear his thought over
By each particular star in heaven, and
By all their influences; you may as well
Forbid the sea for to obey the moon
As or by oath remove or counsel shake
The fabric of his folly, whose foundation
Is piled upon his faith and will continue

414 best!] *Hanmer;* Best: F

410 As As if.

411 vice persuade (like the Vice in a morality drama); usually glossed as 'screw' or 'force', perhaps because 'instrument' suggests a carpenter's tool, but agency can include persons as well as mechanisms, and Shakespeare's coinage (this is the only usage of 'vice' as a verb in the canon) more probably refers to the traditional theatrical tempter he invokes elsewhere: e.g. *TN* 4.2.124 and *1H4* 2.4.453.

412 best blood (1) blood 'essential for life' or (2) 'royal blood'; compare *John* 3.1.343, 'the . . . dearest-valued blood of France'. Shakespeare uses the phrase 'best blood' only here and in *R2* 1.1.149, *1H4* 5.2.94, and *2H6* 4.10.37.

413 jelly Besides 'animal substance' in general, perhaps specifically 'sperm', as in the first two *OED* citations (*n* 2a). If so, Polixenes means that if he has committed adultery with Hermione his noblest sentiments of any sort should be debased into corrupt sexual appetite.

414 his . . . best i.e. the name of Judas, who betrayed Jesus Christ.

416 strike . . . nostril impinge forcibly on the least acute sense of smell.

419–20 Swear . . . heaven Perhaps, as Johnson says, 'overswear his present persuasion, that is, endeavour to overcome his opinion, by swearing oaths as numerous as the stars'. Apparently parallel to *MM* 5.1.243, 'swear down each particular saint', pile up numerous oaths against a contrary position.

421 influences supposed emanations of ethereal fluid from the stars (see 420) that shaped human character and destiny.

422 for to to (Abbott 152).

423 or . . . or . . . shake either efface by swearing the contrary or destabilize through rational dissuasion.

424 fabric edifice (see 'foundation').

425 faith conviction.

The standing of his body.

POLIXENES How should this grow?

CAMILLO I know not; but I am sure 'tis safer to
Avoid what's grown than question how 'tis born.
If therefore you dare trust my honesty
That lies enclosèd in this trunk, which you
Shall bear along impawned, away tonight.
Your followers I will whisper to the business,
And will by twos and threes at several posterns
Clear them o'th'city. For myself, I'll put
My fortunes to your service, which are here
By this discovery lost. Be not uncertain,
For by the honour of my parents, I
Have uttered truth, which if you seek to prove,
I dare not stand by, nor shall you be safer
Than one condemnèd by the king's own mouth,
Thereon his execution sworn.

POLIXENES I do believe thee.
I saw his heart in's face. Give me thy hand.
Be pilot to me, and thy places shall
Still neighbour mine. My ships are ready, and
My people did expect my hence departure
Two days ago. This jealousy
Is for a precious creature. As she's rare
Must it be great; and as his person's mighty,
Must it be violent; and as he does conceive
He is dishonoured by a man which ever

440 condemnèd] F2 (condemned); condemnd F **440–41** mouth, / Thereon] F *(subst.)*; *as one line Capell*

426 The standing . . . body As long as his body lasts.

427–8 'tis . . . born This is a romance premise rather than a tragic one; compare *Lear*, 1.4.328, 'Safer [to fear too far] than trust too far'. Camillo's counsel to seek safety, thereby avoiding the risks posed by a relentless pursuit of whys and wherefores, concisely sums up the tragic dilemma of Oedipus, who suffers the woeful consequences of indeed questioning how he was born.

430–1 trunk . . . impawned body, which you shall take with you as a pledge.

433 several posterns separate side and back gates.

434 Clear them Get them clear (*OED* clear *v* 15b).

436 discovery revelation (to you).

438–9 if . . . by i.e. if you seek to test ('prove') my assertion by asking the king, I won't dare to acknowledge it ('stand by').

441 Thereon . . . sworn And whom he thereupon swore to have executed.

443–4 thy . . . mine i.e. 'you will always have a position near my own in power, prestige, and access to the throne' (Andrews). Steevens reads 'places' as preferments, honours.

445 hence departure departure from here.

Professed to him, why, his revenges must
In that be made more bitter. Fear o'ershades me.
Good expedition be my friend, and comfort
The gracious Queen, part of his theme, but nothing
Of his ill-ta'en suspicion. Come, Camillo,
I will respect thee as a father if
Thou bear'st my life off hence. Let us avoid.

CAMILLO It is in mine authority to command
The keys of all the posterns. Please your highness
To take the urgent hour. Come, sir, away. *Exeunt*

2.1 *Enter* HERMIONE, MAMILLIUS, [*and*] LADIES

HERMIONE Take the boy to you; he so troubles me
'Tis past enduring.

FIRST LADY Come, my gracious lord,
Shall I be your playfellow?

454 Queen | F; Queen's *Warburton* 457 off hence. | *Rowe;* off, hence: F; off. Hence: *Wilson;* off. Hence! *Pafford* 2.1 | F *(Actus Secundus. Scena Prima.)* 0 SD | *Rowe; (Enter Hermione, Mamillius, Ladies: Leontes, Antigonus, Lords.)* F 2, 4, 13, 15 SH | *Rowe (subst., I Lady); Lady.* F 3–4 Shall . . . you. / Why . . . lord? | *Steevens; as three lines* . . . playfellow? / No . . . you. / Why . . . F; *as two lines* . . . playfellow? / No . . . lord? *Folger (after White)*

451 **Professed** Professed friendship, as in *JC* 1.2.77–8, 'That I profess myself in banqueting / To all the rout'.

453–5 **Good . . . suspicion** i.e. Polixenes hopes that his expeditious departure will serve him well and comfort the queen (by removing further occasions for Leontes' jealousy). The concluding phrases about the queen give trouble, since it is hard to see how Polixenes could think Leontes suspects only him and not Hermione; perhaps he means that Hermione is properly of concern to Leontes ('part of his theme', 454), as his wife, but by no means properly the object of his ill-conceived suspicion. ('Part of his theme' is elsewhere glossed as 'object of the king's anger' [Pafford]; 'Leontes' fantasy' [Kermode]; 'the subject of his conversation' [Wilson]; and 'involved in his ill-conceived suspicion' [Orgel].) Heath saw 'expedition' as still the grammatical subject: Polixenes wishes that his speedy withdrawal will benefit him and comfort the queen by taking him out of danger but will not increase Leontes' suspicion of her (207). Schanzer takes 'expedition' more generally, to indicate not only Polixenes' quick departure but also a speedy resolution of Leontes' suspicions, which will benefit both Polixenes and Hermione, befriending him and comforting her. If 'expedition' is not the subject of 'comfort', then Polixenes 'is merely wishing the Queen comfort in the troubles he is leaving her to, and the vagueness of the expression matches the emptiness of the wish' (Kermode).

457 **bear'st . . . hence** get me out of here alive.

457 **avoid** depart, leave.

Act 2, Scene 1

The picture of Mamillius surrounded by women and free to command the conversation suggests a nursery setting, probably in or near the queen's own apartments since Mamillius is not yet 'breeched' and in a separate establishment (see Snyder). Compare *Pandosto* (Bullough, 163): 'Comming to the Queenes lodging, they [the guards dispatched by the king to bring Hermione to prison] found her playing with her young sonne Garinter'. From Kemble's 1802 production to recent ones (e.g. Lewis), either a child's rocking horse or a carousel horse has often been a staple in this brief interlude of 'procreative domesticity' (Ranald, 13). See illustration 2, p. 6.

1–2 Hermione's opening lines indicate as stage action some physical play with Mamillius.

1 **to you** into your care (*OED* take *v* 14).

1 **troubles** wearies, tires.

MAMILLIUS No, I'll none of you.
FIRST LADY Why, my sweet lord?
MAMILLIUS You'll kiss me hard and speak to me as if
I were a baby still. – I love you better.
SECOND LADY And why so, my lord?
MAMILLIUS Not for because
Your brows are blacker; yet black brows, they say,
Become some women best, so that there be not
Too much hair there, but in a semicircle
Or a half-moon made with a pen.
SECOND LADY Who taught' this?
MAMILLIUS I learned it out of women's faces. – Pray now,
What colour are your eyebrows?
FIRST LADY Blue, my lord.
MAMILLIUS Nay, that's a mock. I have seen a lady's nose
That has been blue, but not her eyebrows.
FIRST LADY Hark ye,

6 still.–] *Bevington;* still. F; still. *To another lady Orgel* 7, 11, 19 SH] F *(2. Lady.)* 11 taught'] F; taught F2; taught you *Rowe* 12 faces.–] *Folger;* faces. F

3 **I'll none of you** 'I will have nothing to do with you' (Schanzer).

7 **Not for** Not because.

8–9 **black . . . best** 'The boy is being, perhaps deliberately, rude: black brows were not admired in Shakespeare's day' (Wilson); poets typically idealized female beauty as golden-haired and blue- or grey-eyed. Mamillius, however, may be alluding to an anti-convention formula that was itself part of the English Petrarchan sonnet tradition in the 1590s. See Sidney's *Astrophil and Stella* (7, 9, and 20) and Shakespeare's *Sonnets* 127, 130–132; in *LLL* (4.3.264 ff) Berowne defends Rosalind's black hair.

9–11 The fashion called for ladies of the court to pluck their eyebrows, penning in a highly arched ('semi-circle' or 'half-moon') look, possibly with black lead. See Maggie Angeloglou, *A History of Make-up*, 1970, 18, 45, and 76; also illustration no. 342 in Jacob Burckhardt's *The Civilization of the Renaissance in Italy*, trans. S. G. C. Middlemore (Vienna: Phaidon Press, c. 1937).

11 **taught'** Orgel (after F2 and Collier) drops the apostrophe, but while the idiomatic omission of the initial pronoun in "'Beseech you" (1.1.10) and "'Pray you" (2.1.22, 4.4.260) hardly needs apostrophes, it seems advisable to call attention to the absent 'you' or 'thee' in this less familiar construction. Howard-Hill remarks (129) on Crane's particular fondness for apostrophes in *WT* to denote omission of 'notional words' as well as letters (2.1.12, 2.1.116, 3.2.151, 4.2.41, 4.4.231, 5.2.51, 5.2.130.)

12 Mamillius' pert reply may parody Berowne's argument (*LLL* 4.3.286–340) for the lords' right to recant their vow of celibate study, since true knowledge derives from women's eyes.

14 **that's a mock** you're making fun of me.

15 **blue** livid (*OED adj* 2: 'leaden-colored, as the skin becomes after a blow, from severe cold, from alarm'.) Compare *Wiv.* 5.5.44, 'There pinch the maids as blue as bilberry'. The devastating facial side effects of mercury – the usual medical treatment for syphilis in the period – presumably are behind Norton's linkage of 'blue' noses with disfigurement by venereal disease. The frontispiece to *The Works of Sir William D'Avenant* (1673) shows the poet's disfigured nose, previously mocked by John Suckling ('A Session of the Poets' [*Fragmenta Aurea*, 1646], in *The Poems, Plays and Other Remains of Sir John Suckling*, 2 vols. [2nd edn], ed. W. C. Hazlitt, 1892, 1.8).

The Queen your mother rounds apace; we shall
Present our services to a fine new prince
One of these days, and then you'd wanton with us,
If we would have you.

SECOND LADY She is spread of late
Into a goodly bulk – good time encounter her!

HERMIONE What wisdom stirs amongst you? Come, sir, now
I am for you again. Pray you sit by us,
And tell's a tale.

MAMILLIUS Merry or sad shall't be?

HERMIONE As merry as you will.

MAMILLIUS A sad tale's best for winter. I have one
Of sprites and goblins.

HERMIONE Let's have that, good sir.
Come on, sit down, come on and do your best
To fright me with your sprites; you're powerful at it.

MAMILLIUS There was a man –

HERMIONE Nay, come sit down. Then on.

MAMILLIUS Dwelt by a churchyard – I will tell it softly,
Yond crickets shall not hear it.

HERMIONE Come on then, and give't me in mine ear.

20 her!] *Hanmer;* her.) F **22** Pray] F *(* 'Pray*)* **23** And . . . be?] *Steevens; as two lines* . . . Tale. / Merry . . . F **25–6** A . . . one / Of . . . goblins] *Dyce;* . . . Winter: / I . . . goblins F **29** man –] *Rowe²;* man. F **32** Come . . . ear.] F*; as two lines* Come . . . then, / And . . . ear. *Capell* **32** SD] *Oxford; not in* F*; Enter Leontes* F2*; Enter Leontes . . . Lords Rowe*

16 rounds becomes round; develops to a full round form (as her pregnancy advances). Apparently a Shakespearean coinage (*OED v* 14), this is the first specific textual indicator of Hermione's pregnancy (see 1.2.0 SD.1 n.).

17 prince More often applied to males, the term could be used for royal offspring of either sex; Orgel notes that Bellaria (Hermione's counterpart) is called 'prince' in *Pandosto* (Bullough, 164).

18 wanton play.

20 good . . . her may she have a happy outcome in childbirth. 'Time' was used for the period of gestation (*OED n* 7b [a]), and 'good' signifies its successful completion, as in *H8* 5.1.20–22, 'The fruit she goes with / I pray for heartily, that it may find / Good time, and live'.

22 I . . . again I am ready for you again (Abbott 155).

25 A . . . winter Mamillius seems to ignore the usual meaning of a 'winter's tale' as a trivial story spun out to pass the time (Dent W513.1); his rather prescient call for something serious ('sad') and even frightening responds instead to the bleakness of the season. (See Introduction, pp. 5–7.)

27–8 Come . . . sprites Schanzer notes the poignancy of the dramatic irony: 'Hermione, still happy and unsuspecting, plays at being frightened by the imaginings of her son, unaware that a few moments later she will be truly frightened by the imaginings of her husband', who seemingly on cue answers to the part 'There was a man' (29). Hermione's repetition in 27 of her request that Mamillius sit down (first made in 22 and iterated again in 29) indicates further stage business for the boy.

31 The 'crickets' are the ladies-in-waiting, with their chirping talk and silly jests (like 'blue' in 13).

[*Enter apart* LEONTES, ANTIGONUS, *and* LORDS]

LEONTES Was he met there? His train? Camillo with him?
LORD Behind the tuft of pines I met them; never
Saw I men scour so on their way. I eyed them
Even to their ships.
LEONTES How blest am I
In my just censure, in my true opinion!
Alack for lesser knowledge! How accursed
In being so blest! There may be in the cup
A spider steeped, and one may drink, depart,
And yet partake no venom, for his knowledge
Is not infected; but if one present
Th'abhorr'd ingredient to his eye, make known
How he hath drunk, he cracks his gorge, his sides,
With violent hefts. I have drunk, and seen the spider.
Camillo was his help in this, his pander.
There is a plot against my life, my crown.
All's true that is mistrusted. That false villain
Whom I employed was pre-employed by him;
He has discovered my design, and I
Remain a pinched thing, yea, a very trick

33 Was . . . him?] *as verse Rowe; as prose* F 37 censure, . . . opinion!] *Dyce;* Censure? . . . Opinion? F 38 knowledge!] *Hanmer;* knowledge, F 44 sides,] *Capell;* sides F

32 SD – 55 The text suggests that Leontes, preoccupied with his own fears and suspicions, for a long time addresses no one in the group he has interrupted. Accordingly, a frequent production choice has the lights dim over the female space, as mother and son, frozen in their own private world, continue their tale silently, while a spotlight shines over Leontes and his lords on another part of the stage. Kulick, however, used the image of the spider to bring Leontes into direct and violent contact with Hermione, the king grabbing her at 40 and throwing her to the ground at 45. Although not addressed by Leontes, the women and boy in Cohen manifested alarm as their domestic world was disrupted by the king's entrance at 32 SD (see illustration 3, p. 6).

33 **train** retinue.

35 **scour so** move so rapidly.

38 **Alack . . . knowledge** 'O that my knowledge were less' (Johnson).

39–42 **There . . . infected** Topsell declares that all spiders are poisonous in some degree (*The Historie of Serpents*, 1608, Bb3v), and proverbs agree (Dent S749.1). Leontes' contrary belief that it is not the spider that poisons but knowledge of its presence is harder to document. Possibly, as Schanzer says, Leontes is not invoking accepted belief but creating a 'metaphysical conceit' for his own situation, first blissfully unaware of the adultery corrupting his family life and then, after learning of it, seized with agonies of violent pain.

44 **gorge** throat.

45 **hefts** heavings, retchings.

48 **All . . . mistrusted** Proleptic irony: all *is* true that is mistrusted.

50 **discovered** revealed.

51 **pinched** tortured (*OED* pinch *v* 5); or nipped like a plant, caused to wither (*OED v* 6). Possibly 'pinched' is an early example of *OED* 1d (first recorded use, 1896): 'to be jammed or compressed forcibly between two solid objects so as to be crushed' – a meaning that would match Leontes' sense of double betrayal by wife and friend.

51–2 **a very . . . will** 'Trick' is sometimes glossed as 'plaything', but 'play *with*' is Shakespeare's normal usage in this kind of construction (see *Temp.* 4.1.100 and *1H4* 2.3.92). 'Trick', as in a card game, fits better, especially since the first uses in this sense listed by *OED* (1599, 1602) play on *trick* as deception. Leontes used the card-game metaphor previously (1.2.245), with Hermione as the rich stake and Polixenes as the player who wins

For them to play at will. How came the posterns
So easily open?

LORD By his great authority,
Which often hath no less prevailed than so
On your command.

LEONTES I know't too well.
[*To Hermione*] Give me the boy. I am glad you did not nurse him.
Though he does bear some signs of me, yet you
Have too much blood in him.

HERMIONE What is this? Sport?

LEONTES Bear the boy hence; he shall not come about her.
Away with him, [*Mamillius is led out*] and let her sport herself
With that she's big with, [*to Hermione*] for 'tis Polixenes
Has made thee swell thus.

HERMIONE But I'd say he had not;
And I'll be sworn you would believe my saying,
Howe'er you lean to th'nayward.

LEONTES You, my lords,
Look on her, mark her well; be but about
To say she is a goodly lady, and
The justice of your hearts will thereto add

55 On . . . well.] *Steevens; as two lines* . . . command. / I . . . F **56** SD] *Capell (subst.); not in* F **60** SD] *Bevington (after* swell thus *in* 62, following *Capell subst., after* herself*); not in* F **61** SD] *Oxford; not in* F

her. As the object of their double-dealing, he feels 'played' like a counter in their game (and thus not only deceived but reduced to triviality).

53 his Camillo's.

56–8 I . . . in him There was a widespread belief that character traits were passed to the young through suckling. See, e.g., Thomas Phaer, *The Boke of Chyldren* (1544), ed. Rick Bowers, Medieval and Renaissance Texts and Studies, 201 (Tempe, Arizona: Arizona Center for Medieval and Renaissance Studies, 1999), 31–33.

58 Sport In the following interchange, Leontes plays bitterly on the term Hermione invokes here in all innocence, while she seeks to make sense of his conduct by playing her part in his undefined game (see 62 n.).

60 SD F makes no mention of Mamillius's exit. Some editors mark his departure after 59; others do so after 'swell thus' (62). The repeated (60) order to 'Bear the boy hence' (59) makes placement of the exit after 'Away with him' (as in Howell) attractive. The iteration, coupled with the demand that the boy 'not come about' Hermione (59), suggests that both mother and son try to hold on to each other.

61–2 In Greene, Pandosto learns of Bellaria's pregnancy from the jailer who overhears the incarcerated queen's 'heavie passions' concerning her newly discovered condition (*Pandosto*, Bullough, 165).

62 I'd By using the conditional rather than the indicative, Hermione tries to enter the game she supposes Leontes to be playing, trying out her hypothetical response to his play-accusation. 'She cannot yet believe that the charge is deeply serious' (Pafford).

64 lean to th'nayward incline toward denial.

'Tis pity she's not honest. Honourable;
Praise her but for this her without-door form,
Which on my faith deserves high speech, and straight
The shrug, the hum or ha, these petty brands
That calumny doth use – O, I am out!
That mercy does, for calumny will sear
Virtue itself – these shrugs, these hums and has,
When you have said she's goodly, come between
Ere you can say she's honest. But be't known,
From him that has most cause to grieve it should be,
She's an adultress!

HERMIONE Should a villain say so,
The most replenished villain in the world,
He were as much more villain. You, my lord,
Do but mistake.

LEONTES You have mistook, my lady,
Polixenes for Leontes. O thou thing
Which I'll not call a creature of thy place,
Lest barbarism, making me the precedent,
Should a like language use to all degrees,
And mannerly distinguishment leave out
Betwixt the prince and beggar. – I have said
She's an adultress; I have said with whom.

71 petty brands] F (Petty-brands) 72 out!] *Hudson;* out, F 78 adultress!] *Pafford;* adultresse. F 87 beggar. –] *Folger;* beggar:) F

68 Orgel is probably right in seeing a contrast implied between 'honest' (chaste) and 'honourable' (worthy of respect because of rank and position).

69 **but** only.

71 **petty brands** trivial markings of disgrace (with the accompanying notion of stigmata being burned into flesh), minor ('petty') in implied comparison with calumny's searings at 73–4. For F's hyphenation with noun, see *OED* petty *adj* 3a.

72 **out** (1) confused; or (2) lost, in the sense of losing one's place, forgetting one's lines or part (see *Cor.* 5.3.40–1: 'Like a dull actor now / I have forgot my part, and I am out').

73 **sear** The metaphor carries on from 'brands' (71); the idea of slander searing virtue itself was proverbial (Dent E175).

78 **She's . . . adultress** The play's stylistic feature of loose periodicity in which the main point is held in reserve until the end of the sentence is captured perfectly in 68–78. The effect of the concisely constructed charge is all the more shocking after the prolix and tortured build-up from 64 (Pafford).

79 **replenished** full, complete. *OED* cites *R3* 4.3.18 and this line as the earliest recorded uses of this rare adjectival form.

82–7 **O . . . beggar** Removing F's comma after 'thing' makes the meaning clearer. Leontes denigrates Hermione with the general term 'thing', but forbears putting a more specific label on a person of her high position as queen ('creature of thy place'), lest he allow 'barbarism' to do its worst by setting a 'precedent' for failing to distinguish decently in his language between high and base ('prince and beggar').

83 **place** i.e. in the social hierarchy.

85 **degrees** ranks in society.

More, she's a traitor, and Camillo is
A federary with her, and one that knows
What she should shame to know herself,
But with her most vile principal, that she's
A bed-swerver, even as bad as those
That vulgars give bold'st titles; ay, and privy
To this their late escape.

HERMIONE No, by my life,
Privy to none of this. How will this grieve you,
When you shall come to clearer knowledge, that
You thus have published me? Gentle my lord,
You scarce can right me throughly, then, to say
You did mistake.

LEONTES No. If I mistake
In those foundations which I build upon,
The centre is not big enough to bear
A schoolboy's top. – Away with her to prison!
He who shall speak for her is afar off guilty
But that he speaks.

98 me?] F; me! *Hudson* 103 top. –] *Oxford;* Top. F 104 afar off] F4; a farre-off F

90 **federary** *OED* treats F's 'federarie' as a variant of *fedarie*, a form found only in Shakespeare, who wrongly associated *fedarie* or *feodary* (i.e. feudary) with Latin *foedus* (alliance). Correcting to some form of *feodary*, as in Folios after the first and most later editions, suggests Camillo as Hermione's feudal dependent rather than her accomplice; it, therefore, seems best to stay with Shakespeare's 'federary' (pronounced fed′-a-ry for metrical purposes), whether etymologically erroneous or not. See *MM* 2.4.122 and *Cym.* 3.2.21, where 'fedary' and 'feodary', respectively, also mean confederate or accomplice.

91–2 **What . . . principal** What she should be ashamed of, even if it were known only ('But') to her and her co-criminal Polixenes (and to no condemning onlookers). 'Principal', like 'federary' (90), continues the legal language introduced in 1.1.

93 **bed-swerver** adulteress, one who deviates from marital fidelity.

94 **bold'st titles** After repeating his charge of 'adultress' (88) and then issuing the new one of 'traitor' (89), Leontes again hints at worse names, i.e. those given by the common folk ('vulgars').

98 **published** publicly proclaimed, denounced (*OED* publish *v* 3a).

99 **throughly** thoroughly.

99 **to say** by saying (Abbott 356, the gerundive use of the infinitive). The point that Orgel makes at 2.3.87–8 about the different punishments for slander in relation to a woman's social rank – i.e. whereas a common woman could receive tertiary damages, a noble woman would require a public recantation – might also bear on Hermione's unequivocal statement that Leontes' saying he was mistaken (100) would be insufficient. What emerges in 96–100 is a multivalenced response that carries emotional and moral value (e.g. 'grieve', 'clearer knowledge', 'Gentle my lord') while also touching on legal issues ('published me', 'right me throughly', and 'did mistake').

100–3 **If . . . top** 'If the proofs which I can offer will not support the opinion I have formed, no foundation can be trusted' (Johnson). 'Centre' = the centre of the earth (*OED n* 2a); a boy's 'top' thus balances on a comparatively infinitesimal point.

104–5 **is . . . speaks** is indirectly guilty only for speaking.

HERMIONE There's some ill planet reigns.
I must be patient till the heavens look
With an aspect more favourable. Good my lords,
I am not prone to weeping as our sex
Commonly are, the want of which vain dew
Perchance shall dry your pities; but I have
That honourable grief lodged here which burns
Worse than tears drown. Beseech you all, my lords,
With thoughts so qualified as your charities
Shall best instruct you, measure me; and so
The king's will be performed.

LEONTES Shall I be heard?

HERMIONE Who is't that goes with me? Beseech your highness
My women may be with me, for you see
My plight requires it. – Do not weep, good fools,
There is no cause. When you shall know your mistress
Has deserved prison, then abound in tears
As I come out. This action I now go on

112, 116 Beseech] F (*'beseech*) 118 it. –] *Oxford*; it. F

105 There's . . . reigns Some planet of unfavourable astrological influence is controlling events; Mars and Saturn were especially noted for their maleficent potential.

107 aspect an astrological term meaning 'the relative position of the heavenly bodies as they appear to an observer on the earth's surface at a given time' (*OED n* 4); accented on the second syllable.

111 lodged here possibly an implied stage direction – Hermione may place her hand over her heart.

113 qualified mitigated (rendered less severe than what Leontes' accusations call for).

114 measure judge.

115 Shall . . . heard Hermione's gracious dignity (105–15) has prevented the lords from acting on Leontes' order (103) that the queen be taken to prison, a fact that her own comment ('The king's will be performed') accentuates, riling Leontes even further. See also 124 n.

118 plight situation, i.e. her advanced state of pregnancy.

118 fools As a term of endearment, *fool* connotes both affection and pity (*OED* fool n^1 1c).

119–21 Hermione's admonition is clear until the last phrase, but why could her ladies show their feelings with tears only when she emerges from prison? Perhaps she is reinforcing her main contrast with a secondary one: 'Don't cry as I, innocent, go into prison; if I, guilty, were to come out of prison, *that* would merit tears'.

121 This . . . on 'Action' has been interpreted broadly as a 'course' to be embarked on (Kermode), narrowly as a legal indictment (Johnson) or a military campaign (Wilson), and metaphorically as acting a part (Schanzer). The military meaning fits better with 'go on' but as Orgel says, presents Hermione's action as too voluntary; and no record documents the yoking of 'go[ing] on' and 'action' in a theatrical sense. The best guess is 'legal process' (*OED n* 7a), i.e. commitment to prison, following indictment (Leontes' charges of adultery and treason) and arraignment (Hermione's denial before her judge and prosecutor); compare *Cym.* 2.3.151, 'If you will make 't an action, call witness to 't'. In casting herself as agent rather than victim, Hermione perhaps looks forward to the rest of her statement: she will cooperate in her humiliation in expectation of finally achieving spiritual benefits.

Is for my better grace. – Adieu, my lord.
I never wished to see you sorry; now
I trust I shall. – My women, come, you have leave.

LEONTES Go, do our bidding. Hence!

[*Exeunt Queen, guarded, and ladies*]

LORD Beseech your highness call the Queen again.

ANTIGONUS Be certain what you do, sir, lest your justice
Prove violence, in the which three great ones suffer,
Yourself, your queen, your son.

LORD For her, my lord,
I dare my life lay down – and will do't, sir,
Please you t'accept it – that the Queen is spotless
I'th'eyes of heaven, and to you (I mean
In this which you accuse her).

ANTIGONUS If it prove
She's otherwise, I'll keep my stables where
I lodge my wife; I'll go in couples with her;
Than when I feel and see her, no farther trust her;
For every inch of woman in the world,
Ay, every dram of woman's flesh, is false
If she be.

LEONTES Hold your peaces.

LORD Good my lord –

ANTIGONUS It is for you we speak, not for ourselves.
You are abused, and by some putter-on

122 grace. –] *Oxford;* grace. F **124** shall. –] *Folger;* shall: F **125** SD] *Theobald (subst.); not in* F **136** Than] *Pope*[2]; Then F **138** Ay] F (I) **138** flesh, . . . false] *Orgel;* flesh . . . false, F **139** lord–] *Theobald (subst.);* Lord. F

122 grace divine favour, but also credit in the social sense. The meaning here is closest to *OED* grace *n* 1d, '*to do* (a person or thing) *grace*: to become, reflect credit on . . . also, to do honour to'. For the idea that afflictions are for our own good, see Dent A53 and Rom. 5.3–4: 'but also we rejoyce in tribulations, knowing that tribulation bringeth forthe patience, And patience experience, and experience hope'.

124 My women . . . leave As early as 115 (see n.), it is clear that Hermione controls her own exit; see Leslie Thomson, 'Shakespeare and the Art of Making an Exit', *UTQ* 69 [1999–2000], 540–59). While the editors have placed '*Exeunt*' in its usual place after 125, another possibility, one that asserts Hermione's appropriation of Leontes' authority, is to have the women depart at 124, leaving an exasperated Leontes to repeat his command to attendants who follow the women after the fact (the staging chosen by Howell and Kahn). For another example of a female character's control of her own departure (but to more comic effect), see 2.3.63, 124, and 126–9.

133–6 The note of comic excess in Antigonus' defense of Hermione here, as at 144–50, may be a pointer to general characterization, but more specifically it expresses his sense that the charges of adultery are absurd and must rightly end in 'laughter' (198). Antigonus vows to watch over his wife or hold her in custody like a horse in a stable, or to accompany her everywhere as if they were dogs leashed together, never letting her out of his sight.

138 dram i.e. 'little bit' (Dolan).

141 abused deceived (*OED* abuse *v* 4b).

141 putter-on instigator, inciter (*OED* putter

That will be damned for't; would I knew the villain,
I would land-damn him! Be she honour-flawed –
I have three daughters: the eldest is eleven,
The second and the third, nine and some five;
If this prove true, they'll pay for't. By mine honour,
I'll geld 'em all; fourteen they shall not see
To bring false generations. They are co-heirs,
And I had rather glib myself than they
Should not produce fair issue.

LEONTES Cease, no more!
You smell this business with a sense as cold
As is a dead man's nose; but I do see't and feel't
As you feel doing thus, and see withal
The instruments that feel.

ANTIGONUS If it be so,
We need no grave to bury honesty:
There's not a grain of it the face to sweeten
Of the whole dungy earth.

143 him!] *Kermode;* him: F 143 honour-flawed–] *Capell;* honor-flaw'd, F

n 8). The irony is that Leontes is his own Iago, a character who is the ultimate inciter, a 'setter-on' (see *Oth.* 2.3.210 and 384, 3.3.240, and 5.2.329).

143 **land-damn him** Possible meanings include (1) curse ('land-damn') him vigorously; (2) loudly denounce/proclaim ('land-damn') him a slanderer; or (3) beat (from *lam* = thrash) him severely. Onions (rev. edn) suggests 'give (one) hell on earth, berate sharply'. Malone recommends 'kill him, bury him in earth', but Johnson's general reading – 'condemn him to quit the land' – may be best. Whatever the precise meaning, 'land-damning' is apparently done forcefully and publicly, an act felt/heard throughout the land.

143 **honour-flawed** guilty of adultery, unchaste.

145 **some five** about five.

147 **geld** spay (i.e. remove sexual organs; neuter).

147 **fourteen** Though the contemporary age of consent for girls was twelve, Old Capulet prefers fourteen in *Rom.*

148 **bring . . . generations** i.e. bring forth (*OED* bring *v* 7a) illegitimate ('false') offspring.

148 **co-heirs** joint-heirs; according to the tenets of primogeniture, if a man had sons, the eldest would rightfully inherit the estate; if daughters were his only progeny, they would share equally.

149 Antigonus' willingness to 'glib', or castrate, himself seems irrelevant to his point about women's chastity, but following so closely the reference to daughters as joint heirs, 'glib' likely carries the larger meaning of 'deprive myself of my posterity' (Orgel). Pafford conjectures that 'them' may have dropped out after 'glib'. In his resolve to 'geld' and 'glib' if Hermione proves to be an adulteress, Antigonus gives voice to the etymology of his name (see List of Characters, p. 80).

151 **smell** perceive as if by smell, discern (*OED* *v* 2a).

153 Some stage action is indicated after 'thus', but its exact nature is unclear. Whether Leontes pulls Antigonus' beard, or tweaks his nose, or grasps his arm as in Riverside (after Capell), or perhaps strikes himself as Orgel suggests (following Schanzer in taking 'you' to be impersonal) is up to the actor and director.

153 **withal** as well.

154 **instruments that feel** Leontes' fingers.

157 **dungy** filthy as excrement, i.e. vile, defiling (*OED adj* 2). Shaheen (724) finds a biblical allusion to Ps. 83.10 ('As the whole doung of the earth') and/or Jeremiah 8.2. and 16.4 ('Shalbe as doung vpon the earth'). Compare *Ant.* 1.1.35, 'our dungy earth,' which *OED* records under the first (simply descriptive) meaning: 'of the nature of dung; abounding in dung.'

157 **Lack I credit** Am I not to be believed.

LEONTES What? Lack I credit?
LORD I had rather you did lack than I, my lord,
Upon this ground; and more it would content me
To have her honour true than your suspicion,
Be blamed for't how you might.
LEONTES Why, what need we
Commune with you of this, but rather follow
Our forceful instigation? Our prerogative
Calls not your counsels, but our natural goodness
Imparts this; which if you, or stupefied
Or seeming so in skill, cannot or will not
Relish a truth, like us, inform yourselves
We need no more of your advice. The matter,
The loss, the gain, the ord'ring on't, is all
Properly ours.
ANTIGONUS And I wish, my liege,
You had only in your silent judgement tried it,
Without more overture.
LEONTES How could that be?
Either thou art most ignorant by age,
Or thou wert born a fool. Camillo's flight
Added to their familiarity –
Which was as gross as ever touched conjecture,

160 true than | *Dyce* (than F4); true, then F **160** suspicion, | *Collier;* suspition F **169–70** The loss . . . all / Properly ours. | *Theobald;* . . . on't, / Is . . . F

159 ground circumstance.

159–61 and . . . might I would much rather have her honour vindicated than your suspicions validated, no matter the blame you might incur for suspecting her so unjustly.

162 Commune Consult, confer. For the 'commune . . . of' construction, see *OED v* 6c, where this line is cited.

162–3 but . . . instigation The usual gloss of 'impulse' for 'instigation' suggests that most editors take the subject of 'follow' to be the royal we, Leontes himself. But Shakespeare's other uses of *instigate* (stir up, incite) usually indicate someone other than the speaker as the one being stirred to action (see *2H6* 3.1.51, *Wiv.* 3.5.76, and *Luc.* 43). Leontes' 'follow' may thus be, not a description of his own resolve, but an impatient order to his courtiers to fall in line behind his cause.

163–4 Our . . . counsels My position as king does not call for your advice. Orgel notes Leontes' adherence to King James's position in the contemporary debate over the extent of the royal prerogative; see also Introduction, pp. 20–2.

165 which in regard to which (Abbott 249).

165–6 or . . . or . . . skill either (truly) made stupid or seeming so in cunning ('skill'). See *MM* 2.4.74–5, 'Either you are ignorant, / Or seem so craftily'.

167 Relish Appreciate.

172 overture opening (to public view), i.e. publicity (Pafford). *OED* first records the sense of 'revelation' or 'disclosure' in 1548 (*n* 2), citing *Lear* 3.7.89 ('That made the overture of thy treasons to us') as the second example.

175 their familiarity the public intimacy of Hermione and Polixenes.

176 touched conjecture coincided with suspicion.

That lacked sight only, naught for approbation
But only seeing, all other circumstances
Made up to'th'deed – doth push on this proceeding.
Yet, for a greater confirmation –
For in an act of this importance 'twere
Most piteous to be wild – I have dispatched in post
To sacred Delphos, to Apollo's temple,
Cleomenes and Dion, whom you know
Of stuffed sufficiency. Now from the oracle
They will bring all, whose spiritual counsel had
Shall stop or spur me. Have I done well?

LORD Well done, my lord.

LEONTES Though I am satisfied and need no more
Than what I know, yet shall the oracle
Give rest to th'minds of others such as he
Whose ignorant credulity will not
Come up to th'truth. So have we thought it good
From our free person she should be confined,
Lest that the treachery of the two fled hence
Be left her to perform. Come, follow us;

182 have] F2; hane F 187–8 | F; *as one line Folger (after Keightley)* 191 others . . . he,] *Oxford;* others; . . . he F; others – . . . he, *Kermode*

177–8 That . . . seeing i.e. that left nothing lacking for full proof ('approbation') of the adulterous deed except an eye witness (or, as in *Oth.* 3.3.360, 'ocular proof').

179 Made up to Built a case for.

182 wild rash, lacking in deliberation.

182 in post at express speed. In Greene it is Bellaria who asks Pandosto 'to send six of his noblemen whom he best trusted to the Isle of Delphos, there to inquire of the oracle of Apollo whether she had committed adultery with Egistus, or conspired to poyson with Franion' (*Pandosto*, Bullough, 168–9).

183 Delphos In calling Delos, the island where Apollo was born, 'Delphos', Shakespeare was following not only his source (see Bullough, 169) but the common practice of conflating Delos with Delphi, the site of Apollo's temple and Oracle located on the mainland (see Terence Spencer, 'Shakespeare's Isle of Delphos', *MLR* 47 [1952], 199–202).

185 stuffed sufficiency ample qualification.

185 oracle the priestess (the Pythia) through whom Apollo spoke at his temple in Delphi, or, perhaps, the actual site where the mediation occurred. At 3.1.18 and 3.2.125, 'oracle' refers to the god's response itself, not the human instrument or the location for such instrumentality. See Supplementary note, p. 252.

186 all the whole truth (Schanzer).

186 had once received.

191 he Antigonus. Riverside's SD 'Points to Antigonus' (after Furness's conj.) seems overly prescriptive; some business (as in 153) may be required but it could be nothing more than a nodding of the head, or, as in Howell, an obvious look of disdain. Some editors avoid specifying the pronominal reference, preferring the indefinite 'any person' (Bevington) or 'anyone' (Folger).

193 come up to rise to the level of.

194 free accessible.

195 treachery i.e. the 'plot' of 2.1.47.

We are to speak in public, for this business
Will raise us all.

ANTIGONUS [*Aside*] To laughter, as I take it,
If the good truth were known. *Exeunt*

2.2 *Enter* PAULINA, *a Gentleman,* [*and Attendants*]

PAULINA [*To Gentleman*] The keeper of the prison, call to him.
Let him have knowledge who I am.

[*Exit Gentleman*]

Good lady,
No court in Europe is too good for thee;
What dost thou then in prison?

[*Enter Gentleman and* JAILER]

Now, good sir,
You know me, do you not?

JAILER For a worthy lady,
And one who much I honour.

198 SD *Aside*] *Hanmer; not in* F 2.2] F *(Scena Secunda.)* 0 SD] *Hanmer (subst.); Enter Paulina, a Gentleman, Gaoler, Emilia.* F 1 SD] *Folger; not in* F 2 SD] *Rowe (after 1); not in* F 4 SD] *Rowe (subst., after 5); not in* F

198 raise stir to action, perhaps with specifically political implications if understood as putting 'us on alert for dangers to the state and its citizens' (Andrews).

Act 2, Scene 2

The gathering of women characters at the prison – Paulina and Emilia onstage with the offstage incarcerated Hermione, newly delivered of a daughter, as the subject of conversation – helps to set up a core of female values in opposition to the suspicions and precautions Leontes has been setting up in the previous scene and imposing on his male courtiers. To emphasize this female solidarity, Kulick showed Hermione in a daybed upstage far right, with women attending her and a basket for the baby by her side, while Paulina, the Jailer, and Emilia conversed centre stage. See Supplementary note, p. 252.

0 SD F mentions only a Gentleman accompanying Paulina; but as 13 indicates, other attendants are present as well. As the wife of Lord Antigonus, she is not a lady in waiting as is Emilia or the other ladies in 2.1; rather, she appears as a confidante and friend to Hermione, eager to bring her comfort and moral support. Before we even know her name and that she is the wife of Antigonus, the text offers several clues as to Paulina's elevated social standing: the presence of both a gentleman and attendants, the imperative mode that marks her initial appearance, her own sense of rank (2, 5, 10), and the acknowledgement of it by both the Jailer (5–6) and Emilia (41–42, 45).

1–4 Paulina begins imperatively with two commands addressed to the Gentleman among her attendants, and then shifts her address to the absent Hermione, using the informal 'thee' (3) and 'thou' (4), thereby indicating the close relationship between the two women.

2 Good 'Good' echoes Camillo's moral description of Hermione at 1.2.217, and anticipates Paulina's ringing repetition of the word in the next scene (2.3.58, 59–60, 64–65).

6 who whom (Abbott 274).

PAULINA Pray you then,
Conduct me to the Queen.
JAILER I may not, madam;
To the contrary I have express commandment.
PAULINA Here's ado, to lock up honesty and honour from
Th'access of gentle visitors! Is't lawful, pray you,
To see her women? Any of them? Emilia?
JAILER So please you, madam,
To put apart these your attendants, I
Shall bring Emilia forth.
PAULINA I pray now, call her. –
Withdraw yourselves.
[*Exeunt Gentleman and Attendants*]
JAILER And, madam,
I must be present at your conference.
PAULINA Well, be't so; prithee.
[*Exit Jailer*]
Here's such ado to make no stain a stain
As passes colouring.

[*Enter* JAILER *with* EMILIA]

Dear gentlewoman,
How fares our gracious lady?

7–20] *Alexander; as seventeen lines ending* Queene. . . . (Madam) . . . commandment. . . . from . . . you . . . Emilia? . . .(Madam) . . . I . . . forth. . . . her: . . . selues. . . . Madam, . . . Conference. . . . prethee. . . . staine, . . . Gentlewoman, . . . Lady? F **10** visitors! | *Rowe;* visitors. F **14** her. –| *Oxford;* her: F **15** SD| *Theobald (subst.); not in* F **17** prithee| F *(*prethee*)* **17** SD| *Capell (subst); not in* F **19** SD| *Capell (subst.); not in* F; *Enter Emilia* F2

7–20 Many editors have attempted to improve this metrically irregular sequence by relineation without success.

9 honesty and honour The words 'recall . . . Leontes' charge [2.1.68] that Hermione was "honourable" but not "honest"' (Orgel).

10 access accented on the second syllable.

10 gentle noble.

10–11 Is't . . . Emilia Paulina finds the loophole in Leontes' order. Although this is the first textual reference to one of Hermione's attendants by name, it is possible that Emilia was one of the ladies present in 2.1 (see Mahood, *Bit Parts*, 9–10).

13 put apart send away, dismiss.

15 conference conversation.

19 passes colouring defies dyeing (*OED* colour *v* 1), i.e. disguising, and also excusing (*OED* colour *v* 3).

19 SD In the 1906 production at His Majesty's Theatre, Maude Tree's Paulina introduced the baby at this point. As Bartholomeusz notes (129), the business is 'questionable' but the frequent references to the infant and Paulina's 'This child' (58) lend it theatrical support. The reasoning behind the innovation may have found further prompting in 38–9: i.e. if the sight of the baby could make Paulina's anger 'evaporate . . . at a breath' (*Era*, 8 September 1906), it would similarly dissipate Leontes' wrath.

EMILIA As well as one so great and so forlorn
May hold together. On her frights and griefs,
Which never tender lady hath borne greater,
She is, something before her time, delivered.
PAULINA A boy?
EMILIA A daughter, and a goodly babe,
Lusty, and like to live. The Queen receives
Much comfort in't, says 'My poor prisoner,
I am innocent as you.'
PAULINA I dare be sworn.
These dangerous, unsafe lunes i'th'King, beshrew them!
He must be told on't, and he shall. The office
Becomes a woman best; I'll take't upon me.
If I prove honey-mouthed, let my tongue blister.
And never to my red-looked anger be
The trumpet any more. Pray you, Emilia,
Commend my best obedience to the Queen;
If she dares trust me with her little babe,
I'll show't the King, and undertake to be
Her advocate to th'loud'st. We do not know
How he may soften at the sight o'th'child.
The silence often of pure innocence
Persuades when speaking fails.

27–28 'My . . . you.'] *Capell (subst.)*; my . . . you. F

22 On By reason of, as a result of. The 'frights' that Hermione playfully anticipated (2.1.28) have become real and painful.

23 Which Than which.

25 a boy Why does Paulina raise the issue of the baby's sex? Positing an analogy to Henry VIII's query 'Is the Queen delivered? / Say, 'Ay, and of a boy' (*H8* 5.1.163–4), Thomas Merriam argues for a deliberately subversive meaning related to the Tudor monarchy's failure 'to ensure a lasting male dynasty' ('The Old Lady, Or All Is Not True,' *S. Sur.* 54 [2001], 244.)

26 lusty healthy, strong.

28 innocent as you To be innocent as a baby was proverbial (Dent, B4).

29 dangerous, unsafe If Shakespeare is not simply using the second adjective to iterate the meaning of the first, *dangerous* may have one of its older meanings: 'arrogant' or 'severe' (*OED* 1a), 'hard to please' (1b), 'ready to run into danger' (3), 'injurious' (5).

29 lunes fits of lunacy (etymologically derived from *luna*, the moon).

29 beshrew curse.

30 on't of it.

30 office duty, business, moral obligation; possibly (given the theatrical imagery elsewhere), part or role.

32 Were Paulina to mince words and 'sweeten' her message to Leontes, she would bring on the proverbial result of lying, a blistered mouth (Dent R84).

33–4 And . . . more A herald carrying a (defiant) message to the enemy conventionally wore red and was preceded by a soldier sounding a trumpet.

38 advocate to th'loud'st loudest, most audible advocate.

EMILIA Most worthy madam,
Your honour and your goodness is so evident
That your free undertaking cannot miss
A thriving issue: there is no lady living
So meet for this great errand. Please your ladyship
To visit the next room, I'll presently
Acquaint the Queen of your most noble offer,
Who but today hammered of this design,
But durst not tempt a minister of honour
Lest she should be denied.

PAULINA Tell her, Emilia,
I'll use that tongue I have; if wit flow from't
As boldness from my bosom, let't not be doubted
I shall do good.

EMILIA Now be you blest for it!
I'll to the Queen. Please you come something nearer.

JAILER Madam, if't please the Queen to send the babe,
I know not what I shall incur to pass it,
Having no warrant.

PAULINA You need not fear it, sir;
This child was prisoner to the womb and is
By law and process of great nature thence
Freed and enfranchised, not a party to
The anger of the King, nor guilty of
(If any be) the trespass of the Queen.

JAILER I do believe it.

52 let't] F3; le't F 53 it!] *Hanmer;* it. F

43 **free** generous.

44 **thriving issue** fortunate outcome (with wordplay on 'issue' = baby, child).

46 **presently** immediately.

48 **hammered of** perhaps 'earnestly deliberated' as Pafford argues, but since Emilia is privy more to Hermione's speech than to her mental processes, 'urged repeatedly' or, as Orgel suggests, 'repeatedly discussed' seems more likely.

49 **tempt . . . honour** attempt to use an agent ('minister') of high rank ('honour').

51 **wit** wisdom, good judgment (*OED n* 6).

54 **something nearer** a repetition of Emilia's earlier request (46).

56 **to pass it** 'Pass' as 'allow' finds support in *OED* (*v* 43), for which this line is cited as meaning 'To cause or allow (a person or thing) to go past or through some barrier.' Many editors, with the gerundive rather than infinitive use of 'to' in mind (see Abbott 356), say something like 'by (in or as the consequence of) letting it pass' (i.e. leave the prison).

59 **process** Noting the word 'law' earlier in the line and the reference to 'freed and enfranchised' in the next, Folger finds 'wordplay on "legal proceeding" . . . the doubling of synonymous words being a reflection of legal language'. The editors further suggest that 'law and process', if read to mean 'legal process', may illustrate the figure of speech known as *hendiadys*. As 58–62 indicate, Paulina is already acting as an advocate, one fully aware of the legal argument that holds a foetus, as 'prisoner to the womb', innocent of any crime committed by the mother.

PAULINA Do not you fear; upon mine honour, I
Will stand betwixt you and danger. *Exeunt*

2.3 *Enter* LEONTES

LEONTES Nor night, nor day, no rest. It is but weakness
To bear the matter thus, mere weakness, if
The cause were not in being – part o'th'cause,
She, th'adultress; for the harlot king
Is quite beyond mine arm, out of the blank
And level of my brain, plot-proof; but she
I can hook to me – say that she were gone,

2.3] F *(Scæna Tertia.)* **0 SD**] *Capell (subst.); Enter Leontes, Seruants, Paulina, Antigonus, and Lords.* F; *Enter Leon, Ant, Lords and other Attendants Rowe; Enter Leontes. Antigonus, Lords, and other Attendants, in waiting behind Staunton* **1** weakness,] F; weakness. *Collier* **3** being–] *Johnson;* being: F; being, *Collier*

64–5 Compare Paulina's confident promise to safeguard the jailer with the Abbess's commitment to keep Antipholus of Syracuse in her protective custody (*Err.* 5.1.92–112).

Act 2, Scene 3

As 2.3.197 makes clear, twenty-three days have passed since Cleomenes and Dion were dispatched to the Delphic Oracle. In performance, candles and/or special lighting effects usually designate this as a night scene (but see 11 n.); Granville-Barker's 'intensely impressive' staging made use of a great brazier, its red light picking characters out and then passing them back into the shadows (Bartholomeusz, 153). The scene fuses four separate passages from Greene's narrative: Pandosto's thoughts on revenge against Egistus; the jailer's attempt to 'appease' the king's fury by bringing Pandosto news of Bellaria's pregnancy; a passing reference that Pandosto 'could take no rest, until he might mitigate his choler with a just revenge'; and, after the birth of the child, an account of attempts by the nobles to 'divert [the king] from [his] bloody determination' to kill the infant (Bullough, 165–6).

0 SD F's massed entry (see Collation) must be adjusted for Paulina's later entrance (40) and the soliloquy-like quality of Leontes' opening lines, which explore his own thoughts and are addressed to no one onstage, thus suggesting either a single entrance or some version of the Staunton grouping (see Collation), with Antigonus and the other lords, along with servants, following Leontes on but standing at a distance. In her notes for this edn, Snyder suggested that the placement in F's SD of 'Servants' after 'Leontes' and before 'Paulina' might imply a sequential entrance, with Leontes' servants following behind him at the beginning of the scene but remaining in the background (or, as Bevington and Riverside indicate, 'keeping door') until needed to bar Paulina's forced entry, at which time Antigonus and the lords would appear, chasing after her. See Appendix C, p. 271.

2 mere nothing but; i.e. if the external cause were removed ('not in being,' 3), his sufferings could be mastered by resolution.

3–6 part . . . plot-proof Leontes reminds himself that he can eradicate only part of the external 'cause', Hermione, Polixenes being beyond the reach of his power.

4 harlot lewd; although moving in the direction of gender specificity by the early seventeenth century, the word did not yet apply to women exclusively.

5–6 blank / And level The 'blank' is the white spot in the middle of a target; 'level' refers to the process of shooting or aiming at it. Polixenes, in other words, is beyond Leontes' range.

6 plot-proof safe from any scheme hatched against him.

7 hook to me catch and draw to me, as with a grappling-hook in a sea-battle (Schanzer); or, continuing the imagery of 1.2.180–1, 193, as with a fishing hook.

Given to the fire, a moiety of my rest
Might come to me again. Who's there?

[*Enter a* SERVANT]

SERVANT My lord.
LEONTES How does the boy?
SERVANT He took good rest tonight; 'tis hoped
His sickness is discharged.
LEONTES To see his nobleness,
Conceiving the dishonour of his mother!
He straight declined, drooped, took it deeply,
Fastened and fixed the shame on't in himself,
Threw off his spirit, his appetite, his sleep,
And downright languished. Leave me solely. Go,
See how he fares.

[*Exit Servant*]

Fie, fie, no thought of him!

9 SD] *Oxford (after Rowe [following* lord*], subst.); not in* F; *Enrer* F2 12 His . . . nobleness] *Steevens; as two lines* . . . discharged. / To . . . F 13 mother!] *Pafford;* Mother. F; Mother, F2 17 solely.] *Bevington;* solely: F; solely; *Kermode* 18 SD] *Theobald (subst., after 17); not in* F 18 him!] *Kermode;* him, F

8 **Given . . . fire** Execution by fire was the punishment for women convicted of treason (Schanzer), a charge levelled twice by Leontes at Hermione (2.1.88–9, 3.2.13–19) because adultery 'would cast doubt on the succession and because it would motivate the queen to conspire against her husband's life' (Dolan, 3.2.13 n.; see also her introduction, pp. xxxiii–xxxv). Leontes will actually call for Hermione to be committed to 'the fire' at 2.3.94–5. Death by fire was also the punishment favoured for heretics (see 2.3.113–15 n.).

8 **moiety** (1) small part (*OED* 2b, where this line is cited), or (2) half (*OED* 1), since only one of the two adulterers can be destroyed.

11 **tonight** i.e. on the night just past, last night (*OED* 3); *OED* further notes 'perhaps only said in the morning.' See also 2.3.31.

12 **discharged** cleared away.

12–13 **To . . . mother!** Since the punctuation followed by many editors after Rowe ('To see his nobleness! / Conceiving the dishonour of his mother, . . .') 'provides Leontes with a neater and more rational train of thought, it is dramatically undesirable' (Orgel).

13 **Conceiving** perhaps just 'imagining' or 'comprehending', but the context also supports the stronger 'becoming possessed with' (*OED* conceive *v* 6).

14 **straight** immediately.

15 **on't** of it (Abbott 181).

17 **solely** alone. Snyder, who favoured having the Servants enter behind Leontes at the beginning of the scene, thought that his request 'is perhaps more naturally directed at hovering attendants already onstage than to the messenger reporting on Mamillius, who would not be expecting to attend the king after delivering his message' (Snyder, notes).

18 **Fie . . . him** Leontes takes up his inner monologue where he left off before the interlude with the servant, rejecting the thought of Polixenes against whom he cannot act for 'present vengeance' (22) against Hermione. Lines 18–23 evince Shakespeare's typical compression of passages deriving directly from *Pandosto*: ' . . . yet [Pandosto] saw, that Egistus was not onely of great puissance and prowesse to withstand him, but also had many Kings of his alliance to ayde him, if neede should serve: for he married to the Emperours daughter of Russia. These and the like considerations something daunted Pandosto his courage, so that he was content rather to put up a manifest injurie with peace, than hunt after revenge with dishonor and losse; determining since Egistus had escaped scot-free, that Bellaria should pay for all at an unreasonable price' (Bullough, 164).

The very thought of my revenges that way
Recoil upon me: in himself too mighty,
And in his parties, his alliance. Let him be,
Until a time may serve. For present vengeance,
Take it on her. Camillo and Polixenes
Laugh at me, make their pastime at my sorrow;
They should not laugh if I could reach them, nor
Shall she, within my power.

Enter PAULINA [*carrying a baby*], *Servants*, ANTIGONUS, and LORDS

LORD You must not enter.
PAULINA Nay, rather, good my lords, be second to me.
Fear you his tyrannous passion more, alas,
Than the Queen's life? A gracious, innocent soul
More free than he is jealous!
ANTIGONUS That's enough.
SERVANT Madam, he hath not slept tonight, commanded
None should come at him.
PAULINA Not so hot, good sir,

26 SD] *Folger (subst.); Enter Paulina.* F 29–30 gracious, . . . soul . . . jealous!] *Orgel;* gracious . . . soule, . . . iealous. F

19–20 thought . . . Recoil For lack of agreement between subject and verb, resulting from confusion with the noun most proximate ('revenges'), see Abbott 412.

21 his parties, his alliance his political connections and his allies or friends.

24 pastime sport (in the sense of matter affording mirth, a jest or joke; see *OED* sport *n* 4).

26 SD Many editors specify stage business involving the men's efforts to hold Paulina back.

27 be second to support. In his review of Syer, Armstrong noted (30) a defined 'triangulation' of Paulina's authority in 27–127, her opposition varying in tone as she directed her outrage at three targets: the King, Antigonus, and a sycophantic courtier who had been established in 1.2 as a court spy.

30 free (1) innocent, guiltless (*OED adj* 7); (2) noble, honourable (*OED adj* 4). Since Paulina has already referred to Hermione's 'innocent soul' (29), the second meaning is perhaps more operative.

30 That's enough In trying to stop Paulina from saying anything more, Antigonus appears to reaffirm his wife's praise of the Queen by stating that she is 'gracious, innocent, and noble enough' (Folger).

32 come at come near; approach.

32 Not so hot While the Servant's tone may be sufficient to prompt Paulina's reaction, some stage business is more likely, the Servant being physically ardent or zealous ('hot') in trying to enforce Leontes' wish that he not be disturbed.

I come to bring him sleep. 'Tis such as you
That creep like shadows by him and do sigh
At each his needless heavings, such as you
Nourish the cause of his awaking. I
Do come with words as medicinal as true,
Honest as either, to purge him of that humour
That presses him from sleep.

LEONTES What noise there, ho?

PAULINA No noise, my lord, but needful conference
About some gossips for your highness.

LEONTES How?
Away with that audacious lady! Antigonus,
I charged thee that she should not come about me;
I knew she would.

ANTIGONUS I told her so, my lord,
On your displeasure's peril and on mine
She should not visit you.

LEONTES What? Canst not rule her?

PAULINA From all dishonesty he can; in this –
Unless he take the course that you have done,
Commit me for committing honour – trust it,
He shall not rule me.

39 What] F2; Who F 42 lady!] *Globe;* lady. F 50 me.] *Rowe;* me: F

35 **needless** unnecessary (*OED adj* 2).

35 **heavings** sighs, groans, or sobs uttered with great effort (*OED* heave *v* B8).

36 **awaking** insomnia.

37 **medicinal** pronounced 'med'-ci-nal'.

38 **Honest as either** Paulina is as honest in her intentions as either healing or truthful words (Furness).

38 **humour** mental aberration, thought to result from imbalance of the humours (the four fluids – black bile, yellow bile, phlegm, and blood – that were considered at the time to determine moods and dispositions).

39 **presses** 'keeps', or 'prevents'. The figurative suggestion of pressing to death, the torture by which the accused was crushed under a mass of stones, may also be present: Leontes' mental agitation weighs heavily on him, thereby keeping him from sleep.

39 **What . . . ho?** Leontes, on another part of the stage, with his view of Paulina and the Lords blocked, has heard only commotion and not the actual altercation of 26–39. In Kahn, as the light dimmed over Leontes at 26, the rear mirrored wall became a scrim to reveal Paulina upbraiding Antigonus and his companions; see illustration 8, p. 12.

41 **gossips** godparents, i.e. for the christening of 'your highness['s]' newborn infant. Since the baptismal rite is one of spiritual cleansing and renewal, the line may also indirectly refer to Leontes' present state.

47 **dishonesty** dishonourable behaviour.

49 **Commit . . . honour** Paulina plays on *commit*, 'consign to prison', and *committing*, 'performing', concluding ironically with 'honour' rather than the expected bad action, which in Leontes' mind (like Othello's and Lear's) would be the sin of adultery (see *OED* commit *v* 6c).

ANTIGONUS La you now, you hear,
When she will take the rein, I let her run;
But she'll not stumble.
PAULINA Good my liege, I come –
And I beseech you hear me, who professes
Myself your loyal servant, your physician,
Your most obedient counsellor, yet that dares
Less appear so in comforting your evils
Than such as most seem yours – I say I come
From your good Queen.
LEONTES Good Queen!
PAULINA Good Queen, my lord, good Queen, I say 'good Queen',
And would by combat make her good, so were I
A man, the worst about you.
LEONTES [*To Lords*] Force her hence.
PAULINA Let him that makes but trifles of his eyes
First hand me! On mine own accord, I'll off,
But first I'll do my errand. The good Queen
(For she is good) hath brought you forth a daughter;
Here 'tis. Commends it to your blessing.
[*Laying down the baby*]

52–57 come – . . . yours –] *Capell (after Rowe);* come: . . . yours. F **58** Queen!] *Capell;* Queen? F **59** Good . . . I say good Queen,] *Capell; as two lines* . . . Queene / I . . . F; . . . lord, / Good Queen . . . *Pope* **59** 'good Queen'] *Folger;* good Queene F **60** good, so] *Theobald;* good so, F **61** SD *To Lords*] *Oxford; not in* F **63** me!] *Orgel;* me: F; me. *Kermode* **66** SD] *Rowe (subst.); not in* F

50 La you An underlining exclamation. Schanzer proposes as an equivalent the modern 'There now, you hear how she will talk,' and suggests some accompanying gesture of resignation.

51–2 As at 2.1.133–5, Antigonus uses equine metaphors when speaking of his wife, this time in a more complimentary fashion.

53 professes Abbott (247) lists several examples of the third person verb in relative clauses with antecedents in the first or second person; see also 'dares' (55).

56 comforting in the legal sense, 'abetting criminal activity'. Paulina will risk not appearing as the 'obedient counsellor' (55) because of her refusal to condone Leontes' crimes in the manner of those counsellors who 'most seem yours' (57), i.e. who seem most devoted or loyal to you.

58 good Queen Paulina's phrase, iterated in 59, combines the rhetorical schemes of *ploce* (repetition of a word or phrase within the same line) and *epanalepsis* (repetition of the same word or phrase at the beginning and end of the same line), relentlessly reminding Leontes of what he does not want to hear.

58 Good Queen! Leontes is expressing his strong disdain for the epithet 'good', not inflecting the phrase as a question. In the early modern period the question mark, F's punctuation here, frequently indicates exclamation rather than question.

60 by . . . her prove her 'good' in trial by combat (the reference is to the chivalric rite by which medieval knights would uphold a lady's honour).

61 worst i.e. (even) the most inferior or least valiant (among your entourage).

63 hand lay hands on. The servants and/or lords, perhaps Antigonus himself, apparently attempt to remove Paulina as she vigorously holds her ground.

66 SD Paulina must set down the infant sometime before 2.3.73; this is the likeliest place.

LEONTES Out!
A mankind witch! Hence with her, out o'door!
A most intelligencing bawd!
PAULINA Not so;
I am as ignorant in that as you
In so entitling me, and no less honest
Than you are mad – which is enough, I'll warrant,
As this world goes, to pass for honest.
LEONTES Traitors!
Will you not push her out? [*To Antigonus*] Give her the bastard,
Thou dotard, thou art woman-tired, unroosted
By thy Dame Partlet here. Take up the bastard,
Take't up, I say; give't to thy crone.
PAULINA [*To Antigonus*] For ever
Unvenerable be thy hands, if thou
Tak'st up the Princess by that forced baseness
Which he has put upon't.

66–8 | Out! . . . witch! . . . o'door! . . . bawd!] Kermode *(after Rowe* Out! . . . witch!*; after Capell* bawd!*)*; Out: . . . Witch? . . . o'dore: . . . bawd. F; Out! . . . witch! . . . o'door – . . . bawd. *Oxford* **72** Traitors!] *Rowe;* Traitors; F **73** SD] *Rowe (subst.); not in* F **76** SD] *Oxford; not in* F

67 mankind masculine; pejorative when applied to women and sometimes merging with the other meaning of 'fierce, mad' (*OED* mankind *adj*[2]) to suggest a violent, overbearing woman, a virago. Pafford cites Beaumont and Fletcher, *Monsieur Thomas*, 4.6.50, ''Twas a sound knock she gave me: A plaguey mankind girl.' Reinforced by 'witch', likewise carrying implications of gender barriers transgressed (e.g. the armored Joan of Arc, *1H6* 1.5.6, and the three witches, *Mac.* 1.3.45–7), the epithet marks Paulina's intrusion in this scene on male space and prerogatives.

68 intelligencing carrying secret information, i.e. between Hermione and Polixenes in her capacity as 'bawd', i.e. go-between, pander.

72 As this world goes Proverbial (Dent W884.1).

74 woman-tired henpecked ('tired' = torn at by the beak). The idea is repeated in the next phrase, 'unroosted [i.e. dislodged from your perch, *OED* unroost *v* 1, where this line is cited] by thy Dame Partlet', which picks up the generic name for a hen derived from the Reynard the Fox stories, and perhaps best known from Chaucer's 'Nun's Priest's Tale' (Pertelote or 'Partlet' being the name of Chauntecleer's domineering hen). In *1H4*, Falstaff addresses Mistress Quickly as 'Dame Partlet, the hen' (3.3.52). 'Unroosted' might also suggest wordplay on 'unroost' = 'unrooster-ed' (i.e. castrated), which might then lead to an alternative reading of 'woman-tired' = attired as a woman.

75–6 Take up . . . Take't up As in 2.1 when he ordered Hermione's removal, and in his frequent calls for Paulina's immediate dismissal in this scene, so now in demanding that Antigonus pick up the baby, Leontes is forced to repeat his commands.

76 crone (1) an ugly, withered old woman (possibly, if understood as *hag* [*OED n*[1] 2 and 3], continuing the imagery of 'mankind witch' [67]); and (2) an old toothless ewe (*OED n* 2). Schanzer favours the second meaning alone: 'Paulina's loud reproaches, after being compared to the angry clucking of a hen, are now likened to the bleating of an old ewe'.

78 forced baseness unnaturally imposed title of bastard. Paulina repeats the idea of the appellation's being wrongly thrust upon the infant in 'put upon't' (79). See 3.1.16, where 'forcing' has the same sense.

LEONTES He dreads his wife.
PAULINA So I would you did; then 'twere past all doubt
You'd call your children yours.
LEONTES A nest of traitors!
ANTIGONUS I am none, by this good light.
PAULINA Nor I, nor any
But one that's here, and that's himself: for he
The sacred honour of himself, his Queen's,
His hopeful son's, his babe's, betrays to slander,
Whose sting is sharper than the sword's; and will not
(For as the case now stands, it is a curse
He cannot be compelled to't) once remove
The root of his opinion, which is rotten
As ever oak or stone was sound.
LEONTES A callat
Of boundless tongue, who late hath beat her husband

81 traitors!] *Capell;* Traitors. F 82 I . . . any] *Steevens; as two lines* . . . light. / Nor . . . F

79 **dreads** fears. Paulina's ellipsis in the next line plays on another sense of 'dread' as 'respect' (Folger).

81 **You'd . . . yours** According to English common law, any child born in the state of wedlock was legitimate, the husband's denial of paternity notwithstanding; compare *John* 1.1.116–29. For a discussion of Perdita's 'bastardy' in the context of Elizabeth I's, both 'pure creation[s] of royal will', see Orgel, 30–31.

82 **by . . . light** a conventional oath like 'by heaven', or, perhaps, 'by God's light'.

85–6 **slander . . . sword's** a common expression, perhaps even proverbial, despite Dent's disclaimer (Dent S521.1, 'Slander is sharper than a sword'; and W839, 'Words hurt [cut] more than swords'); compare *Cym.* 3.4.33–4, 'slander, / Whose edge is sharper than the sword'. In the Geneva Bible, note 'q' on Job 5.15 ('He saueth the poore from the sword, from their [q] mouth, and from the hande of the violent man') reads, 'He compareth the slaunder of the wicked to sharpe swordes', thus indicating that *slander* is textually implicit (Shaheen, 725). Shaheen also cites Geneva's Ps. 57.4: 'My soul is among lions, and I lie even among them . . . whose teeth are speares and arrowes, and their tongue a sharpe sworde'. For 'slander figured as theater' in political and dramatic practice in early modern England, see M. Lindsay Kaplan, *The Culture of Slander in Early Modern England*, 1997.

87–8 **as . . . to't** circumstances being what they are (i.e. Leontes having absolute power as king), the hard reality is that he cannot be forced to change his view; in other words, no court has jurisdiction over him. Orgel observes that were Leontes 'not the King, under English law Hermione would have a case. To defame a woman's honour was actionable in both civil and ecclesiastical courts; when the person defamed was a commoner the act was a tort and could be redressed by a fine, but defaming an aristocrat was a more serious matter touching the public good [and requiring a public recantation]. Under Elizabeth, to slander the Queen was treasonable'. See 2.1.99 n.

90 **callat** While the sense of lewd woman (*OED n* 1) may be operative, Leontes' term of abuse (given the following references to 'boundless tongue' and 'beat') seems more indicative of an ill-tongued woman or scold (*OED n* 2, where this line is cited).

91 **beat** pronounced *bait*, thus creating a pun in the next line where Leontes feels Paulina's verbal attack ('baits' = harasses or persecutes 'a person more or less unable to escape', *OED* bait *v* 4) as also physical. For an early audience, the pun might trigger an association with bear-baiting in which dogs attacked a chained bear.

And now baits me! This brat is none of mine,
It is the issue of Polixenes.
Hence with it, and together with the dam
Commit them to the fire.

PAULINA It is yours;
And might we lay th'old proverb to your charge,
So like you 'tis the worse. Behold, my lords,
Although the print be little, the whole matter
And copy of the father – eye, nose, lip,
The trick of's frown, his forehead, nay, the valley,
The pretty dimples of his chin and cheek, his smiles,
The very mould and frame of hand, nail, finger.
And thou good goddess Nature, which hast made it
So like to him that got it, if thou hast
The ordering of the mind too, 'mongst all colours
No yellow in't, lest she suspect, as he does,
Her children not her husband's.

92 me!] *Capell;* me: F

92 mine, Editors have long inclined to emending F's comma to a semi-colon, and in the case of Oxford (followed by Folger) a full stop. Such emendations, however, suggest a logical and grammatical clarity at odds with Leontes' agitated state; the retention of F's comma (as in Riverside and Orgel) seems better suited to a rash running on of thoughts in a turbulent mind.

94 dam See 1.2.136 n.

94–5 Likewise, in *Pandosto* the king, upon hearing that 'Bellaria was brought to bed of a fair and beautiful daughter, . . . determined that both Bellaria and the young infant should be burnt with fire' (Bullough, 165–6). Leontes' lines render his call for the Oracle's message and his decision to have a trial mere formalities; here he is ready to kill the child before Hermione's guilt, and by extension the child's bastardy, are confirmed by the Oracle.

96–7 th'old . . . worse Dent 1.290; Staunton cites Overbury's character of a Sergeant (1614): 'The devil calls him his white son; he is so like him, that he is the worst for it'; and Pafford cites Fletcher's *The Elder Brother*, 'Your eldest son, sir, and your very image, / (But he's so like you, that he fares the worse for't)'.

98 print image, as reproduced by a printing press. The comparison continues with 'matter' and 'copy' (99). In performance, Paulina usually picks the baby up at this moment, showing it to the lords who gather around her, and setting it down again at the end of the speech.

100 trick a distinguishing characteristic or feature, a trait. While the word often has this meaning in Shakespeare's plays, it is used to establish paternity only in *WT*, *John*, 1.1.85, 'He hath a trick of Cordelion's face', and *1H4*, 2.4.402–5, 'That thou art my son I have partly thy mother's word . . . but chiefly a villainous trick of thine eye . . . that doth warrant me'.

100–1 valley . . . cheek The first items of each pair go together, i.e. the valley or cleft in his chin and the dimples in his cheek. For similar respective constructions see 2.1.165–7, 3.2.160–2, 3.2.201–2, 4.1.1–2, and 4.4.357–8.

103 which who (Abbott 265).

104 got begot.

105 colours hues of complexion (*OED* colour *n* 3); Orgel proposes 'natures'.

106 yellow the colour associated with jealousy (*OED adj* 2).

106–7 lest . . . husband's Since the woman who conceives and bears children usually knows the identity of the father, Paulina's gender reversal here comments ironically on Leontes' irrationality: for him to suspect Hermione of infidelity is as mad as for his grown-up daughter to doubt the legitimacy of her own children.

LEONTES A gross hag! –
And, losel, thou art worthy to be hanged,
That wilt not stay her tongue.

ANTIGONUS Hang all the husbands
That cannot do that feat, you'll leave yourself
Hardly one subject.

LEONTES Once more, take her hence!

PAULINA A most unworthy and unnatural lord
Can do no more.

LEONTES I'll ha'thee burnt.

PAULINA I care not.
It is an heretic that makes the fire,
Not she which burns in't. I'll not call you tyrant;
But this most cruel usage of your queen,
Not able to produce more accusation
Than your own weak-hinged fancy, something savours
Of tyranny, and will ignoble make you,
Yea, scandalous to the world.

LEONTES [*To Lords*] On your allegiance,
Out of the chamber with her! Were I a tyrant,

107 hag!–] *Oxford (Rowe, exclamation mark);* Hagge: F **111** hence!] *Orgel;* hence. F **120** SD] *This edn.; not in* F; *To Antigonus Oxford* **121, 123** her!] *Globe;* her. F

107 gross rude or extremely coarse (*OED adj* 14a, 15).

107 hag 'a repulsive old woman' (*OED n*[1] 3). If 'hag', however, conjures the image of a demon, malicious sprite, or witch (*OED n*[1] 1a, 2), then 'gross' may have the sense of 'monstrous' (*OED adj* 4), thereby continuing not only the earlier references to 'mankind witch' (67) and 'crone' (76) but also the idea of frightening sprites and goblins associated with 'winter's tales' (2.1.25–8).

108 losel worthless person, good-for-nothing.

109–11 Antigonus' humour is one of 'many comic touches in the scene by means of which Shakespeare mitigates its tragic impact upon the audience' (Steevens).

113–15 Under both Catholic and Protestant regimes, heretics were burned at the stake; Paulina, the true believer, 'wittily applies the punishment to the heresy of lacking faith in Hermione' (Schanzer).

115 I'll . . . tyrant Paulina makes effective use of paralipsis (the ironic emphasis on something by pointedly pretending to pass over it); see 3.2.215–29 for her more sustained use of the device. The sting of 'tyrant' is keenly felt by Leontes, for whom, it appears, such a charge is the worst thing that could be said about him (121–3); see Introduction, pp. 21–2.

116 accusation evidence.

117 weak-hinged unsupported (probably a reference to the hook-and-eye hinges on which doors of the time were hung); apparently the only recorded use of the word.

120 On . . . allegiance On your sworn duty to obey me, failure of which constitutes treason.

121 chamber (1) a private room or apartment, perhaps a bedroom (which in this instance would make Paulina's intrusion exceptionally bold); (2) a reception room in a palace (*OED n* 1b). See also 5.2.5, where the setting is clearly neither a private study nor a bedroom. The frontispiece to Hudson's 1851 edition depicts 2.3 as the royal presence chamber, Leontes' throne plainly in view. Although Wentworth followed suit (NJSF, 1996), the current performance norm favors domestic settings.

Where were her life? She durst not call me so
If she did know me one. Away with her!

PAULINA I pray you, do not push me; I'll be gone.
Look to your babe, my lord, 'tis yours; Jove send her
A better guiding spirit! What needs these hands?
You that are thus so tender o'er his follies
Will never do him good, not one of you.
So, so. Farewell, we are gone. *Exit*

LEONTES [*To Antigonus*] Thou, traitor, hast set on thy wife to this.
My child? Away with't! Even thou, that hast
A heart so tender o'er it, take it hence
And see it instantly consumed with fire.
Even thou, and none but thou. Take it up straight.
Within this hour bring me word 'tis done,
And by good testimony, or I'll seize thy life,
With what thou else call'st thine. If thou refuse,
And wilt encounter with my wrath, say so;
The bastard-brains with these my proper hands
Shall I dash out. Go, take it to the fire,
For thou set'st on thy wife.

ANTIGONUS I did not, sir;
These lords, my noble fellows, if they please,
Can clear me in't.

126 spirit!] *Capell;* Spirit. F 130 SD] *Oxford;* not in F 131 with't!] *Capell;* with't? F; with't. *Rowe* 143 can; . . . liege,] *Orgel;* can: . . . Liege, F; can, . . . liege. *Folger*

124, 126 The implied stage business in these lines calls for one or more attendants to lay hands on Paulina so as to expel her forcibly. As Folger notes: 'It is possible to stage this scene in several ways . . .: perhaps Leontes' lords repeatedly lay hands on her in response to the king's orders and a physically powerful Paulina resolutely, or even violently, resists their efforts until she has done her "errand." Or perhaps her words combined with her looks freeze Leontes' attendants in their places, and they never presume to approach her until just before she takes her leave'.

126 A . . . spirit (1) A better protector (than Leontes) or, perhaps, (2) a better disposition (than the King's).

127 tender o'er so tolerant of.

129 we . . . gone See Supplementary note, p. 252.

130–41 Throughout the speech Leontes frequently repeats assertions ('set on', 'set'st on') and commands ('take it hence,' 'Take it up,' and 'take it to'), often with a sense of urgency ('instantly,' 'straight' = immediately, and 'Within this hour'). He finds himself mentally and verbally locked in place.

130 set on incited, urged. See note to 'putter-on' (2.1.141).

132 tender o'er considerate of or kindly disposed toward.

136 testimony evidence.

136 seize the legal term for 'take into custody', 'take possession of'. Leontes will 'seize' not only Antigonus himself but all his property, inclusive of his wife and children ('with what thou else call'st thine', 137).

139 proper own.

LORDS We can; my royal liege,
He is not guilty of her coming hither.
LEONTES You're liars all.
LORD Beseech your highness, give us better credit.
We have always truly served you, and beseech'
So to esteem of us; and on our knees we beg,
As recompense of our dear services
Past and to come, that you do change this purpose,
Which being so horrible, so bloody, must
Lead on to some foul issue. We all kneel.
LEONTES I am a feather for each wind that blows.
Shall I live on to see this bastard kneel
And call me father? Better burn it now
Than curse it then. But be it; let it live.
It shall not neither. [*To Antigonus*] You, sir, come you hither,
You that have been so tenderly officious
With Lady Margery, your midwife there,

157 SD] *Rowe (subst.); not in* F

143–4 SH **Lords** Despite the potential awkwardness of the lines' choral delivery, editorial tradition retains F's plural prefix; in performance, however, the practice tends toward dividing the lines.

146 **Beseech** We beseech. The speaker may be the same lord who defended Hermione so chivalrously (2.1.129–33) and disputed Leontes so forthrightly (2.1.158–61).

147 **beseech'** We beseech you (see 2.1.11 n.). Besides indicating an omission, the apostrophe may signify an elision (Orgel) so as to accommodate an essentially trochaic pentameter.

149–50 **services . . . come** E. W. Ives ('Shakespeare and History', *S. Sur. 38* [1985], 25) notes that Leontes' sparing of Perdita from the fire is 'an act of patronage', and that the lords' plea which prompts it echoes 'the standard formula in letters patent: "for services past and to come"'. The lords' services have been 'dear', i.e. loving and valuable.

152 **issue** outcome, with wordplay on 'issue' as offspring (see 2.2.44); the Lords see the consequences, not the baby, as 'foul'.

152 **We all kneel** The kneeling could be literal (as it is in most productions) or figurative. If the courtiers do actually kneel here, it is not clear when they stand again (Folger): in Howell they rose at Leontes' 'But be it; let it live' (156); in Kahn, at 'You, sir, come you hither' (157).

153 Proverbial (Dent F162): 'As wavering as feathers in the wind'.

158 **officious** perhaps, the now obsolete meaning of 'eager to perform kind services, ready to help others' (*OED adj* 1); or, in the modern sense (first recorded in 1602, *OED* adj 3), meddlesome, interfering.

159 **Lady Margery** Possibly a variant of Dame Partlet (see 74n), since 'margery-prater' was a cant expression for a hen. For *Margery* = female private parts, see Williams, who also notes that when combined with 'midwife', a euphemism for bawd that here seemingly refers to one who deals in illegitimate children, the term becomes dismissive of women in general, reducing them to their physical nature. Although it was the role of the midwife to bring the newly delivered baby to the father, here 'midwife' points, not to Paulina's actual assistance at Perdita's birth (as Hoeniger suggests, 42), but to her assumption of command over Leontes and his household. Orgel, however, thinks that the term implicates Paulina not only in the child's delivery but also in the concealment of its true paternity; he cites Thomas R. Forbes, *The Midwife and the Witch* (1966), 145, on the midwife's oath that was part of the licensing process, according to which the midwife promised not to 'permit or suffer that woman being in labour or travail shall name any other to be the father of her child, than only he who is the right true father thereof'.

To save this bastard's life – for 'tis a bastard,
So sure as this beard's gray – what will you adventure
To save this brat's life?

ANTIGONUS Anything, my lord,
That my ability may undergo,
And nobleness impose – at least thus much:
I'll pawn the little blood which I have left
To save the innocent – anything possible.

LEONTES It shall be possible. Swear by this sword
Thou wilt perform my bidding.

ANTIGONUS [*Placing his hand on the sword's hilt*] I will, my lord.

LEONTES Mark, and perform it, seest thou? For the fail
Of any point in't shall not only be
Death to thyself, but to thy lewd-tongued wife
(Whom for this time we pardon). We enjoin thee,
As thou art liegeman to us, that thou carry
This female bastard hence, and that thou bear it
To some remote and desert place, quite out
Of our dominions, and that there thou leave it,
Without more mercy, to it own protection

161 gray – what] *Pope;* gray. What F 168 SD] *Folger (subst.); not in* F

161 **this beard's gray** Leontes is unlikely to be referring to himself since he is little more than thirty (see 1.2.152–5 and 155 n.). Antigonus, on the other hand, alludes to his advanced years (see 2.3.165 n.) and is referred to as an 'old man' by the Shepherd (3.3.97); see also 2.1.173.

161 **adventure** risk, dare.

163 **undergo** undertake, perform.

165 i.e. I'll pledge (as a knight does in facing a challenge to his honour) or hazard (as when one pawns something of value) what little life ('blood', *OED n* 4) I have left on earth. Antigonus alludes to the belief that blood dried as one aged (see A. R. Braunmuller's note on *Mac.* 5.1.39–40, 'Yet who would have thought the old man to have had so much blood in him?' (NCS *Macbeth* [1997]).

167 **Swear . . . sword**. The usual stage business requires Leontes to bring out a sword (the hilt and blade forming a cross) for Antigonus to swear his obedience.

169 **Mark** Pay attention.

169–70 **For . . . in't** For the failure to perform any detail of my command. The line antedates *OED*'s first citation of *failure* in 1641.

171 **lewd-** usually glossed as 'foolish', 'vulgar', 'vile', or 'foul', but the sense of 'rude' = 'ill-mannered' or 'discourteous' (*OED adj* 4) may also be present.

172 **enjoin** order, command; perhaps with ironic overtones of 'join to' (*OED v* 1): 'By carrying out Leontes' commission Antigonus will join himself to his portion of the fate that awaits the king' (Andrews), a complicity that the Third Gentleman notes when he later says of the devoured Antigonus and drowned mariners, ' . . . all the instruments which aided to expose the child were even then lost when it was found' (5.2.60–2).

173 **liegeman** one who has sworn faithful service.

175 **desert** forsaken, uninhabited, desolate.

177 **it** its. 'Occasionally *it*, an early provincial form of the old genitive, is found for *its*, especially when a child is mentioned [as here and at 3.2.98], or when any one is contemptuously spoken of as a child' (Abbott 228).

And favour of the climate. As by strange fortune
It came to us, I do in justice charge thee,
On thy soul's peril and thy body's torture,
That thou commend it strangely to some place
Where chance may nurse or end it. Take it up.

ANTIGONUS I swear to do this, though a present death
Had been more merciful.

[*He picks up the baby*]

Come on, poor babe;
Some powerful spirit instruct the kites and ravens
To be thy nurses. Wolves and bears, they say,
Casting their savageness aside, have done
Like offices of pity. [*To Leontes*] Sir, be prosperous
In more than this deed does require; [*to the baby*] and
blessing
Against this cruelty fight on thy side,
Poor thing, condemned to loss. *Exit*

LEONTES No, I'll not rear
Another's issue.

Enter a SERVANT

SERVANT Please your highness, posts
From those you sent to th'oracle are come

184 SD] *Orgel (after Bevington, subst., at the beginning of* 183*); not in* F 188 SD] *Folger; not in* F 189 SD] *Oxford (subst.); not in* F 192 Please your] F3; Please 'your F

178–82 strange fortune . . . end it 'strange' = 'foreign' or 'alien' (*OED adj* 1), the baby being not his but that of Polixenes, whom Leontes now no longer regards as a close friend but as a stranger; it is therefore only fitting that this foreigner's child be left 'strangely', i.e. 'as a stranger, without more provision' (Johnson) to 'chance' (182). The proverbial 'Fortune is a strumpet' (Dent F603.1) may be implicit.

182 nurse . . . end perhaps, a variant of the proverb 'Either mend or end' (Dent M874); see 3.1.18.

185–8 Some . . . pity Antigonus may allude to either the ravens who fed Elijah (1 Kings 17.4, 6) or the shewolf who suckled Romulus and Remus, the mythical founders of Rome. By praying that the most vicious of beasts and birds of prey like 'kites and ravens' will show mercy toward the infant with similar acts of kindness ('Like offices of pity'), Antigonus (in keeping with the title of the play) hopes for something extraordinary and wondrous.

189 In more . . . require (May you be prosperous) in more ways than this barbarous act deserves or commands in repayment. For a similar use of 'require,' see 3.2.61.

189–91 and blessing . . . loss After wishing Leontes prosperity (188), Antigonus then addresses the baby with a prayer for blessing. Andrews' placement of a period and a dash after 'side' leads to a strained reading by which Leontes becomes the addressee and recipient of Antigonus' call for 'blessing'.

191 loss perdition or destruction (see 3.3.50); perhaps specifically 'being cast away' (see *H8*, 2.2.29). Baret's *Alvearie* (1580) uses *lose* and *loss* to translate both *naufragium*, 'ruin,' and *orbare*, 'to bereave, to take away (a relative) by death'.

192 posts couriers, express messengers.

An hour since. Cleomenes and Dion,
Being well arrived from Delphos, are both landed,
Hasting to th'court.

LORD So please you, sir, their speed
Hath been beyond account.

LEONTES Twenty-three days
They have been absent: 'tis good speed, foretells
The great Apollo suddenly will have
The truth of this appear. Prepare you, lords;
Summon a session that we may arraign
Our most disloyal lady; for as she hath
Been publicly accused, so shall she have
A just and open trial. While she lives
My heart will be a burden to me. Leave me,
And think upon my bidding. *Exeunt [severally]*

3.1 *Enter* CLEOMENES *and* DION

CLEOMENES The climate's delicate, the air most sweet,
Fertile the isle, the temple much surpassing
The common praise it bears.

206 SD *severally*] *Theobald; not in* F **3.1**] F (*Actus Tertius. Scena Prima.*)

195 well safely or, perhaps, successfully.

197 beyond account (1) without precedent, record-breaking; or, as some editors suggest, (2) without explanation.

197 Twenty-three days A little over three weeks pass in the first half of the play, since the trial scene (3.2), anticipated at 2.3.201 and 204, apparently occurs on the heels of Cleomenes and Dion's return.

199 suddenly speedily.

201–2 Summon . . . lady I.e. convene the court for a judicial proceeding so that we may formally indict ('arraign') Hermione. In light of 'trial' (204), 'arraign' may be understood as 'try' or 'judge', an obsolete meaning first recorded in 1623 (*OED v* 4). Since Leontes has already indicted and tried his wife in his own mind and found her 'most disloyal', the so-called 'just and open trial' (204) is patently *pro forma*. In *Pandosto*, the idea of summoning a court session originates with the lords (Bullough, 170).

204–5 While . . . me Faucit notes (358) the proleptic irony: '[Leontes] had yet to learn how much heavier a burden his heart would have to bear'.

206 think upon i.e. see that 'my bidding' is done, or, as Deighton proposes, 'take care that it is performed'.

Act 3, Scene 1
Shakespeare reworks Greene's cut-and-dried reporting of fact (*Pandosto*, in Bullough, 169–70) into a lyrical moment. In their first onstage appearance, Cleomenes and Dion register a sense of awe that adds another layer to the earlier bureaucratic image of them as men of 'stuffed sufficiency' (2.1.185). See Appendix C, p. 272.

1 delicate delightful (*OED adj* 1). The opening lines echo Duncan's arrival at Macbeth's castle (*Mac.* 1.6.1–10), making the scene 'more than functional; it is connected profoundly to Shakespeare's imaginative universe' (Bartholomeusz, 178). See Supplementary note, p. 252.

2 isle Delphos (see 2.1.183 n.).

3 common usual.

DION I shall report,
For most it caught me, the celestial habits –
Methinks I so should term them – and the reverence
Of the grave wearers. O, the sacrifice!
How ceremonious, solemn, and unearthly
It was i'th'off'ring!

CLEOMENES But of all, the burst
And the ear-deaf'ning voice o'th'oracle,
Kin to Jove's thunder, so surprised my sense
That I was nothing.

DION If th'event o'th'journey
Prove as successful to the Queen – O, be't so! –
As it hath been to us rare, pleasant, speedy,
The time is worth the use on't.

CLEOMENES Great Apollo
Turn all to th'best! These proclamations,
So forcing faults upon Hermione,
I little like.

DION The violent carriage of it
Will clear or end the business when the oracle,

6 sacrifice!] *Capell;* sacrifice, F 8 off'ring!] *Rowe;* off'ring? F 12 so!] *Hanmer (subst.);* so F 15 best!] *Rowe;* best: F

4 caught me i.e., captured my attention; perhaps, however, the speaker's sense of awe is better conveyed by 'caught' = charmed (*OED* catch *v* 37). The idea of having the mind arrested by something astonishing is repeated in 10 in a now obsolete usage of 'surprised' = overwhelmed, captivated (*OED* surprise *v* 1b, where this line is cited).

4 celestial habits heavenly raiment.

6 grave dignified.

8 burst (1) 'blast of thunder' (Dolan), or (2) the oracle's shriek (as in Milton's 'On the Morning of Christ's Nativity', 173–8).

9–11 Citing *Cym.* (5.4.92 SD) and *Temp.* (3.3.52 SD), Pafford notes that 'thunder or thunderous noise is usual with' Shakespearean theophanies; the sound effect might cover the noise of machinery lowering the god from the heavens.

10 sense senses.

11 That I was nothing Shakespeare's original audience 'would have recognized [in these words] . . . the self-surrender that was the right prelude to the operation of divine grace' (Mahood, 80).

11 event outcome.

12 successful In addition to the primary meaning of 'beneficial' or 'helpful', the sense of 'propitious', recorded only in Marlowe's *Jew of Malta* (*OED* successful *adj* 3a), would be appropriate.

14–15 Apollo . . . th'best Proverbial: 'God turns all to good' (Dent G227.1).

15–16 Proclamations . . . Hermione Leontes left the stage at the end of 2.1 preparing to 'speak in public' (2.1.197) his case against Hermione, an action apparently performed offstage (2.3.201–2). In any case, Hermione, who felt Leontes' charges as public at 2.1.98 ('published'), will refer to public accusations at 3.2.99–100.

16 forcing unjustly imposing.

17 violent carriage Pafford and Orgel take 'carriage' to mean Leontes' conduct or management of the whole accusation of Hermione, but it is not clear how violence in this respect will 'clear or end the business' (see next n.). More logically, Dion ascribes this decisive effect to their own action of carrying (*OED* carriage *n* 1) the oracle at a 'breakneck pace' (Andrews).

18 clear or end the business i.e., resolve it one way (Hermione's acquittal) or the other (her execution). The expression was proverbial (see Dent M874).

18 oracle the god's response; at 2.1.185 and 2.3.193, 'oracle' indicated either the human figure functioning as the god's instrument or the place of such human mediation.

Thus by Apollo's great divine sealed up,
Shall the contents discover; something rare
Even then will rush to knowledge. Go; fresh horses!
And gracious be the issue. *Exeunt*

3.2 *Enter* LEONTES, LORDS, *and* OFFICERS

LEONTES This sessions, to our great grief we pronounce,
Even pushes 'gainst our heart. The party tried,
The daughter of a king, our wife, and one
Of us too much beloved. Let us be cleared
Of being tyrannous, since we so openly
Proceed in justice, which shall have due course
Even to the guilt or the purgation.
Produce the prisoner.

21 Go; fresh horses!] *Moorman (subst)*; Goe: fresh horses, F; Go–fresh horses – *Johnson* **3.2**] F *(Scœna Secunda.)* **0 SD**] *Theobald (subst.); Enter . . . Officers: Hermione (as to her Triall) Ladies: Cleomines, Dion.* F

19 great divine high priest. It was he who would officiate at the temple's sacrificial rituals and him to whom, in those rare instances when the oracle's message was not spoken directly to the petitioner, the tasks of writing and sealing up (19) the message would have fallen (see Joseph Fontenrose, *The Delphyic Oracle: Its Responses and Operations with a Catalogue of Responses* [1978], 217–18). In both Greene and Shakespeare, the god's words are written down, becoming a text to be read (3.2.129), a change in transmission that may reflect early modern controversies surrounding translations of the bible (see Miola, esp. 40–5).

20 the . . . discover reveal its contents (Orgel).

21 Go . . . horses Dyce[2]'s insertion of 'To Attendant' here (following Johnson's inclusion of attendants in the scene's opening stage direction) is not necessary since Dion may be understood as saying something like 'Let's go. Fresh horses await!'

22 issue outcome (punning on 'issue' = offspring; see 2.2.44 and 2.3.152). Like 'event' (11), 'issue' drives attention forward to resolution. The emphasis on speed, so pronounced at the end of 2.3, continues in Dion's surety that the oracle's revelation will produce a 'rush to knowledge' (21).

Act 3, Scene 2

In what is traditionally known as the trial scene, though it is not technically such since no evidence is presented (Orgel, 'Perspective', 262), Shakespeare compresses *Pandosto*'s two separate court-room episodes.

0 SD Dessen (124–7), who argues against emending F's massed stage entrance here, thinks the theatrical value is enhanced by having Hermione, Cleomones, and Dion onstage from the beginning, with silence being the desired effect (see 3.2.10n. and Collation) when she is formally summoned. Editorial tradition and performance history, however, favour separate entries for Hermione and her ladies (10 SD) and the two emissaries (121 SD). In Doran, Antony Sher's Leontes, exhausted and demented, limped the length of the stage at the end of 2.3 to begin the court session, 'a terrible parody of his opening energetic entrance, stumbl[ing] up the steps of a huge throne' (Smallwood, 'Performances', 264).

1 sessions judicial sitting (*OED session n* 4).

4 Of us By me.

5 tyrannous Paulina's charge of tyranny (2.3.115–20) evidently still rankles, forcing Leontes to justify himself in the eyes of his public, and, perhaps (as Pafford indicates), even in his own.

7 Even to (1) Equal to; (2) indifferent to; (3) all the way to, right up to. Steevens quotes Richard Roderick, 'Justice shall have its due course; equal to the guilt, or the innocence, which shall appear in the queen upon her trial'. Instead of Roderick's 'innocence', however, 'clearing' or 'acquittal' may be a better gloss for 'purgation' (*OED n* 9).

OFFICER It is his highness' pleasure that the Queen
Appear in person here in court. Silence!

[*Enter*] HERMIONE *as to her trial*, [PAULINA, *and*] LADIES

LEONTES Read the indictment.

OFFICER [*Reads*] 'Hermione, queen to the worthy Leontes, King of Sicilia, thou art here accused and arraigned of high treason in committing adultery with Polixenes, King of Bohemia, and conspiring with Camillo to take away the life of our sovereign lord the King, thy royal husband; the pretence whereof being by circumstances partly laid open, thou, Hermione, contrary to the faith and allegiance of a true subject, didst counsel and aid them for their better safety to fly away by night.'

HERMIONE Since what I am to say must be but that
Which contradicts my accusation, and
The testimony on my part no other
But what comes from myself, it shall scarce boot me
To say, 'not guilty'; mine integrity,
Being counted falsehood, shall, as I express it,
Be so received. But thus: if powers divine
Behold our human actions (as they do)
I doubt not, then, but innocence shall make

10 Silence! | *Rowe (subst.); italicized and set as* SD F **10** SD | *Theobald (subst.); included in opening* SD F **12** SD | *Capell; not in* F **12–19** 'Hermione . . . night.' | F *(Hermione . . . night.)* **24** 'not guilty' | *Capell (subst.);* not guilty F **27** human | F *(* humane*)*

10 Silence F prints *Silence* in the margin as a SD, but editors since Rowe and performances generally treat the word as part of the Officer's dialogue; both Pafford and Schanzer point out that it is a long-standing law-court cry. In adhering to Rowe, Folger cites Crane's scribal practice of italicizing certain words for emphasis and the lack of any other similar stage direction in the Shakespeare canon; but see 'Ring the bell', followed by SD *Bell rings* in *Mac.* 2.3.80.

10 SD *Enter Hermione . . . Ladies* In a radical departure from the traditional approach featuring a stately entrance for an elegantly attired Hermione (as in Kean), Goldie Semple (in William) and Alexandra Gilbreath (in Doran) appeared disheveled and visibly exhausted: the former in rags, barefoot and manacled, her hair now bluntly cropped; the latter wearing a bloody prison smock as a graphic reminder of Hermione's recent labour and delivery.

10 *as to her trial* (1) to stand for her trial, or, perhaps, (2) under guard. Pafford, following Wilson subst., emends to 'guarded'. Dessen-Thompson includes the 'as to' SD as a sub-category of 'as [if]' signals that occasionally serve as the opposite of the more common 'as from', but is more often linked to a specific place or event. Compare F's 'As to the Parliament', *R2* 4.1.0.

16 pretence plot, intention (*OED n* 3); see *Pandosto*, 'but their pretence [in reference to the charges of adultery and conspiracy] being partely spyed' (Bullough, 167). See also *TGV* 2.6.36–7, 'I'll give her father notice / Of their disguising and pretended flight'.

17 circumstances circumstantial evidence (Folger).

22 on my part in my behalf.

23 scarce boot hardly avail.

26 thus i.e., since I am required to speak, this is what I say.

False accusation blush, and tyranny
Tremble at patience. You, my lord, best know,
Whom least will seem to do so, my past life
Hath been as continent, as chaste, as true
As I am now unhappy – which is more
Than history can pattern, though devised
And played to take spectators. For behold me,
A fellow of the royal bed, which owe
A moiety of the throne, a great king's daughter,
The mother to a hopeful prince, here standing
To prate and talk for life and honour fore
Who please to come and hear. For life, I prize it
As I weigh grief, which I would spare; for honour,
'Tis a derivative from me to mine,
And only that I stand for. I appeal
To your own conscience, sir, before Polixenes
Came to your court, how I was in your grace,
How merited to be so; since he came,
With what encounter so uncurrent I

31 Whom] F; Who *Rowe*

30 **patience** the capacity to suffer or endure adversity with composure.

31 **Whom . . . so** Most editors accept Rowe's emendation to 'who', but Hermione may mean 'whom least it will befit': i.e. 'Since you yourself have brought this accusation, you will find it inappropriate to acknowledge my spotless past life'. F2 does not alter to 'who', although it makes parallel changes at 4.4.341 and 4.4.403 where 'who' is indicated (thus suggesting that printers understood the construction with the dative-accusative 'whom'). The line may originally have read 'whom least 'twill seem', the repeated 't' omitted by compositorial error.

32 **continent** temperate, self-controlled.

34 **Than . . . pattern** Than is precedented in narrative or drama (see 35). 'History' carried the general sense of story, true or fictive (*OED n* 1).

35 **take** appeal to, captivate.

36 **which owe** who owns.

37 **moiety** share, part. Given the legal context and Hermione's emphasis on her royal pedigree – daughter of, wife of, and mother to a (future) king (36–8) – she may be pointedly using 'moiety' in a legal or quasi-legal sense to indicate that hers is one of two equal parts (*OED* 1a); compare Gertrude as 'imperial jointress' (*Ham.* 1.2.9). See also 2.3.8 n.

38 **hopeful prince** a prince who holds great promise (see 1.1.29–32).

39 **prate** 'plead idly' (Pafford), as in Volumnia's 'yet here he lets me prate / Like one i'th' stocks' (*Cor.* 5.3.159–60).

40–1 **For . . . spare** 'For' = 'as for', 'weigh' = 'value', and 'spare' = 'avoid' or 'do without', thus yielding Johnson's 'Life is to me now only grief, and as such only is considered by me; I would, therefore, willingly dismiss it.'

41–3 **for . . . for** For Hermione life at this point holds little value, but honour is a completely different matter since that involves her reputation, the only legacy or inheritance ('derivative') that flows directly from her to her children; for that ('[a]nd only that') she will fight and defend herself ('stand for').

44 **conscience** personal, inward, knowledge (*OED n* 1).

47–8 **With . . . thus** This difficult passage, found by Johnson and others to be unintelligible, has for some time (see Halliwell, Staunton, and White) been given the reading 'with what behaviour so unacceptable ('encounter so uncurrent') I have sinned ('strained') that I should be required to appear before you in this manner (i.e., on trial)'. See Supplementary note, p. 252.

Have strained t'appear thus; if one jot beyond
The bound of honour, or in act or will
That way inclining, hardened be the hearts
Of all that hear me, and my near'st of kin
Cry fie upon my grave.

LEONTES I ne'er heard yet
That any of these bolder vices wanted
Less impudence to gainsay what they did
Than to perform it first.

HERMIONE That's true enough,
Though 'tis a saying, sir, not due to me.

LEONTES You will not own it.

HERMIONE More than mistress of
Which comes to me in name of fault, I must not
At all acknowledge. For Polixenes,
With whom I am accused, I do confess
I loved him, as in honour he required,
With such a kind of love as might become
A lady like me; with a love, even such,
So, and no other, as yourself commanded;
Which not to have done I think had been in me
Both disobedience and ingratitude
To you and toward your friend, whose love had spoke
Even since it could speak, from an infant, freely,
That it was yours. Now, for conspiracy,
I know not how it tastes, though it be dished

49 **or . . . or will** either in performance or intention.

52–5 Leontes utters a triple negative: 'ne'er', 'wanted' (lacked), and 'less'. If 'wanted / Less' has the sense of 'were less at a loss for', then the passage might be understood to mean 'I have never heard that such bold crimes were at a loss for the perpetrator's shameless denial of culpability'. Kermode offers: 'The point is that if one is bold enough to commit the crime one will be bold enough to deny it'.

56 **due** pertinent, applicable.

57 **own** own up to, admit.

57–9 **More . . . acknowledge** I.e. I must not accept responsibility for faults (see 3.2.83 n.) that are not mine. I can accept responsibility for only those faults that are mine (that I am 'mistress of'); more than that I cannot acknowledge.

61 **he required** he rightly expected as his due. Hermione's suffering exists on several levels, one of which is the social affront to the propriety and decorum she values and prides herself in following as a lady of rank (62–3); see 3.2.99–100 and 2.1.98.

64 **as yourself commanded** Hermione reminds Leontes that it was at his behest she argued for an extension of Polixenes' stay in Sicilia (1.2.27) out of respect for the love he and Polixenes had openly ('freely', 68) shared since boyhood.

70–1 **dished . . . how** served up or set forth as part of the charge against me, to which I must answer. The culinary imagery, typical of Hermione's verbal style, recalls 1.2.38, 81, and 92–7; see also 108 below.

For me to try how. All I know of it
Is that Camillo was an honest man,
And why he left your court the gods themselves,
Wotting no more than I, are ignorant.

LEONTES You knew of his departure, as you know
What you have underta'en to do in's absence.

HERMIONE Sir,
You speak a language that I understand not.
My life stands in the level of your dreams,
Which I'll lay down.

LEONTES Your actions are my dreams.
You had a bastard by Polixenes,
And I but dreamed it! As you were past all shame –
Those of your fact are so – so past all truth,
Which to deny concerns more than avails; for as
Thy brat hath been cast out, like to itself,
No father owning it – which is indeed
More criminal in thee than it – so thou
Shalt feel our justice, in whose easiest passage
Look for no less than death.

HERMIONE Sir, spare your threats.

74 **Wotting** Knowing.

79–80 Since my life lies within the range or aim ('level') of your delusions ('dreams'), I will give it up voluntarily so that you don't have to shoot me down. See 2.3.5–6 n.

80 **Your . . . dreams** Not only have Leontes' ugly thoughts precluded restful sleep (2.3.1–9, 31), those suspicions, being groundless, are also as insubstantial as dreams. Warren cites this line as an example of how amenable Shakespeare's verse can be 'to a variety of stresses': e.g. Colm Feore (in William) and Tim Piggott-Smith (in Hall) sometimes emphasized 'actions' and at other times 'are'; in Wood, Eric Porter inflected the line as a question with the stress on 'dreams' (Warren, 120).

83 **fact** deed or, perhaps, crime (the most common meaning of 'fact' in the early modern period according to *OED n* 1c). See the corresponding passage in *Pandosto* where 'fact' is explicated as 'monstrous crime' and 'fault' (Bullough, 168).

83–4 **truth . . . avails** i.e. to deny the truth of your crime simply calls attention ('concerns', *OED v* 5) to your guilt, thereby hurting your case rather than helping it. The sense of 'implicate' (*OED* concern *v* 6) may also be present, though the earliest recorded usage dates from later in the seventeenth century.

85 **cast out . . . self** The sense is something like 'sent away, literalizing its state as an "outcast", one rejected by family or friends'. The surrounding emphasis on bastardy (81 and 86) reinforces the notion of 'outcast', making unnecessary the emendation of 'like' to 'left' by some nineteenth-century editors.

86 **owning it** acknowledging paternity.

88 **easiest passage** i.e. 'least painful proceeding' (Folger).

89–114 Hermione's final argument belongs to the medieval tradition known as *ars bene moriendi*, the art of dying well, a series of questions posed to the one about to die in order to ready him or her for departure from this life. The Christian ritual, still practiced in the early modern period, appropriated the classical topos *contemptu mundi*, i.e. a contempt of the world expressed by the stoic distancing of oneself from its essential mutability. The priest or minister would use this topos to persuade those about to die that death was preferable to life. See *MM* 3.1.1–43.

The bug which you would fright me with, I seek.
To me can life be no commodity.
The crown and comfort of my life, your favour,
I do give lost, for I do feel it gone,
But know not how it went. My second joy
And first-fruits of my body, from his presence
I am barred like one infectious. My third comfort,
Starred most unluckily, is from my breast,
The innocent milk in it most innocent mouth,
Haled out to murder; myself on every post
Proclaimed a strumpet; with immodest hatred
The childbed privilege denied, which 'longs
To women of all fashion; lastly, hurried
Here, to this place, i'th'open air, before
I have got strength of limit. Now, my liege,
Tell me what blessings I have here alive
That I should fear to die? Therefore proceed.

95 first-fruits] *Rowe;* first fruits F 104 limit] F; limbs F3

90 **bug** 'An object of terror, usually an imaginary one; a bugbear, hobgoblin, or bogey' (*OED* n^1); the word recalls the 'sprites and goblins' of Mamillius' winter's tale (2.1.25–8).

91 **commodity** benefit, advantage, value (in contrast to its pejorative sense in *John* 2.1.561–98, where the meaning is 'self-interest at the expense of honour and the general welfare' (*King John*, ed. L. A. Beaurline [NCS, 1990], 98).

93 **give** regard as, consider.

95 **first-fruits** the earliest issue of anything, the first products of an endeavour (*OED* first-fruit 2).

97 **Starred . . . unluckily** Ill-starred, i.e., born under a most unlucky star; see 2.1.105.

98 **it** its (Abbott 228).

99 **Haled** Dragged.

99 **post** in reference to the general practice of affixing royal and civic proclamations, public notices, and advertisements to posts.

100 **immodest** The adjective plays against two meanings of *modest*: not harsh or domineering (*OED adj* 1), and moderate, not excessive (*OED adj* 4); the suggestion of intrusion on womanly modesty is also present.

101 **childbed privilege** See 104 n.

102 **all fashion** every walk of life or social rank.

103 **open air** It was generally thought that fresh air did not aid the recuperative process. In contrast to the interior court chamber used by such nineteenth-century directors as Kemble and Macready, Noble seized upon 'open air' to justify an outdoor setting in the rain under black umbrellas. Reading the phrase as modifying 'hurried' rather than 'place', Faucit imagined (360) *how* Hermione was transported from the prison – walking through the streets, 'i'th'open air'–to a hall of justice. An ancient theatre 'as vast as Epidauros' (in Kean), with 'serried rows of silent spectators seated up stage left' (Bartholomeusz, 88, 93), suggested a setting open to the air but still architecturally enclosed.

104 **limit** the end of the (typically) month-long period of bedrest ('childbed privilege', 101), which would have allowed Hermione to regain her 'strength'. In Erasmus' 'The New Mother', Fabulla says 'I've been in bed a month now and I'm strong enough to wrestle' (*Colloquies of Erasmus*, trans. Craig R. Thompson, [1965], 270). Since part of the reason for the newly delivered mother's sequestration and rest during this time was to purge the fluids released during and after birth, Hermione's complaint at being called forth to a public appearance before she has acquired 'strength of limit' may refer more specifically to the end of such weakening lochial discharge (Paster, 192–5).

But yet hear this – mistake me not: no life,
I prize it not a straw, but for mine honour,
Which I would free – if I shall be condemned
Upon surmises, all proofs sleeping else
But what your jealousies awake, I tell you
'Tis rigor, and not law. – Your honours all,
I do refer me to the oracle.
Apollo be my judge.

LORD This your request
Is altogether just. Therefore bring forth,
And in Apollo's name, his oracle.

[*Exeunt Officers*]

HERMIONE The Emperor of Russia was my father.
O, that he were alive, and here beholding
His daughter's trial! that he did but see
The flatness of my misery – yet with eyes
Of pity, not revenge.

[*Enter* OFFICERS, *with* CLEOMENES *and* DION]

OFFICER You here shall swear upon this sword of justice
That you, Cleomenes and Dion, have

112 law.–] *This edn;* law. F 116 SD] *Capell (subst.); not in* F 119 trial!] *Capell;* trial: F 120 misery –] *Oxford;* misery; F 121 SD] *Capell (subst.); not in* F

107 no life apparently part of another forward-connecting grammar (like 3.2.47–9): Hear my assertion, in support not of my life, which is no longer worth anything to me, but of my 'honour' (108), which I am concerned to free from this taint. Life and honour as a pair recall 3.2.39–43: there they are parallel, but here set in contrast.

110 else other (modifying 'proofs').

112 rigor . . . law tyranny . . . justice. Hermione's words echo Bellaria's in *Pandosto* (Bullough, 168).

116 SD Exeunt Officers 'It is not strictly necessary to assume that Cleomenes and Dion are off stage. They could quite well have been in the Court from the outset and be simply brought forward at [121]. However, there is perhaps greater dramatic and stage effect in sending officers for them and bringing them in with some ceremonial at [121] than in having them on stage all the time' (Pafford). But see 3.2.0 SD n.

117 Emperor of Russia In *Pandosto*, the Emperor of Russia is not the father of Bellaria (Shakespeare's Hermione), but of the wife of Egistus (Polixenes). Pafford, citing Charlton, thinks the introduction of Russian ancestry here may have been intended (1) to invest Hermione's plight with additional pathos and majesty and (2) to recall the long-held understanding of tragedy as illustrating the fall of princes. Daryl Palmer demonstrates the topical significance of Hermione's paternity in 'Jacobean Muscovites: Winter, Tyranny, and Knowledge in *WT*', *SQ* 46 (1995), 323–39.

120 flatness downrightness, absoluteness (*OED* 5b). Johnson, however, may be right to link it with abject position: '[H]ow low, how *flat* I am laid by my calamity.'

121 pity for Hermione, as opposed to 'revenge' against Leontes.

Been both at Delphos, and from thence have brought
This sealed-up oracle, by the hand delivered
Of great Apollo's priest; and that since then
You have not dared to break the holy seal,
Nor read the secrets in't.

CLEOMENES *and* DION All this we swear.

LEONTES Break up the seals and read.

OFFICER [*Reads*] 'Hermione is chaste, Polixenes blameless, Camillo a true subject, Leontes a jealous tyrant, his innocent babe truly begotten, and the King shall live without an heir if that which is lost be not found.'

LORDS Now blessèd be the great Apollo!

HERMIONE Praised!

LEONTES Hast thou read truth?

OFFICER Ay, my lord, even so
As it is here set down.

LEONTES There is no truth at all i'th'oracle.
The sessions shall proceed; this is mere falsehood.

[*Enter* SERVANT]

SERVANT My lord the King, the King!

LEONTES What is the business?

SERVANT O sir, I shall be hated to report it.
The Prince your son, with mere conceit and fear
Of the Queen's speed, is gone.

LEONTES How? gone?

SERVANT Is dead.

130 SD] *Capell; not in* F 130–3 'Hermione . . . found.'] F *(Hermione . . . found.)* 134 Apollo!] *Hanmer;* Apollo. F 134 Praised!] *Hanmer;* Praised. F 135 Ay] F *(I)* 135–6 so / As] *Capell; as one line* F 138 SD] *Rowe; not in* F 139 King, the King!] *Hanmer (subst.);* King: the King? F; King! the King! *Riverside*

128 SH A SH that names two speakers rather than reading *Both* directs simultaneous 'choric' speech, which would be appropriate here for the emissaries' short formal declaration at a specific moment in a legal ritual (Honigmann, 123).

130–3 Research on extant oracular messages shows that they were usually unambiguous (Miola, 41 n.32). The message in *WT*, however, is both clear and opaque.

137–8 By having Leontes blasphemously deny the oracle's veracity, in contrast to Pandosto's immediate acceptance and repentance, 'Shakespeare is able to punctuate his trial scene with a crescendo of climaxes, culminating in Paulina's report of the Queen's death' (Schanzer, 184).

138 mere absolute, downright (*OED adj*² 4); the usual sense of 'nothing more than' is present in 141.

141–2 conceit . . . speed thought ('conceit') and worry ('fear') as regards ('of,' Abbott, 173) the Queen's fortune ('speed', *OED n* 3b). As to 'conceit', Orgel suggests an overtone of 'a morbid affection or seizure of the body or mind' (*OED n* 11).

LEONTES Apollo's angry, and the heavens themselves
Do strike at my injustice.

[*Hermione faints*]

How now, there?

PAULINA This news is mortal to the Queen. Look down
And see what death is doing.

LEONTES Take her hence.
Her heart is but o'er-charged; she will recover.
I have too much believed mine own suspicion.
Beseech you, tenderly apply to her
Some remedies for life.

[*Exeunt* PAULINA *and* LADIES *with Officers carrying* HERMIONE]

Apollo, pardon
My great profaneness 'gainst thine oracle.
I'll reconcile me to Polixenes,
New woo my queen, recall the good Camillo,
Whom I proclaim a man of truth, of mercy:
For, being transported by my jealousies
To bloody thoughts and to revenge, I chose
Camillo for the minister, to poison
My friend Polixenes; which had been done,

144 SD] *Malone; at end of line Rowe; not in* F 144 now,] *Theobald;* now F 149 Beseech] F *(* 'Beseech*)* 150 SD] *Folger (subst.); Exeunt* Paulina *and Ladies with* Hermione *Rowe; not in* F 153 woo] F2 *(subst.);* woe F

143 Apollo was the god of sudden death as well as the patron of prophecy.

144 SD While this is the usual placement for Hermione's faint, she could collapse instantly either on first hearing the news ('is gone') or on hearing it clarified ('Is dead'); in the latter case, Leontes might well not notice his wife's fall for a moment, being caught up in shock and grief comparable to hers.

145 **mortal** fatal.

147 **o'er-charged** overcome, distressed.

149 Beginning in 149 and continuing to the end of the scene, Shakespeare deftly modulates the pronouns of address in the dialogue between Leontes and Paulina. Leontes signals the sudden collapse of his delusions by the more respectful 'you' in 149. Soon after her reentry (169), Paulina addresses the king with the familiar form 'thou', breaching courtly etiquette in her rage. As she becomes more apologetic at 215, she returns to the conventionally proper 'you'. Leontes, meanwhile, begins at 212 to address her as 'thou', not in contempt (as in 2.3.113) but as a sign of new intimacy. See Randolph Quirk, 'Shakespeare and the English Language', in Muir and Schoenbaum, 70–72.

150 SD, 169 SD No exits are marked in F, but the most likely place for Hermione's removal from the scene, along with the departure of Paulina and the ladies, is at 'tenderly apply to her / Some remedies for life' (149–50). More problematic is the moment of Paulina's re-entry. A return at 155 would allow her to hear of Leontes' attempted suborning of Camillo, to which she refers at 184–6, but it makes more dramatic sense to delay her re-entrance until just before her outburst at 169 (thereby making her the centre of attention as soon as she brings her devastating news) and assume that the audience would not notice her awareness of something they already know but she cannot.

But that the good mind of Camillo tardied
My swift command, though I with death and with
Reward did threaten and encourage him,
Not doing it and being done. He, most humane
And filled with honour, to my kingly guest
Unclasped my practice, quit his fortunes here –
Which you knew great – and to the hazard
Of all incertainties himself commended,
No richer than his honour. How he glisters
Through my rust! And how his piety
Does my deeds make the blacker!

[*Enter* PAULINA]

PAULINA Woe the while!
O, cut my lace, lest my heart, cracking it,
Break too!
LORD What fit is this, good lady?
PAULINA [*To Leontes*] What studied torments, tyrant, hast for me?
What wheels? racks? fires? What flaying? boiling?

162 humane] F; human F4 **165** hazard] F; certain hazard F2 **168** Through] F; Thorough *Malone* **168** rust!] *Rowe*; rust? F **169** blacker!] *Rowe*; blacker? F **169** SD] *Rowe*; *not in* F **169** while!] *Hanmer*; while: F **170** lest] F3; least F **171** Break . . . lady] *Moorman*; *as two lines* . . . too. / What . . . F **171** too!] *Capell*; too. F **172** SD] *Oxford*; *not in* F

159 tardied delayed (in carrying out) (Folger). *OED* gives 158–60 as the earliest of two recorded uses of *tardy* as a verb.

160–2 though . . . done though I threatened him with death if he did not kill Polixenes and encouraged him with the promise of reward if he did. On the frequency of 'respective constructions' in the play, see 2.3.100–1 n.

164 Unclasped my practice Opened up (revealed) my plot ('practice').

165 Many editors since Rowe (including Pafford and more recently Oxford) follow F2's 'certain hazard', which regularizes the meter, but occasional short (as well as long) lines are not uncommon in Shakespeare's late plays. Besides, as Furness notes, the pentameter rhythm would be satisfied by a necessary pause after 'great'.

166 commended committed, entrusted.

167 No . . . honour Without any riches except his honour.

168 Through 'Through' (often spelled 'thorough') could be pronounced as either one or two syllables; many editors (following Malone) indicate their preference for the latter pronunciation by printing the variant 'thorough'. The editor of F2 inserted 'dark' to modify 'rust' for metrical regularity, an emendation adopted by Rowe and Capell. No 'editorial fussing', as Orgel points out, is required since the feminine enjambment of the preceding line allows the first foot of 168 to be heard as a regular iambic unit.

169–229 While Paulina's grief may be read as genuine (Susan Wright's interpretation in William), its 'chilling dash of rant' may also imply a lack of 'earnestness [that] should be hers if she were really convinced that the queen was truly dead' (Furness, 132n); such was Eileen Atkins's more 'calculated' than impassioned outrage in Hall (Warren, 123–5).

170 lace laces (the strings used to pull together the bodice of a dress or the stays of an underbodice, *OED* stay n^2 3a).

173 Pafford argues that no addition on the order of F2's 'burning' is needed to make the nine-syllable line a full pentameter; the required slow delivery of the five fully stressed syllables – enhanced by several internal caesurae – camouflages the missing syllable, as does the 'r' coloured vowel [γ] in the medial 'fires'.

173 wheels, racks instruments of torture or punishment used to break or stretch the body. See *OED* wheel *n* 2 and *OED* rack n^3.

173 flaying skinning alive.

In leads or oils? What old or newer torture
Must I receive, whose every word deserves
To taste of thy most worst? Thy tyranny,
Together working with thy jealousies –
Fancies too weak for boys, too green and idle
For girls of nine – O think what they have done,
And then run mad indeed, stark mad: for all
Thy bygone fooleries were but spices of it.
That thou betrayedst Polixenes, 'twas nothing;
That did but show thee, of a fool, inconstant,
And damnable ingrateful. Nor was't much
Thou wouldst haue poisoned good Camillo's honour
To have him kill a king; poor trespasses,
More monstrous standing by: whereof I reckon
The casting forth to crows thy baby daughter
To be or none, or little, though a devil
Would have shed water out of fire ere done't.
Nor is't directly laid to thee, the death
Of the young prince, whose honourable thoughts –
Thoughts high for one so tender – cleft the heart
That could conceive a gross and foolish sire
Blemished his gracious dam; this is not, no,
Laid to thy answer. But the last – O lords,

174 newer] F; new F2   181 of it] F; for it F2   190 done't] F (don't)   196–7 last – O . . . woe! –] *Moorman (subst.)*; last: O . . . woe: F

174 leads By itself 'leads' might = cauldrons, but in parallel with 'oils' it more likely means 'molten lead'.

178 green simple, immature.

178 idle foolish, baseless (*OED adj* 2b, c).

181 spices small elements, traces.

183 Johnson paraphrases, 'It show'd thee, *first* a fool, *then* inconstant and ungrateful'.

187 More . . . by Either 'in comparison to ("standing by") others that are worse ("monstrous")', or 'given that others that are worse are waiting to be rehearsed ("standing by")'.

189 or . . . or either (no sin) or (merely another poor trespass).

190 shed . . . fire wept even while burning in hell.

194 gross and foolish perhaps 'grossly foolish' (Folger).

195 gracious dam good (perhaps also with the meaning 'grace-filled') mother. Paulina's amelioration of Leontes' term of contempt (1.2.136 and 2.3.94) may suggest a final link to her husband Antigonus, who had hoped that animals, as surrogate mothers, would tenderly care for the helpless infant (2.3.185–8).

196 Laid . . . answer Proposed as a charge you must answer.

196–8 But . . . dead Hermione's death as a result of the loss of her children (188–9, 191–5) would have been credible apart from romance convention: 'contemporaries had no trouble in believing that parents suffered such deep grief at the deaths of their children that they could die themselves' (Patricia Crawford, 'The Construction and Experience of Maternity in Seventeenth-Century England', in *Women as Mothers in Pre-Industrial England*, ed. Valerie Fildes, 1990, 23, citing S. H. Mendelson, *The Mental World of Stuart Women: Three Studies* [1987], 88).

When I have said, cry woe! – the Queen, the Queen,
The sweet'st, dear'st creature's dead, and vengeance for't
Not dropped down yet.

LORD The higher powers forbid!

PAULINA I say she's dead. I'll swear't. If word nor oath
Prevail not, go and see; if you can bring
Tincture or lustre in her lip, her eye,
Heat outwardly or breath within, I'll serve you
As I would do the gods. – But, O thou tyrant,
Do not repent these things, for they are heavier
Than all thy woes can stir; therefore betake thee
To nothing but despair. A thousand knees,
Ten thousand years together, naked, fasting,
Upon a barren mountain, and still winter
In storm perpetual could not move the gods
To look that way thou wert.

LEONTES Go on, go on.
Thou canst not speak too much; I have deserved
All tongues to talk their bitt'rest.

LORD [*To Paulina*] Say no more.
Howe'er the business goes, you have made fault
I'th'boldness of your speech.

PAULINA I am sorry for't;
All faults I make, when I shall come to know them,
I do repent. Alas, I have showed too much
The rashness of a woman: he is touched
To th'noble heart. What's gone and what's past help

199 forbid!] *Hanmer;* forbid. F 202 eye,] *Rowe;* eye F 204 gods. –] *Folger;* Gods. F 210 perpetual] *Orgel;* perpetuall, F 213 SD] *Oxford; not in* F

202 Tincture . . . lustre I.e., colour to her lip or brightness to her eye. See 2.3.100–1 n.

206 woes . . . stir repentant sorrowings ('woes') can displace ('stir').

207 knees kneelings in prayer.

209 still always.

213 Abbott (354) cites this line as illustrating the use of the noun and infinitive as object; for use as subject, see 5.1.42.

215–29 Paulina's sudden shift from castigation to solicitude and remorse is often interpreted in performance as genuine concern to underline how stricken Leontes is. But an ironic reading that seeks not to diminish but in fact to exacerbate the king's grief and guilt finds support in her use of paralipsis, whereby she inventories Leontes' crimes even while saying she will pass over them, perhaps hoping to evoke the response that in fact follows: Leontes refuses comfort and oblivion and promises to remember and do penance. See Gourlay, in Hunt, 268–9.

219–20 What's . . . grief 'Never grieve for that which you cannot help' is the proverbial expression (Dent G453). Compare *Ant.* 1.2.97, 'Things that are past are done with me'.

Should be past grief. – Do not receive affliction
At my petition; I beseech you, rather
Let me be punished, that have minded you
Of what you should forget. Now, good my liege,
Sir, royal sir, forgive a foolish woman.
The love I bore your queen – lo, fool again! –
I'll speak of her no more, nor of your children;
I'll not remember you of my own lord,
Who is lost too. Take your patience to you,
And I'll say nothing.

LEONTES Thou didst speak but well
When most the truth, which I receive much better
Than to be pitied of thee. Prithee bring me
To the dead bodies of my queen and son.
One grave shall be for both. Upon them shall
The causes of their death appear, unto
Our shame perpetual. Once a day I'll visit
The chapel where they lie, and tears shed there
Shall be my recreation. So long as nature
Will bear up with this exercise, so long
I daily vow to use it. Come, and lead me
To these sorrows. *Exeunt*

220 grief. –] *Oxford (subst.)*; greefe: F **225** again!–] *Capell*; again) F **235** perpetual.] *Rowe (subst.)*; perpetuall) F

220–1 Do not . . . petition Do not be tormented at my urging (i.e. at my entreaty that you suffer perpetual despair, 206–7).

222 minded reminded.

227 remember remind.

228 Paulina's declaration that Antigonus is 'lost' (i.e. dead – see 5.3.135 n.), even though it is too soon for her to despair of his return, somewhat parallels her knowledge of Leontes' suborning of Camillo, related when she was offstage. Parry attributes the comment to her intuition; but if 'lost' = 'ruined, esp. morally or spiritually' (*OED ppl* 1), Paulina may mean that he is damned (i.e. his soul 'lost') for his role in Perdita's fate. See Supplementary note to 2.3.129, and 2.3.191 n.

228 Take . . . you Bear your suffering patiently.

234 causes Leontes is the cause, but the plural may signify his tyranny and jealousies (176–7), along with his blasphemous rejection of the oracle.

235 Our Leontes shifts to the 'royal we' construction, perhaps to indicate the repercussions that go beyond the personal to consume the court at large.

237 recreation diversion, pastime (with an underlying sense of restoration and re-creation).

238 exercise as both habitual action and devotional practice (*OED n* 2 and 4, respectively).

239–40 The lines imply some physical contact between these previously polarized figures; perhaps Paulina takes Leontes' hand as they exit together. Mahood (80) thinks that Leontes should depart in the company of Paulina, Cleomenes, and Dion, an exit that makes for an attractive parallel to the entrance of the same quartet at the beginning of Act 5 (see 5.1.0 SD n.).

3.3 *Enter* ANTIGONUS [*with the*] *child*, [*and a*] MARINER

ANTIGONUS Thou art perfect, then, our ship hath touched upon
The deserts of Bohemia?
MARINER Ay, my lord, and fear
We have landed in ill time: the skies look grimly
And threaten present blusters. In my conscience,
The heavens with that we have in hand are angry
And frown upon's.
ANTIGONUS Their sacred wills be done! Go, get aboard;
Look to thy bark; I'll not be long before
I call upon thee.
MARINER Make your best haste, and go not
Too far i'th'land; 'tis like to be loud weather.
Besides, this place is famous for the creatures
Of prey that keep upon't.
ANTIGONUS Go thou away,
I'll follow instantly.
MARINER I am glad at heart
To be so rid o'th'business. *Exit*

3.3] F (*Scæna Tertia.*) 0 SD] *Rowe (subst.); Enter Antigonus, a Marriner, Babe, Sheepeheard, and Clowne.* F 7 wills] F (wil's)

Act 3, Scene 3

The action moves from Sicilia to Bohemia in a scene that assumes generic significance (see Introduction, pp. 7–8). In *Pandosto*, the baby, set adrift in a small boat, is buffeted about for two days before Fortune, finally taking pity, has the boat wash up on the shores of Sicilia.

1 perfect certain.

2 deserts wilderness (see 2.3.175). As with Delphos, Shakespeare's geography may be faulty, but he would have found a Bohemian seacoast in *Pandosto* (Bullough, 167, 169). Hanmer was so chagrined by the error that he changed the place name to Bithynia, an emendation borrowed by Kean in his celebrated 1856 revival. The link between Bohemia and the sea, however, may be moral rather than geographic; see Orgel's (39, 40) discussion and reproduction of the personal *impresa* of Wenceslaus IV, King of Bohemia (1361–1419), which shows a tempest-tossed ship and the motto *Tempestati Parendum* ('stormy weather must be prepared for').

2–6 'For however much they were a law unto themselves, sailors were traditionally held to pay much deference to the powers above. In [*WT*] it is the mariner who recognises in the storm Apollo's anger at the act of abandoning the infant Perdita' (Mahood, 209).

4 present imminent.

4 In . . . conscience (1) In truth, indeed (Schmidt); or (2) in my mind, to my knowledge (*OED* conscience *n* 1). The modern sense of an internal moral compass may also be present.

5 have in hand are doing.

10 i'th'land inland.

10 loud noisy (Orgel), in being 'windy', 'rough', or 'tempestuous' (the usual glosses, though *OED* records no such usage).

12 keep dwell.

13–14 I . . . business As a facilitator in 'ungentle business' (33), the Mariner might recall several reluctant, conscience-stricken executors/murderers who, nevertheless, are willing to carry out malevolent royal orders: see *2H6* 3.2.3–4; *R3* 1.4.107–46, 271–8, and 4.3.1–21; and *John* 4.1.6–7, 85.

14–57 Despite his complicity in a heinous act, lines in this speech encourage a degree of sympathy for Antigonus (14, 26–9, 45, 46–8, and 51–2).

ANTIGONUS Come, poor babe.
I have heard, but not believed, the spirits o'th' dead
May walk again. If such thing be, thy mother
Appeared to me last night, for ne'er was dream
So like a waking. To me comes a creature,
Sometimes her head on one side, some another;
I never saw a vessel of like sorrow
So filled and so becoming. In pure white robes
Like very sanctity, she did approach
My cabin where I lay; thrice bowed before me,
And, gasping to begin some speech, her eyes
Became two spouts; the fury spent, anon
Did this break from her: 'Good Antigonus,
Since fate, against thy better disposition,
Hath made thy person for the thrower-out
Of my poor babe, according to thine oath,
Places remote enough are in Bohemia;
There weep, and leave it crying; and for the babe

26–35 'Good . . . more'] *Theobald (subst.)*; Good . . . more F 28 thrower-out] F2; Thower-out F

15–18 Citing this passage as establishing 'that Hermione is, at this point in the play, dead', Siemon (in Bloom, 56) points out that Shakespearean ghosts who appear in dreams are always those of the dead. But the phenomenon of walking spirits of the living – what in modern parapsychology is called bilocation – would not have been unknown in the seventeenth-century; as an example, Orgel cites Walton's *Life of Donne*, in which we learn 'how in Paris in 1612 the poet was visited by the spirit of his wife, who was alive in London at the time'. Early Catholic hagiography is rich in stories of saints who, while living, were reported present in more than one place at the same time (e.g. St Anthony of Padua, St Ambrose of Milan, and St Severus of Ravenna).

15–16 I . . . be Antigonus' scepticism (like Horatio's in *Ham.* 1.1.23–5) links him to the Protestant tradition, according to which ghosts, if they existed at all, were delusions, demoniacal in origin; the Catholic position was more amenable to walking spirits of the dead, often regarded as souls undergoing the trials of purgatory, the place of temporal punishment for those who die without having fully expiated their sins (see *Ham.* 1.5.10–13).

18 So . . . waking So real.

20 vessel person, as a human receptacle (*OED n* 3); see *JC* 5.5.13, 'Now is that noble vessel [Brutus] full of grief'. The term, however, was frequently used of women (e.g. *Rom.* 1.1.16, 'the weaker vessels' – as derived from 1 Peter 3.7). Pafford, citing *Rom.* 2.4.102, likens a woman in flowing white robes (21) to 'vessel' = 'a ship moving easily under all sail', but 'becoming' in the next line makes such a nautical image problematic (see 21 n.).

21 becoming While some editors gloss 'becoming' as meaning either 'beautiful' (in her sorrow) or 'appropriate' (her fullness of sorrow being 'beautifully appropriate'), others have suspected an error for some word denoting 'overflowing'; Shakespeare, however, seems rather to be thinking of a 'vessel' (see 20 n.) replete with emotion ('filled') yet still augmenting it ('becoming' filled), as in *AWW* 1.3.202–4, 'Yet in this captious and intenible sieve / I still pour in the waters of my love / And lack not to lose still'.

22 very sanctity true saintliness.

23 cabin berth.

25 fury intense passion.

26–35 In recent performances, Hermione is often heard delivering some, if not all, of these lines (e.g. Donnellan, Kulick, Kahn, and Warchus; see illustration 9, p. 13).

31 for because.

Is counted lost for ever, Perdita
I prithee call't. For this ungentle business
Put on thee by my lord, thou ne'er shalt see
Thy wife Paulina more.' And so with shrieks
She melted into air. Affrighted much,
I did in time collect myself, and thought
This was so, and no slumber. Dreams are toys,
Yet for this once, yea superstitiously,
I will be squared by this. I do believe
Hermione hath suffered death, and that
Apollo would, this being indeed the issue
Of King Polixenes, it should here be laid,
Either for life or death, upon the earth
Of its right father. Blossom, speed thee well;

[*He lays down the child*]

There lie, and there thy character; there these,

[*He lays down a bundle and a box*]

Which may, if fortune please, both breed thee, pretty,
And still rest thine. [*Thunder*] The storm begins; poor
wretch,

45 its] F *(* it's*)* 45 SD] *Rowe (subst.); not in* F 46 SD] *Folger (subst.); not in* F*; laying down a bundle Johnson; He lays down a box (after* character*) Oxford* 48 SD] *Wilson (subst.; after* 48 *Dyce); not in* F

32 counted considered, regarded (*OED* count *v* 3).

32 Perdita The name means 'she who is lost'.

33–5 For . . . more Paulina intuited this fatal consequence at 3.2.227–8.

33 ungentle violent, unkind (perhaps with the sense of 'unnatural').

38 was so was real (and not a dream).

38 toys trifles.

39 superstitiously In abandoning the sceptical position of Protestantism regarding ghosts (see 15–16 n.), Antigonus sees himself, at least for the moment, believing like a Catholic, hence 'superstitiously'. For another reference to superstition that contrasts Catholic and Protestant views, see 5.3.42–4.

40 squared ruled, directed (*OED* square *v* 4). Compare 5.1.52.

40–5 Antigonus considers Hermione's appearance to be proof of her death; it's not as clear, however, why he sees it as evidence of her adultery, the baby he now views as the 'right'(= true) 'issue' (= offspring) of Polixenes. Perhaps, in temporarily taking the Catholic view toward ghosts, he sees Hermione as a spirit from purgatory, still in need of expiating her earthly sins, specifically, in his mind, the sin of adultery.

42 would wishes.

44 for . . . death to live or die.

44 earth land.

46 character something written (perhaps a note or a scroll bearing the name Hermione has directed him to give the baby). Folger reads as 'letters' (presumably with 5.2.30–1 in mind), a frequent choice in modern productions (e.g. Howell and Kahn). The infant's name must be graphically indicated because, with Antigonus' death, Perdita's adoptive family would otherwise be ignorant of it; and while the Shepherd may be illiterate (3.3.69), his son is not (see 4.3.36–46).

46–8 these . . . thine 'May this gold not only serve for your upbringing ['breed thee'], but a portion of it remain unspent ['still rest'] for your subsequent use' (Moorman).

46 SD bundle . . . box i.e. the 'fardel' and 'box' referred to in 4.4.718–20.

That for thy mother's fault art thus exposed
To loss, and what may follow! Weep I cannot,
But my heart bleeds, and most accursed am I
To be by oath enjoined to this. Farewell.
The day frowns more and more; thou'rt like to have
A lullaby too rough. I never saw
The heavens so dim by day.

[*Bear roars*]

A savage clamour!
Well may I get aboard.

[*Enter bear*]

This is the chase;
I am gone forever! *Exit pursued by a bear*

[*Enter* a SHEPHERD]

SHEPHERD I would there were no age between ten and three-and-twenty, or that youth would sleep out the rest; for there is nothing in the between but getting wenches with child, wronging the ancientry, stealing, fighting – hark you now! Would any but these boiled-brains of nineteen and two-and-twenty hunt

50 follow!] *Moorman;* follow. F 51 accursed] F *(*accurst*)* 55 SD] *Collier; not in* F; *Noise without of Hunters and Dogs Staunton* 55 clamour!] F3; clamour? F 56 SD] *Sisson; not in* F 57 for ever!] *Pafford;* for ever. F 57 SD *Enter* a SHEPHERD] F2; *not in* F 61 fighting–] *Rowe;* fighting, F 61 now!] *Moorman;* now: F

50 **loss** ruin, abandonment (see 2.3.191).

50 **Weep I cannot** As Hermione's spirit had ordered him to do (31).

55 SD–56 The interpretive issue in these lines has to do with the referent of 'savage clamour'. 'Chase' = hunted animal (*OED n* 4a), and when taken with the Shepherd's comment about a nearby hunting party (61–3), suggested to Johnson that Antigonus may first hear the 'savage clamour' of dogs and hunting horns, and then see the hunted bear. But as Schanzer notes, the roar of the bear better fits 'savage' and motivates Antigonus' fearful response ('Well may I get aboard') as hunting sounds would not. Another possibility is the thunder of the storm (48 SD, 54). Folger follows Orgel in suggesting a combination of hunting sounds and thunder, while Kahn's 2002 production mixed thunder claps with the ferocious growl of a bear. The combination of all three sounds would produce a 'savage clamour'.

57 **gone** For 'gone' = 'dead', see 3.2.142.

57 SD I In what may be the most famous stage direction in the canon, a transformation of sorts takes place as Antigonus, the newly discovered prey or hunted creature, switches places with the bear, literally becoming the 'chase' (56). For the emblematic significance of the bear and the theatrical logistics surrounding it in *WT*'s performance history, see Introduction, pp. 30–3.

58 From here to the end of the scene, verse gives way to prose as befits the social status of the speakers and the shift from tragic turbulence to the more comic everyday concerns of the shepherds (see Vickers, 413, 416–20).

59 **the rest** the years between ten and twenty-three.

61 **ancientry** older generation, elders.

61 **hark** A sound cue may be intended. Anticipating 'hunt' in the next line, Riverside (after White[2]) inserts a SD 'Horns'.

62 **boiled-brains** brains addled by overheating; see *Temp.* 5.1.59–60 and *MND* 5.1.4.

this weather? They have scared away two of my best sheep, which I fear the wolf will sooner find than the master; if any where I have them, 'tis by the seaside, browsing of ivy. Good luck, an't be thy will!

[*He sees the child*]

What have we here? Mercy on's, a bairn! A very pretty bairn. A boy or a child, I wonder? A pretty one, a very pretty one – sure some scape; though I am not bookish, yet I can read waiting-gentlewoman in the scape. This has been some stair-work, some trunk-work, some behind-door work; they were warmer that got this than the poor thing is here. I'll take it up for pity; yet I'll tarry till my son come; he hallooed but even now. Whoa-ho-hoa!

Enter CLOWN

CLOWN Hilloa, loa!

SHEPHERD What, art so near? If thou'lt see a thing to talk on when thou art dead and rotten, come hither. What ail'st thou, man?

CLOWN I have seen two such sights, by sea and by land! but I am not to say it is a sea, for it is now the sky; betwixt the firmament and it you cannot thrust a bodkin's point.

SHEPHERD Why, boy, how is it?

63 scared] *Rowe (subst.)*; scarr'd F 66 an't] Pope[2]; and't F 66 will!] *Capell*; will) F 66 SD] *Schanzer (after Dyce*[2] *subst., following* here*)*; *not in* F 67 bairn!] Rowe *(subst.)*; Barne? F 73 hallooed] F *(* hallow'd*)* 77 land!] *Hudson*; land: F

63–4 Contemporary audiences would likely have recognized the allusion to the parable of the lost sheep (Matt. 18.11–13), later parodied in the Shepherd's 'Let my sheep go' (3.3.111).

65 **ivy** perhaps, sea holly or seaweed (Folger). The young leaves of the former, according to Gerard (*The herball, or generall historie of plantes*, 1597), are 'good to be eaten'; and 'wild sheep . . . will graze on' seaweed (Orgel). Shakespeare's use of 'ivy' recalls *Pandosto*'s 'sea Ivy' (Bullough, 173).

65–6 **Good . . . will** An invocation seeking help from the gods in finding the sheep; or, perhaps, an exclamation at the sight of the baby – a reading that F encourages by treating 'an't be thy will' as a parenthetical expression, the 'what' interrogative of the next line being part of the same sentence.

67 **bairn** child. According to *OED*, the word expresses 'relationship, rather than age', thus ruling out the gloss 'baby'. De Grazia and Parker, respectively, discuss the aural link with 'bear', iterative throughout the text.

68 **child** dialect for female infant (*OED* sv *n* 1b). Pafford cites Greene, *James the Fourth* 5.4.103, 'Hob your sonne, and Sib [a female] your nutbrowne childe' (ed. Norman Sanders, 1970).

69 **scape** sexual transgression (the issue or result of which is the baby).

70–1 **some stair-work . . . behind-door work** i.e. furtive copulation ('work') in out-of-the-way places (like the back-stairs, in [or on] a trunk, behind doors).

72 **got** begot.

73 **hallooed** shouted.

73 SD For the generic name 'Clown', see List of Characters, p. 81.

79 **bodkin** (1) a small pointed instrument, a needle, or (2) a short pointed weapon, a dagger.

CLOWN I would you did but see how it chafes, how it rages, how it takes up the shore – but that's not to the point. O, the most piteous cry of the poor souls! Sometimes to see 'em, and not to see 'em; now the ship boring the moon with her mainmast, and anon swallowed with yeast and froth, as you'd thrust a cork into a hogshead. And then for the land-service, to see how the bear tore out his shoulder-bone, how he cried to me for help and said his name was Antigonus, a nobleman. But to make an end of the ship, to see how the sea flap-dragoned it; but first, how the poor souls roared, and the sea mocked them; and how the poor gentleman roared, and the bear mocked him, both roaring louder than the sea or weather.

SHEPHERD Name of mercy, when was this, boy?

CLOWN Now, now! I have not winked since I saw these sights; the men are not yet cold under water, nor the bear half dined on the gentleman – he's at it now.

SHEPHERD Would I had been by to have helped the old man.

CLOWN I would you had been by the ship side to have helped her; there your charity would have lacked footing.

82 shore–] *Schanzer;* shore, F; shore! *Capell* 83 souls! Sometimes] *Kermode;* souls, sometimes F 94 now!] F *(now:)* 96 gentleman –] *Orgel;* Gentleman: F 98–9] *As aside Theobald*

81 **chafes** fumes, frets (*OED* chafe *v* 10c).

82 **takes up** takes possession of, occupies.

84 **boring** piercing.

85 **anon** immediately.

85 **yeast** foam.

86 **hogshead** a large cask of liquid.

86 **land-service** Continuing his juxtaposition of the awful events 'by sea and by land' (77), the Clown likens Antigonus to a soldier engaged in military service on land in contrast to the mariners. There may also be a pun on 'service' as the food set forth for a meal (*OED* service *n*[1] 27b), Antigonus being the dish served up for the bear; compare *Ham.* 4.3.23–4, 'your fat king and your lean beggar is but variable service, two dishes, but to one table'.

89 **flap-dragoned it** swallowed (the ship) as though it were a flapdragon (= flaming raisin) caught from burning brandy, the flame extinguished by closing the mouth and swallowing (Johnson).

90 **mocked** imitated derisively (i.e. roared back).

94 **winked** blinked.

97 **old** The Shepherd in fact has no way of knowing Antigonus' age, although the reader/spectator might recall 2.1.173 and 2.3.161, 165. Steevens supposes that the Shepherd 'infers the age of Antigonus from his inability to defend himself; or perhaps Shakespeare, who was conscious that he himself designed Antigonus for an old man, has inadvertently given this knowledge to the Shepherd who had never seen him'. Capell thinks it suits the character, the 'father presumes he was *old* because he himself was' (*Notes*, 2.172). Perhaps the same actor played both parts, a doubling found in several modern productions (see Appendix B, p. 266).

98–9 Clown's ironic response (which Theobald thought an aside) suggests that his father's sympathy would have been equally inefficacious in saving Antigonus or the ship's crew. Punning on charitable *foundations*, the Clown points out that his father's charity lacks 'footing' literally in the deep water, figuratively (footing = 'basis in ability') in both cases. The Clown's good nature and compassion in this scene and in 4.3 argue against a reading that would imply a desire on his part for the Shepherd's drowning so that he could inherit.

SHEPHERD Heavy matters, heavy matters! But look thee here, boy. Now bless thyself; thou met'st with things dying, I with things newborn. Here's a sight for thee: look thee, a bearing-cloth for a squire's child;

[*He points to the box*]

look thee here, take up, take up, boy; open't.

[*The Clown picks up the box*]

So, let's see – it was told me I should be rich by the fairies. This is some changeling. Open't; what's within, boy?

CLOWN [*Opening the box*] You're a made old man! If the sins of your youth are forgiven you, you're well to live. Gold, all gold!

SHEPHERD This is fairy gold, boy, and 'twill prove so. Up with't, keep it close. Home, home, the next way. We are lucky, boy, and to be so still requires nothing but secrecy. Let my sheep go. Come, good boy, the next way home.

CLOWN Go you the next way with your findings, I'll go see if the bear be gone from the gentleman, and how much he hath eaten. They are never curst but when they are hungry. If there be any of him left, I'll bury it.

100 matters!] Moorman; matters: F **103** SD] *Oxford; not in* F **104** SD] *Orgel (subst.); not in* F **105** see–] *Orgel;* see, F **107** SD] *Oxford (subst.); not in* F **107** made] *Theobald;* mad F **107** man!] *Orgel;* man: F

100 Heavy . . . matters The Shepherd is perhaps indirectly rebuking the Clown for his jocular attitude toward the suffering he observed.

101–2 thou . . . newborn For the generic and structural significance of this frequently cited passage, see Introduction, pp. 7–8.

102 bearing-cloth a christening gown. Pafford speculates that the garment is Hermione's mantle (see 5.2.29).

106 changeling applicable either to the ugly fairy child secretly left by fairies or to the beautiful human one taken in exchange (the case here and in *MND* 2.1.23); at 4.4.657, the word refers to the one substituted, thus marking Perdita's deflated value in the eyes of her adopted family.

107 Since *OED* records that *mad* could be written as *made*, perhaps Theobald's widely accepted emendation should be seen as a variant spelling (see, e.g., *1H4* 2.4.492, where some later editors follow F3 in emending Q and F's 'made' to 'mad'). That it means 'made' here in the sense of 'assured prosperity' is supported, as Farmer first noted (in Furness), by the parallel wording in *Pandosto*, where the old man tells his wife they are 'made for ever' (Bullough, 174).

107–8 If . . . you The biblical allusion is either to Job 20.11 ('His bones are full of the sinne of his youth') or to Ps. 25.6 ('Oh remember not the sinnes and offences of my youth'); Shaheen prefers the latter.

108 well to live 'well off as regards living' (i.e. prosperous), analogous to the modern expression 'well to do' (Abbott 356); see *MV* 2. 2. 55.

109 'twill . . . so i.e. the prophecy that the fairies will make him rich will turn out to be true.

110–11 close . . . secrecy As in *Pandosto*, the shepherd emphasizes the need to keep his new-found wealth a secret ('close') and urges the nearest ('next') route home. Tradition held that to divulge the news of gold given by the fairies would result in the loss of their favour (Staunton).

111 still always.

115 curst fierce, vicious (*OED* cursed *ppl a* 4b).

115–17 If . . . deed While all religions show respect for the dead, calling burial a 'good deed' may allude specifically to one of the seven 'corporal works of mercy' important in Catholic teaching and a prominent subject in medieval art.

SHEPHERD That's a good deed. If thou mayest discern by that which is left of him what he is, fetch me to th' sight of him.

CLOWN Marry, will I; and you shall help to put him i'th'ground.

SHEPHERD 'Tis a lucky day, boy, and we'll do good deeds on't.

Exeunt

4.1 *Enter* TIME, *the Chorus*

TIME
I that please some, try all; both joy and terror
Of good and bad, that makes and unfolds error,
Now take upon me, in the name of Time,
To use my wings. Impute it not a crime
To me or my swift passage that I slide
O'er sixteen years and leave the growth untried
Of that wide gap, since it is in my power
To o'erthrow law, and in one self-born hour
To plant and o'erwhelm custom. Let me pass

119 Marry] F ('Marry) **120** we'll] F (wee'l) **120** SD] F; *Exeunt severally Capell* **4.1**] F (*Actus Quartus. Scena Prima.*) **2** makes] F; mask *Theobald*

Shakespeare may also have in mind the classical idea (central to Sophocles' *Antigone*) that failure to bury would doom the soul to wander forever and never find peace. Clown's intention, backed by his father, thus might indicate that Antigonus has found redemption.

118 what he is i.e., his identity and social rank.

119 Marry Indeed, certainly (originally a mild oath meaning 'by the Virgin Mary').

Act 4, Scene 1

Many editors and critics have found Time's speech unsatisfactory and suspected that it is an interpolation. Its rhymed couplets stand apart from the rest of the play's verse structure. Kittredge (432), however, is among those who defend it as in character for Time, a long-winded ancient, 'senile but self-assured, ridiculous but triumphant'. See Introduction, pp. 34–40.

1 try test. Time as the tester of all things was proverbial (Dent T336).

1–2 both . . . bad the joy and terror of good and bad alike. As Schanzer notes, 'This accords . . . with the words that follow: by making error, Time is the joy of the bad and the terror of the good; by unfolding it, the terror of the bad and the joy of the good'. See *Luc.* 995, 'O time, thou tutor both to good and bad'.

3–4 Now . . . wings The emblematic figure who has been teasing the audience for two and a half lines with his riddling attributes now reveals his name in the presentational style of medieval morality drama and Tudor moral interludes. See *Per.* 4. Cho. 47, and illustrations 13 and 19 (pp. 16 and 35 respectively).

4–15 Impute . . . it Time stakes out its position as the one to whom law and custom are subject, both coming into existence in time and changing over time, and therefore having no permanent value. Since Capell, many commentators see a more specific allusion to the unity of time, a dramatic convention that required the action of a tragedy to be limited to the hours of the actual performance, or at most to a single day spanning either twelve or twenty-four hours.

6 growth untried Johnson glosses 'growth' as 'progression' and 'untried' as 'unexamined' (see *OED* try *v* 5a). Understood in terms of narrative development, the words indicate that Time intends no detailed explanation of what has happened over the years. But 'growth' – along with its variants 'growing' (16) and 'grown' (24) and the semantically linked 'plant'(9) and 'freshest' (13) – also announces the sense of spring and the power of nature that give Bohemia its atmospheric character. In addition, the sense of 'growth' as moral development may provide the first hint of Leontes' interior progress in the 'wide gap' of sixteen years (see Introduction, pp. 41–7).

8 one self-born hour i.e. one hour to which Time itself has given birth. 'All hours were thought of as the offspring of time' (Schanzer).

9 o'erwhelm overturn, overthrow.

9 pass proceed (in narration) without challenge or censure (*OED* *v* 1e, 15).

The same I am ere ancient'st order was,
Or what is now received. I witness to
The times that brought them in; so shall I do
To th'freshest things now reigning, and make stale
The glistering of this present as my tale
Now seems to it. Your patience this allowing,
I turn my glass, and give my scene such growing
As you had slept between; Leontes leaving –
Th'effects of his fond jealousies so grieving
That he shuts up himself – imagine me,
Gentle spectators, that I now may be
In fair Bohemia; and remember well
I mentioned a son o'th'King's, which Florizel
I now name to you; and with speed so pace

17–19 leaving – . . . himself–] *Staunton (subst.)*; leaving . . . jealousies, . . . himselfe. F

10–11 The same . . . received I.e. I am the same I was before the oldest laws and customs were established or what is now generally accepted ('received'). An early modern audience might have heard in Time's account of himself as forever changeless the scriptural 'I am that I am' (Exodus 3.14) and 'Before Abraham was, I am' (John 8.58). See also *R3* 5.3.183.

13–15 and make . . . it i.e. and make old and dull ('stale') the shiny newness ('glistering') of present custom and convention just as my tale now seems out of fashion. It is unclear whether 'tale' refers to the play as a whole – an old-fashioned 'winter's tale' – or more narrowly to Time's speech, which seems 'stale' in comparison with either the play it interrupts (Kermode) or the 'glistering' of what is to follow in the sheep-shearing sequence (Furness).

16 glass hourglass. In turning the hourglass, Time completes the generic reversal of action begun in 3.3.101–2 (see Introduction, pp. 7–8, and illustration 21, p. 39).

16–17 give . . . between Reading 'scene' = 'play' and 'growing' = advancement, Folger paraphrases as 'advance the action of the play as if you had slept between acts'.

17 Leontes leaving i.e. leaving Leontes. Time as playwright moves the dramatic action away from the character who dominated the Sicilian sequence to a new group of characters, asking his audience to imagine themselves in Bohemia. Wood appears to be the first of several directors (e.g. Lapine and Kulick) to show a mournful Leontes in the background (Bartholomeusz, 205–7).

18 The effects of Leontes' foolish ('fond') jealousy so grieve him ('that he shuts up himself', 19). *Per.* 5.1.23–6 offers a possible clue into the regimen of Leontes' self-imposed isolation: silence and fasting.

21–2 and remember . . . King's Time asks the audience to remember his earlier mention of a son of Polixenes, but this is Time's first appearance in the play as we have it. Consequently, some editors have suggested emendations, most notably Hudson's 'and remember well / A mentioned son o'th'King's' (on the theory that the compositor mistakenly repeated the 'I' of the next line and then interpolated 'a' for sense [Furness]). But if, like Gower in *Per.*, Time is a narrator/playwright, he ventriloquizes the entire dialogue – hence he 'mentions' all that is spoken or represented in the play (see Introduction, pp. 34–8). Mahood speculates (227 n.16) that Shakespeare may have played Time himself, with the 'I' here slipping from character-reference to author-reference; she also points out (35) that 'since all events under the sun are the products of Time, he can legitimately consider himself the originator of the entire action, including the talk about Florizel in [1.2]'.

23 pace proceed or advance (*OED v* 1b, citing this line). Some visual accompaniment to Time's speech, with Florizel and Perdita appearing as they are mentioned, has become the theatrical norm; see also 17 n.

To speak of Perdita, now grown in grace
Equal with wond'ring. What of her ensues
I list not prophesy; but let Time's news
Be known when 'tis brought forth. A shepherd's daughter
And what to her adheres, which follows after,
Is th'argument of Time. Of this allow,
If ever you have spent time worse ere now;
If never, yet that Time himself doth say
He wishes earnestly you never may. *Exit*

4.2 *Enter* POLIXENES *and* CAMILLO

POLIXENES I pray thee, good Camillo, be no more importunate. 'Tis a sickness denying thee anything, a death to grant this.

CAMILLO It is fifteen years since I saw my country; though I have for the most part been aired abroad, I desire to lay my bones

4.2| F *(Scena Secunda.)*

24 grace In this initial reference to the grown-up Perdita, 'grace' enjoys a range of meanings from beauty, physical charm, and favour to virtue and sanctity (a spectrum that picks up on the word's earlier usage by the 'gracious' Hermione [e.g. 1.2.98, 104; 2.1.122]). Shaheen (727) detects a possible allusion to 2 Peter 3.18, 'But grow in grace'.

25 Equal . . . wond'ring 'To a degree demanding admiration' (Kermode). Perdita's capacity to inspire wonder is borne out at 4.4.109–10, 143–6, and 157–9.

26 list not choose not to (for the omission of *to*, see Abbott 349).

27 brought forth While Time is traditionally depicted as an old man, some productions (e.g., Reinhardt, Bergman, Syer, Donellan, and Cohen) represent the role as female.

27 daughter 'Daughter' and 'after' (28) may have been heard as a rhyme in Shakespeare's time; see *Shr.* 1.1.239–40 and *Lear* 1.4.317–21.

28 to . . . adheres (and what) relates to or concerns her.

29 argument subject-matter, theme (*OED n* 6).

29–32 'Allow' governs both 'this' and (elliptically) 'that Time himself doth say' (Pafford), but the meaning shifts from 'admit or acknowledge' to 'permit or grant': Admit this, that you have passed the time less pleasantly before now; if you never have, then permit Time to indulge himself by wishing with deep sincerity that you never will.

Act 4, Scene 2
The second phase of the dramatic action gets under way with a scene reminiscent of 1.1: a private, informal exchange at court, cast in expository prose. Hall detected 'a sense of waste hang[ing] over the scene', the effect of the intervening sixteen years on Camillo and Polixenes (Warren, 129).

1–2 The scene opens in mid-conversation ('be no more importunate'), Camillo evidently persisting with a request that sickens Polixenes to refuse (presumably because of the debt he owes Camillo) but which would kill him to grant (because of the friendship and counsel Camillo has long provided).

3–7 Besides motivating Camillo's later plan to aid Florizel and Perdita (4.4.488–93), these lines (like 4.1.17–19) keep present the image of the penitent Leontes.

3 fifteen years At 4.1.6 Time says 'sixteen.' The contradiction may be explained either by scribal or compositorial misreading of xvi as xv (Orgel), or as the result of Shakespeare's forgetfulness or indecision while writing (Honigmann, *Stability*, 138–9). Shakespeare settles on sixteen at 5.3.31 and 50, which is the temporal span in *Pandosto* (Bullough, 175) and the one recorded in Forman (see Appendix A).

4–5 for . . . there Camillo seems to intend a general contrast between his abode while living and his resting place when he no longer breathes the air. Some editors read 'been aired abroad' as 'breathed foreign air', but that does not account for the puzzling phrase 'for the most part'. Perhaps the phrase can be read as 'for all these years' to indicate that Camillo does not consider Bohemia 'home'.

there. Besides, the penitent king, my master, hath sent for me, to whose feeling sorrows I might be some allay (or I o'erween to think so), which is another spur to my departure.

POLIXENES As thou lov'st me, Camillo, wipe not out the rest of thy services by leaving me now. The need I have of thee thine own goodness hath made. Better not to have had thee than thus to want thee; thou, having made me businesses which none without thee can sufficiently manage, must either stay to execute them thyself or take away with thee the very services thou hast done – which if I have not enough considered (as too much I cannot), to be more thankful to thee shall be my study, and my profit therein the heaping friendships. Of that fatal country Sicilia prithee speak no more, whose very naming punishes me with the remembrance of that penitent, as thou call'st him, and reconciled king my brother, whose loss of his most precious queen and children are even now to be afresh lamented. Say to me, when saw'st thou the Prince Florizel my son? Kings are no less unhappy, their issue not being gracious, than they are in losing them when they have approved their virtues.

11 thee;] *Kermode;* thee, F; thee. *Rowe*

6 **feeling** acute, heartfelt.

6 **be some allay** i.e. bring some comfort, give some relief.

6 **o'erween** presume. Riverside suggests 'am conceited enough'.

8 **As thou lov'st me** A hint of jealousy may be present in Polixenes' dismay over Camillo's continuing affection for his old master.

11 **want** be without.

11–14 **thou . . . done** i.e. 'you, having started affairs for me ["made me businesses"], which no one but yourself can carry out ["sufficiently manage"], must either stay and see these things through yourself or else take away with you the very good ["services"] you have done' (Pafford). 'Made me businesses', 'sufficiently manage', and 'profit' (16) introduce a commercial element that pervades the world of Bohemia both at court and in the country; see also 30–41 n. and Introduction, p. 19.

14 **considered** rewarded.

15 **study** goal, concern.

16 **heaping friendships** Finding the phrase 'irreducibly ambiguous', Folger raises three possibilities: (1) an increase in Camillo's friendly services; (2) an increase in the friendship between the two men; or (3) an increase 'in the friendships, or alliances that Camillo, as Polixenes' agent, will make for the king with others'.

16 **fatal** mortal, death-dealing (to Mamillius, Hermione, and – by design – Polixenes). See *OED adj* 6.

18 **as thou . . . him** Pafford suggests an unspoken 'rightly' after 'thou', a conjecture which finds support in the following references to 'reconciled' and 'my brother', thus indicating a sad but sympathetic Polixenes.

19 **reconciled** Evidently, a rapprochement of some type has occurred, perhaps only on the level of diplomatic relations.

20, 25 **are** i.e. is. The proximity of the plural 'queen and children' (20) and 'affairs' (25) confuses the verb (see Abbott 412).

21 **when . . . son** Polixenes' inquiry about Florizel recalls Bolingbroke asking after his own errant son in *R2* 5.3.1–4, and Cymbeline's query concerning the absent Imogen (*Cym.* 3.5.29–35).

22 **gracious** pleasing in manner and conduct; virtuous; princely. See 4.4.8. Pafford notes Hal's use of the phrase 'ungracious boy' when role-playing his father's likely reception of him (*1H4* 2.4.445).

23 **approved** proved. For Polixenes, Florizel's sudden waywardness is just as much a burden as to have had a difficult son from the beginning (21–3).

CAMILLO Sir, it is three days since I saw the Prince. What his happier affairs may be are to me unknown; but I have missingly noted he is of late much retired from court, and is less frequent to his princely exercises than formerly he hath appeared.

POLIXENES I have considered so much, Camillo, and with some care, so far that I have eyes under my service which look upon his removedness, from whom I have this intelligence: that he is seldom from the house of a most homely shepherd, a man, they say, that from very nothing, and beyond the imagination of his neighbors, is grown into an unspeakable estate.

CAMILLO I have heard, sir, of such a man, who hath a daughter of most rare note. The report of her is extended more than can be thought to begin from such a cottage.

POLIXENES That's likewise part of my intelligence – but, I fear, the angle that plucks our son thither. Thou shalt accompany us to the place, where we will (not appearing what we are) have some question with the shepherd, from whose simplicity I think it not uneasy to get the cause of my son's resort thither. Prithee be my present partner in this business, and lay aside the thoughts of Sicilia.

41 Prithee] F (*'Prethe*)

25 **missingly** i.e. 'regretting his absence', or, perhaps, as Steevens thinks, 'at intervals'.

26 **frequent to** attentive to.

27 **princely exercises** royal activities and duties. Ophelia alludes to such exercises when she speaks of 'The courtier's, soldier's, scholar's, eye, tongue, sword' (*Ham.* 3.1.151).

29–30 **so far . . . removedness** i.e. so much so that I have employed spies to observe where he keeps himself while absent from the court. The use of spies against a family member (see 2.1.33–6) is one of several patterns linking the two halves of the play (see Introduction, pp. 22–4).

30–41 These lines, especially 31–3, 35–6, and 40, introduce issues of class consciousness and social mobility (in this instance, and later in 4.4 and 5.2, defined up, but at 4.3.13–4, down). For how such concerns contribute to making Bohemia a less conventional pastoral world, see Introduction, p. 19.

30 **intelligence** information, news.

31 **homely** simple, unsophisticated.

33 **unspeakable** beyond description or belief. In three phrases – 'from very nothing', 'beyond the imagination' (32), and 'into an unspeakable estate' – Shakespeare compresses Greene's text and substitutes a sense of wonder for what in *Pandosto* is simply a recitation of material facts (see Bullough, 175).

35 **note** distinction, reputation (*OED n*[2] 19).

35–6 **report . . . cottage** i.e. her fame ('report') is too widespread ('extended more') to have originated in such a lowly, humble dwelling ('cottage').

37 **but** Theobald's emendation of 'but' to 'and' reads more easily, but Polixenes may mean that, while Perdita is only *part* of his spies' reports of the shepherd's cottage, she is the main point of Florizel's visits; 'but' was dropped completely in Schlegel-Tieck.

38 **angle** Besides *angle* as baited hook (recalling Leontes' imagery at 1.2.178–79, 193, and 2.3.7), Patricia Parker (unpublished manuscript) suggests a play on *ingle* (to fondle or caress), which could have a heterosexual as well as a homosexual application. Compare Polixenes' paternal echo of the Shepherd's worry about a son's years 'between ten and three-and twenty' (3.3.58–60).

38 **our** the royal 'we' (also in 38 ['us'] and 39 ['we']). Polixenes' shift from the formal detachment of 'our', 'us', and 'we' to the personal 'my' (41) underscores his dilemma as a father who is also a king.

40 **question with** talk with (in the vein of an examination or interrogation).

41 **uneasy** hard, difficult.

CAMILLO I willingly obey your command.
POLIXENES My best Camillo! We must disguise ourselves.
[*Exeunt*]

4.3 *Enter* AUTOLYCUS *singing*

When daffodils begin to peer,
With heigh, the doxy over the dale,
Why then comes in the sweet o'the year,
For the red blood reigns in the winter's pale.
The white sheet bleaching on the hedge,
With heigh, the sweet birds, O how they sing!
Doth set my pugging tooth on edge,
For a quart of ale is a dish for a king.
The lark that tirra-lirra chants,
With heigh, with heigh, the thrush and the jay,
Are summer songs for me and my aunts
While we lie tumbling in the hay.

45 Camillo!] *Theobald;* Camillo, F 45 SD] *Rowe; Exit* F 4.3] F *(Scena Tertia.)* 7 pugging] F; progging *Hanmer;* prigging *Thirlby conj.* 7 on] F *(an)* 10 with heigh, with heigh] F2; *with heigh* F

Act 4, Scene 3
On a footpath (4.3.112) in Bohemia Shakespeare brings together the play's two chief comic figures, the good-hearted Clown and the mercurial Autolycus, whose 'keynote . . . is disguise' (Draper, 66). In keeping with the nature of the characters and the situation, the episode, with the exception of the framing songs, is in prose. A multilayered intertextuality inclusive of Greek myth (0 SD n., 24–5 n.), the bible, Greene's 1592 'Conny-Catching' pamphlets (57–8 n., 71 n., and 87 n.), and a vast body of 'rogue' (89–90 n.) literature lies behind both the scene and the character of Autolycus.

0 SD Autolycus For the classical and mythological sources of the name, see List of Characters, p. 81.

0 SD *singing* For Richard McCabe (Autolycus in Noble), the realization came gradually that 'the singing voice is a fundamental constituent in the natural vitality and freshness that the fourth act brings to the play' (Smallwood, *Players*, 68).

1–12 R. Noble (*Song*, 94) notes how succinctly these lines introduce Autolycus on his first entrance: 'It is the song used as a soliloquy'.

1 peer appear. See 4.4.3.

2 doxy in vagabonds' cant, a beggar's woman or mistress, i.e. a prostitute. See 'aunts' (11).

4 'The meaning is, the red, the *spring* blood, now *reigns o'er* the parts lately under the *dominion* ['pale' = domain, enclosure] *of winter*' (Farmer, cited in Furness). The pun on *pale* = *pallor* leads by further association to 'the white sheet bleaching' in the next line (Edward Armstrong, *Shakespeare's Imagination: A Study of the Psychology of Associations and Inspiration*, 1946, 14, 16). For similar proximity of 'pale,' linen, and red colouring, see *Ven.* 589–90, 'whereat a sudden pale, / Like lawn [linen] being spread upon the blushing rose'.

7 set . . . edge Proverbial (Dent T431). The general sense of 5–8 is that, for Autolycus, the sight of fresh linen drying whets his appetite for stealing; the money he will make from selling the sheets will go toward purchasing ale, 'a dish fit for a king' (Dent D363.1).

7 pugging Steevens cites *The Roaring Girl* (5.1.301) for the use of *puggards* as a type of thief.

9 tirra-lirra an orthographic representation of the skylark's sound (this line is *OED*'s first recorded usage).

10 Most editors accept F2's repetition of '*with heigh*' as a way of filling out F's metrically short '*With heigh, the Thrush and the Iay*'. It may be, however, as Schanzer (following Dyce) suggests, that the name of another bird has dropped out.

11 aunts whores, i.e. doxies (see 4.3.2).

I have served Prince Florizel and in my time wore three pile, but now I am out of service.

But shall I go mourn for that, my dear?
The pale moon shines by night,
And when I wander here and there
I then do most go right.
If tinkers may have leave to live
And bear the sow-skin budget,
Then my account I well may give,
And in the stocks avouch it.

My traffic is sheets; when the kite builds, look to lesser linen. My father named me Autolycus, who being (as I am) littered under Mercury, was likewise a snapper-up of unconsidered trifles. With die and drab I purchased this caparison, and my

14 service] F; suit and service *Thirlby conj.* 15 my dear?] *Pope; (my deere)* F 17 here and there] F3; *here, and there* F; here and there, F4

14 **service** Thirlby's speculation (in Theobald) that the original read 'suit and service', a stock phrase for personal attendance, strengthens by wordplay the link with 'three-pile' = the thickest, richest velvet, and sets up the contrast with Autolycus' present ragged clothes purchased 'with die and drab' (26). Walter Whiter notes the coupling of 'suit and service' in Shakespeare's phraseology (see *MV* 2.2.144–7; *LLL* 5.2.275–6 and 839–40) extended to a more general association between clothing, esp. livery, and service (*A Specimen of a Commentary on Shakespeare* [1794], 86–90).

16–18 Wilson in NS cites Falstaff in *1H4* 1.2.15: 'we that take purses go by the moon and the seven stars'. Lines 17–18 speak specifically to Autolycus' life as a vagabond, pointing up his new-found freedom and mastery in living out his true calling as a con artist: 'for a vagabond, since he has no specific destination, all directions are the right direction, no road is the wrong road' (Pafford) and, thus, he is free 'to do what is best for [him]' (Orgel).

19 **tinkers** itinerant menders of kitchen utensils.

20 **sow-skin budget** pigskin toolbag. Autolycus, however, uses the tinker's bag (usually cow leather rather than pigskin) to carry stolen goods.

21–2 Autolycus hopes that the addition to his wardrobe of a 'sow-skin budget' (20) will prove ('avouch') to authorities that he is a legitimate tinker and not a vagabond, and therefore, if arrested and put 'in the stocks' (a common punishment for vagabonds and beggars), should be released.

23 **traffic** saleable commodities (*OED n* 4), or, perhaps more generally, trade, business (*OED n* 2).

23 **sheets** If Steevens is correct in detecting a pun relating to the selling of broadsheets, i.e. ballads, as well as stealing laundry, the word anticipates a role that Autolycus takes up in the next scene.

23 **When . . . linen** I.e. when the kite (a bird of prey) builds his nest, look to your smaller pieces of laundry ('lesser linen') just as you should attend to your sheets (larger linen) when I am on the prowl.

24–5 **littered . . . Mercury** i.e. born when the planet Mercury was in the ascendant. See Autolycus in List of Characters, p. 81.

25 **snapper-up** thief.

25 **unconsidered** disregarded, unattended (Andrews).

26 **With . . . caparison** Through (losing money by) gambling ('die') and wenching ('drab') I arrived at this (ragged) outfit ('caparison'). Suggestive of ornamental trappings, whether for a horse or a human, 'caparison' (*OED n* 1, 2) recalls the sartorial splendor of 'three pile' (13), apparently one of the things the clothes-conscious Autolycus misses most from his former life at court (see 4.3.53–4, 57–8, and 4.4.696ff).

revenue is the silly cheat. Gallows and knock are too powerful on the highway; beating and hanging are terrors to me. For the life to come, I sleep out the thought of it.

Enter CLOWN

A prize, a prize!

CLOWN Let me see, every 'leven wether tods, every tod yields pound and odd shilling; fifteen hundred shorn, what comes the wool to?

AUTOLYCUS [*Aside*] If the springe hold, the cock's mine.

CLOWN I cannot do't without counters. Let me see, what am I to buy for our sheep-shearing feast? [*Reading out of a note*] Three pound of sugar, five pound of currants, rice – what will this sister of mine do with rice? But my father hath made her mistress of the feast, and she lays it on. She hath made me four-and-twenty nosegays for the shearers: three-man-songmen all, and very

29 SD] F *(after 30)* 31 'leven wether] *Malone;* Leauen-weather F 34 SD] *Rowe; not in* F 35 counters] F *(*Compters*)* 36 SD] *Capell (after* sugar *in 37); not in* F 37 currants] F *(*Currence*)*

27 **silly cheat** Simple (petty) theft (Kermode) is Autolycus's source of income ('revenue').

27 **Gallows and knock** 'The resistance which a highwayman encounters in the fact, and the punishment which he suffers on detection' (Johnson). The two terms are in chiastic synonymy with 'beating and hanging' in the next line.

29 **sleep out** be unmindful of, oblivious to.

30 The standard cry at the sight of valuable booty that belongs to one who wins it by the rules of war (or piracy). The cry is used by pirates in *Per.* 4.1.93, outlaws in *TGV* 5.4.121, and a messenger to Jack Cade in *2H6* 4.7.20.

31–3 Ritson does the arithmetic: the wool of eleven castrated sheep ('wether') would weigh a tod, or 28 lbs., so that, at £1 and 1s for each 'tod', 1500 sheep shorn would produce £143 and 30s (Steevens 1793), a great deal of money and typical of the increasing wealth of sheep-herding estates at the time; see Mowat, 'Rogues', 68–9.

34 **springe** trap (set to catch woodcocks, generally regarded as foolish, easily duped birds). See *Ham.* 1.3.115 and 5.2.306.

35 **counters** disks (often metal) used for arithmetic operations (*OED* counter n^2 1a).

35–46 Sheepshearing feasts were celebrations held anywhere between mid-May and the end of July, this one apparently in late July (4.4.106–7), although Bate (231) pinpoints late June. Contemporary references note the lavishness of the feasts: 'If it be a sheep-shearing feast, maister Baily can entertaine you with his bill of reckonings to his Maister, of three sheapheards wages, spent on fresh cates, besides spices and Saffron pottage' *(Questions of Profitable and Pleasant Concernings* [1594], fo. 4a). *The Booke of Cookerie* (1629) (largely reprinted from Thomas Dawson's 1587 *Good Housewife's Jewel*) has a list of things necessary for a banquet (E2r), including sugar, currants, saffron, nutmegs, ginger, prunes and raisins, all in the Clown's list, as well as dates, which are not but occur to him as appropriate.

37–8 **rice . . . rice** It is not clear why the Clown is surprised at rice, unless it was expensive because imported and thus evidence of Perdita's 'lay[ing] it on' (i.e. being extravagant, *OED* lay *v* 55e) for the sheepshearing feast where Florizel would be present. Charlton speculates that the Clown may be thinking of Florizel's courtship of Perdita and the custom of throwing rice at the bridal couple; Sokol, however, questions such ceremonial usage, finding implications but no definitive proof of the nuptial practice in Elizabethan times (Sokol, 127–8, 227–8 nn. 44–49, esp. n. 49).

40 **three-man-songmen** the trio of countertenor, tenor, and bass who would sing part songs.

good ones, but they are most of them means and basses – but one puritan amongst them, and he sings psalms to hornpipes. I must have saffron to colour the warden pies; mace; dates – none, that's out of my note; nutmegs, seven; a race or two of ginger, but that I may beg; four pound of prunes, and as many of raisins o'th'sun.

AUTOLYCUS [*Grovelling on the ground*] O, that ever I was born!

CLOWN I'th'name of me!

AUTOLYCUS O, help me, help me! Pluck but off these rags, and then death, death!

CLOWN Alack, poor soul, thou hast need of more rags to lay on thee, rather than have these off.

AUTOLYCUS O sir, the loathsomeness of them offend me more than the stripes I have received, which are mighty ones and millions.

CLOWN Alas, poor man, a million of beating may come to a great matter.

45 prunes] F (Prewyns) 46 raisins] F (Reysons) 47 SD] *Rowe; not in* F 48 me!] *Hudson;* me. F; me – *Rowe*

41 means Orgel suggests boy altos or adult countertenors but most editors since Steevens opt for tenors, presumably because the tenor and bass voices are more common.

41–2 but . . . hornpipes except for one puritan who sings 'psalms' even to lively tunes played on shrill wind instruments. Shaheen (195) compares *Wiv.* 2.1.62–3, 'the hundred Psalms to the tune of 'Green-sleeves'. Since puritans were often mockingly depicted as singing in high nasal tones (W. P. Holden, *Anti-Puritan Satire 1572–1640*, 1954, pp. 102–3), Schanzer may be right to assign the treble part to the puritan. On 39–42 as introducing into the play contemporary disputes about rural pastimes, see Phebe Jensen, 'Singing Psalms to Horn-pipes: Fesitivity, Iconoclasm, and Catholicism in [*WT*]', *SQ* 55 (2004), 279–306.

43 saffron a plant whose dried orange yellow stigmas were popular as both a spice and an ingredient for colouring.

43 warden pies pear pies. Cotgrave defines this type of baking pear as a 'winter pear . . . which may be kept very long' (*Dictionarie of the French and English Tongue*, 1632).

43 mace an aromatic spice.

44 out . . . note Usually glossed as 'not on my list', but Gill proposes 'crossed off my list'. White thinks it more likely that the Clown's 'note' (36) is what he has been told rather than a list he consults, since reading was an unusual accomplishment for one of his class; but the Clown 'responds to the list of ingredients given to him by his sister to purchase as if he is reading rather than remembering' (Folger). Besides, one of the conventions of literary pastoral favoured literate shepherds and shepherdesses (see Mopsa's love of 'a ballad in print', 4.4.249).

44 race root.

46 raisins . . . sun raisins dried naturally (by the sun) rather than artificially.

48 If 'me' is not included by accident, perhaps Steevens' parallel of 'before me', a mild oath like 'by my word' or 'on my soul', is relevant (see *TN* 2.3.171 and *AWW* 2.3.26, 2.4.29–30). The 1606 Act of Abuses, which forbade profanity in stage plays, may be accountable for the otherwise untraced, 'and no doubt intentionally comic, form of the exclamation' (Schanzer). Furness cites Johnson's conj. that 'me' should be omitted and quotes Kendrick's lengthy rebuttal proposing that the speaker, in an act of self-censorship, quickly substitutes 'me' for 'Heaven' or 'Mercy'; an interrupted 'mercy', as the Variorum editor notes, may find support in the Shepherd's 'Name of mercy, when was this, boy' (3.3.93).

53 offend i.e. offends (Abbot 412). See 4.2.20 and 25. Many editors follow F2 in emending to 'offends'.

AUTOLYCUS I am robbed, sir, and beaten, my money and apparel ta'en from me, and these detestable things put upon me.

CLOWN What, by a horseman or a footman?

AUTOLYCUS A footman, sweet sir, a footman.

CLOWN Indeed, he should be a footman by the garments he has left with thee; if this be a horseman's coat, it hath seen very hot service. Lend me thy hand, I'll help thee. Come, lend me thy hand [*helping him up*].

AUTOLYCUS O good sir, tenderly. O!

CLOWN Alas, poor soul!

AUTOLYCUS O good sir, softly, good sir! I fear, sir, my shoulder-blade is out.

CLOWN How now? Canst stand?

AUTOLYCUS Softly, dear sir [*picks his pocket*]; good sir, softly. You ha' done me a charitable office.

CLOWN Dost lack any money? I have a little money for thee.

AUTOLYCUS No, good sweet sir; no, I beseech you, sir. I have a kinsman not past three quarters of a mile hence, unto whom I was going. I shall there have money, or anything I want. Offer me no money, I pray you; that kills my heart.

CLOWN What manner of fellow was he that robbed you?

AUTOLYCUS A fellow, sir, that I have known to go about with troll-my-dames. I knew him once a servant of the Prince. I cannot tell, good sir, for which of his virtues it was, but he was certainly whipped out of the court.

58 detestable] F2; derestable F 64 SD] *Rowe; not in* F 70 SD] *Capell (at the end of* 71 *Kermode; at the beginning of* 70 *Bevington; after second* softly *Oxford); not in* F 72 Dost] F3; Doest F

57–8, 71 Parodic allusions to the parable of the Good Samaritan (Luke 10. 30–37). This whole sequence also shows the influence of popular 'cony-catching' pamphlets; for the 'false piety' of 'charitable office', Pafford cites Greene's *Second Conny-Catching* in which the author describes a theft in St Paul's where the con-artist 'as devoutly as if he were som zealous person, standeth soberly, with his eies elevated to heauen, when his hand is either on the purse or in the pocket' (31, 41).

59–63 Wordplay on 'horseman' and 'footman' moves from the initial contrast between a man who robs on horseback (highwayman) and one who robs on foot (footpad) to that between a mounted soldier and a foot soldier. Autolycus' poor clothing suggests to the Clown someone not rich enough to travel on horseback, or, if a mounted soldier, one fresh from the heat of battle ('very hot service'), whose clothing would indicate hard or heavy use. In 60 Autolycus, perhaps again remembering his better days, hints at 'footman' in the sense of 'attendant' (see also 79).

67 softly gently.

68 out dislocated. The line may hint at the doubling of Autolycus and Antigonus; the latter also experienced a shoulder injury (3.3.86–7). See Appendix B, p. 266.

70 SD Editors usually place the picking of the Clown's pocket at or near this point in order to underline the double meaning in Autolycus' following 'You ha' done me a charitable office'.

71 charitable office act of charity.

73 Autolycus refuses money to prevent the Clown from discovering the absence of his purse.

74 past more than.

78–9 troll-my-dames i.e. troll madams, 'literally, a board game [in which balls were rolled through hoops or into holes], but here [in light of

CLOWN His vices you would say. There's no virtue whipped out of the court; they cherish it to make it stay there – and yet it will no more but abide.

AUTOLYCUS Vices I would say, sir. I know this man well; he hath been since an ape-bearer, then a process-server, a bailiff; then he compassed a motion of the Prodigal Son, and married a tinker's wife within a mile where my land and living lies; and, having flown over many knavish professions, he settled only in rogue. Some call him Autolycus.

CLOWN Out upon him! Prig, for my life, prig! He haunts wakes, fairs, and bear-baitings.

AUTOLYCUS Very true, sir; he, sir, he; that's the rogue that put me into this apparel.

CLOWN Not a more cowardly rogue in all Bohemia; if you had but looked big and spit at him, he'd have run.

AUTOLYCUS I must confess to you, sir, I am no fighter. I am false of heart that way, and that he knew, I warrant him.

CLOWN How do you now?

Autolycus' traffic in doxies and 'aunts'] probably meaning whores' (Folger). 'Troll' in the sense of moving about in all directions (*OED v* 1) recalls Autolycus' philosophy as expressed in 17–18.

84 **abide** stay briefly as opposed to stay permanently. No examples of this sense appear after 1535 (*OED v* 2), but some of Shakespeare's uses have a temporary implication (compare *MM* 4.2.24, 5.1.265; *MV* 3.4.32; and *Ant.* 2.2.244); see also Hilda Hulme, 'The Spoken Language and the Dramatic Text', *SQ* 9 (1958), 385. Orgel prefers Staunton's reading 'will barely, or only with difficulty, remain'.

86 **ape-bearer** an itinerant showman featuring a trained monkey in his act.

86 **process-server** a sheriff's official assigned the task of serving summonses; i.e. a 'bailiff' (*OED* bailiff 2), F's parentheses indicating synonymy.

87 **compassed** acquired for touring purposes; or, perhaps, composed, devised.

87 **motion** a puppet show (see *TGV* 2.1.94–5, 'O excellent motion! O exceeding puppet'). As indicated by Autolycus' reference to the parable of the Prodigal Son (Luke 15.11–32), the subject matter was often biblical; compare Jonson's *Every Man Out Of His Humour* (2.1.426–8), 'They say, there's a new motion of the city of Nineveh, with Jonas, and the whale, to be seene at Fleet-bridge' (ed. Helen Ostovich, 2001). For other examples of biblical motions from the period, see *The Control and Censorship of Caroline Drama: The Records of Sir Henry Herbert, Master of the Revels 1623–73*), ed. N. W. Bawcutt (1996), 77, 80, and 83.

87–8 **married . . . wife** Marrying a tinker's wife continues the imputation of unsavoury activity and company, since tinkers were regarded as dishonest bunglers.

88 **living** estate, the income from land 'as productive property' (Orgel).

89–90 **in rogue** i.e. upon the 'knavish' profession of idle vagrant ('rogue', *OED n* 1). By 1572, 'rogue' had become 'the term used in legal statutes to refer to those who, though healthy, were unemployed and who had no other source of income [than to beg for money by pretending to be sick]. To be a rogue – i.e., to be unemployed and destitute – was to be a criminal liable to severe punishment' (Folger, 244–5). For more on the semantics of *rogue* in Shakespeare's time, see Mowat, 'Rogues'.

91 **Prig** Thief.

91 **wakes** country festivals, including the eve of such revels (*OED* wake *n*[1] 4a).

92 **bear-baitings** a popular bloodsport in which dogs attacked a bear chained to a stake.

96 **big** mighty, threatening (presumably by standing tall, with chest thrust out).

97–8 **false of heart** without courage.

AUTOLYCUS Sweet sir, much better than I was. I can stand and walk. I will even take my leave of you and pace softly towards my kinsman's.

CLOWN Shall I bring thee on the way?

AUTOLYCUS No, good-faced sir; no, sweet sir.

CLOWN Then fare thee well. I must go buy spices for our sheep-shearing. *Exit*

AUTOLYCUS Prosper you, sweet sir. – Your purse is not hot enough to purchase your spice. I'll be with you at your sheep-shearing too – if I make not this cheat bring out another, and the shearers prove sheep, let me be unrolled, and my name put in the book of virtue!

Song
Jog on, jog on, the footpath way,
And merrily hent the stile-a;
A merry heart goes all the day,
Your sad tires in a mile-a. *Exit*

4.4 *Enter* FLORIZEL [*and*] PERDITA, [*followed, at a little distance, by*] SHEPHERD, CLOWN; POLIXENES, CAMILLO [*disguised*]; MOPSA, DORCAS, *Servants,* [*Shepherds and Shepherdesses*]

104 good-faced] *Theobald (subst.)*; good fac'd F 106 SD] F; *after* sir *in* 107 *Capell* 107 sir. –] *This edn; not in* F 109 too –] *Orgel*; too: F 4.4 F *(Scena Quarta.)* 0 SD] Pafford; *Enter* Florizel *and* Perdita *Rowe*; *Enter Florizell, Perdita, Shepherd, Clowne, Polixenes, Camillo, Mopsa, Dorcas, Seruants, Autolicus.* F

101 softly carefully or slowly (so as to avoid pain).

106 SD If Clown exits here, then Autolycus' 'Prosper you, sweet sir' in the next line is delivered to his back and potentially takes on a more ironic and dismissive tone than it would if the Clown's departure is postponed until after Autolycus' valediction (as in those editors who follow Capell).

107–8 Your purse . . . spice With wordplay on the hot nature of spices, Autolycus calls attention to the Clown's now cold, i.e. empty, purse. See *1H4* 2.4.323, 'Hot livers and cold purses'.

109 cheat (1) trick; (2) theft.

109 bring out bring about, produce.

110 sheep i.e. to be fleeced or robbed (Folger).

110 unrolled deleted from the roll of famous thieves and vagabonds.

112–15 The song, with two additional stanzas, appears as a catch in *An Antidote against Melancholy . . . witty Ballads, Jovial Songs, and Merry Catches* (1661). An early version of the tune with the title 'Hanskin' survives in the *Fitzwilliam Virginal Book* (1609–19), no. 197; the same tune under the title 'Jog on' is found in John Playford's *Dancing Master* (1651).

113 hent . . . stile-a grab hold of (in order to leap over) a set of steps ('stile') for crossing a fence.

Act 4, Scene 4

From six lines in *Pandosto* relating to a 'merry' country meeting filled with 'homely pastimes . . . and sportes' at which Fawnia (= Perdita) was 'bidden as the mistress of the feast' (Bullough, 177–8), Shakespeare creates an elaborate sheepshearing celebration, the longest scene in *WT* and the second longest in the canon. Like a one-act play, the episode can be divided into exposition (1–54), rising action (55–322), climax (323–421), counter movement (421–641), and denouement (642–796). Early editors (Theobald, Hanmer, and Capell) stipulated the Shepherd's cottage as the setting, occasionally specifying a room within. Many later editors and virtually all directors locate the scene outdoors, sometimes '*before*' a cottage.

0 SD As in the entrance direction to 2.3, the question is how many characters to subtract from Crane's mass entry in F's opening stage direction (see Collation). Autolycus cannot come on yet, but perhaps the others do, with merrymaking in the background while Florizel and Perdita demonstrate their absorption in each other.

1 SH In the stage directions (except that for 5.1.0), F has Florizell; Rowe altered to Florizel throughout, perhaps influenced by F's one exception and by more familiar names such as Daniel, Raphael, and Nathaniel.

FLORIZEL These your unusual weeds to each part of you
Does give a life: no shepherdess, but Flora
Peering in April's front. This your sheep-shearing
Is as a meeting of the petty gods,
And you the queen on't.
PERDITA Sir, my gracious lord,
To chide at your extremes it not becomes me –
O pardon that I name them! Your high self,
The gracious mark o'th'land, you have obscured
With a swain's wearing, and me, poor lowly maid,
Most goddess-like pranked up. But that our feasts
In every mess have folly, and the feeders
Digest it with a custom, I should blush
To see you so attired – sworn, I think,
To show myself a glass.

6–7 me – O . . . them!] *Pafford (subst.)*; me: (. . . them:) F 12 Digest it] F2 *(* Disgest it*)*; Digest F 13 sworn] F; swoon *Hanmer (conj. Theobald)*

1 **weeds** garments ('unusual' because Perdita is dressed not as a simple shepherdess but as the queen of the feast).

2 **Does . . . life** Does impart 'an animation, vitality' (Folger), or, perhaps, 'does make you a different character' (Gill). For use of the singular 'Does' with a plural subject, see Abbott 412; Theobald was the first to adopt the unnecessary emendation 'Do' (followed as recently as Dolan).

2 **Flora** Roman goddess of flowers and spring.

3 **Peering . . . front** (Flora) making her appearance (1) at the beginning of April, or (2) in the guise ('front' = 'brow', 'forehead', hence in this instance 'face') of April.

4 **petty** lesser, minor.

5 **on't** of it.

6 **extremes** exaggerations, extravagances (of praise) (*OED* extreme *n* 5).

8 **mark** The word suggests both a target, something attracting others' looks and aspirations, and a model set up for guidance (*OED n* 5), as is Hotspur, 'the mark and glass, copy and book, / That fashion'd others' (*2H4* 2.3.30–2).

9 **swain's wearing** the garb ('wearing') of a country youth or young shepherd.

10 **pranked up** dressed up, bedecked (*OED* prank v^4). See *TN* 2.4.86, 'That nature pranks her in attracts my soul', and *Cor.* 3.1.23, 'For they do prank them in authority'.

10–12 **But . . . custom** I.e. were it not for our feasts having in every group of diners ('mess', see 1.2.224 n.) some who behave foolishly, and the fools themselves ('feeders' = those who feed, thrive on folly) accepting such behaviour as customary. Because there are no other recorded instances of 'with a custom', Wilson suggests emending to 'accustom' (a word still in use in the seventeenth century meaning 'habit' or 'custom'); Schanzer adopts the emendation, but, as Orgel notes, there are no parallels to 'with accustom' either, the *OED* citing only 'by accustom'.

13 **sworn** The emendation 'swoon', first proposed by Theobald and generally adopted by most subsequent editors, is not only awkward but unnecessary if 'sworn' = 'formally undertaken' (*OED* swear *v* 2). The sense of 13–14 is that Florizel, by defiantly putting on shepherd's garb so as to match Perdita's, presents to her a mirror ('glass', 14).

FLORIZEL I bless the time
When my good falcon made her flight across
Thy father's ground.

PERDITA Now Jove afford you cause!
To me the difference forges dread; your greatness
Hath not been used to fear. Even now I tremble
To think your father by some accident
Should pass this way, as you did. O, the Fates!
How would he look to see his work, so noble,
Vilely bound up? What would he say? Or how
Should I, in these my borrowed flaunts, behold
The sternness of his presence?

FLORIZEL Apprehend
Nothing but jollity. The gods themselves,
Humbling their deities to love, have taken
The shapes of beasts upon them. Jupiter
Became a bull and bellowed; the green Neptune
A ram and bleated; and the fire-robed god,
Golden Apollo, a poor humble swain,
As I seem now. Their transformations
Were never for a piece of beauty rarer,
Nor in a way so chaste, since my desires

20 Fates!] *Capell;* Fates, F 29 fire-robed god] F *(* Fire-roab'd-God*)*

15 her The 'falcon' is the female, the tercel the male. The line derives from a passing reference in *Pandosto* to Dorastus' spying Fawnia on his way home from a day of hawking (Bullough, 178).

16 afford . . . cause (May Jove) give you reason (to 'bless the time').

17–24 In *Pandosto,* both Fawnia and Dorastus wrestle extensively with the 'difference' (17) in their social ranks (Bullough, 179–84).

20 Fates In Greek mythology, the Fates were the three sisters who held the shears of destiny: Clotho spun the thread of life, Lachesis held and fixed it, and Atropos cut it. See *MV* 2.2.60–1, 'according to Fates and Destinies, and . . . the Sisters Three'.

21 work Florizel as 'work' produced by his father, now poorly clothed ('vilely bound up', 22). The metaphor is from bookbinding; compare *Rom.* 3.2.83–4, in which the terms are reversed, 'Was ever book containing such vile matter / So fairly bound?'

23 flaunts finery.

24 Apprehend (1) Anticipate (*OED v* 10) or (2) fear (*OED v* 11).

27–30 Florizel alludes to three gods from classical mythology who disguised themselves in pursuit of a woman. While all three allusions appear in *Pandosto* (Bullough, 184), Shakespeare (like Greene) would have known the stories from Ovid's *Metamorphoses*, especially Book 2, which concludes with an account of the abduction of Europa, and Book 6, which briefly mentions in close proximity the three transformations as tales woven into Arachne's tapestry.

32 piece woman (in the sense of masterpiece, a work of art).

33 Nor . . . chaste I.e. ('their transformations') were never undertaken in so chaste an endeavour. Florizel's counterpart, Dorastus, briefly suggests using his rank to force Fawnia to be his concubine, an argument she firmly rejects (*Pandosto*, in Bullough, 182–3).

Run not before mine honour, nor my lusts
Burn hotter than my faith.

PERDITA O, but sir,
Your resolution cannot hold when 'tis
Opposed, as it must be, by th'power of the King.
One of these two must be necessities,
Which then will speak, that you must change this purpose
Or I my life.

FLORIZEL Thou dearest Perdita,
With these forced thoughts I prithee darken not
The mirth o'th'feast. Or I'll be thine, my fair,
Or not my father's. For I cannot be
Mine own, nor any thing to any, if
I be not thine. To this I am most constant,
Though destiny say no. Be merry, gentle;
Strangle such thoughts as these with anything
That you behold the while. Your guests are coming.
Lift up your countenance, as it were the day
Of celebration of that nuptial which
We two have sworn shall come.

PERDITA O Lady Fortune,
Stand you auspicious!

[SHEPHERD, CLOWN, MOPSA, DORCAS, *and others come forward, with the disguised* POLIXENES *and* CAMILLO]

FLORIZEL See, your guests approach.
Address yourself to entertain them sprightly,
And let's be red with mirth.

39 speak, that] F; speak that *Oxford* 40 dearest] F2 *(* deerest*)*; deer'st F 52 SD] *Pafford; Enter* ALL F2; *not in* F

35 faith fidelity (to Perdita, her trust in him, and his promise to marry her); see 49–51, 150–3. Compare 33–5 and *Temp.* 4.1.23–31, 54–6.

39–40 change . . . life i.e. (either you must) change your purpose to marry me, or, if you cling to it, I will be required to change my life. Perhaps Perdita anticipates being forcibly separated from Florizel through prison or exile; Sokol (129), however, thinks 'change my life' means 'become your concubine', while Wilson, among others, suggests that Perdita is referring to her own death.

41 forced strained (*OED ppl adj* 3b).

42–3 Or . . . Or Either . . . Or.

44 any anyone.

46 gentle an endearment, perhaps comparable to 'dearest' (Schanzer). Orgel cites as a parallel Antony's address to Cleopatra, 'Gentle, hear me' (*Ant.* 4.15.47).

51 Lady Fortune In classical mythology, the goddess Fortuna personified chance, bringing good and bad luck at will.

54 red red-faced, i.e. flushed.

SHEPHERD Fie, daughter, when my old wife lived, upon
This day she was both pantler, butler, cook,
Both dame and servant; welcomed all, served all;
Would sing her song and dance her turn; now here
At upper end o'th'table, now i'th'middle;
On his shoulder, and his; her face o'fire
With labour, and the thing she took to quench it
She would to each one sip. You are retired,
As if you were a feasted one, and not
The hostess of the meeting. Pray you bid
These unknown friends to's welcome, for it is
A way to make us better friends, more known.
Come, quench your blushes and present yourself
That which you are, mistress o'th'feast. Come on,
And bid us welcome to your sheep-shearing,
As your good flock shall prosper.

PERDITA Sir, welcome.
It is my father's will I should take on me
The hostess-ship o'th'day. You're welcome, sir.
Give me those flowers there, Dorcas. Reverend sirs,
For you there's rosemary and rue; these keep
Seeming and savour all the winter long.

60 o'fire] F; afire *Oxford*

55–62 Since her counterpart in *Pandosto* enters the narrative more fully, having both a name, Mopsa, and a personality (Bullough, 174–5), the brief mention of Shepherd's dead wife appears deliberate, perhaps indicative of Shakespeare's proclivity for absent mothers (see Mary Beth Rose, 'Where are the Mothers in Shakespeare?', *SQ* 42 [1991]:291–314).

56 **pantler, butler** household servants responsible for the pantry and the wine cellar who served bread and liquor, respectively.

57 **dame** mistress of the household.

60 **On** At.

60 **o'fire** on fire (i.e. flushed as a result of her 'labour').

61–2 **and . . . sip** i.e., and with the drink she took to satisfy the thirst (worked up by her labours) she would toast ('sip') each guest in turn.

62 **retired** withdrawn.

63 **feasted one** one of the guests.

65 **unknown . . . to's** i.e., (welcome these friends) unknown to us. For the transposition of adjectives, see Abbott 419a. The act of welcoming makes 'unknown friends' better acquainted ones (66).

68–70 **Come on . . . prosper** Theobald thinks that Polixenes speaks these words to Perdita (see John Nichols, *Illustrations of the Literary History of the Eighteenth Century*, 1817, 2: 363). But the Shepherd is prompting her, giving her lines to say to the strangers.

70–2 **Sir . . . sir** Although many editors have Perdita address the first 'Sir' to Polixenes and the second to Camillo, we have no way of knowing which one Perdita addresses first. Folger interpolates stage directions of address on the assumption that the king's costume would indicate social superiority (p. 245), but Polixenes' status would not necessarily be evident in disguise. In Donellan, for example, the black garbed, 'blind' strangers were socially indistinguishable, as were the poncho-clad visitors in Cohen.

75 **Seeming and savour** Appearance (colour) and scent.

[*Giving flowers*] Grace and remembrance be to you both,
And welcome to our shearing.

POLIXENES
Shepherdess
(A fair one are you!), well you fit our ages
With flowers of winter.

PERDITA
Sir, the year growing ancient,
Not yet on summer's death nor on the birth
Of trembling winter, the fairest flowers o'th' season
Are our carnations and streaked gillyvors,
Which some call nature's bastards; of that kind
Our rustic garden's barren, and I care not
To get slips of them.

POLIXENES
Wherefore, gentle maiden,
Do you neglect them?

76 SD] Bevington *(subst., after* shearing *in 77); not in* F 78 you!), well] *Riverside;* you:) well F*;* you. Well *Oxford* 83 bastards; of] *Pierce;* bastards) of F

76 **Grace and remembrance** The usual associations of rue (also known as herb of grace) and rosemary, respectively. The former linked divine favour with sorrow and repentance, while the latter was 'anciently supposed to strengthen the memory, and [therefore] prescribed for that purpose in the books of ancient physic' (Steevens); Ophelia likewise associates rosemary with remembrance (*Ham.* 4.5.175–81). Throughout the distribution of floral gifts (73–135), Perdita's presentation accords with traditional flower symbolism; see 'A Nosegay Always Sweet', in Clement Robinson's *Handful of Pleasant Delights* (1584); Sokol, 133–7; and Charles Forker, who argues for the 'dramaturgical parenthesis' as a thematic microcosm of the play ('Perdita's Distribution of Flowers and the Function of Lyricism in [*WT*]', in *Fancy's Images*, 1990, 117).

79 **the year . . . ancient** i.e. perhaps, in the autumn or when autumn comes (the flowers of that season better suiting the ages of the 'unknown friends' than the rosemary and rue that will 'keep . . . all the winter long'). Sheepshearing would not occur in autumn (see 4.3.35–46 n.), so the line does not mean that it is *now* autumn as some commentators suggest; the phrasing, however, allows the passing of seasons to register subliminally, thus underscoring time as cyclic.

82 **gillyvors** i.e. gillyflowers. Acknowledging that the name was variously applied to pinks, carnations, sweet-williams, wallflowers, and stocks, Moorman votes for clove-carnation; Charlton, for clove-scented pink. Behind Perdita's vehement disavowal of gillyflowers is perhaps not only the hybridizing process that produces their streaks but the association of these flowers with loose women. Although *OED's* first entry for this meaning is 1797, a note by Steevens (4.4.98) cites Rowley's *A Woman Never Vex'd* (1632), in which Robert, a forward suitor, asks Jane if she has fair roses, to which she replies reprovingly, 'Yes, sir, roses; but no gilliflowers' (3.1); the whole passage of sexual aggression and defense plays on the names and associations of garden plants. *Gillyvor* suggests a relation to *gill-flirt* or *flirt-gill* (as in *Rom.* 2.4.153, 'Scurvy knave, I am none of his flirt-gills' [i.e. loose women]). The spelling itself may reflect rustic pronunciation, 'gillyvors' being the term used by 'low people in Sussex to denote a wanton' (Steevens).

83 **bastards** (1) hybrids (*OED* bastard *adj* 2); (2) things that are not genuine, i.e. counterfeit (*OED* bastard *adj* 4).

PERDITA For I have heard it said
There is an art which in their piedness shares
With great creating nature.
POLIXENES Say there be;
Yet nature is made better by no mean
But nature makes that mean: so over that art
Which you say adds to nature is an art
That nature makes. You see, sweet maid, we marry
A gentler scion to the wildest stock,
And make conceive a bark of baser kind
By bud of nobler race. This is an art
Which does mend nature – change it rather – but
The art itself is nature.
PERDITA So it is.
POLIXENES Then make your garden rich in gillyvors,
And do not call them bastards.
PERDITA I'll not put
The dibble in earth to set one slip of them;
No more than, were I painted, I would wish
This youth should say 'twere well, and only therefore
Desire to breed by me. Here's flowers for you:
Hot lavender, mints, savory, marjoram,

93 scion] *Steevens;* Sien F 96 nature – . . . rather –] *Pafford;* Nature: . . . rather, F 98 your] F2; you F

86–103 The nature/art debate was a commonplace. Perdita's position reflects the thinking of Montaigne, while Polixenes' owes much to Puttenham (see Supplementary note, p. 252). Cut by directors from Kemble to Tree, the debate was restored to the stage by Ames in 1910 (Bartholomeusz, 134–5).

87–8 Perdita distinguishes between streaking or parti-colour ('piedness') produced by a natural process and that (like the gillyvor's) resulting from horticultural skill or 'art'.

89 mean means, i.e. instrument or agency.

90–2 over . . . makes i.e. subsuming this horticultural skill that enhances nature is nature itself which creates its own means of improvement.

92–5 we marry . . . race Polixenes explains the means used to create gillyvors as the process of grafting by which a twig ('scion' = slip for grafting offshoot) from a cultivated or domesticated plant is joined to 'wildest stock' to yield a nobler flower.

97 So . . . is Furness imagines Perdita to give 'a swift, furtive, smiling glance at Florizel' as she agrees, but her assent 'may be merely polite . . . without real conviction' (Schanzer).

100 dibble a tool used to make holes in the ground for seeds, bulbs, or cuttings.

101 painted i.e. with cosmetics (thus creating an artificial rather than a natural beauty). Perdita's argument recalls her earlier unease at being 'pranked up' (10).

103–8 Here's . . . age Pafford thought these lines were directed at other men, visibly younger than the two visiting strangers, but Schanzer and Orgel argue persuasively that by offering Polixenes and Camillo flowers of 'middle summer' for middle age, Perdita is making amends for her earlier attribution to them of advanced age (see 4.4.74–5, 78–9).

104 Hot Deighton proposed 'strongly smelling', but most commentators relate the description to the temperature of plants (*OED adj* 4), citing herbal miscellanies of the period that describe either all lavender as 'hot' (e.g. Dodoens 1578 *Herbal* [265], and Cogan's 1589 *Haven of Health* [56]) or (as in Gerard's 1597 *Herball* [468, 470]) only a specific type, lavender spike in contrast to French lavender. Herbs were also divided at the time between 'hot' and 'cold' on the basis of when they bloomed. Cold herbs and flowers were said to bloom early and 'have a quicker perception of the heat . . . than the hot herbs have' (Bacon, *Sylva Sylvarum*, in

The marigold that goes to bed wi'th'sun,
And with him rises, weeping. These are flowers
Of middle summer, and I think they are given
To men of middle age. [*She gives flowers*]
Y'are very welcome.

CAMILLO I should leave grazing, were I of your flock,
And only live by gazing.

PERDITA Out, alas!
You'd be so lean that blasts of January
Would blow you through and through. [*To Florizel*]
Now, my fair'st friend,
I would I had some flowers o'th'spring that might
Become your time of day; [*to the Shepherdesses*] and yours, and yours,
That wear upon your virgin branches yet
Your maidenheads growing – O Proserpina,
For the flowers now that, frighted, thou letst fall
From Dis's wagon! Daffodils,
That come before the swallow dares, and take

105 wi'th'] *White* [2]*;* with' F **108** SD] *Wilson (subst., after* 108*; after* 103 *Bevington); not in* F **112** SD] *Wilson (after* friend*); not in* F **114** SD] *Wilson (subst. , after second* yours*); not in* F **116** growing –] *Orgel;* growing: F*;* growing. *Kermode*

Works, ed. James Spedding [1857], 2: 519, 520). Although rosemary and rue are classified as 'hot' in Gerard (1072, 1110), perhaps Perdita furthers her conciliatory project here by the deliberate choice of an adjective suggesting more vigorous life in lavender than in the sober rosemary and rue.

105–6 The marigold . . . weeping The petals of the marigold (called *Sponsus Solis*, i.e. the spouse of the sun) close up at sunset and reopen, 'weeping' (i.e. wet with dew), at sunrise.

110 Out An exclamation of reproach, often followed by 'alas' (*OED interj* 2).

111 blasts . . . January cold winds of winter (would blow). Intervening between the floral sumptuousness of middle summer and that of spring (118–27) is the reminder that, even in festive Bohemia, the chill of winter is known. Snyder thought that there might also be a hint at Camillo's size, Perdita possibly poking fun at his non-'lean' (middle-age) girth.

115 virgin branches virginal tresses (long hair worn down being the favoured hair style of young unmarried women).

116–18 The daughter of Ceres (goddess of agriculture), Proserpina, while gathering flowers, was 'frighted' by Dis/Pluto, the god of the underworld, who, enamoured of her beauty, abducted her in his chariot ('wagon'): As he 'caught her up . . . And as she from the upper part her garment would have rent, / By chance she let her lap slip down, and out the flowers went' (Ovid, *Metamorphoses*, 5.491 ff). Jupiter, taking pity on the grieving mother who sought his assistance, forged a compromise allowing the young girl to spend six months of the year on earth with her mother (a time of bounty marking the seasons of spring and summer) and six in the underworld with Pluto (a period of decline and barrenness associated with fall and winter). See Introduction, pp. 70–1.

118–20 Daffodils . . . beauty Blooming from early February until late April (Gerard's *Herbal* [1597] . . . amended by Thomas Johnson, 1633, vol. I, pp. 123–37, esp. 123, 131, and 137), the daffodil appears as the first sign of spring. Unlike the 'swallow', it risks ('dares') adverse conditions (the 'winds of March'), which its beauty captivates or bewitches ('take', *OED v* 10; see *Ham.* 1.1.163, 'No fairy takes, nor witch hath power to charm').

The winds of March with beauty; violets, dim,
But sweeter than the lids of Juno's eyes
Or Cytherea's breath; pale primroses
That die unmarried ere they can behold
Bright Phoebus in his strength (a malady
Most incident to maids); bold oxlips and
The crown imperial; lilies of all kinds,
The flower-de-luce being one. O, these I lack
To make you garlands of, and my sweet friend,
To strew him o'er and o'er.

FLORIZEL What, like a corpse?

PERDITA No, like a bank for love to lie and play on,
Not like a corpse; or if, not to be buried,
But quick, and in mine arms. Come, take your flowers.
Methinks I play as I have seen them do
In Whitsun pastorals; sure this robe of mine
Does change my disposition.

125 bold] F; gold *Hanmer*

120 dim less brilliantly coloured (than daffodils).

121–2 sweeter . . . breath 'sweeter to *behold* than the lids of Juno's eyes, sweeter to *smell* than the breath of Venus' (Schanzer). Female eyelids were often singled out for praise, as evidenced by Spenser in *The Faerie Queene*, 'Upon her eyelids many graces sat, / Under the shadow of her even brows' (2.3.25) and *Amoretti*, 'when on each eyelid sweetly doe appeare / an hundred Graces as in shade to sit' (Sonnet 40); see also *Per.*, 5.1.110–11, 'her eyes as jewel-like / And cas'd as richly, in pace another Juno'.

122 Cytherea Venus, the goddess of love, who was born of the seafoam near the island of Cythera.

122–5 pale . . . maids The early-blooming primroses, pale greenish yellow in colour, which fade before their bridegroom, the sun, reaches full potency, are like unmarried girls ('maids') afflicted with the 'malady' of green sickness (chlorosis, a form of anemia), which makes their complexions pallid. Schanzer notes a legend from the period claiming that those young girls who died from this condition were turned into primroses.

124 Phoebus Apollo, the sun god.

125 incident to likely to happen to, common or prevalent among (*OED* incident *adj*[1] 1).

125 bold Hanmer's emendation 'gold' was followed by some other eighteenth-century editors, but it is typical of this passage that the colours of flowers are conveyed only indirectly, i.e. as qualities of action and effect. Here 'bold' brings out the yellowness directly expressed in Peele's *The Arraignment of Paris*, 'yellow Oxslips bright as burnished gold' (1.3.40). Some editors (e.g. Steevens, Pafford), however, prefer to read 'bold' as an adverb indicating how the flower, with its sturdy stalk, stands tall and confident in contrast to the delicate cowslip.

126 crown imperial yellow fritillary, whose leafy stalk is encompassed by a cluster of drooping, bell-shaped flowers, a form Gerard likened to an 'imperial crown' (*Herbal*, 1597, 153–4).

127 flower-de-luce the fleur-de-lis (the heraldic lily displayed on the French royal coat of arms) or the iris, which 'was not uncommonly classed among the lilies' (Schanzer).

129 corpse *Corpse* or *corse* (F's spellings here and in 131, but *corps* in 5.1.58) could mean either a living or a dead body (*OED* *n* 1). The custom of the time called for bedecking both the bodies of the dead (*Cym.* 4.2.218–29, 283–7) and the bed of the newly married with flowers (*Ham.* 5.1.245–6).

130 bank i.e. a heap (of flowers).

132 quick alive.

134 Whitsun pastorals Presumably open-air festivities (*OED* pastoral *n* 2) held during the late spring feast of Pentecost, or Whitsunday (White Sunday), the seventh Sunday after Easter so called, as Andrews notes, because of the

FLORIZEL What you do
Still betters what is done. When you speak, sweet,
I'd have you do it ever. When you sing,
I'd have you buy and sell so, so give alms,
Pray so, and for the ord'ring your affairs,
To sing them too. When you do dance, I wish you
A wave o'th'sea, that you might ever do
Nothing but that: move still, still so,
And own no other function. Each your doing,
So singular in each particular,
Crowns what you are doing in the present deeds,
That all your acts are queens.
PERDITA O Doricles,
Your praises are too large. But that your youth
And the true blood which peeps fairly through't
Do plainly give you out an unstained shepherd,
With wisdom I might fear, my Doricles,
You wooed me the false way.
FLORIZEL I think you have
As little skill to fear as I have purpose
To put you to't. But come, our dance, I pray.
Your hand, my Perdita; so turtles pair
That never mean to part.

white robes worn by those to be baptized. In *TGV* (4.4.158–61), the male-disguised Julia refers to 'pageants of delight' held 'at Pentecost', during which time she performed a role in 'Madame Julia's gown'.

135–6 What . . . done Your manner of doing things is even better than the effect of your actions, or perhaps each action of yours is even better than the last. Both ideas are present in what follows: first, her singing redeems mundane affairs like buying and selling; then, her dancing succeeds and betters her singing. In Florizel's eyes, each act of Perdita's is perfect, subsequent acts paradoxically improving upon perfection.

142 move . . . so be constantly in motion and always in this manner (dancing). 'Still' = always but 'with wordplay on the stillness of the wave as it crests' (Folger).

143 own . . . function i.e. have no other purpose or reason for being.

143–5 Each . . . deeds Every act you perform, unique ('singular') in each detail ('particular'), brings to perfection ('crowns') whatever you are presently doing; or, perhaps, as Johnson paraphrases, with the emphasis on performative process rather than completed performance, 'Your manner in each act crowns the act.'

146 Doricles Florizel's name while disguised as a country swain. 'Doric, from Doris, in Greece, was used to mean rustic, as the Doric order was the simplest of the Greek architectural orders' (Orgel).

147 large much, extravagant.

147 But that If it were not for the fact that.

148 true blood with the double sense of noble heritage and virtuous disposition (both of which show beautifully through your youth, proclaiming you a pure and honourable ['unstained'] shepherd [149]).

151 false way (1) by flattery; or (2) with a dishonourable intent.

152 skill cause, reason.

154–5 turtles . . . part Turtledoves mate for life (thus typifying 'conjugal affection and constancy' [*OED* turtle n^1 1]).

PERDITA I'll swear for 'em.
POLIXENES [*To Camillo*] This is the prettiest low-born lass that ever
Ran on the greensward. Nothing she does or seems
But smacks of something greater than herself,
Too noble for this place.
CAMILLO He tells her something
That makes her blood look on't – good sooth, she is
The queen of curds and cream.
CLOWN Come on, strike up!
DORCAS Mopsa must be your mistress; marry, garlic to mend her kissing with!
MOPSA Now, in good time!
CLOWN Not a word, a word; we stand upon our manners.
Come, strike up!

[*Music*]. *Here a dance of shepherds and shepherdesses*

POLIXENES Pray, good shepherd, what fair swain is this
Which dances with your daughter?

156 SD] *Bevington; not in* F 157 greensward] F *(*greene-sord*)* 160 on't] F*;* out *Pope*[2] *(conj. Theobald)* 163 marry,] *Theobald;* marry F 164 with!] *Cam.;* with. F 167 SD *Music*] *Malone; not in* F

155 I'll . . . 'em I'll be sworn they do. Pafford finds the expression 'typical of Perdita's downright country speech'.

157 greensward green way, i.e. the turf on which grass grows.

157 Nothing . . . seems Nothing in her actions or appearance.

160 on't Sisson remarks (200) that 'out', Theobald's often-adopted emendation for 'on't' (first conjectured in his *Shakespeare Restored* [1726], and then adopted in Pope[2] before Theobald's own 1733 edn), means almost the same thing – Perdita's blood coming to the surface (as a blush) – but lacks the additional implication of coming out to look on something unexpected. Wells and Taylor find both readings 'strained' but think the emendation 'better suggests Perdita's confusion' (*Companion*, 602).

160 good sooth a mild oath meaning 'in truth'.

161 curds and cream a custard-like dish called 'white-pot' made with cream, eggs, apples, sugar, and various spices. In some May games the queen was given the name 'white pot queen' (Wilson).

162–7 Although set as prose in F, most editors follow Pope in arranging these lines as verse, presumably because they lend themselves to a fairly regular metrical pattern. But as Pafford and Orgel note, none of these three characters elsewhere speaks in verse.

163 marry Originally the name of the Virgin Mary used as an oath, which, by the sixteenth century was apprehended as nothing more than a 'mere interjection' (*OED interj*).

163–4 garlic . . . with Dorcas, perhaps in imitation of Perdita's distribution of flowers, hands garlic to Mopsa, her rival for the Clown's affections, to improve ('mend') her breath for kissing. The sarcasm is not lost on Mopsa, who responds with an indignant 'in good time' (165) = indeed.

166 stand upon must mind, observe (our manners).

167 SD The dance of shepherds and shepherdesses is probably a brawl, with steps going alternately left and right, perhaps in a circle or chain (as in Howell and Bedford). In contrast to this orderly display, the later satyrs' dance (4.4.322) features 'wild leaps and outlandish gestures' (Brissenden, 89, 124–5; see also Sorell, 380–1). Nunn in 1969 emphasized the 'juxtaposition between decorous lyricism and raucous energy' by reordering the satyrs' dance to appear fifteen lines after the first dance (Draper, 66). See Supplementary note, p. 252.

SHEPHERD They call him Doricles, and boasts himself
To have a worthy feeding; but I have it
Upon his own report, and I believe it –
He looks like sooth. He says he loves my daughter;
I think so too; for never gazed the moon
Upon the water as he'll stand and read,
As 'twere, my daughter's eyes; and, to be plain,
I think there is not half a kiss to choose
Who loves another best.

POLIXENES She dances featly.

SHEPHERD So she does anything, though I report it
That should be silent. If young Doricles
Do light upon her, she shall bring him that
Which he not dreams of.

Enter SERVANT

SERVANT O master, if you did but hear the peddler at the door you would never dance again after a tabor and pipe; no, the bagpipe could not move you. He sings several tunes, faster than you'll tell money; he utters them as he had eaten ballads, and all men's ears grew to his tunes.

170 and] F; and he *Rowe;* he *Capell;* 'a *Malone Suppl. conj.* 171 feeding] F; breeding *Hanmer* 171 but I] F; I but *Thirlby conj.*

170 **boasts himself** either, continuing the report of what others have related, 'they say he boasts himself' (Schanzer), or Doricles is understood as the subject (see Abbott 399). The potential difficulty with the latter is that it appears to make 'upon his own report' (172) redundant. 'But' (171), however, implies that 'boasts himself' differs somehow from 'his own report': perhaps the subject is meant to be something more like 'his appearance'–i.e. his clothes and bearing–suggests he owns 'a worthy feeding' (171), i.e. extensive, valuable pasturage.

173 **like sooth** truthful, honest.

175 **as** i.e. in the same fixed way as.

178 **another** the other.

178 **featly** nimbly, with graceful agility (*OED adj* 2b).

179–80 **though . . . silent** proverbial (Dent S114).

181 **light . . . her** i.e. choose her (for his bride).

183 **master** The addressee of the servant's message is ambiguous. 'Master' would suggest the old Shepherd who has just been speaking (see also 4.4.306), but the son could be so addressed (as in both Howell and Kahn).

183 **peddler . . . door** Schanzer cites this line (reinforced by 4.4.322) as indicating an indoor setting for the scene; Orgel restricts its interiority to the first part, claiming that by 4.4.652 the action seems to have moved outside.

184 **after . . . tabor** to the music of a small drum (and the whistle-'pipe' it accompanied). For an illustration of these instruments associated with rustic dances, see William Kemp, *Kempes nine daies wonder* (1600), title page.

186 **tell** count.

186 **ballads** tabloid-like stories in irregular verse and printed on one side of a large sheet of paper known as a broadside or broadsheet (*OED* ballad *n* 3), hence called 'broadside ballads'. They were frequently set to popular tunes, and pedlars would both sing and sell them.

187 **grew** Dolan's 'listened' conveys the basic idea but omits the sense of something irresistible, i.e. 'all men's ears' becoming attached through strong attraction ('to his tunes'). The image alludes generally to Orpheus and his mesmerizing music and more specifically to Midas, who, because he favoured the music of Pan over that of Apollo, had his ears changed into those of an ass. Both stories are found in Ovid's *Metamorphoses*, Books 10 and 11.

CLOWN He could never come better; he shall come in. I love a ballad but even too well, if it be doleful matter merrily set down, or a very pleasant thing indeed and sung lamentably.

SERVANT He hath songs for man or woman of all sizes; no milliner can so fit his customers with gloves. He has the prettiest love-songs for maids, so without bawdry (which is strange), with such delicate burdens of dildos and fadings, 'jump her and thump her'; and where some stretch-mouthed rascal would, as it were, mean mischief and break a foul gap into the matter, he makes the maid to answer, 'Whoop, do me no harm, good man' – puts him off, slights him, with 'Whoop, do me no harm, good man.'

POLIXENES This is a brave fellow.

CLOWN Believe me, thou talkest of an admirable conceited fellow. Has he any unbraided wares?

194 'jump . . . her'] *Capell (subst.)*; Iump . . . her F 197, 198 'Whoop . . . man'] F *(Whoop . . . man)* 200 admirable conceited] F; admirable-conceited *Theobald*

188 come better come at a better or more opportune time.

189–90 doleful . . . lamentably Compare Thomas Preston's *A Lamentable Tragedy, Mixed Full of Pleasant Mirth, Containing the Life of Cambyses, King of Persia* (*c.* 1569–70), and the 'very tragical mirth' of Pyramus and Thisby (*MND* 5.1.57).

191 sizes kinds.

191 milliner 'a vendor of fancy wares and articles of apparel [e.g. bonnets, gloves, and ribbons], esp. of such as were originally of Milan manufacture' (*OED* 2a).

193–5 so . . . thump her Although he sets out to prove the pedlar's songs are without indecency ('bawdry'), the servant takes up ballad catchwords ('dildos' and 'fadings') and expressions ('jump' and 'thump') whose sexual connotations make the refrains ('burdens') anything but 'delicate'. 'Dildo', first recorded in *OED* in 1610, refers to an artificial penis. 'With a fading' was the refrain of a popular song of an indecent character (*OED* fading *n*); 'fading' was also the name of a dance or jig. 'Jump' and 'thump' here carry the bawdy sense of copulating with vigour (Partridge).

195 stretch-mouthed Both Rolfe's 'broad-spoken' (*broad* = gross, indecent, loose – *OED adj* 6c) and Dolan's 'foul mouthed' fit the context better than Schanzer's 'wide-mouthed' or Orgel's 'bigmouth'.

196 break . . . matter interrupt by inserting something obscene, either in words or in action. It was evidently common in ballads sung by a man and a maid for the former to pause at various times, thus creating a 'gap' (*OED n*[1] 2b, 6b) to be filled by something scurrilous; the maid, however, would preempt the indecency by saying 'Whoop, do me no harm' (see next n.). Finding 'gap' problematic, some editors have substituted 'jape', a form, however, not recognized by *OED* as a variant. Although Pafford retains 'gap', he speculates that 'break a jest' (see *Ado* 5.1.187 and *Shr.* 4.5.72) might be the intended phrase.

197, 198 Whoop . . . harm Most likely the refrain of one or more popular ribald songs of the time. The tune is in William Corkine, *Ayres, to Sing and Play to the Lute and Basse Violl* (1610), sig. F1v.

199 brave an epithet of praise meaning 'fine, excellent, capital'. It's unclear whether Polixenes refers to the versatile pedlar being heralded or (mockingly) to the servant whose choice of words in defending 'delicate burdens' is unusual.

200 admirable conceited 'wonderfully ingenious' (Moorman).

201 unbraided new (hence not faded or soiled). For *braided OED* (*adj* b) gives an obsolete meaning of *braided wares* as 'goods that have changed colour, tarnished, faded'.

SERVANT He hath ribbons of all the colours i'th'rainbow; points, more than all the lawyers in Bohemia can learnedly handle, though they come to him by th'gross; inkles, caddisses, cambrics, lawns – why, he sings 'em over as they were gods or goddesses. You would think a smock were a she-angel, he so chants to the sleeve-hand and the work about the square on't.

CLOWN Prithee bring him in, and let him approach singing.

PERDITA Forewarn him that he use no scurrilous words in's tunes.

[*Exit Servant*]

CLOWN You have of these peddlers that have more in them than you'd think, sister.

PERDITA Ay, good brother, or go about to think.

Enter AUTOLYCUS [*wearing a false beard, carrying his pack,*] *singing*

Lawn as white as driven snow,
Cypress black as e'er was crow,
Gloves as sweet as damask roses,
Masks for faces and for noses,

209 SD] *Capell; not in* F 212 SD *wearing . . . pack*] *Oxford (subst.); like a peddler Capell; not in* F

202 points tagged laces used to fasten hose to a doublet or to lace a bodice (with a pun on legal details or arguments).

204 inkles linen tapes.

204 caddises ribbons of worsted tape or binding used for garters (*OED* caddis[1] 2c). *Caddis* was 'short for caddis-ribbon'; see *1H4* 2.4.70, 'caddis-garter'.

205 cambrics, lawns often glossed as fine or delicate linen fabrics, though 'cambric' could refer to a heavy cotton imitation of the fine white linen originating in Cambray, Flanders. 'Cambric' comes into the Shakespeare lexicon only in the later plays (see *Cor.* 1.3.84 and *Per.* 4. Cho. 24).

205–6 sings . . . goddesses i.e. (he) celebrates them in song as though he were paying homage to divine beings.

206 smock woman's undergarment, with possible wordplay on 'smock' as a loose woman (*OED n* 1c, 3b).

207 sleeve-hand sleeve's cuff or wristband (*OED* sleeve *n* 8b).

207 work . . . on 't needlework decorating the yoke or breast piece ('square', *OED n* 10a) of the smock.

210 You have of There are some of.

212 go about to am going to, intend to.

212 SD wearing . . . beard This is the only textual information given as to Autolycus' disguise at the sheepshearing feast. With the money taken from the Clown he presumably bought a 'pedlar's look' for himself (along with all the goods he plans on selling), but that costume 'in terms of the standards of realism in force in the modern theater . . . is . . . entirely at the modern director's discretion' (Folger). The point is that Autolycus must appear different in this scene so as to avoid being recognized by the Clown.

213–24 This song and the later 'Will you buy' (4.4.300–5) are typical of contemporary pedlars' songs. Pafford thinks that Shakespeare may have had in mind a song from Mundy's *Downfall of Robert Earl of Huntingdon* (1601): 'What lacke ye? What lacke yee? What ist ye wil buy? / Any points, pins, or laces, any laces, points or pins? / Fine gloues, fine glasses, any buskes, or maskes? Or any other prettie things. . . .' (ed. John C. Meagher, 1980, lines 1556–65). For a setting of Autolycus' song, see John Wilson, *Cheerfull Ayres or Ballads*, 1660, 64–6 (transcribed in Turner, 862–3).

213 Lawn See 4.4.205 n.

214 Cypress A light, transparent fabric resembling crape, here black (to be used for mourning attire) (*OED* cypress[3] 1c).

216 Masks Masks were worn to protect the face from the sun or, as Norton notes, to hide the ravages of syphilis.

Bugle-bracelet, necklace amber,
Perfume for a lady's chamber,
Golden coifs and stomachers
For my lads to give their dears,
Pins and poking-sticks of steel:
What maids lack from head to heel
Come buy of me, come, come buy, come buy;
Buy, lads, or else your lasses cry; come buy!

CLOWN If I were not in love with Mopsa, thou shouldst take no money of me; but being enthralled as I am, it will also be the bondage of certain ribbons and gloves.

MOPSA I was promised them against the feast, but they come not too late now.

DORCAS He hath promised you more than that, or there be liars.

MOPSA He hath paid you all he promised you; maybe he has paid you more, which will shame you to give him again.

CLOWN Is there no manners left among maids? Will they wear their plackets where they should bear their faces? Is there not milking-time, when you are going to bed, or kiln-hole to whistle of these

222 heel] *Schanzer; heele:* F 234–35 milking-time, . . . bed,] *Rowe* ²; milking-time? . . . bed? F 235 kiln-hole] F *(kill-hole)*

217 **Bugle-bracelet** Bracelet made of (usually black) glass beads.

219 **coifs . . . stomachers** tight fitting caps and stiff, ornamental V-shaped coverings for the stomach and chest.

221 **poking-sticks** rods which, after being heated in the fire, were used to repleat and stiffen ruffs.

222 In the omission of any punctuation, this edn follows Schanzer, who found F's colon at the end of the line (often replaced with a full stop by later editors) 'intrusive'.

226 **enthralled** captivated (the etymological meaning 'enslaved' figuratively anticipates the 'bondage' of ribbons and gloves [227] that, when purchased, will be tied up in parcels).

228 **against** in time for.

231–2 Clown has paid Dorcas more than he promised, i.e. by making her pregnant, an allegation Proudfoot (in Hunt, 281) finds support for in Dorcas's subsequent horror at marrying a usurer (4.4.256); she may be in need of a husband but not at the risk of giving birth to moneybags. Donnellan's 1999 production, however, while having a 'statuesque' Dorcas, showed a visibly pregnant Mopsa, the Clown's current girlfriend (see Holland). The sixteen years that have seen Perdita grow from infancy to young womanhood have apparently left the Clown at much the same age of feckless youth described by his father in 3.3.58–63, there hunting in bad weather, here 'getting wenches with child'.

233–4 **Will . . . faces** i.e. will they wear where it can be seen a garment that should be concealed ('plackets' = petticoats, or under-petticoats, with slits implying female genitalia). Although 'bear' is here understood as *bare* (reveal, display), F's spelling implicitly continues the previous allusions to pregnancy, thus reinforcing the multiple valences of the *bear/bare/burden* iteration noted by De Grazia and Parker, respectively.

235 **kiln-hole** fireplace (defined literally in *OED* [kiln *n* 2] as the opening or fire-hole of an oven or kiln), presumably a more fitting location for the gossip that offends the Clown's sense of decorum. 'Kill-hole' (F's spelling here and in *Wiv.* 4.2.59–Shakespeare's only other usage) indicates the seventeenth-century pronunciation, still recorded as acceptable in U.S. dictionaries.

235 **whistle** talk secretly, whisper (*OED v* 10).

secrets, but you must be tittle-tattling before all our guests? 'Tis well they are whisp'ring. Clamor your tongues, and not a word more.

MOPSA I have done. Come, you promised me a tawdry-lace and a pair of sweet gloves.

CLOWN Have I not told thee how I was cozened by the way and lost all my money?

AUTOLYCUS And indeed, sir, there are cozeners abroad; therefore it behoves men to be wary.

CLOWN Fear not thou, man, thou shalt lose nothing here.

AUTOLYCUS I hope so, sir, for I have about me many parcels of charge.

CLOWN What hast here? Ballads?

MOPSA Pray now, buy some. I love a ballad in print alife, for then we are sure they are true.

AUTOLYCUS Here's one to a very doleful tune, how a usurer's wife was brought to bed of twenty money-bags at a burden, and how she longed to eat adders' heads and toads carbonadoed.

MOPSA Is it true, think you?

AUTOLYCUS Very true, and but a month old.

DORCAS Bless me from marrying a usurer!

239 promised] F *(* ptomis'd*)* 249 ballad] F3; ballet F 249 alife] F *(* a life*)*

236–7 'Tis . . . whisp'ring Howell foregrounds the rustic trio; Autolycus and the other shepherds and shepherdesses remain in the background, with Shepherd, Polixenes, and Camillo out of the frame.

237 Clamor Silence. See *OED* clamour v^2 2, where this line and one from John Taylor, the Water Poet, 'Clamour the promulgation of your tongues', are given as examples.

239 tawdry-lace i.e. St Audrey's lace, a popular silk neckerchief deriving its name from St Audrey, who believed a tumour in her throat was punishment for her youthful indulgence in fancy neck adornments.

241 cozened cheated, robbed.

246–7 parcels of charge i.e., expensive goods; see Greene, *Second Conny-Catching*, 'parcels of worth' (44, 46).

249 ballad in print See 187n.

249 alife dearly, or, perhaps, indicative of an oath = 'on my life' (Abbott 24). Andrews favours a third possibility, 'from life' (i.e. based on actual incidents).

251–2 usurer's . . . burden In her focus on the play's concern with birthing and various kinds of bearing, Parker (175) argues for the lexical and thematic relevance of this bizarre tale of a usurer's wife delivered ('brought to bed') of twenty money-bags ('a fitting issue for a usurer', Andrews) in one birth ('at a burden'), and of the testimony to its truth by a 'Mistress Tale-Porter' (257–8). See also Parker, 'Promissory Economies', 30–1. On the significance of words like 'usurer' and 'money-bags' for the kind of pastoral world Bohemia represents, see Introduction, p. 19.

253 longed Proudfoot (in Hunt, 281) finds 'a small but typical example' of the linkage between the play's two halves in the echoing here and in 4.4.639 of the pregnant Hermione's 'I long' (1.2.100).

253 carbonadoed cut up for broiling or grilling.

AUTOLYCUS Here's the midwife's name to't, one Mistress Tale-Porter, and five or six honest wives that were present. Why should I carry lies abroad?

MOPSA Pray you now, buy it.

CLOWN Come on, lay it by, and let's first see more ballads. We'll buy the other things anon.

AUTOLYCUS Here's another ballad, of a fish that appeared upon the coast on Wednesday the fourscore of April forty thousand fathom above water, and sung this ballad against the hard hearts of maids. It was thought she was a woman and was turned into a cold fish for she would not exchange flesh with one that loved her. The ballad is very pitiful, and as true.

DORCAS Is it true too, think you?

AUTOLYCUS Five justices' hands at it, and witnesses more than my pack will hold.

CLOWN Lay it by too. Another.

AUTOLYCUS This is a merry ballad, but a very pretty one.

MOPSA Let's have some merry ones.

AUTOLYCUS Why, this is a passing merry one, and goes to the tune of 'Two maids wooing a man'. There's scarce a maid westward but she sings it; 'tis in request, I can tell you.

MOPSA We can both sing it. If thou'lt bear a part, thou shalt hear; 'tis in three parts.

DORCAS We had the tune on't a month ago.

257 Mistress] F *(* Mist.*)* 260 Pray] F *(* 'Pray*)* 276 'Two . . . man'] *Theobald (subst.)*; Two . . . man F

257–8 Tale-Porter The midwife's name indicates that she is a carrier of tales, a gossip. Wordplay on 'tail' = female genitalia (*OED n*[1] 5c) implies that she is also a bawd (one who traffics in 'tails').

264 fourscore the eightieth (of April). The parodic treatment of the 'wonders' associated with broadside ballads continues through the description of one dealing with the transformation of a frigid woman 'turned into a cold fish' (266–8).

267 exchange flesh have sexual intercourse.

269 Snyder thought there was something wrong here and wondered whether 'as true' in the previous line was an error for something else, possibly 'It is true' being read as '& as true'.

270 Five . . . it i.e., the signatures of five justices of the peace attest to its truth.

270 witnesses testimony, evidence (*OED* witness *n* 2).

273 pretty (1) pleasing, nice; (2) proper (*OED adj* 3b). Mopsa, however, prefers 'merry' to 'pretty' ones (274).

275 passing extremely, exceedingly.

276 'Two . . . man' A song of this title was set to music by Boyce in 1759 (Moorman), but no tune or allusion to the music for 'Get you hence' under the title 'Two maids wooing a man' has survived from Shakespeare's time (Orgel). Autolycus may be improvising a title that fits both the lyrics to 'Get you hence' and the rustic love triangle of Clown, Mopsa, and Dorcas (Pafford).

276 westward in the western part of the country, 'a pointer' (Schanzer) that Bohemia in Shakespeare's imagination was simply another name for England (as the references to Whitsun pastorals, the ingredients for the sheepshearing feast, and specific flowers and herbs also indicate).

278 bear carry, join in singing.

280 on't of it.

AUTOLYCUS I can bear my part; you must know 'tis my occupation. Have at it with you.

Song

AUTOLYCUS Get you hence, for I must go
Where it fits not you to know.
DORCAS Whither?
MOPSA O whither?
DORCAS Whither?
MOPSA It becomes thy oath full well
Thou to me thy secrets tell.
DORCAS Me too; let me go thither.
MOPSA Or thou goest to th'grange or mill,
DORCAS If to either thou dost ill.
AUTOLYCUS Neither.
DORCAS What, neither?
AUTOLYCUS Neither.
DORCAS Thou hast sworn my love to be.
MOPSA Thou hast sworn it more to me.
Then whither goest? Say whither?

CLOWN We'll have this song out anon by ourselves. My father and the gentleman are in sad talk, and we'll not trouble them. Come,

282 SD *Song*] F4; *before* 283 F **283** SH AUTOLYCUS] *Rowe; before* 284 F *(* Aut.*)* **285**] *Capell; as three lines* F **291**] *Capell; as three lines* F **296** gentleman] F *(* Gent.*)*; Gentlemen *Rowe*

281 bear my part In addition to the literal meaning of singing the lines assigned to him, his 'part' (see 4.4.278 n.), there is sexual wordplay both in 'bear' as the carrying or bearing a 'burden' (refrain) and in the pun on 'part' as male organ.

281 occupation In his disguise as a pedlar hawking ballads, Autolycus would be accustomed to singing (especially if, as is generally thought, the role was originally played by the actor-singer Robert Armin). A bawdy sense of 'occupation' may also be present (as in Pompey's claim that 'your whores, sir, being members of my occupation, using painting [cosmetics], do prove my occupation a mystery [i.e. an art or skilled craft]', *MM* 4.2.37–8).

282 Have at it I'll try it, or 'Let's have a go at it'.

283–94 A contemporary musical setting for the song, along with two sets of lyrics (one comparable to those found here and the other including additional verses), survives in manuscript form in the Drexel Collection of the New York Public Library. See also appendices in Pafford and Orgel, along with Pafford's 'Music, and the Songs in *The Winter's Tale*', *SQ* 10 (1959):161–75, and John P. Cutts's 'An Unpublished Contemporary Setting of a Shakespeare Song', *S. Sur.* 9 (1956): 86–9.

289 Or . . . or Either you will go to the farm ('grange') or to the mill.

290 dost ill do evil, commit sin.

295 We'll . . . ourselves This may refer to having it out in the sense of fully airing a quarrel (Dorcas and Mopsa's fighting over Clown) as well as the three of them carrying the song (with additional lyrics) to its conclusion in private.

296 gentleman This expands F's abbreviation 'Gent.', which, given the verb 'are' that follows, could be plural (Rowe, followed by many editors). 'My father', however, as part of a compound subject could make the verb plural without requiring the same of 'gentleman', and earlier (see 168–82) Polixenes and Shepherd are in dialogue with no contribution from Camillo.

296 sad serious.

bring away thy pack after me; wenches, I'll buy for you both. Peddler, let's have the first choice. Follow me, girls.

[*Exit with Dorcas and Mopsa*]

AUTOLYCUS And you shall pay well for 'em.

Song

Will you buy any tape, or lace for your cape?
My dainty duck, my dear-a?
Any silk, any thread, any toys for your head
Of the new'st and fin'st, fin'st wear-a?
Come to the peddler, money's a meddler
That doth utter all men's ware-a. *Exit*

[*Enter a* SERVANT]

SERVANT Master, there is three carters, three shepherds, three neatherds, three swineherds that have made themselves all men of hair. They call themselves saltiers, and they have a dance which the wenches say is a gallimaufry of gambols, because they are not in't; but they themselves are o'th'mind, if it be not too rough for some that know little but bowling, it will please plentifully.

297 me; wenches,] *Orgel;* me, Wenches F 298 SD] *Dyce; not in* F 300–305] F; *as nine lines Johnson (ending* tape, cape, dear-a, thread, head, wear-a, peddler, meddler, ware-a*)* 300 cape] F2; *Crpe* F 305 SD2] *Rowe; not in* F

300–5 On the crowdedness of the F page where this song appears, see Textual Analysis (pp. 257–8).

301 duck a term of endearment analogous to 'my pet'; the first recorded use of this figurative sense appears in *MND* 5.1.281, 'O dainty duck! O dear!' (see *OED* duck n^1 3).

302 toys trifles, trinkets. The proverbial 'To have toys in one's head' (Dent T456.1) cautioned against indulgence in trivial fashions.

304–5 money's . . . ware-a i.e. money, the go-between ('meddler') that facilitates selling (*OED* utter v^1 1) goods ('ware-a'), is involved in everything. 'Meddler' may also carry the meanings of one who mixes wares fraudulently and one who engages in sexual intercourse (*OED* meddle *v* 1b, 5), with additional wordplay on 'medlar'(the fruit that becomes edible only when decayed and which is often associated with prostitutes – e.g. *MM* 4.3.174).

306 carters drivers of carts.

307 neatheards cowherds.

308 saltiers leapers (from Fr. *saultier* = vaulter). The servant (whose grasp of semantics is questionable–see 4.4.193–5 n.) may be misspeaking since the stage direction at 4.4.322 specifies 'satyrs' (mythological creatures who are human from the waist up and goat from the waist down), to which he seemingly alludes in his description (307–8) of the rustic entertainers as having 'made themselves all men of hair' (i.e. dressed themselves up in animal skins). The word may hint at the type of dance to come: something along the lines of the running and leaping Jonson stipulates for his satyrs on their first entrance in *Oberon,* their later dance described as 'antic . . . full of gesture, and swift motion' (H&S, 7:342, 351). See illustration 11, p. 15.

309 gallimaufry . . . gambols confused, ridiculous jumble of leaps and capers.

310 o'th'mind of the opinion.

311 bowling i.e. lawn bowling, a gentler activity than the gymnastic dancing just mentioned.

SHEPHERD Away! We'll none on't; here has been too much homely foolery already. I know, sir, we weary you.

POLIXENES You weary those that refresh us. Pray, let's see these four threes of herdsmen.

SERVANT One three of them, by their own report, sir, hath danced before the King; and not the worst of the three but jumps twelve foot and a half by th'square.

SHEPHERD Leave your prating; since these good men are pleased, let them come in – but quickly now.

SERVANT Why, they stay at door, sir.

[He lets the herdsmen in]
Here a dance of twelve satyrs

POLIXENES *[To Shepherd]* O Father, you'll know more of that
hereafter.
[To Camillo] Is it not too far gone? 'Tis time to part them.
He's simple and tells much. *[To Florizel]* How now, fair
shepherd!

319 square] F *(squire)* 320 prating;] *Rowe (subst.)*; prating, F 322 SD1] *Wilson; not in* F 323 SD] *Pierce (subst.); not in* F 324 SD] *Cam.; not in* F 325 SD] *Wilson; not in* F

313 homely simple, rustic (see 4.2.31).

315 You . . . us You tire the patience of those who offer us entertainment.

316 four threes four groups of three countrymen each – the carters, shepherds, neatherds, and swineherds mentioned in 4.4.306–7.

317–18 One . . . King Since it was common for anti-masque dances in court masques to be performed by professional actors, the servant's statement has suggested to some that three of the King's Men had danced in the antimasque of satyrs in Jonson's *Masque of Oberon* performed at court on 1 January 1611 (see H&S, 10: 521). Brissenden adds that, with so many company actors needed onstage in 4.4 (ten speaking parts plus additional shepherds and shepherdesses), the other nine dancers may have been hired only for this scene (91). See Introduction, p. 62.

319 by th'square with extreme accuracy, precisely (*OED* square *n* 1b, figuratively derived from *square* = a carpenter's ruler).

322 SD 'The satyrs . . . in their wild celebration must contain a hint of danger, for their dancing goes just before the explosion caused by Polixenes' (Bartholomeusz, 190); to demonstrate such menace the satyrs in Evans reached out for the young lovers, who, on different sides of a wide stage, reached out for each other. See Appendix C, p. 273.

323 Polixenes and the Shepherd appear to have been talking privately during the dance sequence, perhaps resuming their earlier 'sad' conversation (4.4.296); Polixenes now answers the Shepherd as a way of easing back into onstage dialogue.

324 The question, whether delivered as an aside (Johnson) or to Camillo (the choice of most modern editors), might indicate a conclusion either based on watching the lovers or (as Rann thought) resulting from Polixenes' having assimilated the Shepherd's (privately expressed) expectation of a marriage between Perdita and Florizel. In 'far gone', Knowles (cited by Turner) observes an echo of Leontes' words at 1.2.215.

325 simple honest, forthcoming (in reference to the Shepherd who, living up to Polixenes' earlier description, has yielded the information desired by the king [see 4.2.39–41]).

325 How . . . shepherd In a break from theatrical tradition, Syer advanced Florizel's recognition of his disguised father from its usual place at 4.4.397 to Polixenes' direct address here. As a result, Florizel's words in the betrothal sequence (4.4.336–97) 'became veiled defiances aimed at his watching father, making him more dramatically interesting, but at some cost to Perdita, who faded from view as . . . attention fixed instead on the mounting tension between father and son' (Armstrong, 31).

Your heart is full of something that does take
Your mind from feasting. Sooth, when I was young
And handed love, as you do, I was wont
To load my she with knacks; I would have ransacked
The peddler's silken treasury and have poured it
To her acceptance. You have let him go
And nothing marted with him. If your lass
Interpretation should abuse, and call this
Your lack of love or bounty, you were straited
For a reply, at least if you make a care
Of happy holding her.

FLORIZEL Old sir, I know
She prizes not such trifles as these are.
The gifts she looks from me are packed and locked
Up in my heart, which I have given already,
But not delivered. [*To Perdita*] O hear me breathe my life
Before this ancient sir, who, it should seem,
Hath sometime loved. I take thy hand, this hand,
As soft as dove's down and as white as it,
Or Ethiopian's tooth, or the fanned snow that's bolted
By th'northern blasts twice o'er.

335 reply, at least] *Dyce;* reply at least, F 340 SD] *Bevington (conj. Pafford); not in* F 341 who] F2; whom F

327 **Sooth** Indeed, in truth.

328 **handed** handled, engaged in (anticipating the pledging of love by the hand at 4.4.363, 370–1).

329 **load . . . knacks** i.e. overwhelm my beloved with knick-knacks, trinkets. For only the second time in the play (see 1.2.77) we hear of Polixenes' wife and Florizel's absent mother, whose amenability to material things (as Turner notes) contrasts with Perdita's rejection (4.4.337–9) of what Juliet Dusinberre calls 'the courtship of bribery' (*Shakespeare and the Nature of Women*, 1975, 124).

332 **nothing marted** did no bargaining or trading (with the pedlar).

333 **Interpretation . . . abuse** Should misinterpret.

334 **were straited** would be placed in a difficult position.

335–6 **make . . . / Of** really care about.

336 **happy . . . her** Folger suggests two possibilities: (1) keeping her happy, and (2) happily keeping her.

338 **looks** looks for, expects.

339–40 **given . . . delivered** Florizel here distinguishes the private promise of his heart to Perdita from a formal ratification requiring contractual delivery (*OED* delivery 4b, 'the legal handing over of anything to another'). He intends for the hand-fasting that begins at 4.4.342 (but which is ultimately aborted at 4.4.397) to be that formal transfer.

340 **breathe . . . life** vow my lifelong love (Pafford).

344 **fanned . . . bolted** blown . . . sifted. For 'fanned snow', see *MND* 3.2.141–2, 'That pure congealed white, high Taurus' snow, / Fann'd with the eastern wind', and *TNK* 5.1.139–40, 'white as chaste, and pure / As wind-fann'd snow'.

345 **northern blasts** i.e. cold wintry winds as coming from the north (as in *Luc.* 1334–5, 'to hie as fast / As lagging fowls before the northern blast').

POLIXENES What follows this?
How prettily th'young swain seems to wash
The hand was fair before! I have put you out;
But to your protestation – let me hear
What you profess.

FLORIZEL Do, and be witness to't.

POLIXENES And this my neighbour too?

FLORIZEL And he, and more
Than he, and men: the earth, the heavens, and all;
That were I crowned the most imperial monarch
Thereof most worthy, were I the fairest youth
That ever made eye swerve, had force and knowledge
More than was ever man's, I would not prize them
Without her love; for her, employ them all,
Commend them and condemn them to her service
Or to their own perdition.

POLIXENES Fairly offered.

CAMILLO This shows a sound affection.

SHEPHERD But my daughter,
Say you the like to him?

PERDITA I cannot speak
So well, nothing so well – no, nor mean better.
By th'pattern of mine own thoughts, I cut out
The purity of his.

SHEPHERD Take hands, a bargain.
And, friends unknown, you shall bear witness to't.

361 better. | *Rowe;* better F

345 What . . . this? (1) Why the need for this elaborate preface? (2) Where is this leading?

346–7 to wash . . . before Through his poetic and proverbial comparisons in 4.4.343–5 (see Dent D576.1 and D573.2), Florizel is said to make Perdita's fair hand even whiter. Some gesture may also be implied such as Florizel's washing Perdita's hand with his kisses. Orgel specifies Camillo as the addressee of this comment (which Keightley thought an aside), but there could be a wider audience, possibly beginning with Camillo, then taking in Shepherd, and finally concluding with the focus on Florizel (as in Howell).

347 was that was (Abbott 244).

347 put you out distracted or confused you (as in 'put you out' of your part).

352–3 crowned . . . worthy i.e. the most majestic, exalted (*OED* imperial *adj* 5) monarch most deserving of honour. The following references to physical attractiveness, power, and knowledge recall *Ham.* 3.1.151–2 (see 4.2.27 n.).

357–8 Either commend them (i.e. my good qualities) to her service or condemn them to destruction (see 2.3.100–1 n.). 'Perdition' sets up wordplay on Perdita's name.

362–3 Using a sewing metaphor, Perdita says that the purity of her thoughts validates the purity of Florizel's since her feelings are the same as his.

363 Take . . . bargain The Shepherd proposes a 'handfasting': couples who clasped hands as they exchanged vows before witnesses were considered legally married (though a church wedding was expected to follow). See 1.2.102–3 n. and 1.2.274–5 n.

I give my daughter to him, and will make
Her portion equal his.

FLORIZEL O, that must be
I'th'virtue of your daughter. One being dead,
I shall have more than you can dream of yet;
Enough then for your wonder. But come on,
Contract us fore these witnesses.

SHEPHERD Come, your hand,
And, daughter, yours.

POLIXENES Soft, swain, awhile, beseech you,
Have you a father?

FLORIZEL I have; but what of him?

POLIXENES Knows he of this?

FLORIZEL He neither does nor shall.

POLIXENES Methinks a father
Is at the nuptial of his son a guest
That best becomes the table. Pray you once more,
Is not your father grown incapable
Of reasonable affairs? Is he not stupid
With age and alt'ring rheums? Can he speak? hear?
Know man from man? Dispute his own estate?

372–3] *Steevens; as four lines* F

366 portion dowry.

367 One . . . dead i.e. when my father dies.

368 yet now.

369 Enough . . . wonder (1) There'll be time enough *then* for your wonder; or, perhaps, (2) And even more to amaze you in the future (presumably when the Shepherd learns of Florizel's royal identity).

370 Contract . . . witnesses Because Polixenes puts an end to the 'handfasting' at 4.4.397, it is unclear which of the two kinds of marriage contracts in Shakespeare's time Florizel has in mind: the *sponsalia per verba de futuro* (a betrothal or promise to marry at some time in the future) or the *sponsalia per verba de praesenti* (a legally valid marriage contract because the couple declared themselves husband and wife from that time forth). Polixenes' reference to his son's 'nuptial' (4.4.375), however, may suggest the latter (Schanzer).

371 Soft An imperative exclamation meaning 'not so fast', 'wait' (*OED adv* 8).

373 Editors have generally linked 4.4.372–3, keeping 4.4.374 as a separate line. Some (e.g. Bevington) adopt Walker's recommendation (3:109) that the single line should be 'Knows . . . this', followed by the linked 'He . . . shall. / Methinks . . .'

377–82 The passage recalls Jacques' seventh age of man: 'second childishness, and mere oblivion, / Sans teeth, sans eyes, sans taste, sans every thing' (*AYLI* 2.7.165–6).

379 alt'ring (1) weakening (Moorman relates to Fr. *alterer*, which when used in regard to health, means 'impair'); (2) affecting the mind (Schanzer).

379 rheums Usually glossed as the secretions associated with colds and catarrhs, though Hoeniger connects the word to 'chronic rheumatism resulting from gradual bone decay' (217).

380 Dispute . . . estate (1) Maintain his legal right to control his property (as not incapacitated by age), perhaps further specifying being of sound mind to draw up a last will and testament; or, more generally, (2) discuss his own affairs (see *Rom.* 3.3.63, 'Let me dispute with thee of thy estate').

Lies he not bedrid, and again does nothing
But what he did being childish?

FLORIZEL No, good sir,
He has his health, and ampler strength indeed
Than most have of his age.

POLIXENES By my white beard,
You offer him, if this be so, a wrong
Something unfilial. Reason my son
Should choose himself a wife, but as good reason
The father (all whose joy is nothing else
But fair posterity) should hold some counsel
In such a business.

FLORIZEL I yield all this;
But for some other reasons, my grave sir,
Which 'tis not fit you know, I not acquaint
My father of this business.

POLIXENES Let him know't.

FLORIZEL He shall not.

POLIXENES Prithee let him.

FLORIZEL No, he must not.

SHEPHERD Let him, my son; he shall not need to grieve
At knowing of thy choice.

FLORIZEL Come, come, he must not.
Mark our contract.

POLIXENES [*removing his disguise*] Mark your divorce, young sir,
Whom son I dare not call. Thou art too base
To be acknowledged – thou a sceptre's heir,

397 SD] *Rowe (subst.); not in* F 399 acknowledged] F2 *(* acknowledg'd*)*; acknowledge F

384 **white beard** Earlier references to the disguised Polixenes as 'old' (4.4.336) and 'ancient' (4.4.341) are now explained by the false white beard he wears (and which he likely removes at 4.4.397).

386 **Something** For adverbial use as 'somewhat', see Abbott 68.

386 **Reason** There is good reason that, it is reasonable that. Rolfe cited a similar ellipsis in *John* 5.2.130, 'He is prepar'd, and reason too he should.'

386 **my** Dyce conjectured that 'my' should be 'the', but as it stands Polixenes' first person possessive pronoun can be seen as a momentary (and anxious) lapse in his disguise (understandable given the legality of what seems to be unfolding), a lapse he quickly corrects with the more impersonal article, 'the' (388).

389 **fair posterity** reputable lineage. See also 4.4.409.

392 **not acquaint** do not inform. Some editors suggest 'cannot' or 'will not'. See Abbott 305.

397–421 The abrupt change of tone in these lines parallels the explosion of rage in 1.2, providing a major link between the two halves of the play (see Introduction, pp. 22–4).

399 **acknowledged** F's 'acknowledge' is an easy error for 'acknowledgd' in Elizabethan script.

399 **sceptre's** i.e. king's.

That thus affects a sheep-hook! [*To Shepherd*]
Thou, old traitor,
I am sorry that by hanging thee I can
But shorten thy life one week. [*To Perdita*] And thou, fresh piece
Of excellent witchcraft, who of force must know
The royal fool thou cop'st with –

SHEPHERD O, my heart!

POLIXENES I'll have thy beauty scratched with briars and made
More homely than thy state. [*To Florizel*] For thee, fond boy,
If I may ever know thou dost but sigh
That thou no more shalt see this knack (as never
I mean thou shalt), we'll bar thee from succession,
Not hold thee of our blood, no, not our kin,
Farre than Deucalion off. Mark thou my words.
Follow us to the court. [*To Shepherd*] Thou, churl, for this time,
Though full of our displeasure, yet we free thee
From the dead blow of it. [*To Perdita*] And you, enchantment,

400 sheep-hook!] *Hanmer;* sheep-hook? F **400** SD] *Oxford (after Bevington subst.); not in* F **402** SD] *Oxford (after Bevington subst.); not in* F **403** who] F2*;* whom F **404** with –] *Pope;* with. F **406** SD] *Oxford (after Bevington subst.); not in* F **408** shalt see] *Rowe;* shalt neuer see F **412, 414** SD] *Oxford (after Bevington subst.); not in* F

400 affects . . . sheep-hook desires (or loves) a shepherd's crook. The antithesis of 'sceptre's heir' and 'sheep-hook' encourages a metonymic reading of the shepherd's crook as representing both the shepherd's way of life in general and, more particularly, the shepherdess Perdita, now reduced to nothing more than an inanimate rustic tool.

402–3 fresh . . . witchcraft young woman of bewitching seductiveness (Dolan subst.). Orgel and Folger read 'piece' not as 'woman' or 'girl' (*OED* piece *n* 9b) but as 'masterpiece' (*OED* piece *n* 17). Pafford (citing R. A. Foakes, ed., *Henry VIII*, 1957, 5.4.26 n.) points out the frequency with which 'piece' is associated with the heroines of the final plays.

403 who . . . know i.e. who had of necessity ('of force') to have known.

404 cop'st (you) have to do (with) (*OED* cope v^2 5), possibly with the added sense of 'make a bargain with' (*OED* cope v^3 3). The latter would continue the commercial implications of 'bargain' (4.4.363) and 'business' (4.4.390, 393).

406 homely plain, ugly (in being as unrefined as her low social 'state').

406 For As for.

406 fond (1) foolish; (2) infatuated.

408 knack (1) trifle (*OED* *n* 3); (2) delicacy (*OED* *n* 3b); (3) clever device (*OED* *n* 1), this last meaning having relevant overtones of deceitfulness (Orgel).

411 Farre . . . off i.e., further removed in kinship from me than Deucalion, Noah's counterpart in classical mythology. 'Farre' = comparative of *far*.

412 churl (1) peasant, rustic; (2) base fellow, villain. See *OED* *n* 4, 5.

414 dead fatal. Compare *MND* 3.2.57, where a murderer is said to look 'dead', i.e. deadly. Andrews reads 'dead blow' as 'execution'.

414 enchantment See 4.4.402–3 n.

Worthy enough a herdsman – yea, him too,
That makes himself (but for our honour therein)
Unworthy thee – if ever henceforth thou
These rural latches to his entrance open,
Or hoop his body more with thy embraces,
I will devise a death as cruel for thee
As thou art tender to't. *Exit*

PERDITA Even here undone!
I was not much afeared, for once or twice
I was about to speak and tell him plainly
The selfsame sun that shines upon his court
Hides not his visage from our cottage, but
Looks on alike. [*To Florizel*] Will't please you, sir, be gone?
I told you what would come of this. Beseech you,
Of your own state take care; this dream of mine
Being now awake, I'll queen it no inch farther,
But milk my ewes and weep.

CAMILLO Why, how now, father!
Speak ere thou diest.

417 thee–] *Capell;* thee. F 419 hoop] F (hope) 421 undone!] *Capell;* vndone: F; undone, *Johnson* 426 SD] *Rowe; not in* F

415–17 Worthy . . . thee i.e. 'You are a worthy mate for a herdsman, indeed worthy of him (Florizel) who has made himself through his conduct unworthy of you except that he shares royal honour (blood, dignity) with us.'

418 latches fastenings for a door or a gate. Sexual wordplay may be present if, as Andrews suggests, Polixenes implies a 'groundless suspicion that Perdita has parted more than the latches of her cottage'.

419 hoop enclose, encompass. Pope first discerned the meaning of F's 'hope', although his 'emendation' turns out to be a variant spelling (see *OED* hoop v^1 2, where this line is cited).

421 tender vulnerable, sensitive (to pain).

421 Even . . . undone! If we accept F's colon (usually emended to an exclamation mark or a full stop) and not Johnson's comma linking this to what follows, Perdita may be responding immediately to Polixenes' threat of death, asserting that his action right here, in separating her from Florizel, has destroyed her in any case. Thirlby (in Theobald) sees an allusion to her name.

426 Looks . . . alike Pafford follows Malone (1790) and Anon. in Cam. to hypothesize an omitted object after 'on', e.g. 'us' or 'all', but see Abbott 382 on ellipsis in general. The sentiment in 4.4.424–6 is both proverbial (Dent S985) and biblical (Eccles. 42.16 and Matt. 5.45); compare *R3* 5.3.286–7, 'for the self-same heaven / That frowns on me looks sadly upon him', and *R2* 1.3.145, 'That sun that warms you here shall shine on me'.

427–30 Beseech . . . weep Perdita says they should both abandon their disguises, Florizel removing shepherd-dress to resume the rich clothing appropriate to his rank (*OED* state *n* 17a) and she giving up her role as goddess and queen of the feast to resume her humble station as a shepherdess.

431 Pafford, Schanzer, and Orgel all take 'ere thou diest' as a reference to Polixenes' recent condemnation of the Shepherd to death and wonder why Camillo doesn't remember its revocation; his qualifier 'ere' is more likely prompted by the belief that holding in strong emotion instead of venting it could be lethal (as in *Mac.* 4.3.209–10, 'The grief that does not speak / Whispers the o'er-fraught heart, and bids it break'). The Senecan proverb, 'curae leves loquuntur, ingentes stupent' ('slight griefs talk, great ones are speechless') may also be relevant (A. R. Braunmuller, correspondence).

SHEPHERD I cannot speak nor think,
Nor dare to know that which I know. [*To Florizel*] O sir,
You have undone a man of fourscore-three
That thought to fill his grave in quiet; yea,
To die upon the bed my father died,
To lie close by his honest bones; but now
Some hangman must put on my shroud and lay me
Where no priest shovels in dust. [*To Perdita*] O cursed wretch,
That knew'st this was the prince, and wouldst adventure
To mingle faith with him! Undone, undone!
If I might die within this hour, I have lived
To die when I desire. *Exit*

FLORIZEL [*To Perdita*]
Why look you so upon me?
I am but sorry, not afeared; delayed,
But nothing altered. What I was, I am:
More straining on for plucking back, not following
My leash unwillingly.

CAMILLO Gracious my lord,
You know your father's temper. At this time
He will allow no speech (which I do guess
You do not purpose to him), and as hardly
Will he endure your sight as yet, I fear.
Then, till the fury of his highness settle,
Come not before him.

432 SD] *Rowe; not in* F 438 SD] *Rowe; not in* F 442 SD] *Oxford; not in* F 447 your] F2; my F 450 sight . . . yet,] *Hanmer;* sight, . . . yet F

432 An echo of Camillo's words at 1.2.371 and in a similar context, i.e. two enraged kings threatening violence (Pafford).

433 **fourscore-three** eighty-three.

437–8 A reference to the Christian burial service, denied to hanged men, who, as felons, were buried near or under the gallows.

440 **mingle faith** exchange marriage vows.

441–2 Compare *Mac.* 2.3.89–90, 'Had I but died an hour before this chance, / I had liv'd a blessed time'. The entire speech, in its expression of anger, betrayal, and loss, reveals a more serious layer to the Shepherd's essentially comic ethos, the invocation of his deceased father (4.4.435–6) adding to the play's roster of father-son relationships.

445 **More . . . back** More pushing forward because held back. Florizel uses the image of a hunting dog to convey his determination to move forward ('straining on') despite the restraints of a leash (4.4.446) dragging or pulling (*OED* pluck *v* 2) him back.

451 **highness** Schanzer reads this as 'haughtiness' rather than the royal title.

FLORIZEL I not purpose it.
I think, Camillo?
CAMILLO Even he, my lord.
PERDITA [*To Florizel*] How often have I told you 'twould be thus?
How often said my dignity would last
But till 'twere known?
FLORIZEL It cannot fail but by
The violation of my faith; and then
Let nature crush the sides o'th'earth together
And mar the seeds within! Lift up thy looks.
From my succession wipe me, father; I
Am heir to my affection.
CAMILLO Be advised.
FLORIZEL I am, and by my fancy. If my reason
Will thereto be obedient, I have reason;
If not, my senses, better pleased with madness,
Do bid it welcome.
CAMILLO This is desperate, sir.
FLORIZEL So call it, but it does fulfil my vow;
I needs must think it honesty. Camillo,
Not for Bohemia nor the pomp that may
Be thereat gleaned, for all the sun sees or
The close earth wombs or the profound seas hides

453 think, Camillo?] *Johnson;* thinke Camillo. F 454 SD] *Oxford; not in* F 462–3 fancy. . . . obedient,] *Theobald (after Rowe);* fancie, . . . obedient: F

453 **I . . . lord** At some point in this shared line Camillo's disguise is removed, possibly as early as Florizel's saying the name 'Camillo', with the Prince being the agent, or as late as the end of the line with Camillo himself taking off his disguise (as in Howell). Orgel (followed by Folger) inserts a stage direction to that effect before 'Even he'.

455 **dignity** i.e. the honour of being (1) queen of the feast/goddess (see 4.4.1–5, 10), or (2) the prince's beloved.

456–9 **It . . . within** Schanzer notes that the destruction invoked is not only of all actual life but of all potential life. Compare *Lear* 3.2.8, 'Crack nature's moulds, all germains [i.e. seeds] spill at once', and *Mac.* 4.1.58–60, 'though the treasure / Of nature's germains tumble all together, / Even till destruction sicken'. In contrast to Shakespeare's earlier use of similar images, Florizel claims that universal disorder will follow, not from the violation of degree (see *Tro.* 1.3.75–137), but 'if he *fails* to violate Degree' (by disregarding his father's wishes and marrying a shepherdess) (C. L. Barber, '[*WT*] and Jacobean Society', in *Shakespeare in a Changing World: Essays on his Times and his Plays*, ed. Arnold Kettle, 1964, 241).

461 **affection** profound love (in contrast to the passion or lust that is one of several possible meanings in 1.2.137).

461 **advised** cautious (Folger). Florizel replies as if 'advised' means 'counselled'.

462 **fancy** (1) imagination; (2) love.

462–5 **If . . . welcome** If his reason (a higher mental power than the emotions or the apprehension of images) refuses to obey his fancy, then Florizel would value madness over sanity. For the psychology involved, Kermode cites *MND* 5.1.2ff.

469 **thereat gleaned** reaped by becoming king of Bohemia.

470 **wombs** holds, encloses as in a womb (*OED* womb *v* 1).

470 **hides** See Abbott 333 for the old form of the third person plural ending in -s.

In unknown fathoms, will I break my oath
To this my fair belov'd. Therefore, I pray you,
As you have ever been my father's honoured friend,
When he shall miss me (as in faith I mean not
To see him any more), cast your good counsels
Upon his passion. Let myself and fortune
Tug for the time to come. This you may know
And so deliver: I am put to sea
With her who here I cannot hold on shore,
And most opportune to her need, I have
A vessel rides fast by, but not prepared
For this design. What course I mean to hold
Shall nothing benefit your knowledge, nor
Concern me the reporting.

CAMILLO O my lord,
I would your spirit were easier for advice
Or stronger for your need.

FLORIZEL Hark, Perdita.
[*Drawing her aside*]
[*To Camillo*] I'll hear you by and by.

CAMILLO He's irremovable,
Resolved for flight. Now were I happy if
His going I could frame to serve my turn,
Save him from danger, do him love and honour,
Purchase the sight again of dear Sicilia,
And that unhappy king, my master, whom
I so much thirst to see.

474 me (as . . .] *Rowe (subst.)*; me, as (. . . F 479 who] F; whom F2 480 her] F; our *Theobald* 486 SD] *Capell (subst.)*; *not in* F 487 SD] *Theobald*; *not in* F

473 A regular alexandrine often emended to produce a pentameter: e.g. Rowe follows F2 in omitting 'honoured'; Schanzer, following Dyce, favours elision and prints 'As you've e'er been'.

477 **Tug** Wrestle, have it out. Compare *Mac.* 3.1.112, 'So weary with disasters, tugg'd with fortune', where the First Murderer feels pulled about by fortune.

478 **deliver** report.

479 **who** Many editors adopt F2's 'whom', but as Abbott observes (274), the inflection is often neglected.

480 **opportune** accent on the second syllable.

480 **her** Theobald's emendation 'our' may be right but 'her need' works well enough as an objective genitive, i.e. 'the need we have of her'. Compare 'her medal' (1.2.304), or 'The deep damnation of his taking-off' (*Mac.* 1.7.20).

481 **rides . . . by** is anchored nearby.

483–4 **Shall . . . reporting** It will not serve you to know nor will it concern me to tell.

485–6 **easier . . . need** more inclined to heed advice or more focused on what's best for you.

487 **irremovable** immovable, unyielding.

491 **Purchase** Obtain (*OED v* 3).

FLORIZEL Now, good Camillo,
I am so fraught with curious business that
I leave out ceremony.
CAMILLO Sir, I think
You have heard of my poor services i'th'love
That I have borne your father?
FLORIZEL Very nobly
Have you deserved. It is my father's music
To speak your deeds, not little of his care
To have them recompensed as thought on.
CAMILLO Well, my lord,
If you may please to think I love the King,
And, through him, what's nearest to him, which is
Your gracious self, embrace but my direction,
If your more ponderous and settled project
May suffer alteration. On mine honour,
I'll point you where you shall have such receiving
As shall become your highness; where you may
Enjoy your mistress, from the whom, I see
There's no disjunction to be made but by –
As heavens forfend! – your ruin; marry her,

510 forfend!] *Steevens;* forfend F

494 **curious business** matters causing worry (*OED* curious *adj* 1b) or demanding care (*OED* curious *adj* 8, 9).

495 **leave . . . ceremony** i.e. forget my manners (by talking privately with Perdita). Such a breach of etiquette, however, is required for Camillo to voice his narrative-advancing aside that reminds audience and reader again of the 'unhappy' Leontes.

498 **music** delight.

499–500 **not . . . on** i.e. caring greatly to reward them (1) as soon as he reflects on them or (2) as richly as he appreciates their worth.

503 **embrace . . . direction** take my advice (a volitional imperative further softened by the framing 'if' clauses). Camillo's use of the conditional 'if' and 'may' (4.4.501, 504, 505) conveys a humility that suggests respect for Florizel's judgement. See next n.

504 **more ponderous** 'Camillo is tactfully and deferentially referring to Florizel's "project" as being weightier and of greater importance than his own "direction"'–'a delicate emphasis of the characters of the skilled . . . Camillo and the headstrong Florizel who needs to be handled in this way' (Pafford).

505 **suffer** permit, be open to.

506 **receiving** reception. Beginning with this line, Camillo turns from the classical ethical argument (the projection of an image of good will, good sense, and good nature) to the pathetic as he emphasizes what Florizel desires.

507 **highness** Florizel's royal rank (but see 4.4.451 n.).

508–9 **from . . . made** from whom you obviously cannot be separated.

510–12 **marry . . . strive** Malone reads a double command to Florizel, 'marry . . . and strive . . .', interrupted by a parenthetical phrase which means 'with my most fervent assistance, while you are absent'. But as Orgel observes, Florizel's sense of being in the presence of a miracle worker (4.4.514–16) suggests that he assumes the striving (to reconcile father and son) will be done by Camillo.

And, with my best endeavours in your absence,
Your discontenting father strive to qualify
And bring him up to liking.

FLORIZEL How, Camillo,
May this, almost a miracle, be done?
That I may call thee something more than man,
And after that, trust to thee.

CAMILLO Have you thought on
A place whereto you'll go?

FLORIZEL Not any yet;
But as th'unthought-on accident is guilty
To what we wildly do, so we profess
Ourselves to be the slaves of chance, and flies
Of every wind that blows.

CAMILLO Then list to me.
This follows, if you will not change your purpose
But undergo this flight: make for Sicilia
And there present yourself and your fair princess
(For so I see she must be) fore Leontes;
She shall be habited as it becomes
The partner of your bed. Methinks I see
Leontes opening his free arms and weeping
His welcomes forth; asks thee the son forgiveness
As 'twere i'th'father's person; kisses the hands

525 fore | F (*'fore*) 529 thee the son forgiveness | F3; thee there 'Son, forgiveness' *Alexander;* there the son forgiveness *Ritson conj.;* thee there Sonne forgiuenesse F

512 discontenting discontented.

512 qualify mollify.

513 bring . . . liking bring him round (i.e. persuade him) to approval.

518–19 th'unthought-on . . . do i.e. the unexpected or unforseen misfortune of being discovered by Polixenes is responsible for ('guilty to') our imprudent endeavours ('what we wildly do'). For the 'guilty to' construction, see Abbott 188. Folger glosses 'wildly' as 'in confusion'.

520–1 flies . . . blows Shakespeare's choice of *flies* for things to be buffeted by the winds may have been influenced by their association with *blowing* in other later plays (compare *Temp.* 3.1.63 and *Ant.* 5.2.59–60), providing a somewhat unpleasant undertone here; see also 4.4.751.

526 habited attired (and thus accorded the respect that comes with being your wife). Camillo's ironic artfulness in planning a royal disguise (which is in fact no disguise) for the 'anti-artificial Perdita' recalls Polixenes' earlier claim that 'the art itself is nature' (Felperin, 240).

528 free noble, generous (*OED adj* 4a).

529 the son F3's emendation, followed in this edn, balances 'th' father's person' (530) with the son here and avoids the awkwardness of suddenly predicting Leontes' very words and having him call Florizel son, as though seeking forgiveness from the lost Mamillius – a reading implicit in Alexander's emended punctuation, 'there "Son, forgiveness!"' (followed by Pafford). F's 'there son' may have come about by a scribe or compositor thinking 'the' a mistaken repetition of a previous word, possibly spelt the same, and substituting 'there'. Ritson conjectures transposition of the original 'thee there' to read 'there the'.

Of your fresh princess; o'er and o'er divides him
'Twixt his unkindness and his kindness – th'one
He chides to hell, and bids the other grow
Faster than thought or time.

FLORIZEL Worthy Camillo,
What colour for my visitation shall I
Hold up before him?

CAMILLO Sent by the King your father
To greet him, and to give him comforts. Sir,
The manner of your bearing towards him, with
What you, as from your father, shall deliver,
Things known betwixt us three, I'll write you down,
The which shall point you forth at every sitting
What you must say, that he shall not perceive
But that you have your father's bosom there
And speak his very heart.

FLORIZEL I am bound to you –
There is some sap in this.

CAMILLO A course more promising
Than a wild dedication of yourselves
To unpathed waters, undreamed shores – most certain
To miseries enough; no hope to help you,

544 you–] *Orgel;* you: F

531 **fresh** young, springlike, lovely; possibly even 'new', since from Camillo's perspective marriage to Florizel makes her a recent, newly-made princess (*OED* fresh *adj* 2a).

531–2 **divides . . . kindness** constantly goes back and forth in his speech between his unkindness to his boyhood friend so many years ago and his present feelings of kindness to him and you (either as representing Polixenes or simply because he is Bohemia's son). In Shakespeare's time 'kindness', as a natural bond of affection linking members of the human race, enjoyed a wider and deeper meaning than it does today.

534 **Faster . . . time** 'As swift as thought' was proverbial (Dent T240); see also 4.1.3–4 n.

535 **colour** pretext.

536 **Sent** (Tell him you were) sent.

537–44 **Sir . . . heart** This seven-line sentence, its syntax lacking a main verb as it goes off in a different direction after 'him' in 538 (an example of anacolouthon), may be paraphrased as follows: The combination of Florizel's courteous manner and the well crafted message he supposedly brings from his father, which will include information available only to Polixenes, Camillo, and Leontes, should convince Sicilia that Florizel has his father's confidence (see 543 n.) and therefore speaks what Polixenes really thinks and feels.

539 **as** as if.

541 **point . . . sitting** guide you in every session you have with Leontes.

542 **that** so that.

543 **bosom** personal confidence (i.e. Florizel will be perceived as being entrusted with his father's innermost thoughts, *OED* *n* 6a).

544 **I . . . you** As was his father to Camillo sixteen years before.

545 **sap** life, hope.

545–6 Pafford, citing Maxwell, notes an echo of *Cor.* 4.1.35–7, 'Determine on some course / More than a wild exposture to each chance / That starts i'th' way before thee'.

But as you shake off one to take another;
Nothing so certain as your anchors, who
Do their best office if they can but stay you,
Where you'll be loath to be. Besides, you know
Prosperity's the very bond of love,
Whose fresh complexion and whose heart together
Affliction alters.

PERDITA One of these is true:
I think affliction may subdue the cheek,
But not take in the mind.

CAMILLO Yea? Say you so?
There shall not at your father's house these seven years
Be born another such.

FLORIZEL My good Camillo,
She's as forward of her breeding as
She is i'th'rear'our birth.

CAMILLO I cannot say 'tis pity
She lacks instructions, for she seems a mistress
To most that teach.

PERDITA Your pardon, sir; for this
I'll blush you thanks.

FLORIZEL My prettiest Perdita!
But O, the thorns we stand upon! Camillo,
Preserver of my father, now of me,
The medicine of our house, how shall we do?

561 She . . . pity] *Steevens; as two lines* . . . birth. / I . . . F 563 sir; for this] *Hanmer;* Sir, for this, F

550 **Nothing** In no way, by no means.

551–2 **but . . . be** but hold you where you hate to be.

553 Proverbial: 'Prosperity gets friends, but adversity tries them' (Dent P611).

555 **alters** changes for the worse.

556–7 Perdita's sentiment that adversity may overcome ('subdue') one physically (i.e. make the cheek pale, thus altering the complexion) but not conquer ('take in') one's moral disposition or soul (*OED* mind *n* 15, 17) recalls parts of Son. 116, 'Let me not to the marriage of true minds'(see lines 2–3, 5–6, and most notably 9–12). See also Supplementary note, p. 252.

558–9 **There . . . such** With Florizel the likely addressee (as conjectured by Wilson, Pafford, and Riverside, and as shown in Howell), Camillo notes that even among royalty, a person as noble as Perdita is a rarity. (Bethell, however, emphasizes the dramatic irony if Perdita is the addressee.) Rather than a literal statement of fact, 'these seven years' = a proverbial expression indicating a long time (Dent Y25).

560–1 **She's . . . birth** Her personal qualities place her as far beyond ('as forward of') her family origins ('her breeding') as she falls short of ('is i'th'rear') our high birth. F's apostrophe following 'rear' may indicate that a word ('of') has been omitted (Schanzer).

562 **instructions** education.

562 **mistress** instructress.

565 **thorns . . . upon** 'To sit or stand upon thorns' was proverbial (Dent T239). Florizel is saying that he is impatient to get on with Camillo's plan.

567 **medicine** physician (in that he brings healing to Florizel's royal troubles); disyllabic. See *Mac.* 5.2.27 and *AWW* 2.1.71.

We are not furnished like Bohemia's son,
Nor shall appear in Sicilia.

CAMILLO My lord,
Fear none of this. I think you know my fortunes
Do all lie there; it shall be so my care
To have you royally appointed, as if
The scene you play were mine. For instance, sir,
That you may know you shall not want – one word.

[*They talk aside*]

Enter AUTOLYCUS

AUTOLYCUS Ha, ha, what a fool honesty is! And trust, his sworn brother, a very simple gentleman. I have sold all my trumpery; not a counterfeit stone, not a ribbon, glass, pomander, brooch, table-book, ballad, knife, tape, glove, shoe-tie, bracelet, horn-ring, to keep my pack from fasting. They throng who should buy first, as if my trinkets had been hallowed and brought a benediction to the buyer; by which means I saw whose purse was best in picture, and what I saw, to my good use I remembered.

569 Nor . . . lord] *Steevens; as two lines* . . . Sicilia. / My . . . F 574 want –] *Pafford (subst.)*; want: F 574 SD 1] *Rowe; not in* F

569 **appear** appear as such. Florizel's practical question about sartorial matters (567) may indicate that Camillo's counsel is having some effect on the young man's earlier impulsive behaviour.

570 **fortunes** stock of wealth, possessions taken collectively (*OED* fortune *n* 6). Camillo speaks as though he knows that his estate (which he was forced to leave behind when he fled Sicilia) has remained intact.

572 **royally appointed** furnished as befits a prince.

574 SDD The talking aside, followed immediately by the return of Autolycus, suggests that the scene, if initiated indoors (see 4.4.183 n.), has by now moved to an exterior setting. For Autolycus to reenter the Shepherd's cottage to brag aloud about his trickery seems unlikely.

575–94 In this extended speech on the wiles of a con-artist and the gullibility of his victims, Shakespeare draws upon Greene's cony-catching pamphlets.

575 **what . . . is** The notion that 'honesty is a fool' was proverbial (Dent H539.1).

575–6 **trust . . . gentleman** The personification of 'trust' as a 'gentleman' recalls another opportunist's speech on the gentleman 'commodity' (see *John* 2.1.573).

576 **simple** (1) innocent, undesigning; (2) foolish, stupid (*OED adj* 1, 10).

577–9 **glass, pomander . . . table-book . . . horn-ring** looking glass, a perfumed ball worn around the neck to guard against infection . . . writing tablet . . . inexpensive ring made from the animal's horn and thought to have magic powers.

579 **my . . . fasting** my bag ('pack') from going hungry, i.e. being empty.

580–1 **hallowed . . . buyer** sacred and brought a blessing ('benediction') to the purchaser. Citing Harold Brooks, Pafford associates Autolycus here with 'that other traditional comic cheat on the pre-Shakespearian stage, the Pardoner' (see Chaucer's 'The Pardoner's Tale' in *The Canterbury Tales*.)

582 **best in picture** i.e. best in prospect or in appearance because of plumpness and position for stealing. Greene provides an extensive account of how the clever pick-pocket spies the well stocked purse before seizing it (see *Second Part of Conny-Catching*, 30–2, and *Third Part*, 27). There may also be a pun on 'picture' = 'slang for a coin, from the portrait of the sovereign that it often bore' (Fischer, 105); compare Jonson's *Bartholomew Fair*, 3.5.46–7, 'to pick the pictures out o'your pockets' (ed. Eugene M. Waith, 1963).

My clown (who wants but something to be a reasonable man) grew so in love with the wenches' song that he would not stir his pettitoes till he had both tune and words, which so drew the rest of the herd to me that all their other senses stuck in ears. You might have pinched a placket, it was senseless; 'twas nothing to geld a codpiece of a purse; I would have filed keys off that hung in chains – no hearing, no feeling, but my sir's song, and admiring the nothing of it. So that in this time of lethargy I picked and cut most of their festival purses; and had not the old man come in with a hubbub against his daughter and the King's son, and scared my choughs from the chaff, I had not left a purse alive in the whole army.

[*Camillo, Florizel, and Perdita come forward*]

CAMILLO Nay, but my letters by this means being there
So soon as you arrive, shall clear that doubt.
FLORIZEL And those that you'll procure from King Leontes?
CAMILLO Shall satisfy your father.
PERDITA Happy be you!
All that you speak shows fair.
CAMILLO Who have we here?
We'll make an instrument of this, omit
Nothing may give us aid.

588 would] F; could *Globe (anon. conj. Cam.)* 588 filed] F3 (*fil'd*); fill'd F 588 off] F3; of F 594 SD] *Theobald; not in* F

585 **pettitoes** i.e. feet or toes (the word indicates Autolycus's contempt since it typically refers to pig's feet).

586–7 **stuck . . . ears** gave way to the auditory. Moorman compares the expression 'I was all ears'; see 4.4.186–7.

587 **placket** (1) woman's undergarment, (2) woman's genitals (Dolan). See 4.4.234.

588 **geld . . . purse** cut a wallet ('purse') hanging from the front pouch of a man's breeches ('codpiece'). Dolan's 'castrate men of their purses' derives from the sexual connotations of 'geld', 'codpiece' = male genitals, and 'purse' = 'scrotum' (see Williams). Folger points out the continuing sexual wordplay in 'keys', slang for 'penis'. 'Geld' recalls Antigonus' usage in 2.1.147.

588 **would** Hudson suggests that 'would' = 'could', Globe's emendation (which Oxford adopts), but Autolycus may be saying 'I would have filed them off had I wanted to' (Furness).

589 **my sir's** the clown's (i.e. the Shepherd's son's).

590 **nothing** nonsense (with wordplay on 'noting' in the musical sense of setting forth notes).

590 **lethargy** i.e. dullness of the senses (except that of hearing 'my sir's song' [589]).

591 **picked and cut** Autolycus works as both pick-pocket and cut-purse.

591 **festival purses** wallets filled with money to spend at the sheep-shearing feast.

593 **choughs** chattering birds of the crow family like jackdaws (*OED* chough 1). Folger also suggests 'chuffs' = 'rustics' (*OED* chuff *n*[1] 1).

594 **army** assemblage.

598 **Happy be you** i.e. may good 'hap' (= fortune) smile upon you.

599 **shows fair** (1) looks promising; (2) makes sense.

AUTOLYCUS [*Aside*] If they have overheard me now – why, hanging.

CAMILLO How now, good fellow, why shak'st thou so? Fear not, man, here's no harm intended to thee.

AUTOLYCUS I am a poor fellow, sir.

CAMILLO Why, be so still; here's nobody will steal that from thee. Yet for the outside of thy poverty we must make an exchange; therefore discase thee instantly – thou must think there's a necessity in't – and change garments with this gentleman. Though the pennyworth on his side be the worst, yet hold thee, there's some boot.

[*He gives Autolycus money*]

AUTOLYCUS I am a poor fellow, sir. [*Aside*] I know ye well enough.

CAMILLO Nay, prithee dispatch; the gentleman is half flayed already.

AUTOLYCUS Are you in earnest, sir? [*Aside*] I smell the trick on't.

FLORIZEL Dispatch, I prithee.

602 SD] *Theobald; not in* F **603** as prose] *Malone; as three verse lines* . . . fellow) / . . . (man) / . . . thee F; *as two verse lines* . . . so? / Fear . . . *Hanmer* **611** SD] *Dyce (subst.); not in* F **612, 614** SDD] *Hanmer; indicated by parentheses in* F **613** flayed] F *(* fled*)*

602 SD Autolycus enters after 574 and speaks in soliloquy; the others come forward at 594, and at 602 he fears that his self-incriminating soliloquy may have been overheard, a seeming violation of the same convention still operative in the aside here (and again at 612 and 614). Camillo's soliloquy at 634–9 cannot be overheard by Florizel and Perdita, who are talking apart, or by Autolycus, who raises the possibility of telling the King of the elopement (650–1), apparently unaware that Camillo is already planning to do so. What 602 SD illustrates, then, is the fluidity of convention when dramatic effect is at issue, in this instance the comic stage business suggested by Autolycus' alarm and made explicit in Camillo's 'why shak'st thou so?' (603).

602 hanging a punishment in Shakespeare's time for thefts of items valued at more than twelve pence.

606 that i.e. your poverty.

607 the outside . . . poverty i.e. your clothing.

608 discase thee remove your outer casing, i.e. undress yourself. In *Pandosto*, the narrator describes Dorastus as 'uncasing himself [of his shepherd's attire] as secretly as might be' (Bullough, 186).

609 change garments exchange clothes. See Supplementary note, p. 253, and Appendix C, p. 273.

610–11 some boot something extra to make the bargain even more desirable. See 4.4.646 nn.

612 I . . . fellow Coming right after Camillo's proffer of a tip, the expression suggests that Autolycus is hinting for a bit more; compare Feste in *TN* 5.1.27–44.

612 I . . . enough Proverbial (Dent K171.1). Usually addressed 'to supposed knaves, villains', the proverb here assumes comic force in the reversal (Turner).

613 flayed skinned, i.e. stripped of his clothing (see 'discase', 4.4.608). Florizel has evidently begun to remove his outfit. Rowe's widely adopted emendation recognizes F's 'fled' as an obsolete spelling (see *OED* flay *v*). Patricia Parker (unpublished manuscript), however, citing Pafford's observation that F knows how to spell 'flayd' or 'flay'd' when it wants to, argues that F's 'fled' has the advantage of simultaneously suggesting 'the haste of Florizel's intended flight and his only partial state of undress', the latter prompting Camillo's further urging in 618 to 'Unbuckle, unbuckle'. That Compositor A set 'fled' here (and at 5.1.183) and 'flayd'/flay'd at 4.4.745, 763, and 772 (along with 'flaying', 3.2.173) strengthens the argument.

614 on't of it (Abbott 181).

AUTOLYCUS Indeed, I have had earnest, but I cannot with conscience take it.

CAMILLO Unbuckle, unbuckle.

[*Florizel and Autolycus exchange garments*]

Fortunate mistress – let my prophecy
Come home to ye! – you must retire yourself
Into some covert; take your sweetheart's hat
And pluck it o'er your brows, muffle your face,
Dismantle you, and, as you can, disliken
The truth of your own seeming, that you may
(For I do fear eyes over) to shipboard
Get undescried.

PERDITA I see the play so lies
That I must bear a part.

CAMILLO No remedy. –
Have you done there?

618 SD] *Capell; not in* F 627 remedy. –] *Folger (after Oxford subst.); not in* F

616 earnest the money he has already received from Camillo as a partial payment for entering into the bargain (with wordplay on 'earnest' in 614).

618 SD Camillo's following speech to Perdita allows for the prince and Autolycus to move offstage briefly to complete the exchange (as in Kahn); the query in 4.4.628, however, suggests that they simply step aside, possibly moving behind a tree or hedge property. In Howell, television permitted both men to be out of the frame for a few moments.

619–20 prophecy . . . ye forecast of your good fortune come true.

620–3 you . . . Dismantle you Thirlby (in Theobald) wonders whether these lines (1) indicate Perdita's withdrawal for the purpose of undressing in order to disguise herself or (2) simply describe the manner in which she will cover up her beauty.

621 covert a hiding place, possibly a thicket (*OED n* 2, 3).

621 sweetheart's hat A brimmed hat sufficient to covering Perdita's brow is the only textual clue provided for Florizel's 'swain's wearing' (4.4.9). See *LLL* 3.1.17–8, 'with your hat penthouse-like o'er the shop of your eyes'; also title page in Robert Burton, *The Anatomy of Melancholy*, 1638.

623 Dismantle you Change the holiday attire making you queen of the sheepshearing feast; perhaps, literally, remove your mantle (possibly the jewelled one mentioned in 5.2.29–30); see 4.4.665 n.

623–4 disliken / . . . seeming i.e. (as much as possible) alter your actual appearance. The dramatic irony of these lines derives from the audience's awareness – and the onstage characters' ignorance – of Perdita's true identity: Perdita's 'seeming' (the costume she still wears signifying her royal appearance as the 'queen of curds and cream') 'reveals the truth of her birth – the truth of [her] own seeming' (Folger).

625 eyes over overseeing (i.e. watchful, perhaps spying) eyes (see 4.2.29–30). Compare *LLL* 4.3.77–8, 'here sit I in the sky, / And wretched fools' secrets heedfully o'er-eye'.

626 undescried undetected.

627 I . . . part 'A breathtaking understatement given the importance of [Perdita's] role in connecting both halves of [*WT*], made possible by being borne across its "vast" or "great difference" between Bohemia and Sicilia, in both directions' (Patricia Parker, unpublished manuscript). Compare 4.4.281 where the sense of bearing a part is sexual rather than theatrical.

FLORIZEL Should I now meet my father
He would not call me son.
CAMILLO Nay, you shall have no hat.

[*He gives Florizel's hat to Perdita*]

Come, lady, come. Farewell, my friend.
AUTOLYCUS Adieu, sir.
FLORIZEL O Perdita, what have we twain forgot?
Pray you, a word [*drawing her aside*].
CAMILLO What I do next shall be to tell the King
Of this escape, and whither they are bound;
Wherein my hope is I shall so prevail
To force him after, in whose company
I shall re-view Sicilia, for whose sight
I have a woman's longing.
FLORIZEL Fortune speed us!
Thus we set on, Camillo, to th'seaside.
CAMILLO The swifter speed the better.

[*Exeunt* FLORIZEL, PERDITA, *and* CAMILLO]

AUTOLYCUS I understand the business, I hear it. To have an open ear, a quick eye, and a nimble hand is necessary for a cutpurse; a good nose is requisite also, to smell out work for th'other senses. I see this is the time that the unjust man doth thrive. What an

629 SD] *Capell (subst.); not in* F 633 Pray] F ('Pray) 633 SD] *Capell (subst.); not in* F 639 us!] *Hanmer;* us: F 641 SD] *Capell; Exit* F

631 **Adieu, sir** Like Bevington and Orgel, we follow F's lineation; most editors, however, link the valediction to the preceding line, following 'friend'.

632 **what . . . forgot** Rather than speculating on what has been forgotten, it seems best to follow Steevens who perceived the expedience of a dramatic device permitting 'a conversation apart' or 'a sudden exit'. Compare *Wiv.* 1.4.62–3 and 165.

639 **woman's longing** Female longing was proverbial (see Dent L 421.1, 'To have a woman's longing') and generally regarded as all consuming, overwhelming, but the implication of a pregnant woman's intense cravings may also be present.

641 SD Florizel and Perdita should perhaps exeunt in one direction, and Camillo exits in another, since they are going to the ship while he is going to tell the King of their plans. On the other hand, Camillo may accompany them to provide the promised letters and instructions. F's SD *Exit* led Rowe to stipulate a separate exit for Florizel and Perdita after 640.

645 **unjust . . . thrive** The prosperity of the wicked was a commonplace that carried biblical overtones: e.g. Ps. 37.35, 73.3; Jer. 12.1; and Job 21.7 (see Shaheen, 730).

exchange had this been without boot! What a boot is here, with this exchange! Sure the gods do this year connive at us, and we may do anything extempore. The Prince himself is about a piece of iniquity, stealing away from his father with his clog at his heels. If I thought it were a piece of honesty to acquaint the King withal, I would not do't; I hold it the more knavery to conceal it; and therein am I constant to my profession.

Enter CLOWN *and* SHEPHERD

Aside, aside, here is more matter for a hot brain. Every lane's end, every shop, church, session, hanging, yields a careful man work.

CLOWN See, see, what a man you are now! There is no other way but to tell the King she's a changeling, and none of your flesh and blood.

646 boot!] *Hanmer;* boot? F 647 exchange!] *Hanmer;* exchange? F 656 now!] *Hanmer;* now? F

646–7 exchange . . . exchange An example of the rhetorical scheme known as antimetabole, a form of chiasmus in which the same words or phrases are repeated in reversed order; here, 'exchange' and 'boot'.

646 without boot i.e. without the extra tip or reward provided by Camillo.

646 What . . . boot What a profit or boon. For Parker ('Promissory Economies', 36), '"boot" here is simultaneously the term for the surplus . . . or profit that [Autolycus] receives in this exchange and the punining "boot" or article of clothing that transforms him from vagabond into an apparent courtier [4.4.713–14], able with these new garments to fool the Shepherd and his son into adopting him as their "advocate" to the "court" [4.4.705–96].'

647 connive at wink at, look at with secret sympathy (*OED v* 3, where this line is cited).

648 extempore without rehearsal or forethought.

648–52 Autolycus' reasoning may be paraphrased as follows: The Prince is acting against his father's will, and I'm tempted to betray him to the King (especially since he will be slowed somewhat in his flight by the presence of Perdita, a 'clog at his heels'). But that betrayal, knavery in itself, might be construed as an honorable action in that it would forestall the Prince's guilty intentions. Hence I shall be truer to my knavish profession by not revealing the Prince's plans.

648 about engaged in.

649 clog impediment (used here figuratively of Perdita, see *OED n* 3). The literal meaning is something heavy, like a block of wood, attached to the leg or neck of a man or beast to hinder movement or prevent escape (*OED n* 2). 'To have a clog at one's heels' was proverbial (Dent C426.1); compare 'ball and chain', slang for a wife (as in *AWW* 2.5.53).

650 If Even if.

651 withal with this information (Folger).

653 Aside, aside A stage direction may be implied here calling for Autolycus to move aside so as to be out of clear view by the newly arrived Shepherd and Clown; Folger, however, places it after 655.

653 hot sharp, eager.

653–4 lane's end corner (and thus a gathering place like a shop, church service, court session, and public execution – all promising venues for a cony-catcher). Peter Blayney calls to our attention a notice (3 July 1561) that copies of a proclamation of the Court of Aldermen are to be posted at Soper Lane End as well as Cheapside, St. Magnus Corner, and other common places (Corporation of London Records Office, Repertory 14, fol. 502v).

654 careful shrewd, observant (*OED adj* 4).

657 changeling a child secretly substituted by the fairies. See 3.3.106 n.

SHEPHERD Nay, but hear me –

CLOWN Nay, but hear me.

SHEPHERD Go to, then.

CLOWN She being none of your flesh and blood, your flesh and blood has not offended the King, and so your flesh and blood is not to be punished by him. Show those things you found about her, those secret things, all but what she has with her. This being done, let the law go whistle, I warrant you.

SHEPHERD I will tell the King all, every word, yea, and his son's pranks too; who, I may say, is no honest man, neither to his father nor to me, to go about to make me the King's brother-in-law.

CLOWN Indeed, brother-in-law was the farthest off you could have been to him, and then your blood had been the dearer by I know not how much an ounce.

AUTOLYCUS [*Aside*] Very wisely, puppies!

SHEPHERD Well, let us to the King. There is that in this fardel will make him scratch his beard.

AUTOLYCUS [*Aside*] I know not what impediment this complaint may be to the flight of my master.

CLOWN Pray heartily he be at'palace.

659 me –] *Orgel;* me. F 660 *me.*] F; *me. Offord;* me! *Orgel* 672–3 know not] *Hanmer (conj. Thirlby);* know F 674 SD] *Rowe; not in* F 675, 685 fardel] *Steevens;* Farthell F 677 SD] *Hudson; not in* F 679 Pray] F (*'Pray*)

662–4 The Clown's attempt at logical reasoning would seem to refute earlier comments about his lack of intelligence. 'Flesh and blood' = offspring (662), physical body (662–3), and, perhaps, both (663), if the Clown is thinking of himself as well.

665 what . . . her Thirlby (in Warburton) suspects a bawdy reference to the secret thing Perdita always has with her, i.e. her vagina; see Williams on 'thing' and 'secret'. Schanzer and Orgel, however, think 'what she has with her' may be Hermione's jewel, which Perdita wore for the feast, and which is later said to be attached to her mother's mantle (see 5.2.29–30; also 4.4.623 n.).

666 go whistle 'go its own futile way' (Andrews). See Dent W313 for the proverbial expression.

669 go about to pursue a course that would.

669–70 brother-in-law 'A humorous misuse of brother-in-law to mean the father of the king's daughter-in-law' (Folger).

672–3 Editors who reject Hanmer's insertion of 'not' (e.g. Pafford, Orgel) see a conscious joke in F's 'I know how much', i.e. not at all; but the Clown is seldom witty by design, and the joke seems rather to reside in his naive revaluing ('dearer') of the very blood – of his father and himself – that he fears will be forfeited in their punishment.

675 fardel bundle, parcel.

677 complaint statement of grievance. The Shepherd and Clown will claim that they are unjustly punished for the misdeeds of a foundling not related to them and the King's son (see 4.4.793).

678 my master Prince Florizel, in whose service Autolycus evidently still sees himself. See 4.3.13–14 and 4.4.789–90.

679 at'palace F's apostrophe before 'palace' probably indicates the omission of 'the' (see Abbott 90). To Kermode (following Cam.), however, the Clown appears to be speaking of the King 'as he might of an ordinary man being "at home"'.

AUTOLYCUS [*Aside*] Though I am not naturally honest, I am so sometimes by chance. Let me pocket up my peddler's excrement.

[*He takes off his false beard*]

How now, rustics, whither are you bound?

SHEPHERD To th'palace, an it like your worship.

AUTOLYCUS Your affairs there, what, with whom, the condition of that fardel, the place of your dwelling, your names, your ages, of what having, breeding, and anything that is fitting to be known, discover!

CLOWN We are but plain fellows, sir.

AUTOLYCUS A lie, you are rough and hairy. Let me have no lying; it becomes none but tradesmen, and they often give us soldiers the lie; but we pay them for it with stamped coin, not stabbing steel, therefore they do not give us the lie.

CLOWN Your worship had like to have given us one, if you had not taken yourself with the manner.

680 SD] *Hudson; not in* F 681 SD] *Steevens; not in* F 684–6 there, . . . having,] *Pope; question marks throughout* F 687 discover!] *Pafford;* discover? F

681 **excrement** his false beard. Outgrowths such as hair, beards, nails, and feathers were called excrements. The word is often used for comic effect; see *Err.* 2.2.77–8, 'Why is Time such a niggard of hair, being . . . so plentiful an excrement?', and *LLL* 5.1.103–4, 'thus, dally with my excrement, with my mustachio'.

684–7 In an effort to intimidate the Shepherd and Clown, Autolycus, using a mock-voice of authority, parodies the terms and methods of a legal inquiry. Whether or not he is nobly dressed (see 4.4.609 n.), his voice, manner, and outward appearance correspond to the Shepherd's idea of a nobleman ('your worship', 683).

684 **condition** nature.

686 **having** property, estate.

686 **breeding** perhaps with both senses of lineage and upbringing (Folger).

687 **discover** reveal.

688 **plain** simple, ordinary. In his response, however, Autolycus quibbles on 'plain' = smooth (*OED adj*[1] 2), the reference to 'rough and hairy' echoing the earlier mention of the 'men of hair' (4.4.307–8) who performed the satyrs' dance.

689–92 Tradesmen are at first said to 'give the lie' = misrepresent their wares by overcharging for goods of inferior quality or under-supplying what was promised. Perhaps realizing that he may have revealed too much in the reference to tradesmen, Autolycus quickly links himself to a new occupation, that of soldier. Retracting his first statement, he then says that tradesmen do not *give* soldiers the lie because the latter pay for the goods that tradesmen lie about. The choice of payment, money ('stamped coin') rather than swords ('stabbing steel'), implicitly acknowledges 'giving the lie' in the martial sense of telling someone to his face that he lies, a charge requiring the one insulted to issue a challenge to a duel; see *Oth.* 3.4.5–6, 'He's a soldier, and for me to say a soldier lies 'tis stabbing.'

694 'To be taken with the manner' means to be caught in the act, from the legal term *mainour*, hand-work. Capell thinks the Clown means that Autolycus has caught himself in telling a lie, i.e. first saying that tradesmen give the lie and then that they do not (*Notes* 2. 179). He has already given Shepherd and Clown the lie in the usual sense, i.e. accused them of lying (689). Compare *LLL* 1.1.203, where Costard, having been discovered in a compromising position with Jaquenetta, admits 'The manner of it is, I was taken with the manner'.

SHEPHERD Are you a courtier, an't like you, sir?

AUTOLYCUS Whether it like me or no, I am a courtier. Seest thou not the air of the court in these enfoldings? Hath not my gait in it the measure of the court? Receives not thy nose court-odour from me? Reflect I not on thy baseness court-contempt? Think'st thou for that I insinuate to toze from thee thy business, I am therefore no courtier? I am courtier cap-à-pie, and one that will either push on or pluck back thy business there; whereupon I command thee to open thy affair.

SHEPHERD My business, sir, is to the King.

AUTOLYCUS What advocate hast thou to him?

SHEPHERD I know not, an't like you.

CLOWN [*Aside to Shepherd*] Advocate's the court word for a pheasant: say you have none.

SHEPHERD None, sir. I have no pheasant, cock nor hen.

AUTOLYCUS How blessed are we, that are not simple men!
Yet nature might have made me as these are;
Therefore I will not disdain.

CLOWN [*Aside to Shepherd*] This cannot be but a great courtier.

SHEPHERD His garments are rich, but he wears them not handsomely.

CLOWN He seems to be the more noble in being fantastical. A great man, I'll warrant; I know by the picking on's teeth.

695 like] F2; lke F 700 to toze] *Capell;* at toaze F; or toaze *Dolan (after* F2*);* and toaze *Folger (after Malone)* 707 SD] *Capell (subst.); not in* F 709 pheasant, cock] *Capell;* Pheazant Cock, F 713 SD] *Capell (subst.); not in* F

695 courtier Autolycus' manner and apparel strike the Shepherd as belonging to a man of the court (see 4.4.609 n.). Kermode glosses as 'Autolycus is wearing Florizel's festive clothes.'

695 an't like you if you please. See also 4.4.706 and 743.

697 enfoldings garments.

698 measure a formal, elegant motion or step (possibly carrying the further specification of 'a grave or stately dance' known as a 'measure', *OED n* 20).

700 for that because.

700 insinuate penetrate or probe subtly.

700 toze search out, elicit.

701 cap-à-pie from head to foot, i.e. completely. See Dent T436.1 and *Ham.* 1.2.200.

703 open . . . affair disclose your business.

707 pheasant 'A brace of pheasant continues to this day to be a "court word" for advocate in some country circles' (Alan Dent, *The World of Shakespeare: Animals and Monsters*, 1976, 109).

710–12 How . . . disdain Pafford thinks that F's verse setting is part of Autolycus' pose as a courtier. Observing an embedded iambic pentameter in the Clown's preceding line, Schanzer supposes an intentional couplet in 'hen' / 'men' (most editors, however, print 4.4.709 as prose; Oxford is a recent exception). The passage was delivered as an aside in Howell, a choice that Oxford (seemingly alone) incorporates.

713–17 The Clown and Shepherd speak these lines as a shared aside, during which Autolycus likely preens and engages in bits of business like the affectation indicated in 717.

714 garments . . . rich See 4.4.609 n.

716 fantastical amazingly eccentric (in both attire and behaviour) (*OED* fantastic *adj* 4).

717 picking . . . teeth The ostentatious picking of one's teeth with a toothpick was a practice imported from abroad and associated with well travelled gentlemen. See the Bastard's ridicule in *John* 1.1.189–93, 'Now your traveller, / He and

AUTOLYCUS The fardel there, what's i'th'fardel? Wherefore that box?

SHEPHERD Sir, there lies such secrets in this fardel and box which none must know but the King, and which he shall know within this hour if I may come to th'speech of him.

AUTOLYCUS Age, thou hast lost thy labour.

SHEPHERD Why, sir?

AUTOLYCUS The King is not at the palace; he is gone aboard a new ship to purge melancholy and air himself; for if thou beest capable of things serious, thou must know the King is full of grief.

SHEPHERD So 'tis said, sir – about his son, that should have married a shepherd's daughter.

AUTOLYCUS If that shepherd be not in handfast, let him fly; the curses he shall have, the tortures he shall feel, will break the back of man, the heart of monster.

CLOWN Think you so, sir?

AUTOLYCUS Not he alone shall suffer what wit can make heavy and vengeance bitter, but those that are germane to him, though removed fifty times, shall all come under the hangman – which, though it be great pity, yet it is necessary. An old sheep-whistling rogue, a ram-tender, to offer to have his daughter come into grace! Some say he shall be stoned, but that death is

736 germane] *Theobald (subst.)*; Iermaine F 739 whistling] F2; whistiing F

his toothpick at my worship's mess, / And when my knightly stomach is suffic'd, / Why then I suck my teeth, and catechize / My picked man of countries'.

718–19 fardel . . . box The 'fardel' is the bundle or parcel holding the infant clothing of Perdita when she was found, along with the 'character' (3.3.46) identifying her and/or Antigonus' letters (5.2.30). The 'box' contains whatever is meant by 'these' (3.3.46), most likely the remainder of the original gold left by Antigonus with the baby and perhaps some jewels (presumably part of the 'many other evidences' of Perdita's royal lineage cited in 5.2.33–4). The box may be what the Shepherd had in mind when he boasted of Perdita's dowry (see 4.4.366 and 3.3.46–8 n.).

720 there lies For a quasi-singular verb before a plural subject, see Abbott 335.

723 Age Autolycus' affected personification of the Shepherd as an old man. The proverbial 'lost thy labour' (Tilley L9) and the following comment about Polixenes' going to sea (725–6) are remarkably similar to *Pandosto*: 'But (quoth Capnio) you lose your labour in going to the pallace, for the king meanes this day to take the aire of the sea, and to goe aboord of a shippe that lies in the haven' (Bullough, 189).

726–7 beest . . . of can understand.

729 should have was to have.

731 in handfast i.e. under arrest, in custody.

735 wit ingenuity.

735 heavy excruciating, difficult to bear.

736 germane related. The reference to relations 'removed fifty times' recalls Polixenes' hyperbole about Deucalion (4.4.411).

739 rogue in the general sense of rascal, or knave (without the more specific meaning discussed in 4.3.89–90 n.).

739 offer presume.

740 grace i.e. the social favour of nobility (were she to wed Florizel).

too soft for him, say I. Draw our throne into a sheepcote! All deaths are too few, the sharpest too easy.

CLOWN Has the old man e'er a son, sir, do you hear, an't like you, sir?

AUTOLYCUS He has a son, who shall be flayed alive, then 'nointed over with honey, set on the head of a wasps' nest, then stand till he be three-quarters and a dram dead; then recovered again with aqua vitae or some other hot infusion; then, raw as he is, and in the hottest day prognostication proclaims, shall he be set against a brick wall, the sun looking with a southward eye upon him, where he is to behold him with flies blown to death. But what talk we of these traitorly rascals, whose miseries are to be smiled at, their offences being so capital? Tell me (for you seem to be honest, plain men) what you have to the King. Being something gently considered, I'll bring you where he is aboard, tender your persons to his presence, whisper him in your behalfs; and if it be in man, besides the King to effect your suits, here is man shall do it.

748 aqua vitae] F (Aquavite)

741 **sheepcote** a sheephouse, i.e. a shelter for sheep.

745–51 The death predicted by Autolycus suggests the influence of both Boccaccio's *Decameron* 2.9 (a source for *Cym.*) and widely known stories of barbaric tortures inflicted by Spaniards on the inhabitants of the New World. One such tale notes the burning of a native, followed by an anointing with honey before being subjected to the merciless stinging of mosquitoes (see J. D. Rogers, 'Voyages and Exploration', in *Shakespeare's England*, ed. Sidney Lee and C. T. Onions, 2 vols. [1916], 1:184–5). Pafford (citing J. C. Maxwell) reports a similar torture in William of Malmesbury's *Historiae Novellae*.

745, 46, 47, 48 **then** Vickers (416) calls this 'a gloating anaphora' (repetition of the same word at the beginning of a series of clauses).

745 **'nointed** anointed (i.e. drenched, covered).

747 **a dram** a small amount.

748 **aqua vitae** distilled liquor such as brandy and whiskey in contrast to some other stimulant ('hot infusion').

749 **prognostication proclaims** i.e. forecast in the almanac.

751 **with flies blown** stung by insects and consequently swelled up. See 4.4.520–1.

753 **capital** (1) injurious and (2) 'punishable by death'.

754 **plain** straightforward, plainspoken (in contrast to the previous meanings of ordinary and smooth [4.4.688 n.]).

755 **Being . . . considered** Steevens reads as 'I having a gentlemanlike consideration given me, i.e. a bribe', and cites John Wilson, *The Three Ladies of London* (1584):' – sure sir. I'll consider it hereafter if I can. *Dissimulation*. What, consider me? dost thou think that I am a bribe-taker' (ed. H. S. D. Mithal, 1988, lines 460–1).

755–6 **bring . . . aboard** Shepherd and Clown understand Autolycus to mean that he will take them to the king who they suppose has boarded a ship, but Pafford thinks that Autolycus is being deliberately ambiguous as he begins to formulate his plan to help Florizel, the only royal family member who at this point is indeed 'aboard' (see 4.4.791–3).

756 **tender . . . presence** present you to him.

CLOWN [*Aside to Shepherd*] He seems to be of great authority. Close with him, give him gold; and though authority be a stubborn bear, yet he is oft led by the nose with gold. Show the inside of your purse to the outside of his hand, and no more ado. Remember 'stoned' and 'flayed alive'.

SHEPHERD An't please you, sir, to undertake the business for us, here is that gold I have. I'll make it as much more, and leave this young man in pawn till I bring it you.

AUTOLYCUS After I have done what I promised?

SHEPHERD Ay, sir.

AUTOLYCUS Well, give me the moiety [*taking money from Shepherd*]. [*To Clown*] Are you a party in this business?

CLOWN In some sort, sir; but, though my case be a pitiful one, I hope I shall not be flayed out of it.

AUTOLYCUS O, that's the case of the shepherd's son – hang him, he'll be made an example.

CLOWN Comfort, good comfort! [*Aside to Shepherd*] We must to the King and show our strange sights. He must know 'tis none of your daughter nor my sister; we are gone else. – Sir, I will give you as much as this old man does when the business is performed, and remain, as he says, your pawn till it be brought you.

AUTOLYCUS I will trust you. Walk before toward the seaside, go on the right hand. I will but look upon the hedge, and follow you.

CLOWN [*To Shepherd*] We are blessed in this man, as I may say, even blessed.

759 SD] *Capell (subst.); not in* F 763 'stoned' . . . 'flayed alive'] *Globe;* ston'd . . . flay'd aliue F 769 SD] *Bevington (subst.); not in* F 770 SD] *Oxford; not in* F 773 son –] *Orgel;* son: F; son. *Riverside;* son! *Folger* 775 comfort!] *Hudson;* comfort: F; comfort. *Oxford* 775 SD] *Orgel (at beginning of line in Oxford, subst.); not in* F 777 else. –] *Orgel (after Capell, subst.); not in* F 783 SD] *Oxford; not in* F

759 **Close** Come to terms, make a bargain.

760–1 **though . . . with gold** i.e. even the most resistant authority can be bribed. 'To lead by the nose' was proverbial (Dent N233), and tame bears were literally so led (Folger). Whereas a bear (hostile to Antigonus and kind or at least indifferent to Perdita) introduced the Bohemian phase of the action (3.3), the image of a bear, in its contradictory aspects of 'stubborn' and tame, ushers the sequence to its close. See 4.4.781 n.

766 **in pawn** as pledge, security.

769 **moiety** half (of what has been promised as a deposit in 765–6).

771–2 **case . . . flayed** with wordplay on 'case' as (1) plight, situation, and (2) skin. See earlier nn. on 'disease' (4.4.608) and 'flayed' (4.4.613).

777 **gone** undone, lost (perhaps with the sense of 'dead'). See 3.2.142, 3.3.57, and Supplementary note to 2.3.129.

781 **the seaside** The explicit mention of Bohemia's fictive seacoast frames the pastoral phase of the dramatic action (see 3.3.1–2).

782 **I . . . you** Autolycus's desire for privacy while he urinates functions, like his clothing and his toothpick, as a marker of elevated rank (Paster, 27); it also works practically as a means of providing him with an exit soliloquy.

SHEPHERD Let's before, as he bids us. He was provided to do us good. [*Exeunt Shepherd and Clown*]

AUTOLYCUS If I had a mind to be honest, I see Fortune would not suffer me. She drops booties in my mouth. I am courted now with a double occasion: gold, and a means to do the Prince my master good – which who knows how that may turn back to my advancement? I will bring these two moles, these blind ones, aboard him; if he think it fit to shore them again, and that the complaint they have to the King concerns him nothing, let him call me rogue for being so far officious, for I am proof against that title and what shame else belongs to't. To him will I present them; there may be matter in it. [*Exit*]

5.1 *Enter* LEONTES, CLEOMENES, DION, PAULINA, [*and*] *Servants*

CLEOMENES Sir, you have done enough, and have performed
A saint-like sorrow. No fault could you make

786 SD] *Rowe; Exeunt* F2; *not in* F 796 SD] *Rowe; Exeunt* F 5.1] F (*Actus Quintus. Scena Prima.*) 0 SD] *Rowe; Enter . . . Seruants: Florizel, Perdita.* F

788 suffer me allow me to be so (i.e. honest) (*OED* suffer *v* 15).

788 booties gains, prizes.

788–9 I . . . occasion Fortune has doubly wooed ('courted') Autolycus with a 'twofold opportunity of gain' (Schanzer).

790 turn back redound.

791 moles . . . ones 'Blind as a mole' was proverbial (Dent M1034).

792 aboard him i.e. aboard Florizel's ship.

792 shore them put them ashore.

794–5 proof . . . title impervious to being called such a name as 'rogue' (Folger). See 4.3.89–90 n.

796 SD F's 'Exeunt' for all at 796 is not impossible, since Autolycus's last speech may be spoken as an aside, but since he has already instructed the Shepherd and Clown to go on before and that he will follow, Rowe's revision here seems preferable.

Act 5, Scene 1

With the return of the action to the Sicilian court, G. F. Waller ('Romance and Shakespeare's Philosophy of Time in [*WT*]', *SoRA* 4 [1970], 134) senses a time of autumnal harvest, a season suggested in some productions by falling leaves (e.g. Noble and Kahn). Bate's seasonal preference for the first part of the scene is winter (233). In Brook and Phillips, the four characters who open Act 5 looked noticeably older and were dressed in sombre black and grey; funeral wreaths actually hung from the stage balconies in Brook. But as John Lawlor ('*Pandosto* and the Nature of Dramatic Romance', *PQ* 41 [1962], 103) notes, the scene's emotional range takes us 'all the way from a sadly penitent Leontes to a magnanimous host, taking the part of the young against the old'. The first 177 lines differ greatly from Greene's narrative; for the significance of the changes, especially as they affect the characterization of Leontes, see Introduction, pp. 41–7.

0 SD Leontes Peter Holland describes a 1992 production by Theatre de Complicité that had Leontes crawl into the scene on his knees 'as if he really has spent the intervening years doing nothing else', a pointed reminder of Paulina's 'A thousand knees' at 3.2.207 ('Shakespeare Performances in England', *S. Sur.* 46 [1994], 171).

0 SD Cleomenes, Dion The inclusion of these figures, especially if they were last seen exiting with Leontes and Paulina at the end of 3.2, suggests that along with the strong moral presence of Paulina, 'Leontes has had the support through the intervening years of two characters who have themselves been deeply touched by Apollo', the divine force introduced into the play in 3.1 (Mahood, 80).

2 saint-like sorrow rigorous penance (the kind associated with saints). Beginning with 'saint-like' and continuing over the next few lines with 'fault', 'redeemed', 'penitence', 'trespass', 'evil', and 'forgive', the diction reveals 'a much stronger tinge of Christian reference than anything found earlier in the play. [These words] begin to shift the balance away from things Greek or pagan toward things Christian' (Louis Martz, 'Shakespeare's Humanist Enterprise: *The Winter's Tale*', in John Carey, ed., *English Renaissance Studies Presented to Dame Helen Gardner in Honour of her seventieth birthday*, 1980, 129).

2 No . . . make There is no sin (see 'trespass' in 4) you could commit.

Which you have not redeemed; indeed, paid down
More penitence than done trespass. At the last,
Do as the heavens have done, forget your evil;
With them, forgive yourself.

LEONTES Whilst I remember
Her and her virtues, I cannot forget
My blemishes in them, and so still think of
The wrong I did myself: which was so much
That heirless it hath made my kingdom, and
Destroyed the sweet'st companion that e'er man
Bred his hopes out of, true.

PAULINA Too true, my lord.
If one by one you wedded all the world,
Or from the all that are took something good

5 done,] *Theobald;* done; F 12 of, true. / PAULINA Too] F; of. / *Paul.* True, too *Theobald;* of. True? / PAULINA Too *Oxford*

3 **redeemed** (1) made amends for already; or (2) paid off (anticipating the commercial language of 'paid down' = 'paid in full').

4 **penitence** penance (*OED* 1). Turner notes *OED*'s comment that this now rare meaning usually includes the prevailing sense of 'repentance' (*OED* 2).

4 **At . . . last** Now at last (Boorman).

5 **Do . . . evil** Imitate the gods in forgetting your sin. R. Noble (248) observes an allusion to the Visitation of the Sick ritual in BCP, 'O most merciful God, which . . . dost so put away the sins of those which truly repent, that thou rememberest them no more'. See Shaheen (731–2) for additional references to BCP and the scriptures.

6 **With them** As with 'the heavens', i.e. the gods.

7 **Her** Hermione.

8 **in them** in regard to them (i.e.'her virtues'). For this construction, see Abbott 162 and compare *Mac.* 3.1.50–1, 'Our fears in Banquo / Stick deep'. Or, perhaps, with an implicit metaphor of gazing at Hermione's picture, Leontes is saying 'while I dwell on her virtues I cannot forget my sins ["blemishes", *OED* blemish *n* 3] which were so implicated with her goodness or so brought out her virtues'.

12 Most editors, starting with Theobald, reassign 'true' at the end of Leontes' speech to the opening of Paulina's. James Hammersmith ('Two Speech-Assignments in [*WT*]', *PBSA* 75 [1981], 172–3), arguing for F, envisions the scene opening in mid-argument between Cleomenes and Leontes, the latter responding that he can't forgive himself and then – as Cleomenes starts to object – emphasizing his unalterable position with 'true', truncated from 'I tell you true'. The proximity of 'true' to the breeding of heirs may also suggest Leontes' acute awareness that 'out of [Hermione] he had bred . . . true' (Porter and Clarke [1908], as cited by Turner). Oxford (followed by Orgel) keeps the word as part of Leontes' speech but as a separate interrogative, to which Paulina answers affirmatively.

14 **from . . . good** i.e. from each woman now living took a single good trait. Calling this a 'favourite thought' in Shakespeare, Johnson cites Orlando's rhapsody on Rosalind in *AYLI* 3.2.141–52 and Ferdinand's praise of Miranda in *Temp.* 3.1.46–8, 'But you, O you, / So perfect and so peerless, are created / Of every creature's best'; see also Cloten's description of Imogen in *Cym.* 3.5.73–5, 'from every one / The best she hath, and she, of all compounded, / Outsells them all'.

To make a perfect woman, she you killed
Would be unparallelled.

LEONTES I think so. Killed!
She I killed! I did so; but thou strik'st me
Sorely to say I did. It is as bitter
Upon thy tongue as in my thought. Now, good now,
Say so but seldom.

CLEOMENES Not at all, good lady.
You might have spoken a thousand things that would
Have done the time more benefit, and graced
Your kindness better.

PAULINA You are one of those
Would have him wed again.

DION If you would not so,
You pity not the state, nor the remembrance
Of his most sovereign name; consider little
What dangers by his highness' fail of issue
May drop upon his kingdom and devour
Incertain lookers-on. What were more holy
Than to rejoice the former Queen is well?
What holier than, for royalty's repair,
For present comfort, and for future good,
To bless the bed of majesty again
With a sweet fellow to't?

PAULINA There is none worthy,
Respecting her that's gone. Besides, the gods

16–17 Killed! . . . killed!] *Capell (subst.)*; Kill'd? . . . kill'd? F 31 holier than,] *Capell (subst)*; holyer, then F

17 **thou** Throughout the scene Leontes refers to Paulina with the informal second person pronoun, not to demean (as in 2.3), but to register the private bond they now share. See 3.2.149 n.

18 **Sorely** Severely (*OED adv* 2).

19 **good now** an interjectional expression of entreaty (*OED*), often read as 'if you will be so good now' (Andrews) or 'I pray you' (Dolan).

22 **graced** (1) befitted, or, perhaps, (2) set off (in the sense of counterbalancing her 'kindness' with a less harsh choice of words).

25 Furness notes the use of zeugma, 'You pity not the state, nor [regard] the preservation ('remembrance') of the dynastic line ('his most sovereign name' [26]).

26 **consider little** give little consideration to

27 **fail of issue** failure to produce an heir.

29 **Incertain lookers-on** i.e. persons not directly involved in dynastic conflicts but 'uncertain' (anxious) because there is no known succession and because they can do nothing to affect the situation.

30 **well** i.e. at rest in heaven. The euphemism for 'dead' was proverbial (Dent H347, 'He is well since he is in heaven').

31 **royalty's repair** the restoration of the broken dynastic succession (with, perhaps, the suggestion of the king's personal healing).

34 **fellow** companion, partner.

35 **Respecting** In comparison with.

Will have fulfilled their secret purposes;
For has not the divine Apollo said,
Is't not the tenor of his oracle,
That King Leontes shall not have an heir
Till his lost child be found? Which that it shall
Is all as monstrous to our human reason
As my Antigonus to break his grave
And come again to me, who, on my life,
Did perish with the infant. 'Tis your counsel
My lord should to the heavens be contrary,
Oppose against their wills. [*To Leontes*] Care not for issue;
The crown will find an heir. Great Alexander
Left his to th'worthiest; so his successor
Was like to be the best.

LEONTES Good Paulina,
Who hast the memory of Hermione,
I know, in honour, O that ever I
Had squared me to thy counsel! Then, even now
I might have looked upon my Queen's full eyes,
Have taken treasure from her lips.

PAULINA And left them
More rich for what they yielded.

LEONTES Thou speak'st truth.
No more such wives, therefore no wife. One worse,

37 said,| F4; said? F 41 human| F (humane) 46 SD| *Theobald (subst.); not in* F 52 counsel!| *Johnson;* councell: F 54 lips.| F; lips – *Capell (subst.)*

36 By transposing 'fulfilled' and 'their . . . purposes' in his gloss, Orgel clarifies the sense of the gods' insistence on the fulfilment of their will.

40 **Till** The word used in the oracular message was 'if' (3.2.132). Rudolph P. Almasy ('"Go Together You Precious Winners All": A Reading of Shakespeare's [*WT*]', *WVUPP* 27 [1981], 126) claims that the change in wording reflects Paulina's movement 'beyond grief to hope in believing the Oracle offers a promise that Perdita will be found'.

41 **all . . . to** altogether as unnatural ('monstrous') from the point of view of (Folger).

42 **As** As it would be for.

43 **on . . . life** I would swear on my life.

45 **contrary** with the accent on the second syllable.

46 **Oppose against** A redundant formation as in *John* 3.1.170–1, 'I alone, alone do me oppose / Against the pope'; see also *Shr.* 3.2.9, *Tim.* 3.4.79, and *Lear* 4.2.74 and 4.7.31.

46–9 **Care not . . . best** What seems to begin as an allusion to the anxiety surrounding Elizabeth I's lack of concern for 'issue' (by virtue of her refusal to marry) can be seen as ending in a compliment to James I, a 'happy succession to the throne' despite Elizabeth's dying without an heir (Pafford).

49 **like** likely.

50 **hast** holds.

52 **squared me to** directed myself by (*OED* square *v* 4). See 3.3.40.

53 **full** large and rounded (*OED adj* 10).

56 **No more** There are no more.

And better used, would make her sainted spirit
Again possess her corpse, and on this stage
(Where we offenders now) appear, soul-vexed,
And begin, 'Why to me?'

PAULINA Had she such power,
She had just cause.

LEONTES She had, and would incense me
To murder her I married.

PAULINA I should so.
Were I the ghost that walked, I'd bid you mark
Her eye and tell me for what dull part in't
You chose her; then I'd shriek, that even your ears
Should rift to hear me, and the words that followed
Should be, 'Remember mine.'

LEONTES Stars, stars,
And all eyes else dead coals! Fear thou no wife;
I'll have no wife, Paulina.

PAULINA Will you swear
Never to marry but by my free leave?

59 (Where . . . now) appear] *Knight;* (Where . . . appeare) F; (Were we offenders now) appear *Rann* 60 'Why to me?'] *Capell (subst.);* why to me? F 61 just] F3; iust such F 67 'Remember mine.'] *Capell (subst.);* Remember mine. F 68 coals!] *Capell;* coales: F

59 The contrast is between sinful living human beings, offenders in a general sense, and the 'sainted spirit' of the dead Hermione, now in heaven. The awkwardness of the line's syntax has long been debated, and editors offer many emendations (see Turner) of F's parenthetical 'Where we offenders now appear'. The syntax, however, becomes less strained if (1) 'now', functioning elliptically, is understood as 'now are' or (continuing the theatrical metaphor as in Dolan) as 'now play our parts'; or (2) 'appear' is seen as serving both 'we offenders' and the revivified Hermione, i.e. Hermione will appear where we appear right now (essentially Henley's view in Steevens). (Snyder contemplated accepting Rann's emendation of 'where' to 'were', thus making Leontes hypothesize that 'were we [the royal 'we'] to be guilty of so gross an offence as remarriage now, Hermione's spirit would appear soul-vexed'.)

60 **Why to me** i.e. Why inflict such cruel treatment on me (when a worse wife is treated better)?

60 **Had . . . power** Paulina's use of the subjunctive 'reflects . . . [her] own secret consciousness that Hermione has not such power [to reanimate her corporeal body], because she is not yet dead' (Porter and Clarke [1908], cited in Turner).

61 F3 regularizes the meter and is generally accepted on the assumption that F's 'such' in the previous line was repeated by the compositor.

63 **mark** observe.

64 **dull** unattractive. Perhaps, in anticipation of 'dead coals' (68), lifeless or lacking lustre.

65 **shriek** Shrieking is commonly associated with ghosts, but in recalling Antigonus' description of the queen as she exited his dream (3.3.35–6), it may support the idea that through magical powers, Paulina had enabled Hermione to invade Antigonus' subconscious mind; such was the thinking of Lise Bruneau (Hermione) and Tana Hicken (Paulina) in Kahn (from a conversation with the actors).

66 **rift** split (*OED* v^1 1a, where this line is cited).

67 **mine** i.e. my eyes.

68 **eyes else** other eyes.

70 **but . . . leave** i.e. unless I will it. Andrews observes an 'appropriately Pauline' quality to Paulina's admonition not to rush into marriage (1 Cor. 7).

LEONTES Never, Paulina, so be blessed my spirit.
PAULINA Then, good my lords, bear witness to his oath.
CLEOMENES You tempt him over-much.
PAULINA Unless another
As like Hermione as is her picture
Affront his eye.
CLEOMENES Good madam, I have done.
PAULINA Yet if my lord will marry – if you will, sir,
No remedy but you will – give me the office
To choose you a queen. She shall not be so young
As was your former, but she shall be such
As, walked your first queen's ghost, it should take joy
To see her in your arms.
LEONTES My true Paulina,
We shall not marry till thou bidd'st us.
PAULINA That
Shall be when your first queen's again in breath;
Never till then.

75 Good . . . done.] F; Good madam – *Pau.* I . . . done *Capell* 78 you a] F; your *Oxford (after Hudson; conj. Walker)*

73 **tempt** try, test.

73–84 In a curious passage, which commentators tend to ignore, Paulina appears to be rehearsing a possible scenario for restoring Hermione to Leontes, perhaps something on the order of the Friar's plan in *Ado*, where Hero is presented to Claudio in the final act as her look-alike cousin. Paulina's lines may also be a trial gambit in the original writing or rewriting before Shakespeare had fully worked out how to bring Hermione back, i.e. before he thought of the 'statue' scenario. Ultimately (5.1.82–4) Paulina rejects substitutes, insisting that Leontes may only have a wife when his former one lives again (i.e. is 'in breath').

75 **Affront** Come before, meet (compare *Ham.* 3.1.30–1, 'That he . . . may here / Affront Ophelia'). Many editors follow Hanmer in glossing 'affront' as 'confront', which typically suggests a defiant meeting face to face, the sense found in the only other instances of the word in Shakespeare; see *Cym.* 4.3.29–30 and 5.3.86–7. Since Paulina is the play's voice of conscience and justice, a confrontational edge may be implicit in her usage of 'affront'.

75 **Good . . . done** Most editors follow Capell in reassigning 'I have done' to Paulina. Capell argued that nothing could be more characteristic of Paulina than saying she was finished and then going right on (*Notes*, 2.180). See Collation.

77 **No remedy** If there is no other way. The close iteration of 'will' (rhetorical ploce) in 76–7, along with its range of meaning (antanaclasis) – i.e. as a simple auxiliary verb and then with the multiple senses of 'desire', 'being determined', and 'stubbornly exercising volition' – recalls the king's tyrannical will in the first half of the play while underscoring its taming as he defers to Paulina (5.1.82).

77 **office** task, duty.

80 **walked . . . ghost** i.e. if the ghost of your first queen were to walk once again. As with 'shriek' in 65, Paulina's words recall Antigonus' dream (3.3.15–36).

Enter a SERVANT

SERVANT One that gives out himself Prince Florizel,
Son of Polixenes, with his princess – she
The fairest I have yet beheld – desires access
To your high presence.
LEONTES What with him? He comes not
Like to his father's greatness. His approach,
So out of circumstance and sudden, tells us
'Tis not a visitation framed, but forc'd
By need and accident. What train?
SERVANT But few,
And those but mean.
LEONTES His princess, say you, with him?
SERVANT Ay – the most peerless piece of earth, I think,
That e'er the sun shone bright on.
PAULINA O Hermione,
As every present time doth boast itself
Above a better gone, so must thy grave
Give way to what's seen now. [*To the Servant*] Sir, you yourself
Have said and writ so, but your writing now
Is colder than that theme: she had not been,
Nor was not to be equalled; thus your verse

94 Ay–] *This edn;* I: F 98 SD] *Oxford; not in* F

84 SD Some editors follow Theobald in altering 'Servant' to 'Gentleman', since the character is later found to have written poetry honoring Hermione (5.1.99–102); F's term, however, may indicate a gentleman in the royal service. Mahood suggests (230 n.4) identifying this character with the First Gentleman in 5.2.

88 **What . . . him** Schanzer, noting the repeated query in 5.1.92, explains as 'What are those with him?'; in other words, what retinue comes with him.

89 **Like to** As befits.

90 **out of circumstance** unceremonious (*OED* circumstance *n* 7, where this line is cited). A royal state visit would be filled with dignity and ceremony; compare *Oth.* 3.3.354, 'Pride, pomp, and circumstance of glorious war!'

91 **framed** planned.

91 **forc'd** compelled. Folger suggests 'enforced'.

93 **mean** poor, lowly (in status).

94 **piece of earth** (1) creature; (2) masterpiece. Kittredge-Ribner proposes 'the human body', [which] being composed of the same four elements as the physical earth [air, water, fire, clay], was often treated as analogous to it'.

97 **Above . . . gone** i.e., 'As being superior to a better time that is past' (Deighton). Andrews cites Son. 59, which treats this idea at length.

97 **must . . . grave** Perhaps, as Warburton suggests, we should understand 'grave' as 'epitaph'; or, perhaps, 'must thy grave' means 'you, being dead, must. . . .'

99 **so** The word refers forward to 'she . . . equalled' (100–01).

100 **theme** the beautiful Hermione, the subject of your poetry, who is now lifeless.

100–1 **she . . . equalled** Hanmer thinks that Paulina is directly quoting the Servant's verse and punctuates accordingly. But as Schanzer notes, the choice of tense, which should otherwise read 'she has not been, nor is not to be, equalled', points to indirect discourse.

Flowed with her beauty once. 'Tis shrewdly ebbed,
To say you have seen a better.

SERVANT Pardon, madam.
The one I have almost forgot – your pardon;
The other, when she has obtained your eye,
Will have your tongue too. This is a creature,
Would she begin a sect, might quench the zeal
Of all professors else, make proselytes
Of who she but bid follow.

PAULINA How? not women!

SERVANT Women will love her that she is a woman
More worth than any man; men, that she is
The rarest of all women.

LEONTES Go, Cleomenes,
Yourself, assisted with your honoured friends,
Bring them to our embracement.

Exeunt [*Cleomenes and others*]

Still, 'tis strange
He thus should steal upon us.

PAULINA Had our prince,
Jewel of children, seen this hour, he had paired
Well with this lord: there was not full a month
Between their births.

LEONTES Prithee no more, cease; thou know'st
He dies to me again when talked of. Sure

109 women!] *Oxford (conj. Furness)*; women? F 114 SD] *Capell (subst.)*; *Exit* F *(after* vpon vs *115)* 118 Prithee] F *(*'Prethee*)*

102 shrewdly politicly. *OED*'s meanings of 'wickedly' (*adv* 1) and 'grievously' (*adv* 5a) are also possible.

106 tongue voice (of praise).

107–9 i.e. Were she to begin a new religion ('sect'), she might extinguish or cool (*OED* quench *v* 1, 2) the zeal of all those who declare allegiance to other faiths ('professors else'), making them converts ('proselytes') simply by inviting them to follow her. Regarding 'professors', Pafford, citing *H8* 3.1.115, stipulates professors of Christianity, while Kermode specifies Puritans; Orgel includes the meaning 'of a professed member of a religious order' (*OED* professor 1).

109 not women! F places a question mark after 'women', but Paulina is most likely exclaiming disbelief: 'Proselytes the new Beauty might make of men, but of a woman – never!' (Furness). See 'Good Queen!' (2.3.58 n.).

113 assisted with accompanied by. See Abbott 193 for examples (including 5.2.55) of 'with' = 'by'.

115 steal . . . us i.e. come in such quiet and low-key fashion. Maxwell suggests 'come unannounced'.

116 paired matched. Paulina's words are the first of several invocations of the dead prince's memory (see 119–22, 131–2, and 176). The linkage of Mamillius with Florizel recalls 1.2.162–70.

119 The idea that talk of griefs renewed the original sorrow was proverbial (Tilley R89).

When I shall see this gentleman, thy speeches
Will bring me to consider that which may
Unfurnish me of reason. They are come.

Enter FLORIZEL, PERDITA, CLEOMENES, *and others*

Your mother was most true to wedlock, Prince,
For she did print your royal father off,
Conceiving you. Were I but twenty-one,
Your father's image is so hit in you,
His very air, that I should call you brother,
As I did him, and speak of something wildly
By us performed before. Most dearly welcome,
And your fair princess – goddess! O, alas!
I lost a couple that 'twixt heaven and earth
Might thus have stood, begetting wonder, as
You, gracious couple, do; and then I lost –
All mine own folly – the society,
Amity too, of your brave father, whom,
Though bearing misery, I desire my life
Once more to look on him.

130 princess–goddess!] *Dyce (subst.)*; Princesse (Goddesse) F 130 O, alas!] *Steevens*; oh: alas, F

122 **Unfurnish** Deprive.

122 SD Parry thinks that 'the entry of Florizel and Perdita introduces a long, still and speechless pause . . . as the young couple stand "begetting wonder" [5.1.132]'. In Doran, Antony Sher's Leontes had been on the ground, hunched over a book; as youth and love returned to his kingdom, he fell backwards, 'gazing at Florizel and Perdita with a moving intensity that starkly conveyed the despair of his own sense of childlessness' (Smallwood, 'Performances', 265). See Supplementary note, p. 253.

124 **print . . . off** make an exact copy of your father. See 2.3.99.

125 **twenty-one** As Snyder notes (2), this comment provides a textual clue to Mamillius' age at the beginning of the play. Since Florizel and Mamillius are the same age (5.1.117–18), and since the former now reminds Leontes of himself and Polixenes when they were twenty-one, the passage of sixteen years between Act 3 and Act 5 indicates that in the early scenes Mamillius would have been five (or thereabouts, if the numerical figure is not to be taken literally). In *Pandosto*, Dorastus (= Florizel) is said to be 'about the age of twenty yeeres'(Bullough, 176).

126 **hit** exactly represented. Deighton thinks the metaphor comes from archery (hitting the mark), but the proximity to 'print . . . off' (124) lends more credence to Bethell's figurative link to a stamp or seal.

131 **couple** For Kahn, the sight of the young couple was meant to remind Leontes not only of the two children he had lost (the probable sense of 'couple' here) but of the wife and best friend also lost to him. See Supplementary note to 122, 124 n., and illustrations 18 and 23 on pp. 29 and 45.

131 **'twixt heaven and earth** A difficult phrase that may simply signify 'in this world', or, perhaps, imply the mixing of heavenly and earthly attributes (Happé). See next n.

132 **begetting wonder** generating awe in onlookers. Fusing this phrase with the preceding ''twixt heaven and earth', Theobald suggests 'the Wonder of two Worlds, the Objects of Admiration to Gods and Men'.

135 **brave** noble.

135–7 **whom . . . him** i.e. whom, the misery of my life notwithstanding, I desire to live long enough to see once more. 'Him' is redundant.

FLORIZEL By his command
Have I here touched Sicilia, and from him
Give you all greetings, that a king, at friend,
Can send his brother; and but infirmity,
Which waits upon worn times, hath something seized
His wished ability, he had himself
The lands and waters 'twixt your throne and his
Measured to look upon you, whom he loves –
He bade me say so – more than all the sceptres
And those that bear them living.

LEONTES O my brother,
Good gentleman, the wrongs I have done thee stir
Afresh within me, and these thy offices,
So rarely kind, are as interpreters
Of my behindhand slackness. Welcome hither,
As is the spring to th'earth. And hath he too
Exposed this paragon to th'fearful usage –
At least ungentle – of the dreadful Neptune
To greet a man not worth her pains, much less
Th'adventure of her person?

139 at] F; as F2 145 bade] F (bad)

139 at friend (1) as a friend (Abbott 143); (2) being friendly. See *Ham.* 4.3.44, 'the wind at help'– i.e. the wind helping Hamlet.

140 but but that, except for.

141 waits . . . times attends old age. Compare Polixenes' hypothetical, which Florizel had denied (4.4.375–84), but now adapts to his own purposes.

141–2 something . . . ability i.e. somewhat stolen ('seized') from him the physical strength he would like still to have (Pierce); Schanzer and Folger gloss 'seized' as 'taken prisoner'.

144 Measured Travelled.

145–6 sceptres . . . living i.e. (more than all) 'those living kings who bear them [sceptres]' (Kittredge-Ribner); or, taking a cue from 'living', (more than all) 'the kings that ever lived and those now living who bear sceptres'. Either way, in a kind of syllepsis (the use of a word having two different meanings, although the word is not repeated), 'sceptres' first serves figuratively as a metonym for royal rulers and then assumes its literal meaning as a royal instrument.

148 offices courtesies.

149 rarely extraordinarily (given Leontes' earlier offenses).

149–50 interpreters . . . slackness i.e. commentators reproaching me for my insufficiencies (toward Polixenes). *OED* cites this line as the only example of 'behindhand' = 'tardy' (*adj* 4); coupled with 'slackness', the negative modifier intensifies Leontes' remiss behaviour. Compare the opening banter between Camillo and Archidamus on the competitive impulses underlying hospitality (1.1.1–18); Leontes now trades places with Polixenes as the slacker.

150–1 Welcome . . . earth The proverbial expression is 'welcome as flowers in May' (Dent F390). 'It is almost as though Perdita had become the goddess whose part she had assumed' (Kenneth Muir, *Last Periods of Shakespeare, Racine, Ibsen*, 1961, 49).

152–3 fearful . . . ungentle i.e. dangerous or at least rough 'usage'.

153 Neptune Roman god of the sea.

155 adventure risk.

FLORIZEL Good my lord,
She came from Libya.
LEONTES Where the warlike Smalus,
That noble honoured lord, is feared and loved?
FLORIZEL Most royal sir, from thence; from him whose daughter
His tears proclaimed his, parting with her; thence,
A prosperous south wind friendly, we have crossed
To execute the charge my father gave me
For visiting your highness. My best train
I have from your Sicilian shores dismissed,
Who for Bohemia bend to signify
Not only my success in Libya, sir,
But my arrival and my wife's in safety
Here where we are.
LEONTES The blessed gods
Purge all infection from our air whilst you
Do climate here! You have a holy father,
A graceful gentleman, against whose person,
So sacred as it is, I have done sin,
For which the heavens, taking angry note,

158 Most . . . daughter] *Hanmer; as two lines* . . . Sir, / From thence . . . F 159 his, parting] *Hanmer;* his parting F 169 here!] *Hanmer;* here: F

156 Libya In this change from Greene's Padua to the more exotic world of Africa, Norman Holland detects 'a kind of underworld, a dark, African world like the underworld from which Proserpina . . . emerges to bring the spring, as indeed [Perdita] does bring the spring to Sicily, which has been a Waste Land these past sixteen years' (*The Shakespearean Imagination*, 1964, 297). Florizel's fiction concerning Perdita's Libyan background recalls another European princess's connection with Africa, Alonso's unseen daughter, Claribel, who marries the King of Tunis (*Temp.* 2.1.71, 245, 258; 5.1.209).

156 Smalus Like so many of the names in this play, this one (possibly the result of compositorial misreading) may derive from Plutarch who in the life of Dion (*Lives of the Noble Grecians and Romans*) recounts a journey from Libya to a town in Sicily ruled by a Carthaginian called Synalus (Pafford).

158–9 whose . . . her 'whose tears, when he was parting with her, proclaimed her to be his daughter' (Schanzer).

160 friendly being favorable (Abbott 380). Florizel's description of the south wind (either part of Camillo's script or his own invention) is contradicted by Autolycus in 5.2.100–2.

162 My best train The better part (i.e. either in number or in rank) of my retinue.

164 for . . . bend are now bound for Bohemia.

169 climate sojourn (*OED v*, where this line is the only example). Although the sense is different from that in 3.1.1, 'climate', in conjunction with 'air' and the overall religious vocabulary pervading 5.1.167–75, recalls the atmosphere surrounding Apollo's temple in the earlier scene.

169 holy i.e. 'of high and reverend excellence' (*OED adj* 3c).

170 graceful (1) full of divine grace (*OED adj* 1), and (2) virtuous (*OED adj* 2). As in 5.1.156–7, Leontes articulates his view of an ideal monarch, emphasizing in 169–75 the sanctity associated with 'divine right' kingship.

Have left me issueless; and your father's blessed,
As he from heaven merits it, with you,
Worthy his goodness. What might I have been
Might I a son and daughter now have looked on,
Such goodly things as you!

Enter a LORD

LORD Most noble sir,
That which I shall report will bear no credit
Were not the proof so nigh. Please you, great sir,
Bohemia greets you from himself by me,
Desires you to attach his son, who has –
His dignity and duty both cast off –
Fled from his father, from his hopes, and with
A shepherd's daughter.

LEONTES Where's Bohemia? Speak.

LORD Here in your city; I now came from him.
I speak amazedly, and it becomes
My marvel and my message. To your court
Whiles he was hast'ning in the chase, it seems,
Of this fair couple, meets he on the way
The father of this seeming lady and
Her brother, having both their country quitted
With this young prince.

FLORIZEL Camillo has betrayed me,
Whose honour and whose honesty till now
Endured all weathers.

LORD Lay't so to his charge;
He's with the King your father.

177 you!] *Hanmer;* you? F 188 hast'ning in] *This edn;* hastning (in F

173 issueless without an heir (ironic, given Perdita's presence before Leontes).

173 and on the other hand.

175 Worthy (Who are) worthy of.

176 son . . . daughter Shakespeare continues to italicize the dramatic irony inherent in this scene with words that in early Modern English could refer, respectively, to son-in-law (which Florizel is soon to be) and daughter-in-law (Florizel's meaning in 5.1.207–8).

178 will bear no credit would not be believed. For 'will' instead of 'would', see Abbott 371.

180 Bohemia Polixenes.

181 attach arrest.

183 his hopes Either his father's hopes for a suitable marriage or Florizel's own prospects as heir apparent to the throne.

186–7 amazedly . . . marvel (I speak) in a bewildered manner, which befits ('becomes') my own amazement. George T. Wright finds a possible hendiadys in 'marvel . . . message' = 'my astonishing message' ('Hendiadys and *Hamlet*', *PMLA* 96 [1981], 190).

194 Endured . . . weathers Proved steadfast. Compare Olivia's ''twill endure rain and weather' (*TN* 1.5.237–8).

194 Lay't . . . charge Accuse him to his face (of betrayal).

LEONTES Who? Camillo?
LORD Camillo, sir. I spake with him, who now
Has these poor men in question. Never saw I
Wretches so quake; they kneel, they kiss the earth,
Forswear themselves as often as they speak;
Bohemia stops his ears and threatens them
With divers deaths in death.
PERDITA O my poor father!
The heaven sets spies upon us, will not have
Our contract celebrated.
LEONTES You are married?
FLORIZEL We are not, sir, nor are we like to be.
The stars, I see, will kiss the valleys first.
The odds for high and low's alike.
LEONTES My lord,
Is this the daughter of a king?
FLORIZEL She is
When once she is my wife.
LEONTES That 'once', I see by your good father's speed,
Will come on very slowly. I am sorry,
Most sorry, you have broken from his liking
Where you were tied in duty: and as sorry
Your choice is not so rich in worth as beauty,
That you might well enjoy her.
FLORIZEL Dear, look up.
Though Fortune, visible an enemy,
Should chase us with my father, power no jot
Hath she to change our loves. Beseech you, sir,

201 father!] F *(* father: *)* **209** 'once'] *Johnson (subst.)*; once F

197 in question under judicial interrogation.

199 Deny everything they swear to.

201 divers . . . deaths different tortures culminating in death. Happé reads as 'many deaths in one'.

203 contract See 4.4.363 n. and 370 n.

206 Douce observes that dice loaded to throw high or low numbers were called 'high and low'; compare *Wiv.* 1.3.85–6, 'for gourd and fullam [types of false dice] holds, / And high and low beguiles the rich and poor'. Citing this example, Wilson reads 206 as 'Fortune is a cheater who beguiles princes and shepherds alike with his false dice'. Schanzer, however, rejects the dicing expression and argues (following Capell) for a reading that links with the preceding line to suggest that the odds for high joining to low in marriage are like the odds of stars kissing valleys – both are long shots. A third possibility, perhaps recalling 4.4.424–6, is that the chances of good fortune are the same (and poor) no matter what one's social rank.

213 in worth in rank.

214 look up proverbial for 'cheer up' (Dent L431.1).

215 visible visibly, i.e. clearly. For the adverbial use of adjectives, see Abbott 1.

216 power . . . jot not the slightest bit of power.

Remember since you owed no more to time
Than I do now. With thought of such affections,
Step forth mine advocate; at your request
My father will grant precious things as trifles.

LEONTES Would he do so, I'd beg your precious mistress,
Which he counts but a trifle.

PAULINA Sir, my liege,
Your eye hath too much youth in't. Not a month
Fore your queen died, she was more worth such gazes
Than what you look on now.

LEONTES I thought of her
Even in these looks I made. [*To Florizel*] But your petition
Is yet unanswered. I will to your father;
Your honour not o'erthrown by your desires,
I am friend to them and you; upon which errand
I now go toward him. Therefore follow me,
And mark what way I make. Come, good my lord. *Exeunt*

5.2 *Enter* AUTOLYCUS *and a* GENTLEMAN

AUTOLYCUS Beseech you, sir, were you present at this relation?

FIRST GENTLEMAN I was by at the opening of the fardel, heard the old shepherd deliver the manner how he found it; whereupon,

225 Fore] F (*'Fore*) 227 SD] *Theobald; not in* F 5.2] F (*Scœna Secunda.*) 2 SH] F (*Gent. 1.*/ *and throughout scene*) 2 fardel] F (*farthell*)

218–19 Remember . . . now Think back on the time when you were as young as I am now.

219 affections (youthful) feelings of love.

222–7 These lines are all that remain from the protracted incestuous passion Pandosto feels for Fawnia in Greene. Shakespeare not only reduces an entire narrative segment to a single moment but also changes its emotional tenor (see Introduction, pp. 46–7).

226–7 I . . . made Leontes' quick rejoinder assumes added resonance and credibility if (1) the roles of Hermione and Perdita are doubled, or (2) Perdita is represented so as to resemble the Hermione of 1.2 (see Supplementary note to 5.1.122 SD).

229 Florizel has already testified to his honourable intentions and behaviour (4.4.33–5, 151–3). Compare Prospero's admonition to Ferdinand in *Temp.* 4.1.13–23.

230 If both Perdita and Florizel visibly recall the younger Hermione and Polixenes of Act 1 (see illustrations 18 and 23, pp. 29 and 45), Leontes' desire to help Florizel wed Perdita may register on some level his desire to harmonize relations between Hermione and Polixenes; see 5.3.147–9.

232 way progress.

Act 5, Scene 2

Kean in 1856 staged the scene at the Tombs of Syracuse at sunset. Many editors and directors follow Capell in locating it directly before Leontes' palace. Pyle (110) thinks 5.2 might occur in a waiting area outside the royal chamber where Leontes received everyone, and Ralph Berry reports (169) in Phillips a court anteroom into which 'cigarette-smoking officers burst . . . dying to light up as a relief from the big emotional scene upstairs'. Autolycus's presence, however, supports an outdoor setting somewhere on the way between the palace and the chamber mentioned in 5.2.5 (see also 5.2.79 n.), thus making Theobald's more general 'near the Court in Sicily' preferable to Capell's specificity. For the scene's relevance to the revision theory see Introduction, pp. 63–6; and for a sampling of performance choices, see Appendix C, p. 274.

1 this relation the account of this story.

3 deliver report.

after a little amazedness, we were all commanded out of the chamber. Only this, methought I heard the shepherd say he found the child.

AUTOLYCUS I would most gladly know the issue of it.

FIRST GENTLEMAN I make a broken delivery of the business; but the changes I perceived in the King and Camillo were very notes of admiration. They seemed almost with staring on one another to tear the cases of their eyes. There was speech in their dumbness, language in their very gesture; they looked as they had heard of a world ransomed, or one destroyed. A notable passion of wonder appeared in them, but the wisest beholder that knew no more but seeing could not say if th'importance were joy or sorrow; but in the extremity of the one it must needs be.

Enter another GENTLEMAN

Here comes a gentleman that haply knows more. The news, Rogero?

SECOND GENTLEMAN Nothing but bonfires. The oracle is fulfilled: the King's daughter is found! Such a deal of wonder is broken out within this hour that ballad-makers cannot be able to express it.

17 haply | F *(happily)* **19** SH | F *(Gent. 2. / and throughout scene)* **20** found! | *Folger;* found: F

4 after . . . amazedness i.e. after a short time ('little', *OED adj* 6b, *n* 5) of overwhelming astonishment (*OED* amazedness 4, first recorded in 1607). 'Little' = 'some' (OED adj 11) is also possible. A loose paraphrase might read, 'after the initial shock of the astonishing revelations'.

7 issue outcome (*OED n* 10), with wordplay (in light of 'child' in 6) on 'issue' = offspring (*OED n* 6).

8 broken delivery disjointed telling.

9–10 notes of admiration signs of wonder, perhaps spoken or shouted.

10 on at.

11 cases lids (as in *Per.* 3.2.98).

11–12 speech . . . gesture See *Cor.* 3.2.76, 'Action is eloquence'. Throughout the narrative account that follows of the reunion not seen, Shakespeare relies on the language of gesture, paradoxically stressing 'the inadequacy of language in words that are eloquent and moving' (Bevington, *Action*, 19).

15 but seeing than what he saw.

15 importance import, meaning (*OED n* 4, where this line is cited).

16 the one one or the other.

17 haply The spellings of 'haply'(= 'perhaps') and 'happily' were interchangeable.

18 Rogero The name of the Second Gentleman stands out because of its dissimilarity to the names of other male characters, most of which derive from Plutarch. Ross Duffin ('An Encore for Shakespeare's Rare Italian Master', *Elizabethan Review* 2 [1994], 21–5, esp. 23–4) explores a connection between the name and a ballad titled 'The Torment of a Jealious minde', which was sung to a tune called *Rogero* (*The Shirburn Ballads* [c. 1585–1616], ed. Andrew Clark [Oxford, 1907], no. 44). See also Duffin, *Shakespeare's Songbook*, 2004, 342–5.

19 bonfires large open-air fires to mark festive public occasions. Shakespeare borrowed this detail directly from *Pandosto* (Bullough, 198–9).

21 ballad-makers The association of ballads with wonders recalls the outlandish tenor of Autolycus's ballads (see 4.4.251–68); now, however, the incredible (which defies balladry) becomes awesome fact rather than farcical fiction, its truth confirmed orally rather than 'in print' (see 4.4.249–50).

Enter another GENTLEMAN

Here comes the Lady Paulina's steward; he can deliver you more. – How goes it now, sir? This news, which is called true, is so like an old tale that the verity of it is in strong suspicion. Has the King found his heir?

THIRD GENTLEMAN Most true, if ever truth were pregnant by circumstance. That which you hear you'll swear you see, there is such unity in the proofs. The mantle of Queen Hermione's; her jewel about the neck of it; the letters of Antigonus found with it, which they know to be his character; the majesty of the creature in resemblance of the mother; the affection of nobleness which nature shows above her breeding; and many other evidences proclaim her, with all certainty, to be the King's daughter. Did you see the meeting of the two kings?

SECOND GENTLEMAN No.

THIRD GENTLEMAN Then have you lost a sight which was to be seen, cannot be spoken of. There might you have beheld one joy crown another, so and in such manner that it seemed sorrow wept to take leave of them, for their joy waded in tears. There was casting up of eyes, holding up of hands, with countenance of such distraction that they were to be known by garment,

24 more. –] *Oxford;* more. F 27 SH] F *(Gent. 3./ and throughout scene)*

25 old tale incredible, amazing story. Rann specifies 'a romance', while Andrews, noting the allusion to the play's title, suggests 'an ancient legend (embellished by time)'. The phrase recurs in 5.2.53 and 5.3.117 and recalls references to strange tales in 2.1.23–30 and 4.1.13–15.

27–8 pregnant . . . circumstance made full and obvious (*OED* pregnant *adj*[1]) by convincing particulars (i.e. circumstantial evidence). The pregnancy metaphor figuring truth as 'filling out' with the weight of cogent details picks up on the preceding 'deliver' (23), which casts the Third Gentleman in the role of midwife to the truth (Deighton).

29 unity . . . proofs agreement among the evidentiary facts (enumerated in 29–34).

31 character handwriting. Citing 3.3.46 where the word refers to Perdita's identity as graphically represented, Turner observes that 'her character is thus confirmed by his character'.

31 creature i.e. Perdita.

32 affection of usually read as inclination toward (*OED* affection *n* 5), though perhaps 'property or quality of' (*n* 12, first recorded in 1625). The idea that true nobility would shine through humble disguise was a commonplace.

39 crown add the finishing touches to (*OED v*[1] 9, where this line is cited).

39 so . . . that as if (Deighton). Ritson notes 'the technical language of conveyancers' (those who draw up deeds, leases, etc.).

39–40 sorrow . . . tears 'They were weeping because their sorrow had been turned to joy, so the ingenious Third Gent. personifies sorrow and makes her weep at parting from them. It is not a helpful figure' (Bethell).

41 countenance (1) appearance, or (2) faces (if understood as the plural of a noun ending in 'ce' – see Abbott 471). Dolan reads 41–3 as 'with their faces so altered by emotion that they must be distinguished by their clothes rather than their features ["favour"]'.

not by favour. Our King, being ready to leap out of himself for joy of his found daughter, as if that joy were now become a loss, cries, 'O, thy mother, thy mother!' Then asks Bohemia forgiveness, then embraces his son-in-law; then again worries he his daughter with clipping her. Now he thanks the old shepherd, which stands by like a weather-bitten conduit of many kings' reigns. I never heard of such another encounter, which lames report to follow it and undoes description to do it.

SECOND GENTLEMAN What, pray you, became of Antigonus, that carried hence the child?

THIRD GENTLEMAN Like an old tale still, which will have matter to rehearse though credit be asleep and not an ear open: he was torn to pieces with a bear. This avouches the shepherd's son, who has not only his innocence, which seems much, to justify him, but a handkerchief and rings of his that Paulina knows.

FIRST GENTLEMAN What became of his bark and his followers?

THIRD GENTLEMAN Wracked the same instant of their master's death, and in the view of the shepherd, so that all the instruments

45 'O . . . mother!'] *Capell (subst.)*; Oh . . . mother: F 48 weather-bitten] F; weather-beaten F3 51 pray] F (`pray) 59 Wracked] F (Wrackt); Wreck'd *Hanmer*

43–4 **leap . . . joy** a variant of 'leap/jump out of his skin for joy' (Dent S507).

46 **worries he** i.e. he vehemently kisses and hugs (*OED* worry *v* 3c, where this line is cited). The etymology of 'worry' emphasizes violence, usually in the form of throttling or tearing to pieces. Turner speculates that 'he' may have been intended 'to give weight to the clause or in anticipation of the next sentence'.

47 **clipping** embracing.

48 **which** who (see Abbott 265).

48 **weather-bitten** nipped or gnawed by the weather (*OED ppl adj*, where this line is the first of two recorded usages). Steevens, citing *Ham.* 1.4.1 ('The air bites shrewdly') and *AYLI* 2.1.8 ('the winter's wind, / Which when it bites and blows upon my body'), suggests 'corroded by the weather', the reading adopted in Folger. The word is not a variant of F3's emendation 'weather-beaten', the editorial choice of Rowe through Johnson, and more recently of Orgel.

48 **conduit** The general sense of a pipe for conveying water is here understood as a water spout on the order of church gargoyles having the shape of an old man's head (Pafford). While the image figures the old Shepherd weeping, the liquid flowing through him may be more than his own tears, namely, the 'reigns' (with wordplay on 'rains') of the many kings he has outlived.

49–50 **lames . . . it** disables any attempt to report on it later and defies ('undoes') the power of description to render or express ('do' – see also 'done' in 5.2.85) it.

53–4 **matter . . . rehearse** subject matter to relate.

54 **credit** belief.

55 **with** by (compare 5.1.113). The usual sense of instrumentality may also be present (see 58–62), thus making the bear (like the storm) an agent of divine retribution for the crimes against Hermione and the baby Perdita.

56 **innocence** simplicity, artlessness ('such that he would be unable to invent such a story' [Bevington]).

56–7 **justify him** confirm his account.

60 **view . . . shepherd** What seems to be an error (it was the Clown, not his father the Shepherd, who witnessed the shipwreck, 3.3.77–96) is, in fact, accurate since both father and son are shepherds.

60–1 **instruments which** agents who. The Mariner had anticipated as much at 3.3.2–6; see also 5.2.55 n.

which aided to expose the child were even then lost when it was found. But O, the noble combat that 'twixt joy and sorrow was fought in Paulina! She had one eye declined for the loss of her husband, another elevated that the oracle was fulfilled. She lifted the princess from the earth, and so locks her in embracing as if she would pin her to her heart, that she might no more be in danger of loosing.

FIRST GENTLEMAN The dignity of this act was worth the audience of kings and princes, for by such was it acted.

THIRD GENTLEMAN One of the prettiest touches of all, and that which angled for mine eyes (caught the water, though not the fish) was when at the relation of the Queen's death, with the manner how she came to't – bravely confessed and lamented by the King – how attentiveness wounded his daughter, till (from one sign of dolour to another) she did, with an 'Alas!', I would fain say bleed tears; for I am sure my heart wept blood. Who was most marble there changed colour; some swooned, all sorrowed; if all the world could have seen't, the woe had been universal.

FIRST GENTLEMAN Are they returned to the court?

63 Paulina!] *Hanmer;* Paulina. F 67 loosing] F; losing F2 75 'Alas!'] F *(Alas)* 77 swooned] F *(swownded)*

63 **declined** cast down in sorrow. The proverbial expression was 'To cry (or look down) with one eye and laugh (or look up) with the other' (Dent E248). Compare *Ham.* 1.2.11, 'With an auspicious and a dropping eye'.

67 **loosing** (1) being lost (*OED* gives 'loose' as a variant of 'lose'/'lost', common in Shakespeare's time); (2) becoming separated from (i.e. the fastening indicated by 'pin' [66] coming undone). F's spelling (frequently emended to 'losing') keeps both senses in play. For the use of '-ing' as the equivalent of the passive participle '-en', see Abbott 372. Folger concurs with the usual reading of 'she' at the beginning of the line as referring to Perdita but raises the possibility of Paulina being the subject who fears losing Perdita.

68 **dignity** nobleness, excellence.

68 **act** i.e. all that has been reported, not simply the last image of Paulina embracing Perdita. 'The further . . . meaning of "performance of part of a play" is also present, and is responsible for the play-house metaphors in the rest of the sentence' (Schanzer).

71 **angled** fished (see 1.2.178).

71 **water** i.e. his tears.

72–4 **with . . . King** Rather than running the King's praised behaviour ('bravely . . . King') into an extended parenthesis (as many modern editors do by eliminating F's comma after 'to't'), F's punctuation (replaced here by a dash) draws attention to Leontes' perceived remorse.

74 **attentiveness** listening (to the account of her mother's death).

74–5 **from . . . another** moving from one manifestation of grief ('dolour') to another. In Brook, John Moffatt, in the role of Paulina's steward, 'began as a simpering, comic courtier, then turned utterly and movingly sincere at this line' (Bartholomeusz, 178).

75–6 **'Alas!' . . . tears** 'Perhaps suggested by the belief that sighs did cost the heart blood' (Pafford).

77 **most marble** most hardened, i.e. least likely to be moved emotionally. The image of marble undergoing change, following so closely on the account of Hermione's death, 'sets up, in dramatic terms, the mysterious finale' (Marjorie Garber, *Shakespeare's Ghostwriters*, 1987, 139).

79 This question indicates that at the end of 5.1 Leontes leaves the palace to meet Polixenes who is somewhere in the city (5.1.184–5). Thus, the chamber mentioned in 5.2.5 is not a palace chamber but a room where Polixenes and Camillo have stopped on their way to the court (5.1.187–9).

THIRD GENTLEMAN No. The Princess hearing of her mother's statue which is in the keeping of Paulina – a piece many years in doing and now newly performed by that rare Italian master Giulio Romano, who (had he himself eternity and could put breath into his work) would beguile nature of her custom, so perfectly he is her ape. He so near to Hermione hath done Hermione that they say one would speak to her and stand in hope of answer. Thither, with all greediness of affection, are they gone, and there they intend to sup.

SECOND GENTLEMAN I thought she had some great matter there in hand, for she hath privately, twice or thrice a day ever since the death of Hermione, visited that removed house. Shall we thither, and with our company piece the rejoicing?

FIRST GENTLEMAN Who would be thence that has the benefit of access? Every wink of an eye, some new grace will be born; our absence makes us unthrifty to our knowledge. Let's along.

Exeunt Gentlemen

95 SD] *Capell; Exit.* F; *Exeunt Rowe*

80 The sentence beginning 'The Princess . . .' is incomplete. The full answer to the First Gentleman's question (79) does not come until a separate sentence once removed (87–8).

82 **performed** finished (*OED* perform *v* 2a). *OED* 2b gives a sense last recorded in 1612, the completion of something 'by addition of ornament', which may, in the case of Hermione's statue, be the application of paint since the hand (5.3.47–8), veins (5.3.64–5) and lips (5.3.81–3) suggest colour, the first and last specifically described as 'not dry' or 'wet'. Turner cites Tollet's (1778) reference to Jonson's *The Magnetic Lady* (5.7.90–2) as evidence of painted marble statues in the period; see also Smith, 'Sermons', 9, 19.

83 **Giulio Romano** Shakespeare's only mention of a contemporary visual artist is usually thought to refer to a sixteenth-century Italian (c. 1499–1546) celebrated as a painter rather than a sculptor. In what appears to be the only known English text printed before the composition of *WT* that refers to Giulio Romano by name – *The Necessarie, Fit, and Convenient Education of a yong Gentlewoman* (a 1598 translation of Michele Bruto's 1555 treatise on female education) – the artist, along with Dürer, Michelangelo, and Raphael, is cited as a model worthy of imitation, all four 'be[ing] esteemed most excellent painters' (Georgianna Ziegler, 'Parents, Daughters, and "That Rare Italian Master": A New Source for *WT*', *SQ* 36 [1985], 204–12). See Supplementary note, pp. 253–4.

84 **beguile . . . custom** i.e. cheat the goddess Nature of her trade (in living human beings by creating them himself).

85 **ape** imitator.

85–7 **He . . . answer** It is not clear who 'they' are or how the speaker would know this since the unveiling does not occur until 5.3.

87 **greediness of affection** eager love or desire.

88 **sup** The literal meaning is 'have supper', but the word may be intended more figuratively as part of the metaphor begun with 'greediness of affection' (87), i.e. feast on the sight of Hermione's likeness.

91 **removed** secluded.

92 **piece** join (with the added sense of 'piece out' = 'augment').

93 **thence** elsewhere.

94 **Every . . . eye** (With) every blinking of an eye. The emphasis is on many fast appearing graces.

94 **grace** blessing.

95 **unthrifty of** wasteful of the opportunity to increase.

AUTOLYCUS Now, had I not the dash of my former life in me, would preferment drop on my head. I brought the old man and his son aboard the prince; told him I heard them talk of a fardel and I know not what; but he at that time overfond of the shepherd's daughter – so he then took her to be – who began to be much seasick, and himself little better, extremity of weather continuing, this mystery remained undiscovered. But 'tis all one to me, for had I been the finder-out of this secret it would not have relished among my other discredits.

Enter SHEPHERD *and* CLOWN

Here come those I have done good to against my will, and already appearing in the blossoms of their fortune.

SHEPHERD Come, boy, I am past more children, but thy sons and daughters will be all gentlemen born.

CLOWN [*To Autolycus*] You are well met, sir. You denied to fight with me this other day because I was no gentleman born. See

104 SD] F; *Enter . . . in fine apparel* Wilson 109 SD] *Oxford; not in* F

96 dash trace, touch (*OED n*[1] 5b). Following Schmidt's (1874) 'mark of infamy', Pafford reads as 'stain', and Orgel as 'taint'. Happé thought the line marked a change in Autolycus toward a more 'reflective . . . and perhaps regretful' position – the interpretation captured in Howell's glum-looking Autolycus. Other actors, however, appear to support Bethell's reading of the line as 'witty understatement': e.g. in Syer, Autolycus pulled from beneath his coat a silver tray that he had apparently stolen while inside the palace.

97 preferment advancement (presumably a return to 'three-pile' service at court).

98 prince the prince's ship.

100 so as.

101 extremity . . . weather As in 3.3, Perdita once again faced stormy weather at sea before Fortune smiled on her.

102 undiscovered unrevealed.

103 finder-out both 'detector' and 'revealer'.

104 relished found favour (*OED* relish *v*[1] 6). Bevington suggests 'tasted well', and Riverside similarly with 'had a pleasing taste'.

104 discredits misdeeds.

104 SD The 'colloquy [that follows] . . . is sandwiched between the account of Perdita's restoration and the unveiling of her mother's statue, providing the relief of laughter. It insures that the audience will come to the final scene with high expectation, acute judgment, and refreshed emotion' (David Richman, *Laughter, Pain, and Wonder: Shakespeare's Comedies and the Audience in the Theatre*, 1990, 113–14). Surprised by the arrival of the new gentlemen-born, Autolycus in Donnellan 'jumped up onto a plinth and affected the pose of a Grecian statue. His resourcefulness and subsequent sneeze were lightly comic but clearly [the director] was also prompting us towards the resurrection scene of Hermione' (P. Smith, 105).

106 blossoms . . . fortune i.e. their newly acquired sartorial splendour (often ill-fitting, as in Kahn, and thus the occasion of laughter).

107 past . . . children past fathering more children.

108 gentlemen born born gentlemen. In the comic exchange that follows, the Clown shows a complete misunderstanding of the phrase – but perhaps an accurate, satirical one – defining it in terms of behaviour, i.e. wearing rich clothes, knowing the art of quarrelling, swearing, and lying for a friend.

109 ff. Snyder observed a reversal of power-relations between Autolycus and Clown / Shepherd that reprises a similarly placed scene between Parolles and the Clown in *AWW* (5.2), with the same inversion of pronouns: Autolycus now uses 'you' for the 'gentlemen born' (115), and the Clown, who begins with 'you', switches to 'thou' after he tells of his and his father's elevation, and Autolycus pleads for their assistance (132). 'Your worship' (128) and 'Ay, an it like your . . . worship' (133) also switch direction, now said by Autolycus to the Clown and the Shepherd. In conclusion, they promise to be his 'good masters' (150–1), as Lafew does with Parolles.

109–10 You . . . born Perhaps a reference to an offstage incident, or simply the Clown's general recollection of Autolycus' earlier insistence on the social gap between them (see 4.4.684 ff, esp. 695–6).

you these clothes? Say you see them not and think me still no gentleman born, you were best say these robes are not gentlemen born. Give me the lie, do, and try whether I am not now a gentleman born.

AUTOLYCUS I know you are now, sir, a gentleman born.

CLOWN Ay, and have been so any time these four hours.

SHEPHERD And so have I, boy.

CLOWN So you have. But I was a gentleman born before my father: for the King's son took me by the hand and called me brother; and then the two kings called my father brother; and then the Prince my brother and the Princess my sister called my father father, and so we wept; and there was the first gentlemanlike tears that ever we shed.

SHEPHERD We may live, son, to shed many more.

CLOWN Ay, or else 'twere hard luck, being in so preposterous estate as we are.

AUTOLYCUS I humbly beseech you, sir, to pardon me all the faults I have committed to your worship, and to give me your good report to the Prince my master.

SHEPHERD Prithee, son, do; for we must be gentle now we are gentlemen.

130 Prithee] F (*'Prethee*)

112 were . . . say might as well say (see Abbott 352).

113 Give me the lie i.e. accuse me of lying. See 4.4.689–94 nn.

116 these four hours i.e. for several hours (as in *Ham.* 2.2.160, 'sometimes he walks four hours together'). 'Four' was 'commonly used for "several" and hence not to be taken precisely' (Harold Jenkins, ed., *Hamlet*, 1982, p. 245).

118–23 The lines parody the royal family reunion narrated in the first part of the scene (see Draper, 40, and Pyle, 117).

119 took . . . hand On the play's iterative hand imagery, see Introduction, p. 23.

125 preposterous The Clown's blunder for 'prosperous' underlines the inversion of position from low to high, and specifically his becoming a 'gentleman born' before his father. 'Preposterous' literally means 'reversed', i.e. placing in the rear what should be in the front ('the cart before the horse'). See Patricia Parker, *Shakespeare from the Margins: Language, Culture, Context*, 1996, 20–2.

128 me on my behalf.

128–9 good report recommendation.

130 gentle (1) generous, kind; (2) acting as befits a gentleman. In light of 'pardon' (127), Turner, citing Knowles, suggests 'mild' or 'forgiving'. The Shepherd's understanding of what it means to be a gentleman contrasts with the Clown's (see 5.2.108 n.).

CLOWN Thou wilt amend thy life?

AUTOLYCUS Ay, an it like your good worship.

CLOWN Give me thy hand. I will swear to the Prince thou art as honest a true fellow as any is in Bohemia.

SHEPHERD You may say it, but not swear it.

CLOWN Not swear it, now I am a gentleman? Let boors and franklins say it, I'll swear it.

SHEPHERD How if it be false, son?

CLOWN If it be ne'er so false, a true gentleman may swear it in the behalf of his friend. And I'll swear to the Prince thou art a tall fellow of thy hands, and that thou wilt not be drunk; but I know thou art no tall fellow of thy hands, and that thou wilt be drunk; but I'll swear it, and I would thou wouldst be a tall fellow of thy hands.

AUTOLYCUS I will prove so, sir, to my power.

CLOWN Ay, by any means prove a tall fellow. If I do not wonder how thou dar'st venture to be drunk, not being a tall fellow, trust me not. Hark, the kings and princes, our kindred, are going to see the queen's picture. Come, follow us. We'll be thy good masters. *Exeunt*

150 us. We'll] F *(us: wee'le)*

132 Among the passages cited by Shaheen (733) as sources for this line are BCP's opening sentences in Morning and Evening Prayer, 'Amend your liues, for the kingdome of God is at hand'. McCabe's Autolycus (Noble) used the line to steal the Clown's watch, while the rogue in Bergman knelt to the Clown before picking his pocket (stage business that recalled their first encounter in 4.3).

133 **an . . . like** if it please.

135 **honest . . . true** worthy . . . honest (Riverside).

136 For a similar distinction between swearing and saying – the former, binding in carrying the weight of an oath – see 1.2.35–6, 2.1.62–3, and *Cym.* 2.3.90–3. The Clown's response rests on the assumption that swearing (like duelling) was a prerogative reserved for gentlemen; compare *Cym.* 2.1.10–11, 'When a gentleman is dispos'd to swear, it is not for any standers-by to curtal his oaths'.

137 **boors . . . franklins** peasants . . . small landowners.

140 **If . . . false** No matter how false it is (Folger).

141–2 **tall . . . hands** a valiant (*OED* tall *adj* 3) man. 'Tall of his hands' was proverbial (Dent M163), sometimes meaning 'stout of arm, formidable with weapons' (the Clown's usage) but more generally 'deft with his hands' (*OED* tall *adj* 4). See next n.

146 **to . . . power** to the best of my ability. While the line leaves open the possibility of reform, it seems more likely that Autolycus is secretly promising to use his hands boldly as both cut-purse and pick-pocket (Schanzer). Having already demonstrated his dexterity (see 132 n.), the Autolycus in both Noble and Bergman ultimately returned what had been stolen, the latter doing so after being caught stealing from the Shepherd, and the former after making a pragmatic decision that his 'preferment' was dependent on the 'innate goodness' of the two 'gentlemen-born' (McCabe, in Smallwood, *Players*, 69).

149 **Hark** Turner thinks that Collier may be right to suggest that a flourish has sounded, but acknowledges that most editors read 'Hark' as meaning 'Listen to me'. In Howell, the Clown responds to the distant cries of the people cheering the recent good news.

149 **princes** i.e. Florizell and Perdita (the term was applicable to both males and females).

150 **picture** statue or monumental effigy (*OED n* 2d). Perhaps thinking of the earlier reference to Giulio Romano, some editors (e.g. Pafford, Bevington, and Andrews) specify 'painted statue'.

150–1 **good masters** To be or to stand 'good master' or 'good lord' was to be advocate for a suitor or client. Compare *Shr.* 4.4.21, 'I pray you stand good father to me now', and Kyd's *The Spanish Tragedy* 3.4.150–1,'To stand good Lord and help him in distress' (ed. Philip Edwards, 1959).

5.3 *Enter* LEONTES, POLIXENES, FLORIZEL, PERDITA, CAMILLO, PAULINA, *Lords, etc.*

LEONTES O grave and good Paulina, the great comfort
That I have had of thee!
PAULINA What, sovereign sir,
I did not well, I meant well; all my services
You have paid home. But that you have vouchsafed,
With your crowned brother and these your contracted
Heirs of your kingdoms, my poor house to visit,
It is a surplus of your grace, which never
My life may last to answer.
LEONTES O Paulina,
We honour you with trouble. But we came
To see the statue of our Queen. Your gallery
Have we passed through, not without much content
In many singularities; but we saw not

5.3] F *(Scæna Tertia.)* 0 SD *Enter . . . Lords, etc.*] *Rowe (subst.); Enter Leontes, Polixenes, Florizell, Perdita, Camillo, Paulina: Hermione (like a Statue:) Lords, &c.* F 2 thee!] F *(thee?)*

Act 5, Scene 3

The scene takes place in the 'removed house' mentioned at 5.2.91, where Paulina keeps both an art gallery (5.3.10) and a chapel (5.3.86). Although Paulina refers to 'my poor house' (5.3.6), the site is not her domicile, since she 'privately' visits it only 'twice or thrice a day' (5.2.90–1). Some productions favour a gallery setting (Syer), while others a chapel (Howell). Kean (1856) chose a sculpture gallery in the peristyle of Paulina's house. Wherever located, the space, in belonging to Paulina and housing the statue of Hermione, is a female domain, the first such space since 2.1; the difference now is that the male presence is invited rather than intrusive.

0 SD. 2 etc. Editors frequently expand to 'and Attendants', though some prefer 'and Others'. Proudfoot (in Hunt, 297 n.8) proposes extending 'etc.' to include the six characters in 5.2, all of whom exit with the clearly stated intention of seeing the unveiling of Hermione's statue (5.2.91–5, 149–51). Among recent productions showing Shepherd, Clown, and Autolycus are Syer, Freeman, Kulick, Lewis, and Cohen; in Howell, only the three gentlemen are brought back. See Supplementary note, p. 254.

1 grave esteemed. The combination of primary stresses and alliteration ('grave', 'good', and 'great') gives aural emphasis to Paulina's worth.

4 paid home fully repaid. 'To pay home' was proverbial (Dent H535.1); see 5.1.3 for a related commercial expression.

5 your contracted Kermode (after Staunton) suggests that 'your' was a compositorial interpolation, caught either from the preceding 'your crowned' or from the following 'your kingdoms' (6).

7 It . . . grace Your visit is an extra manifestation of your kindness.

7–8 which . . . answer which I may never live long enough to reciprocate ('answer'). See 1.2.3–9 for a similar fear.

9 with trouble with imposition on your hospitality by causing you extra work. Compare Duncan's use of 'trouble' as he addresses his hostess, Lady Macbeth, 'The love that follows us sometime is our trouble . . . Herein I teach you / How you shall . . . thank us for your trouble' (*Mac.* 1.6.11–14).

12 singularities notable objects, rarities.

That which my daughter came to look upon,
The statue of her mother.

PAULINA
As she lived peerless,
So her dead likeness I do well believe
Excels whatever yet you looked upon,
Or hand of man hath done; therefore I keep it
Lonely, apart. But here it is: prepare
To see the life as lively mocked as ever
Still sleep mocked death. Behold, and say 'tis well.

[*Paulina draws a curtain and reveals*] *Hermione like a statue*

I like your silence; it the more shows off
Your wonder. But yet speak: first you, my liege.
Comes it not something near?

LEONTES
Her natural posture!
Chide me, dear stone, that I may say indeed
Thou art Hermione; or rather, thou art she

18 Lonely] *Hanmer;* Louely F 20 SD *Paulina . . . reveals*] *Rowe (subst.); not in* F 20 SD *Hermione . . . statue*] *included in* opening SD F 22 speak:] *Collier (subst.);* speake, F; speak. *Johnson;* speak– *Orgel* 23 posture!] *Folger;* posture. F

15 dead Boorman and Orgel find a possible double meaning in the sense of 'dead' as 'perfect', 'exact' (*OED adj* 31b, c).

18 Lonely, apart i.e. not in the gallery that displays Paulina's other works of art, but in the chapel (86), by itself. Hanmer's emendation is now the editorial norm, but F's 'Louely' for 'Lonely' (in Secretary hand *u* and *n* could be easily confused) is possible, either in the modern adjectival sense of 'lovely' referring to the statue's beauty or, as Warburton suggests, adverbially to mean 'with more than ordinary regard and tenderness' (though the parallel meaning of 'lovingly, affectionately' recorded in *OED* [lovely *adv* 1] was perhaps obsolete by the early seventeenth century).

19 lively mocked vividly (*OED* lively *adv* 4) counterfeited (*OED* mock *v* 4, where this line is cited).

20 Still . . . death Proverbial (Dent S527).

20 well well done, i.e. satisfactory in appearance.

20 SD draws . . . curtain On the early seventeenth-century stage, the statue would probably have been revealed in 'the discovery space . . . generally an open tiring-house doorway within which curtains . . ., or in front of which hangings . . . had been fitted up' (Richard Hosley, 'The Playhouses and the Stage', in Muir and Schoenbaum, 32). Rowe was the first to stipulate the curtain mentioned in 68. For other examples in Shakespeare of a curtained discovery space 'becom[ing] a place of *anagnorisis*' (Bevington, *Action*, 116–7), see *Per.* 5.1.36, *Temp.* 5.1.171, and *H8* 2.2.62 and 5.2.35. The atmosphere surrounding the unveiling of Hermione's 'statue' may be related to similar veneration in remembered scenes of the old religion (as in Roger Martyn's nostalgic recollection of the ceremonial uncovering of sculpture at Long Melford church, quoted in David Cressy and Lori Anne Ferrell, eds., *Religion and Society in Early Modern England: A Sourcebook*, 1996, 11).

20 SD like a statue The play's performance history reveals a preference for a standing Hermione (as indicated by 'posture'[23] and 'stood' [34]), but a number of recent productions have her sitting (e.g. Donnellan, Kretzu, and Cohen). Campbell (1958) appears to have been the first to show Hermione recumbent on a tomb (Bartholomeusz, 188). See Supplementary note, p. 254.

21 shows off displays (*OED* show *v* 12b).

23 something near somewhat close to her likeness.

In thy not chiding, for she was as tender
As infancy and grace. But yet, Paulina,
Hermione was not so much wrinkled, nothing
So aged as this seems.

POLIXENES O, not by much.

PAULINA So much the more our carver's excellence,
Which lets go by some sixteen years and makes her
As she lived now.

LEONTES As now she might have done,
So much to my good comfort as it is
Now piercing to my soul. O, thus she stood,
Even with such life of majesty – warm life
As now it coldly stands – when first I wooed her.
I am ashamed. Does not the stone rebuke me
For being more stone than it? O royal piece!
There's magic in thy majesty, which has
My evils conjured to remembrance, and

37 Does] F *(Do's)* 38 piece!] *Hanmer;* Peece: F

26–7 tender . . . grace Leontes may be treating the softness of a baby and the comfort of grace as two distinct comparisons, or he may mean 'tender as a graceful (i.e. innocent, pleasing) baby' (an example of hendiadys). Either way, the image recalls Paulina's strategy in 2.2.39–41.

28 nothing not at all. While much has been made of the artist's talent for rendering life-like depictions in 5.2 and here (19 and 23), 'wrinkled' is the first graphic clue that a surprise might be in the making.

29 O . . . much Brent Harris (Polixenes in Kahn) had trouble with this line, ultimately abandoning an ironic reading for a simple validation of Leontes' blunt observation. In Howell, Robert Stephenson delivered the line as a gentle rebuke to Leontes' lack of tact.

31 lets . . . by indicates the passage of.

32 As As if.

33 it (1) the life-like statue or (2) Hermione's actual death.

36 when . . . her For a contrasting memory of Leontes' courtship, see 1.2.100–4.

38 more stone more unfeeling. See Dent H310.1 and H311 for the proverbial 'heart of stone'. The repetition of 'stone' after a few intervening words is an example of *ploce*, used in 37–8 to express intense emotion (Joseph, 85).

38 piece work of art, masterpiece.

39–44 Of two dangerous tendencies skirted in this scene, the first is defused here, i.e. idolatry associated with Roman Catholicism, specifically the 'superstition' of venerating images of Christ, Mary, and the saints before whom the faithful would kneel in prayer. See Alençon's promise to Joan of Arc, *1H6* 3.3.14–16, 'We'll set thy statue in some holy place, / And have thee reverenc'd like a blessed saint. / Employ thee then, sweet virgin, for our good'. A photograph of Edith Wynne Matthison's Hermione from Ames' New York revival in 1910 suggests the iconic Virgin Mary (see Bartholomeusz, 138); Armstrong, viewing the 'statue' in Syer, immediately thought of 'the Madonna without the infant' (32). The second tendency, forbidden magic used to raise the dead (hinted at in 'magic' and 'conjured'), is dealt with below (see 90–1, 96–7, and 110–11).

40 conjured . . . remembrance summoned up to my memory.

From thy admiring daughter took the spirits,
Standing like stone with thee.

PERDITA And give me leave,
And do not say 'tis superstition, that
I kneel and then implore her blessing. [*She kneels*] Lady,
Dear queen, that ended when I but began,
Give me that hand of yours to kiss.

PAULINA O, patience!
The statue is but newly fixed; the colour's
Not dry. [*Perdita rises*]

CAMILLO My lord, your sorrow was too sore laid on,
Which sixteen winters cannot blow away,
So many summers dry. Scarce any joy
Did ever so long live; no sorrow
But killed itself much sooner.

POLIXENES Dear my brother,
Let him that was the cause of this have power

44 SD] *Folger; not in* F; *after* Lady *Bevington* 46 patience!] *Hudson;* patience: F 48 SD] *This edn.; not in* F

41 admiring awestruck.

41 spirits i.e. substances or fluids thought to permeate the blood and chief organs of the body (*OED* spirit *n* 16). There were three types: animal, natural, and vital. Bevington and Riverside gloss as 'vital (i.e. animating) forces', but the description of Perdita 'standing like stone' in the following line supports Folger's 'animal spirits', the principle of sensation and voluntary motion that mediated between mind and body (see *OED* animal spirits 1).

44 If Perdita kneels during this line, as seems likely, when does she rise? Folger has her do so at 5.3.84–5, but that requires a long period of kneeling. In Howell, Perdita begins to rise after Paulina stays her attempt to touch the statue's hand (46). A practicable choice may be after 48 (as in this edn).

46 patience (have) patience, i.e. not so fast. In Paulina's admonition to Perdita to refrain from touching the statue, repeated to Leontes at 5.3.80, Cynthia Lewis ('Soft Touch: On the Renaissance Staging and Meaning of the "*Noli me tangere*" Icon', *CompD* 36 [2002–3]: 53–73, esp. 67–70) detects a biblical allusion to the moment when the risen Christ says to Mary Magdalene, 'Touch me not: for I am not yet ascended to my Father' (John 20.17). For another example of this biblical icon, see Viola's 'Do not embrace me' (*TN* 5.1.251).

47 fixed Generally read as 'painted', but Folger's 'put (set) in place' may be preferable since the meaning of 'colour being made permanent' is not recorded in *OED* until 1665 (fix *v* 5a).

47 colour's paint is. On painted statues in Shakespeare's time, see 5.2.82 n.

49 sore . . . on rigorously imposed or inflicted ('laid on', see *OED* lay *v*[1] 55a, c). The immediately surrounding words 'colour', 'dry' [twice], and 'blow away' lead some editors to detect a metaphor drawn from painting that permits a double reading of 'sore' = 'heavily', 'thickly' (Schanzer), and 'laid on' = 'applied as a coat of paint' (Folger).

51 So . . . dry Nor sixteen summers dry up.

51–3 Scarce . . . sooner i.e. just as scarcely any joy can live so long, no sorrow can last sixteen years.

54 Let . . . this By accepting responsibility for Leontes' suffering, Polixenes demonstrates the magnanimity mandated by ideal friendship in Shakespeare's time. Pafford compares Valentine's forgiveness of Proteus at the end of *TGV*, *JC* 4.3.86, 'A friend should bear his friend's infirmities', and *Son.* 88, 'Such is my love, to thee I so belong, / That for thy right myself will bear all wrong'.

To take off so much grief from you as he
Will piece up in himself.

PAULINA Indeed, my lord,
If I had thought the sight of my poor image
Would thus have wrought you – for the stone is mine –
I'd not have showed it.

LEONTES Do not draw the curtain.

PAULINA No longer shall you gaze on't, lest your fancy
May think anon it moves.

LEONTES Let be, let be.
Would I were dead, but that methinks already –
What was he that did make it? – See, my lord,
Would you not deem it breathed? and that those veins
Did verily bear blood?

POLIXENES Masterly done:
The very life seems warm upon her lip.

LEONTES The fixure of her eye has motion in't,
As we are mocked with art.

PAULINA I'll draw the curtain.
My lord's almost so far transported that
He'll think anon it lives.

LEONTES O sweet Paulina,
Make me to think so twenty years together!

62 already–] *Rowe;* alreadie. F 65 Masterly] F *(*'Masterly*)* 67 fixure] F*;* fixture F4 71 together!] *Staunton;* together: F

56 piece . . . himself incorporate into himself (thereby adding to his own grief).

57 image i.e. the statue.

58 wrought stirred, overwhelmed.

58 for . . . mine Thirlby (in Theobald) queried the need of this parenthetical statement. Perhaps Paulina feels compelled to exert control; such was the reading of the subtext by Eileen Atkins (in Hall): 'Hermione will remain stone, under my control, until such time as you're ready to accept her' (Warren, *Staging*, 148). Or the parenthesis may have been intended simply to clarify 'my poor image' as the statue rather than Paulina herself (Turner).

62 May I die, if I do not think it moves already (Staunton). Remembering Macready's performance, Faucit writes (388): 'Has he seen something that makes him think the statue lives? Mr. Macready indicated this, and hurriedly went on [with "What was he . . ."]. His eyes have been so riveted upon the figure, that he sees what the others have not seen, that there is something about it beyond the reach of art'.

63 What Who (Abbott 254).

65 Masterly F's apostrophe (see Collation), which Furness could not explain, is omitted by most editors; Turner proposes an ellipsis = 'It is'.

67 fixure an early form of 'fixture' = 'fixedness'. *OED*, which records the first usage in 1603, cites this line. Shakespeare uses the word once elsewhere, *Tro.* 1.3.101.

68 So that we are fooled by artistic illusion (Bevington, subst.). For the demonstrative meaning of 'as', see Abbott 110. In Donnellan, Leontes atypically snarled the line as a 'furious denouncement of fraud' rather than as the usual 'exclamation of enrapture' (P. Smith, 105).

69 transported carried away.

71 twenty . . . together (for) twenty uninterrupted years (i.e. forever).

No settled senses of the world can match
The pleasure of that madness. Let't alone.

PAULINA I am sorry, sir, I have thus far stirred you; but
I could afflict you farther.

LEONTES Do, Paulina,
For this affliction has a taste as sweet
As any cordial comfort. Still methinks
There is an air comes from her. What fine chisel
Could ever yet cut breath? Let no man mock me,
For I will kiss her.

PAULINA Good my lord, forbear.
The ruddiness upon her lip is wet;
You'll mar it if you kiss it, stain your own
With oily painting. Shall I draw the curtain?

LEONTES No, not these twenty years.

PERDITA So long could I
Stand by, a looker-on.

PAULINA Either forbear,
Quit presently the chapel, or resolve you
For more amazement. If you can behold it,
I'll make the statue move indeed, descend
And take you by the hand – but then you'll think,
Which I protest against, I am assisted
By wicked powers.

89 hand–] *Kermode;* hand: F

72 settled senses untroubled mental faculties. Orgel and Folger follow Schanzer in reading the line as 'No calm mind in the world'. Pafford, citing Harold Brooks, notes a parallel with Florizel in 4.4.462–5.

75 afflict Perhaps 'affect' (Warburton) but more likely 'torment' or 'distress', the sense Leontes understands in 75–7 where he presumably plays on the same stock phrase about affliction's sour cup that Costard mangles in *LLL* 1.1.213–15.

77 cordial restorative.

78 an air a breath.

79 cut breath carve stone so as to imitate breath. Felperin ('Tongue-tied', 175) praises the onomatopoeia of 'What . . . breath', finding in the 'succession of monosyllabic words composed of short vowels chopped off by dental stops . . . [the imitation of] the sharp clicks of a chisel tapping through its medium'.

80 For . . . her Neely (206) contends that Leontes' 'determination to kiss the statue signals Paulina that he is ready for reunion with the woman Hermione'.

83 painting paint.

84 not . . . years not for at least twenty years (see 5.3.71).

85 forbear withdraw. 'Forbear' = 'refrain' (see 80) is possible if Paulina is not using the word in apposition with the following command to leave the chapel but rather as a separate order to stop from touching the statue (Turner).

86 presently immediately.

86 chapel As Orgel emphasizes, the statue is kept not only apart but in a religious, though not necessarily Christian (*OED* 6), setting.

86 resolve you prepare yourselves.

87 behold it stand it.

91 wicked powers i.e. black magic. See 5.3.96, 105, and 110–11.

LEONTES What you can make her do
I am content to look on; what to speak
I am content to hear; for 'tis as easy
To make her speak as move.

PAULINA It is required
You do awake your faith. Then all stand still.
On! Those that think it is unlawful business
I am about, let them depart.

LEONTES Proceed.
No foot shall stir.

PAULINA Music, awake her, strike!

[*Music*]

'Tis time: descend; be stone no more; approach;
Strike all that look upon with marvel. Come,
I'll fill your grave up. Stir; nay, come away;

96 On!] *This edn;* On: F; Or *Hanmer* 98 Music, awake her, strike!] *This edn;* Music; awake her: Strike: F 98 SD *Music*] *Rowe; not in* F

94–5 It . . . faith In Kretzu, Paulina addressed the line to Leontes alone, 'stressing that it is his faith that is crucial to this scene'; in productions where she turns directly to the audience at large (as in Syer and Whitney), the spectators' 'collective faith in theatre's miraculous powers to create life [becomes] the issue' (Shurgot, Kretzu review, 27).

96 On Let us go on (Knight). Most editors follow Hanmer's emendation, 'Or', presumably because (like Pafford) they sense a required alternative to Paulina's command that 'all stand still'. But as Snyder perceived, Knight's reading fits the assertive voice of a character who controls the choreography of the spectacle.

96 unlawful business i.e. occult activities, sorcery. 'Parliament made conjuring evil spirits a secular crime punishable by death in 1563 and added necromancy to the roll of capital offenses in the second witchcraft statute of 1604' (Michael MacDonald, 'Science, Magic, and Folklore', in John Andrews, ed. *William Shakespeare: His World, His Work, His Influence*, I, 1985, 185). Citing Martin Ingram (*Church Courts, Sex and Marriage in England, 1570–1640* [1987], 97), Orgel remarks that despite the illegality of occult practices, prosecutions declined significantly after about 1585, and few cases are recorded in the early seventeenth century. Paulina's disclaimer here and in 90–1 and 105 recalls Leontes' charge of 'mankind witch' (2.3.67). In Cohen, Paulina pointedly delivered 96–7 to the audience, and in Kulick, Leontes looked out at the spectators as he responded 'No foot shall stir' (98).

98 strike Paulina calls for musicians to 'strike' up, i.e. to begin playing their instruments.

99–103 Paulina's eight separate commands, whether punctuated with colons as in F or with semicolons and periods as here, yield a slow delivery, marked with strong pauses, thereby concluding the theme of waiting (see Introduction, p. 23). While Anna Calder Marshall (in Howell) moves only when the text stipulates (the second half of 103), Pernilla August (in Bergman) moved her fingers at 'be stone no more' and then sat up from her recumbent position (see illustration 27, p. 51); Lise Bruneau (in Kahn) found 'redeems' the pivot for what appeared as a sudden shaking off of a spell. See Supplementary note, p. 254.

101 I'll . . . up The primary meaning refers to the immediate occasion that no longer requires Hermione to be dead, but there may be a secondary application to Paulina herself, who in 132–5 looks forward to her own death, as a substitute for Hermione: the Queen, who regains a husband and a daughter, is replaced in the grave by Paulina, whose loss of her husband has recently been confirmed and whose sustaining mission is now completed.

Bequeath to death your numbness, for from him
Dear life redeems you. – You perceive she stirs.

[*Hermione descends*]

Start not. Her actions shall be holy as
You hear my spell is lawful. [*To Leontes*] Do not shun her
Until you see her die again, for then
You kill her double. Nay, present your hand.
When she was young you wooed her; now in age
Is she become the suitor?

LEONTES O, she's warm!
If this be magic, let it be an art
Lawful as eating.

[*Hermione and Leontes embrace*]

POLIXENES She embraces him.

CAMILLO She hangs about his neck.
If she pertain to life, let her speak too.

POLIXENES Ay, and make it manifest where she has lived,
Or how stol'n from the dead!

PAULINA That she is living,
Were it but told you, should be hooted at

103 you.–] *Folger;* you) F; you. [*To Leontes*] *Oxford* **103** SD] *Rowe (subst.); not in* F **105** SD] *Pafford; not in* F **109** warm!] *Capell;* warme: F **111** SD] *Rowe (subst., after* 109*); not in* F **115** dead!] *Staunton;* dead. *Capell;* dead? F

102 him i.e. death.

104 Start not Do not be startled.

106–7 Until . . . double i.e. do not shun Hermione until her (future) death, for if you do you kill her twice. Even now Paulina reminds Leontes of his grievous offense, and with the root word that pained him earlier (5.1.15–20). In Paulina's caution against a double killing, Shakespeare may be remembering Eurydice's 'double dying' in Ovid (*Metamorphoses*, 10. 64–69).

107–9 Nay . . . suitor These lines suggest potential stage business for Hermione (see Introduction, pp. 52–3).

110–11 If . . . eating See 'unlawful business' (96 n.).

111–12 She embraces . . . neck Having heightened Hermione's return by an aura of sanctity, the use of music, talk of magic, and Paulina's formal incantation, Shakespeare turns to the amazement of on-lookers who (having not said anything for some time) now speak, while the focus of their attention – Leontes and Hermione coming together – is silent, beyond words.

113 pertain . . . life belong among the living. Orgel notes the legal overtone 'be entitled' (*OED* pertain *v* 1b).

113 let . . . speak Compare Prince Hal's similar desire for oral/aural verification of a living Falstaff, 'I prithee speak, we will not trust our eyes / Without our ears' (*1 H4* 5.4.136–7).

114–15 make . . . dead Speaking for the audience, not to mention the critics who have written extensively on whether Hermione really died in Act 3 (see Introduction, pp. 47–9), Polixenes poses two alternatives, one connecting Hermione to the ordinary (albeit puzzling) human realm – where and how has she been living all this time – and the other to the heightened world of classical myth, specifically the tales of Alcestis and Eurydice, wives who were 'stol'n from the dead' (115).

Like an old tale; but it appears she lives,
Though yet she speak not. Mark a little while.
[*To Perdita*] Please you to interpose, fair madam; kneel
And pray your mother's blessing [*Perdita kneels*].
[*To Hermione*] Turn, good lady;
Our Perdita is found.

HERMIONE You gods look down,
And from your sacred vials pour your graces
Upon my daughter's head! [*Raising Perdita*] Tell
me, mine own
Where hast thou been preserved? where lived? how found
Thy father's court? For thou shalt hear that I,
Knowing by Paulina that the oracle
Gave hope thou wast in being, have preserved
Myself to see the issue.

PAULINA There's time enough for that,
Lest they desire upon this push to trouble

119 SD] *Pafford; not in* F **120** SD *Perdita kneels*] *This edn.; not in* F **120** SD *To Hermione*] *Pafford; not in* F **122** vials] F *(* Viols*)* **123** head!] *Hanmer;* head: F **123** SD] *This edn; not in* F **126** the] F2*;* rhe F **128** time] F2*;* ttme F **129** Lest] F3*;* Least F

118 Mark Pay attention.

119 interpose i.e. position yourself between Leontes and Hermione (an embedded blocking cue).

121 Our . . . found 'This succinct line, with the contrast in meaning between *Perdita* (she who was lost) and *found* marks the fulfillment of the Oracle' (Happé).

121–8 You . . . issue Hermione speaks only once in this scene and to Perdita alone, leading some critics and directors to question the fullness of spousal reconciliation (see Introduction, p. 55).

121–2 You . . . graces A frequently cited parallel is the invocation of divine blessings ('graces') in *Temp.* 5.1.202–1, 'Look down, you gods, / And on this couple drop a blessed crown'; see also *Cym.* 5.5.350–1, 'The benediction of these covering heavens / Fall on their heads like dew'.

125–28 For . . . issue 'This is the only explanation of Hermione's sixteen-year-long sequestration that Shakespeare provides, and not a few readers have felt that he ought to have thought up a better one' (Schanzer). But as Turner argues, 'Raising her own questions . . . Hermione here anticipates Perdita's and ours. She remained silent so that which was lost could be found, not only Perdita but Leontes as well, whose regeneration is a major part of the triumph of time'. See Introduction, pp. 41–7.

126 Knowing . . . Paulina Hermione in fact heard the oracle herself. If this scene was added some time after the original composition, what appears to be a misrecollection becomes more understandable. See Introduction, pp. 63–6.

127 in being alive.

128 issue (1) the prophecy's fulfillment, and (2) Perdita herself ('issue' = 'offspring').

128 There's . . . that Paulina acts as a surrogate dramatist, recognizing that too many logical questions and the exposition they prompt, particularly as regarding Hermione's narrative, would shatter the wonder of the moment.

129 upon . . . push 'at this critical juncture' (*OED* push *n*[1] 6). But a reading of 'push' as 'provocation' (Folger) or 'prompting' (Andrews) is attractive in establishing Hermione's questions to Perdita as the impetus for 'like relation' (see 130 n.).

129 trouble interrupt (*OED v* 2).

Your joys with like relation. Go together
You precious winners all; your exultation
Partake to everyone. I, an old turtle,
Will wing me to some withered bough and there
My mate, that's never to be found again,
Lament till I am lost.

LEONTES O peace, Paulina!
Thou shouldst a husband take by my consent
As I by thine a wife. This is a match,
And made between's by vows. Thou hast found mine –
But how is to be questioned, for I saw her
(As I thought) dead, and have in vain said many
A prayer upon her grave. I'll not seek far –
For him, I partly know his mind – to find thee
An honourable husband. Come, Camillo,
And take her by the hand, whose worth and honesty

135 Paulina! | *Collier;* Paulina: F

130 with . . . relation with similar stories and inquiries of their own. Schanzer, however, proposes 'by asking you similarly to tell your story'. Retaining F's 'Least' (129), Riverside (1974, 1997) reads as 'The last thing they want, at this critical moment, is to trouble your happiness with such an account'. Bevington, who earlier (1980) offered a similar interpretation, emends to the usual 'Lest' in his 4th edn (1997) and suggests both narrative possibilities: 'Lest they insist, at this critical juncture, on interrupting this moment of joy with your relating of your story or with their telling of what has happened to them.' If Shepherd and Clown are present, Paulina's admonition might take on added force (Proudfoot, in Hunt, 297 n.8).

132 Partake to Make known to, share with.

132 turtle turtledove (traditionally regarded as a symbol of fidelity). See 4.4.154–5. Few things moved Granville-Barker more than the lines about the lone turtledove, to which he responded, 'Plucky Paulina, such a good fellow' ('Preface', in Hunt, 79). Bartholomeusz (156) detects the 'ironic, haunting echo' of the 'Song of Solomon' (2.11–12): 'The winter is past and gone . . . the time of singing has come . . . the voice of the turtle is heard in our land'. For a different response to 5.3.132–5, see 135 n.

133 wing me fly.

135 lost dead. Having spoken of the others as 'precious winners' (131), Paulina may also be thinking of 'lost' in reference to herself as one who has 'lost what can never be recovered' (Johnson). During rehearsals Kahn interpreted Paulina's lamentation as one of the scene's 'embedded jokes': 'It's like here she goes again. We've been through this for sixteen years.'

136–8 Thou . . . vows That Paulina has agreed to marry a suitor chosen by Leontes as part of a mutual agreement with the king is new information (see 5.1.69–71, 81–4). The Paulina-Camillo coda (5.3.136–46) strikes many critics as being problematic and several directors omit the business: e.g. Brook, Bergman, and Donnellan – the last abruptly ending the play after Hermione blesses her newly restored daughter (5.3.123). See Introduction, pp. 58–9 and Appendix B, p. 266.

138 between's between us.

142 For As for

144 whose . . . honesty i.e. Camillo's (Mason's reading [139], followed by Wilson, Schanzer, and Kermode, but disputed by Pafford and Orgel). That the praise logically – if not grammatically, given the pronominal antecedent – refers to Camillo rather than Paulina is borne out by the next two lines: Polixenes and Leontes are both able to validate Camillo's probity through his long service to each, but only Leontes can similarly attest to Paulina's worth. 'Come . . . kings' (143–6) may be read as Leontes' making good on his promise to find Paulina 'an honourable husband' (143).

Is richly noted, and here justified
By us, a pair of kings. Let's from this place.
[*To Hermione*] What! Look upon my brother. Both your
pardons
That e'er I put between your holy looks
My ill suspicion. This your son-in-law,
And son unto the king, whom heavens directing,
Is troth-plight to your daughter. Good Paulina,
Lead us from hence, where we may leisurely
Each one demand and answer to his part
Performed in this wide gap of time since first
We were dissevered. Hastily lead away. *Exeunt*

147 SD] *Pafford; not in* F 147 What!] *Collier;* F What?

145 **richly noted** abundantly celebrated.

145 **justified** vouched for.

146 **from** i.e. go from.

147 **Look . . . brother** With this command, the action comes full circle – especially if Hermione and Polixenes take hands – since looks and the touching of hands fuelled Leontes' initial jealous rage. Hermione has perhaps shown some natural embarrassment about greeting Polixenes (Kermode), either not wishing to remember what started her travail or fearing to restart it should Leontes misinterpret her look.

148 **holy** chaste.

149 **ill** evil.

149 **This** The insertion in Dyce[2] of an apostrophe to mark the omission of 'is', a popular emendation, is unnecessary since the syntax makes it clear that 'This your son-in-law' is the subject of 'Is troth-plight to your daughter'.

150 **whom . . . directing** with the heavens guiding him (Orgel).

151 **troth-plight** betrothed. See 1.2.275 and 4.4.370, 397.

153–4 **demand . . . Performed** i.e. ask questions and provide answers about the parts we have performed (Folger). Leontes' proposal – a tactic Shakespeare frequently uses – deftly spares the audience needless exposition; for its opposite, see the conclusion to *Err.*

154 **wide . . . time** An echo of 4.1.7.

155 **dissevered** separated.

SUPPLEMENTARY NOTES

1.1 Headnote As evidenced by a Padua promptbook belonging to a group of amateur thespians performing in 1620s, the theatrical practice of deleting 1.1 seems to have originated as early as the seventeenth century (Bartholomeusz, 13); modern directors who have followed suit include Tree, Brook, Nunn, Lapine, and Lewis. Syer retained several of the lines, reassigning them to the interpolated figure of Time, who stood flanked by Leontes and Polixenes. When the first scene is fully included, Camillo and Archidamus frequently appear as part of a larger group inclusive of Leontes, Hermione, Mamillius, Polixenes, and often a goodly number of extras; the two courtiers usually move downstage for their conversation, blending into the background after its completion (e.g., Bergman, Doran, and Kahn).

1.1.28 malice or matter Both words also carry legal implications: 'malice' is wrongful intention, which aggravates the guilt of an offence (*OED n* 6); 'matter' is something which is to be tried or proved (*OED n* 16b). While the primary meanings – along with those of 'justified' (1.1.8) and 'attorneyed' (1.1.23) – may not be legal in 1.1, all four words register a legal subcurrent appropriate to a play the first half of which is given to charges of adultery and treason, evidentiary queries, and a trial; even the pastoral world of Bohemia raises issues related to crime and punishment. Finally, if 'malice' is understood as an astrological reference to the baleful influence of certain stars (*OED n* 3), it becomes the first indicator of Fortune's negative spiral, so pervasive from 1.2 through 3.2.

1.1.29–30 of your . . . Mamillius As a way of rendering the sudden reference to Mamillius less abrupt, Howell (1980) shows the boy running onstage during the 'heavens continue their loves . . . either malice or matter to alter it' exchange. He was in pursuit of a ball he had presumably thrown from offstage at the beginning of Camillo and Archidamus' dialogue, and which Camillo held until Mamillius' entrance, when he playfully returned it to the prince, who then ran off, thereby precipitating the praise of Archidamus. Nothing is said of Polixenes' son, who we hear in the next scene is the same age as Leontes'. In his claim that Mamillius is a nonpareil (1.1.30–1), Archidamus either engages in the hyperbole of diplomatic fawning or perhaps implies that the son of his king lacks the same obvious promise of Leontes' heir, a possibility that only adds to the irreplaceable and haunting loss of Mamillius in the final scene.

1.2 Headnote Since 1856, when Charles Kean took Archidamus' effusive praise of Sicilian hospitality as a cue for staging an extravagant banquet, complete with a hymn to Apollo and a Pyrrhic dance (the vestiges of which were still visible in Tree's 1906 staging), the scene's performance history has favoured, if not on the same scale, a well-attended and well-dressed public, formal celebration, often marked by dancing, dining, and toasting – e.g. Phillips, Lapine, Bergman, Doran, Kulick, and Hytner. Nunn's choice of a nursery setting remains a notable exception. According to Warren (102), the rehearsal process led Hall to abandon his initial concept of a 'a court of listeners and watchers' for something more intimate and private. See illustrations 6 and 7 (pp. 10 and 11) for contrasting stagings.

1.2.33 Collier's stage direction perhaps comes too early, as Hermione addresses Leontes at 1.2.42–4. Furness and Wilson place the withdrawal after that address, while Schanzer has it after line 37: he thinks the later lines should be spoken by Hermione to herself rather than her husband (whom she elsewhere never addresses by his name but only as 'sir', 'my lord', etc.). Howell showed a loving relationship between husband and wife throughout Hermione's first two speeches, having Leontes withdraw at her 'Verily' (1.2.45). Rolfe thinks Leontes is occupied playing with Mamillius, a popular choice of stage business that in *WT*'s performance history is rivaled only by Leontes' retreat upstage or to the side to confer with aides or engage in paper work. Gielgud's Leontes (in Brook), however, did nothing but glare at the conviviality of his wife and best friend (see illustration 17, p. 27). Hall's decision to include Tim Pigott-Smith's Leontes in the gaiety of the Hermione-Polixenes exchange that follows ('translating the verbal wit into physical expressions of affection') departs from the norm of having Leontes either exit completely or simply withdraw to another part of the stage. While Hall acknowledged that Leontes' later question 'Is he won yet' (1.2.85) 'suggested someone re-entering the conversation, . . . as rehearsals progressed, the line emerged quite naturally as a request for confirmation that Polixenes would stay, after the conversation had moved away from that specific point into a much wider discussion of boyhood friendships and subsequent marriages' (Warren, 99).

2.1.185 oracle The human instrument ('oracle') was always a woman. As Plutarch, himself a priest at the temple in the first century CE, records in his *Moralia* (tr. Philemon Holland, 1603): '[T]hen ech [*sic*] prophetess is mooved according as she is disposed to receive his inspiration. . . . For surely, that voice is not the gods, nor the sound, nor the phrase, ne yet the meeter and verse, but a womans they be all. As for him [Apollo], he representeth unto her, fancies onely and imaginations, kindling a light in the soule to declare things to come: and such an illumination as this, is that which they call Enthusiasmos' (1189). See also the entry for Delphos in Thomas Cooper's list of proper names, 'Dictionarium Historicum & Poeticum propria locurum & Personarum', included in his *Thesaurus Linguae Romanae et Britannicae* (1565).

2.2 Headnote Given the scene's location between Leontes' dispatching of Cleomenes and Dion to Apollo's oracle at 2.1.182–4 and the news of the emissaries' return after twenty-three days at 2.3.192–8, it would appear that Hermione has been incarcerated for approximately three weeks. The problem with such a temporal sequence arises, however, when we think about the 'audacious' nature of Paulina's character (2.3.42) and the strong bond between her and Hermione – presumably the reason for Leontes' order that she, in particular, be barred from the prison (2.2.7–8). The sense of urgency and incomprehension suggested by 'Here's ado' (2.2.9) and 'Here's such ado' (2.2.18) gives the impression that Paulina has rushed to the prison immediately upon hearing the news. Perhaps 2.2 illustrates Shakespeare's fondness of double time, whereby the passage of days or weeks is suggested without losing a sense of immediacy (as in the Cyprus scenes in *Oth.*).

2.3.129 we are gone Why does Paulina use the plural pronoun? The text does not indicate (as it does for 2.2) that attendants accompany her, and she obviously leaves without the baby. Perhaps, as the emissary for the Queen, she appropriates the royal formula on the model of the Bastard who speaks for King John in 5.2 of that play. Or, if 'gone' is understood as a synonym for 'dead' – the meaning it carries in Antigonus' last words in the play, 'I am gone forever' (3.3.57), she may be acknowledging the end of her marriage, saying something like 'Because I hold you responsible for what happens to the baby, we are dead to each other from this time on'. Such was the choice of Tana Hicken (Kahn) who fixed her gaze on Antigonus at 128, emphatically singling him out for contempt with the words 'not *one* of you'. In both Syer and Kulick, Paulina's tender touching of Antigonus' arm before she exited poignantly implied spousal closure. (I am grateful to Patricia Parker ('Polymorphic Bears', 175) for reminding me of the repetition of the semantic linkage between 'gone' and 'dead' at 3.2.142 and 4.4.777). In a post-performance interview (19 October 2002), Hicken said that had there been more time to fine-tune the business, she would have liked to pick up the baby at 'We are gone', only to have Leontes sternly gesture that she was to leave the infant where she had placed her at 2.3.107.

3.1.1 The climate's delicate, the air most sweet In the section of his *Moralia* entitled 'Why Oracles cease to give answers', Plutarch describes the fragrant odour permeating the oracle's chamber as surpassing the 'most pretious ointments and sweetest perfumes in the world' (1349). On the qualities of the air itself in Delphi, see the section 'Why Pythia giveth no more answers in verse' (1187).

3.2.47–8 With . . . thus Part of the difficulty with this passage seems to inhere in 'strained' understood as an intransitive, meaning 'transgressed' or 'sinned'. If, however, 'strained' functions as a transitive verbal, the problem of a missing object would be solved by looking ahead to 'bound of honour' in the next line. (See also 5.1.99–102 and 5.3.141–3.) Orgel thinks that the obscurity may be 'essential' to the meaning and thus part of a 'poetics of incomprehensibility' peculiar to *WT* (see also his 'Poetics').

4.4.86–103 In his essay 'Of the Cannibals,' Montaigne praises the properties of wild fruit *vis à vis* those of cultivated or 'bastardized' fruit and asserts that 'there is no reason art should gain the point of honour of our great and puissant mother Nature' (*Essays*, trans. John Florio, 1603, Book I, 102). For Puttenham, however, 'art is an aid and coadjutor to nature, or peradventure a mean to supply her wants . . ., an alterer of them, and in some sort a surmounter of her skill, so as by means of it her own effects shall appear more beautiful or strange and miraculous' (*The Art of English Poesy*, ed. Gladys D. Willcock and Alice Walker, 1936, 303–7).

4.4.167 SD According to reviews of Granville-Barker's 1912 revival at the Savoy (Bartholomeusz, 158), the director reversed the usual contrast by showing first a riotous and 'uncouth' folk dance marked by lots of 'rustic bumping and jerking' and then a satyrs' piece that reminded several critics of a court masque instead of the antimasque (an anarchic interlude burlesquing the idealized style of the masque proper) with which it is usually associated (see 4.4.317–18 n.).

4.4.556–7 Last formally addressed at 4.4.486 Perdita has been a silent stage presence for sixty-eight lines. What to do with a character who is mute for such a long stretch of stage time is a challenge for both director and actress. In Howell, the television medium camouflages the problem by often showing only Camillo in the frame; when all three are visible, Camillo frequently motions toward Perdita (especially at those occasional cues offered in the dialogue – e.g. lines 4.4.508–9, 524–7), the actress' facial expression alternating between dismay at Florizel's rash inclinations and relief at Camillo's welcome (because thought out) scenario. When Camillo envisions Leontes' reception of the young couple, both Perdita and Florizel fix their eyes in the direction in which Camillo gestures as though visualizing the scene themselves.

4.4.609 What garments the pedlar and the prince exchange has long been an issue for editors and directors. Obscuring his royal identity with a 'swain's wearing' (4.4.8–9), Florizel would seem to appear in the humble attire of a country youth or young shepherd (4.4.13, 21–2, 149, and 346). Autolycus, however, expresses delight in the new apparel that fortuitously comes his way (4.4.646–7), clothing which the Shepherd later describes as 'rich' (4.4.714). That shepherds may have 'dress-up' clothes for special occasions (as borne out in many productions) offers one answer to the question raised by the exchange of garments. Such holiday apparel (see 4.4.695 n.) might well appear richer than a pedlar's garb – especially if Florizel's 'swain's wearing' reflects the country gentleman look of a prince on holiday (e.g. the gold-trimmed blue vest and white linen pants worn in Lewis and the stylish straw hat, bolero, and ruffled shirt in Kahn). Their contact with men of the court presumably limited at best, the rustics might then easily mistake Autolycus' social status. The fact that they do not recognize the stranger's apparel as something they had seen a short while before is, perhaps, the result of Autolycus' failure to wear his 'courtier' guise handsomely. The Folger editors, who address this costume crux in some detail, rightly conclude that 'the discrepancy is for directors to resolve'. On how some of them have done so, see Appendix C, pp. 273–4.

5.1.122 SDPerdita. In the 1999 Tygres Heart production in Portland, OR, Paulina audibly gasped at the sight of Perdita, suggesting that she recognized the young woman as Hermione's daughter (Shurgot, 'Kretzu', 27). The visual resemblance would obviously be enhanced if the roles were doubled as was the case with Mary Anderson (Lyceum, 1887) and Judi Dench (in Nunn), among others. But even when two actresses are involved, some directors, perhaps beginning with Brook, go out of their way to emphasize the similarity by having Perdita appear coifed and costumed like Hermione in Act One. Smallwood reports a resemblance in Noble's 1992 production so uncanny that 'for a moment one shared Leontes' puzzled wonder' ('Shakespeare 1992', 351). In Kahn, Perdita (now with her hair up) not only appeared in a burgundy dress similar to her mother's but also occupied the same piano bench where her mother had sat in 1.2 and 2.1 (see illustrations 18 and 23, pp. 29 and 45).

5.2.83 Giulio Romano Shakespeare's choice of a contemporary artist known more for his paintings than his sculptures has occasioned much comment. Some editors and critics, troubled by what they perceive as an error (Turner cites Tollet's 1778 edition and S.C. Chew's 1947 *The Virtues Reconciled*), have suggested that Shakespeare was thinking of Giulio as the painter who finished a sculpture made by someone else (see 5.2.82 n.). Others, however – beginning with Elze (*Essays on Shakespeare*, 1874, 284–9) – have pointed to the artist's epitaph quoted in Vasari's *Lives of the Artists*, 1550 (but not available in English until the mid-nineteenth century), which highlights his fame as a sculptor at the time: 'Jupiter saw sculpted and painted bodies breathe . . . by the skill of Giulio Romano', an explanation Orgel finds sufficient for the artist's selection as the carver of Hermione's statue. For Barkan, who discusses the allusion at some length (655–8), the praise of the eminent Giulio as an 'ape' of nature (5.2.85) signifies not so much a specific artist as 'the multiplicity of the arts, the rivalry among them, and the *paragone* of art and nature' (657).

Following a suggestion made by Terence Spencer ('The Statue of Hermione', *Essays and Studies*, NS 30 [1977], 42–3), several recent critics have focused on the obscene pictures Giulio Romano supplied for Pietro Aretino's *Sonnetti Lussuriosi* (1524), detecting in the Giulio allusion either a hint of Hermione's former eroticism that counterpoints her desexualization as a statue (Richard Halpern, *Shakespeare Among the Moderns*, 1997, p. 152 n.73) or 'a dash of comedy, a joke for those who know the Romano Shakespeare had in mind' (Stanford S. Apseloff, *SN* 52.3 [Fall 2002], 87). In his investigation of the artist's pornographic pictures, Orgel ('Ideal') draws no direct connection to the play but reproduces and examines some of the illustrations from the Aretino volume. See also Raymond B. Waddington, *Aretino's Satyr: Sexuality, Satire, and Self-Projection in Sixteenth Century Literature and Art*, 2003.

Ultimately, it may be enough simply to acknowledge that the dramatist's 'most celebrated anachronism, in a work which is full of similar, if less glaring, anachronisms' (Schanzer), is part of the 'old tale' wonder of the play and reflective of the fluidity of Time, who with one gesture can make years pass.

5.3.0 SD. 2 *etc*. As a 'permissive stage direction', *etc.* is one of 'many signals [e.g. *attendants*, *followers*, *lords*, *men*, *others*, *train*, *and the rest*] that leave key details indeterminate . . . most commonly the specific number of actors required for an entrance' (Dessen-Thomson). If understood here as 'attendants' (as in *R2* 2.1.0 SD) or 'other members of the royal train' (as in *R2* 2.1.68 SD and *Temp.* 3.3.0 SD), 'etc.' (especially following 'Lords') suggests a formal, public scene, the sense conveyed in the frontispiece to the play in Rowe's 1709 edition and the effect achieved in elaborate nineteenth-century productions like Macready's and Kean's, traces of which still linger (e.g. Hall's numerous courtiers and Kulick's formally attired couples who were present at the beginning of the play). Most modern directors, however, prefer a more private, intimate atmosphere.

But whether *etc.*, a term appropriate for generic attendants and other figures intended to swell the ranks of the entering royal party, would apply to such important and recently prominent characters as Shepherd, Clown, and Autolycus is questionable; nowhere else in the canon is it so used. As Turner points out (p. 533), in the SD at *R2* 2.1.68, *etc.* in the 1597 Q indicates a half-dozen members of the royal party who are subsequently named in F; and in the SH at *Wiv.* 3.2.50, it 'represents several characters whose names are omitted . . . for want of space'. With respect to the latter, a similar rationale may operate here where F's SD and Leontes' opening lines of dialogue are somewhat crowded, and the white space between the scene heading and the initial SD less than that following scene headings elsewhere in the text. This possibility, however, runs counter to Crane's practice in *WT*'s other mass entries. The omission of specific names at the beginning of 5.3 would thus appear deliberate.

As to why, after explicitly saying that they are on their way to see 'the queen's picture' (5.2.149–50), the trio from Bohemia is not given even a silent part to play in the final scene (along the lines, let us say, of Florizel), hypotheses include: (1) a concern that the characters would appear out of place in a world of 'aristocratic, "high", classical' art (see Martin Orkin, 'A sad tale's best for South Africa?', *Textual Practice* 11 [1997], 16), and undermine an atmosphere of sanctity and awe; (2) a feeling that Autolycus' presence might too strongly indicate a reformation better left open; and (3) a logistical limitation imposed by the theatrical practice of doubling. While there is no evidence that the original actors playing Autolycus, Shepherd, and Clown doubled any of the roles involved in the final scene, a number of modern actors have done so (see Appendix B).

5.3.20 SD. *like a statue* Glynne Wickham appears to be the first to claim that the chapel setting in Shakespeare's time required a tomb property that in this instance 'took the form of the normal sarcophagus surmounted by a niche containing a standing effigy' (*Shakespeare's Dramatic Heritage*, 1969, 264–5); Smith also argues for tomb sculpture as the model for Hermione's 'statue' since 'the sculptor's art in Elizabethan England was almost exclusively the tomb-maker's art' ('Sermons', 2). ('Almost exclusively' is an important qualifier since the early seventeenth century saw a growing interest in private collections of classical sculpture as attested by the sensation-stirring Earl of Arundel's collection – see Orgel ['Ideal'] and the introduction to his edition [pp. 53–7]). Belsey persuasively speculates on the miraculous implications of an effigy-like statue, Hermione's animation visually suggesting her resurrection from the dead (*Loss of Eden*, 114–20). Notably, several of the effigies illustrated in Belsey's book depict the deceased sitting (e.g. fig. 24, p. 109), and although standing effigies were not common early in the seventeenth century, 'there was always . . . a certain ambiguity about the position of the recumbent figures . . . as if their standing [forms] had been laid down to fit the space available' (see fig. 15, p. 93 and fig. 27, p. 114). The painted tomb sculptures of Elizabeth I and Mary Queen of Scots commissioned by King James for their monuments in Westminster Abbey, both of which were completed before 1612, lend topical support for an effigy-like statue of Hermione. For a detailed study of effigies in the period, see Nigel Llwewellyn, *Funereal Monuments in Post-Reformation England* (2000), esp. his discussion of recumbent, standing, kneeling, and seated effigies (pp. 97–114).

5.3.99–103 The earliest and most celebrated example of the literary convention involving a statue coming to life can be found in the Ovidian tale of Pygmalion and his ivory maiden Galatea. Medieval renditions of the popular legend of the cleric Theophilus, a forerunner of Faust, suggest the presence of an animated statue of the Virgin (see Introduction, p. 3 n. and illustration 1, p. 4). Possible dramatic analogues from the late sixteenth and early seventeenth centuries include Lyly's *The Woman in the Moone* (1595–7); Greene's *Friar Bacon and Friar Bungay* (*c.* 1589–90), scene 11; Jonson's *Sejanus* (1603), 5.4; and the anonymous *The Trial of Chivalry* (printed in 1605).

A major influence on the statue scene was the court masque with its emphasis on spectacle, special effects, and the appearance of statue-like, silent figures who eventually enter into the action (Thomas M. Parrott, *Shakespearean Comedy*, 1949, 386); McGuire (169) specifically notes 'the practice in Jacobean court masques of having aristocratic women pose as statues'. Snyder ('[*WT*] Before and After', in *Journey*, 228, 232 n.16) cites Bacon's 'Of Masques and Triumphs', written some time after 1612, as evidence 'not only [of] the royal taste for masques . . . but [of] moving statues as a familiar element'. Although Ewbank links the animation of the statue to 'the central movement of a masque' ('Triumph', in Hunt, 152), she points out (155 n.19) that the masques usually cited as involving living statues – Campion's *Earl of Somerset's Masque* (26 December 1613), his *Lords' Masque* (14 February 1613), and Beaumont's *Masque of the Inner Temple and Gray's Inn* (20 February 1613) –were composed after the usual date assigned to *WT* (1610–11). If, however, Hermione's statue sequence was composed as an afterthought (see Introduction, p. 63) – perhaps in conjunction with the play's inclusion in a list of royal festivities marking Princess Elizabeth's wedding to the Elector Palatine (December–February 1612–13) – then such masques (two of which also appeared on the same entertainment list) assume added relevance.

TEXTUAL ANALYSIS

The Winter's Tale was first printed in the 1623 Folio and set by compositors A and B in a sequence which, on account of early modern printing requirements, is different from the order in which we read the play. The setting order is as follows: 2.1.29–142/TLN 623–754 (Compositor A); 2.1.143–2.2.50/TLN 755–878 (Compositor B); 1.2.384–2.1.28/TLN 497–622 (A); 2.2.50–2.3.83/TLN 879–1004 (B); 1.2.270–383/ TLN 365–496 (A); 2.3.84–199/ TLN 1005–136 (A); 2.3.200–3.2.76 / TLN 1137–255 (A); 1.2.153–1.2.269/TLN 233–364 (A); 1.2.44–1.2.152/TLN 101–232 (A); 3.2.77–197/TLN 1256–1387 (A); 1.1.0–1.2.43/TLN 1–100 (A); 3.2.198–3.3.69/TLN 1388–513 (B); 4.4.307–414/TLN 2147–278 (B); 4.4.415–521/TLN 2279–410 (B); 4.4.191–307/TLN 2016–2146 (B); 4.4.526–632/ TLN 2411–542 (A); 4.4.77–190/TLN 1884–2015 (B); 4.4.633–753/TLN 2543–674 (A); 4.3.82–4.4.77/TLN 1759–883 (B); 4.4.753–5.1.62/TLN 2675–800 (A); 4.2.18–4.3.81/TLN 1635–758 (B); 5.1.62–170/TLN 2801–932 (A); 3.3.69–4.2.17/TLN 1514–634 (B); 5.1.171–5.2.43/TLN 2933–3058 (A); 5.2.43–5.3.2/TLN 3059–187 (A); 5.3.2–110/TLN 3188–319 (A); 5.3.111–55/TLN 3320–3369 (B).[1]

The previous play, *Twelfth Night*, ends on the recto, followed by a blank page (z6v). The *Winter's Tale* then begins, with a new set of signatures, Aa1-Cc2 (Cc2v blank), followed by the first of the histories, *King John*, beginning a1. According to Charlton Hinman's analysis,[2] compositors A and B turned to work on quire c in the histories (part of *Richard II*) after B had completed *Twelfth Night*, presumably because the copy for *The Winter's Tale* was not yet available, though it soon became so. They then set *The Winter's Tale*, completing the comedies section.

The Folio text is unusually clean, with little obvious need for correction. Later editors, when moved to emend, were usually responding to a certain obscurity and ellipticality notable in the language of the play's first part, though much less so in the second. Most of the emendations, especially in Leontes' notorious apostrophe on 'Affection' (1.2.137–45), have gained little support, and the trend more recently has been to try to explicate the text as we have it. Stephen Orgel has argued that incomprehensibility may itself be the main message in such passages,[3] though in his own Oxford edition of *The Winter's Tale* he provides speculative glosses, as any editor must.

Certain features of the Folio *Winter's Tale* make it almost certain that the copy provided to the printers was a transcript by Ralph Crane, a professional scrivener: typical of Crane's work are the elaborate punctuation, especially lavish in brackets,

[1] See Peter Blayney's introduction to *The Norton Facsimile: The First Folio of Shakespeare*, 2nd edn, 1996, xxxv.

[2] *The Printing and Proof-Reading of the First Folio of Shakespeare*, 2 vols., 1963, 2.521.

[3] 'The Poetics of Incomprehensibility', *SQ* 42 (1991), 431–7.

hyphens, and apostrophes; the 'massed entries' at the beginnings of many scenes listing all characters who will appear even if they are to enter later; the sparse stage directions; the careful act-scene division; the list of 'The Names of the Actors' following the end of the play identifying the characters. Detailed analysis of Crane's extant transcripts by T. H. Howard-Hill demonstrates that in imposing these preferences Crane typically worked over his material quite thoroughly.[4]

That heavy editing hand makes it difficult to determine what kind of manuscript of *The Winter's Tale* Crane was copying. Further complicating any speculation is the entry recorded by Malone[5] from the office-book, since lost, of Sir Henry Herbert, Master of the Revels:

> For the king's players, An olde playe called Winters Tale, formerly allowed of by Sir George Bucke, and likewyse by mee on Mr. Hemmings his worde that there was nothing prophane added or reformed, thogh the allowed booke was missinge; and therefore I returned itt without a fee, this 19 of August, 1623.

Given this absence of the original 'allowed' book (perhaps, though not necessarily, a book used to prompt) in August of 1623, W. W. Greg supposed that it had been found to be missing some months earlier when copy was being gathered for the Folio printers, and that Crane had consequently been commissioned to transcribe the play from the other version in playhouse possession, Shakespeare's foul papers.[6] If the loss was a last-minute discovery, that might account for the slight delay in printing previously noted. Since the minimal and incomplete stage directions of the Folio text suggest that Crane's version would not have been a workable prompt book, Howard-Hill hypothesized a two-stage transcription, first from foul papers to prompt copy, then from the prompt copy to a more literary version – downplaying stage directions – for the printers.[7] But Wells and Taylor point out that Crane might well have worked from the original prompt book, which then went missing as a result of the copying process.[8] No conclusions can be drawn about what sort of manuscript lies behind the transcript, because – as in the case of other Crane plays like *The Tempest*, *The Two Gentlemen of Verona*, and *Measure for Measure* – the scribe's thoroughness has effaced the marks that might have indicated prompt copy or foul papers.

The same scribal orderliness also seems to have obviated difficulties in casting off copy, and the Folio text of *The Winter's Tale* has little in the way of expansions and compressions to make up for faulty calculations. The single exception, noted by J. H. P. Pafford, is Bb3, which becomes crowded toward the end of the second column: a comment by a new character, Autolycus, is printed on the same line (4.4.298) as the one just finished by the Clown (itself densely set), and the heading

[4] *Ralph Crane and Some Shakespeare First Folio Comedies*, 1972. Generalizations about Crane practices and citations of Crane statistics, unless otherwise identified, are from this volume.

[5] *The Plays and Poems of William Shakespeare*, 10 vols., ed. Edmond Malone, 1790, 1.2.226.

[6] *The Editorial Problem in Shakespeare*, 1951, 416–17.

[7] 'Knight, Crane and the Copy for the Folio *Winter's Tale*', *N&Q* 211 (1966), 139–40.

[8] Stanley Wells and Gary Taylor, with John Jowett and William Montgomery, *William Shakespeare: A Textual Companion*, 1987, 601.

'Song' stands beside the first line of 'Will you buy' (4.4.300) rather than above. (Something similar occurs at 4.4.283 where the heading 'Song' actually displaces the speech heading for the first singer to the second line of 'Get you hence'.) This local crowding may have been caused by late insertion of the second song, 'Will you buy',[9] perhaps originally inscribed on a separate sheet and then, on second thought, printed in full rather than just the opening line plus 'etc.' as in *Mac.* 3.5.33 SD and 4.1.43 SD.

Thanks to Howard-Hill's work with Crane's dramatic transcripts that survive in manuscript, his scribal habits can be examined in some detail.

Accuracy: Crane's average is one error every 52 lines. There are various small substitutions, most of little significance, also occasional interchanging of singular and plural nouns, and a couple of incorrect speech headings. Except perhaps for the latter, many such slight modifications are too hard to detect to have any impact on editing choices. Even where errors are more apparent, they are of this general nature and offer no model of guidance for other possible emendations: e.g. 'A' for 'And' (1.2.103), 'Who' for 'What' (2.3.39), 'you' for 'your' (4.4.98), 'acknowledge' for 'acknowledged' (4.4.399), and 'my' for 'your' (4.4.447).

Spelling: Some characteristic Crane spellings show up in *The Winter's Tale*: 'councels' (1.2.234), 'extreames' (4.4.6), 'physicks' (1.1.33), 'powrefull' (1.2.200 and 2.1.28), and 'wayting' (1.2.92). Another idiosyncratic Crane spelling that does not appear in the Folio text may explain what does appear. The odd 'Holy-Horse' where 'hobby-horse' seems clearly intended (1.2.273) is understandable if Crane originally had 'Hobby' in the copy and the word was misread by Compositor A as 'holly', which he took to mean 'holy', as in Crane's usual spelling, and set as such.

Punctuation: Crane favoured the colon over other stops. There are 839 colons in *The Winter's Tale*, one every 31 words: a ratio significantly higher than in the five comedies Howard-Hill used as controls, where the average is 1:54 words, but approximating the average in the Crane dramatic manuscripts, 1:27. Noteworthy here are two lines with multiple colons:

> 'Tis time: descend: be Stone no more: approach: (5.3.99)
> Ile fill your Graue vp: stirre: nay, come away: (5.3.101)

E. A. J. Honigmann points out that, apart from *Othello*, which may be based on a Crane transcript, the only other Folio examples of lines with three or more colons are in Crane comedies: two in *The Tempest*, one in *The Two Gentlemen of Verona*, and the two cited above.[10]

Crane also used parentheses liberally: once every 69 words as opposed to the average of the control plays, 1:923. *The Winter's Tale* has the highest incidence

[9] '*The Winter's Tale*: Typographical Peculiarities in the Folio Text', *N&Q* 206 (1961), 173. Another reason for the typographical crowding may have to do with the possible late addition of the satyrs' dance sequence (see Introduction, p. 64), which closely follows 'Who will buy'. Although Snyder thought it 'tempting' to connect the two, she concluded that '[t]his would assume that the typesetter's calculations were thrown off by a late insertion into the copy text, . . . and Crane's transcript is most likely later than 1613' ('[*WT*] Before and After', in *Shakespeare: A Wayward Journey*, 232 n.).

[10] *The Texts of 'Othello' and Shakespearian Revision*, 1996, 66–7.

of parentheses around a single word (76 is the total), a feature that Honigmann has found to be especially typical of Crane transcripts.[11] The majority of 'swibs' (Honigmann's abbreviation for single words in brackets) are instances of direct address (e.g. 'sir', 'madam', 'brother', 'boy', or various proper names); the seven non-vocatives are 'indeed' (1.1.33), 'good deed' (hyphenated in F) (1.2.42), 'priestlike' (1.2.234), 'counsaile' (1.2.423), 'alas' (2.3.28), 'missingly' (4.2.25), and 'frighted' (4.4.117). The compositor for the first four was A; for the last three, B.

Apostrophes are also frequent in Crane plays. *The Winter's Tale* takes the lead on this front as well, with an apostrophe every 26 words. They function to indicate not only letters omitted but also notional words ("'Beseech you", "'Pray you"); there is one example here of the Jonsonian elision that occurs often in Crane manuscripts, in which the apostrophe signals elision but the complete spelling is retained – *Verely'is* (1.2.49). Crane's characteristic *it's* for the possessive appears five times in *The Winter's Tale* (1.2.150, 151, 156, 263; and 3.3.45).

Also evident are Crane's fondness for and unusual uses of hyphens. The Howard-Hill total of 264 for *The Winter's Tale* includes idiosyncratic compounds constructed from verb and pronoun ('*auouch-it*' [4.3.22], '*made-me*' [4.3.39]) and from verb and adverb ('*come-on*', twice in 2.1.27 and at 4.4.261; '*push-on*' or '*pluck-back*' [4.4.702]; '*seal'd-vp*' [3.2.125]) as well as standard adjective-noun combinations.

'*Names of the Actors*': The appended list of characters is another mark of Crane's work. Similar lists appear in his transcript of Middleton's *The Witch* and in the 1623 quarto of *The Duchess of Malfi*, based on a Crane transcript. Of the seven Folio plays followed by character lists, four – *The Tempest*, *The Two Gentlemen of Verona*, *Measure for Measure*, and *The Winter's Tale* – are agreed to be Crane plays. Two more, *Othello* and *2 Henry IV*, have been claimed for him (partly, but not entirely, on this basis). The copy for *The Merry Wives of Windsor*, the only Crane-transcript play that lacks a list, might well have contained a character-list like the others. Its omission in printing is explainable by lack of space: the text of the play ends close to the end of the page.

The provenance of the lists is unclear. We don't know whether Crane drew them up himself or copied them from some authorial manuscript. The identification of the Duke in *Measure for Measure* as 'Vincentio', a name that appears nowhere in the text, points to the latter; the fact that most of these lists omit a few minor characters perhaps points to the former, or at least points away from any practical playhouse function. *The Winter's Tale* compilation lacks several characters: not only the generically labelled jailer and mariner, the performing satyrs, and various lords, ladies, and servants, but also Mopsa, Dorcas, and Time.[12] Such incompleteness reinforces the conclusion that the Crane transcript was not for playhouse use; *The Winter's Tale* list like the others seems aimed at a more 'literary' presentation, on the model of Jonson's plays in the 1616 Folio.

[11] *Texts of 'Othello'*, 59–63, 162–3.

[12] Perhaps the reason for the absence of these three named figures has something to do with doubling; the roles of Time, Mopsa, and Dorcas seem ready-made for that theatrical practice (see Introduction, pp. 34–8 and Appendix B).

Speech headings: Jeanne Roberts notes that the Crane dramatic manuscripts show considerable toleration of variety and a tendency to begin by using a longer form and later shortening it.[13] This accords with his practice in *The Winter's Tale*, where initial *Antig.* is later varied with *Ant.* and *Perd.* with *Per. Paul.* varies with *Pau.* throughout. Some compositor preference is probably influential in this area. B uses both longer and shorter forms; A uses only the longer. The single instance of a longer form for Leontes, *Leon.* as opposed to the usual *Leo.*, occurs on a page set by A.

Stage directions: the Crane dramatic manuscripts indicate that the scribe first wrote out the dialogue and then inserted stage directions. This practice might well lead to some misplacings and omissions (though absent stage directions, especially exits, are common in other Folio plays). Crane's most striking practice in stage directions, the massed entry, is not uniformly applied in the Folio plays: *The Tempest* and *Measure for Measure* have conventional entries throughout, and *The Winter's Tale* itself has two scenes with conventional entries mixed among the eight that introduce at the beginning of the scene characters who come onstage only later (sometimes with separate entrance directions). Here, too, the Jonsonian model was apparently decisive, since, as Howard-Hill notes (79), constructing these groups meant extra labour with no obvious benefit to the reader.

Crane's treatment of stage directions in his copy seems to have varied considerably. Although the most famous one in Shakespeare occurs here (*Exit pursued by a Beare*), stage directions are generally as sparse in *The Winter's Tale* as they are elaborate and descriptive in *The Tempest*. From the non-Shakespearean dramatic transcripts, Howard-Hill concluded that Crane could shorten as well as embellish stage directions, though he adds that 'there is little evidence that he omitted directions' (24). John Jowett, who suspects that the two parenthetical phrases in *The Winter's Tale* stage directions – both describing Hermione (*as to her Triall* [3.2.10; TLN 1174–5] and *like a Statue* [5.3.20; TLN 3185]) – may be Crane's additions, conjectures that the scribe's general habit was to elaborate stage directions but not to notice and supply needed directions when they were absent from his copy.[14] Noting that the quartos and Folio plays that seem to derive from Shakespeare's foul papers have directions for offstage sounds while Folio plays that lack such directions are associated firmly or conjecturally with Crane, Gary Taylor concluded that Crane deliberately removed them from the plays he transcribed.[15] Not many offstage sounds seem required in *The Winter's Tale*: the trial of Hermione in 3.2 would presumably be introduced by a formal instrumental signal, though perhaps less elaborate than the *trumpets, sennet, and cornets* that begin the comparable trial in *Henry VIII*. Other royal scenes are more in the off-duty vein, probably including 1.2.[16] One scene, however, calls fairly clearly for noises off. When Antigonus interrupts his apostrophe to the baby Perdita

[13] 'Ralph Crane and the Text of *The Tempest*', *Shakespeare Studies* 13 (1980), 219.

[14] 'New Created Creatures: Ralph Crane and the Stage Directions in *The Tempest*', *Shakespeare Survey* 36 (1983), 114–15.

[15] Gary Taylor and John Jowett, *Shakespeare Reshaped 1606–1623*, 1993, 71–2.

[16] See also 5.2.149 n. for the possibility of another offstage sound cue.

he is leaving on the Bohemian shore to announce 'The storm begins' (3.3.48), he presumably reacts to the sound of thunder or wind; a few lines later, his exclamation 'A savage clamour?' (3.3.55) marks an even clearer response to offstage noise, either the horns and cries of the hunters or the roars of the bear itself (see 3.3.55 SD–56 n.).[17] In any case, with stage directions as with his other scribal habits, knowledge of Crane's characteristic way with dramatic texts provides reasoned grounds to the editor for undoing at least some of his work: simplifying punctuation, rationalizing stage entries, supplying other directions when needed.

[17] The trial scene might also call for the sound of thunder, a cue often heard in performance immediately following Leontes' blasphemous denial of the oracle's veracity (3.2.137–8) and thus anticipating the storm at the beginning of 3.3. In his 1906 revival at Her Majesty's Theatre, Tree, who had introduced distant thunder as early as 1.2.309–15, increased its audibility after 3.2.137 (Bartholomeusz, 130). Trewin (263) proposes a slightly later sound cue, between the announcement of Mamillius' death (3.2.142) and Leontes' 'Apollo's angry, and the heavens themselves/Do strike at my injustice' (3.2.143–4).

APPENDIX A SIMON FORMAN'S NOTES ON *THE WINTER'S TALE*, PERFORMED AT THE GLOBE, 15 MAY 1611[1]

Observe there how Leontes, the king of Sicilia, was overcome with jealousy of his wife with the king of Bohemia, his friend that came to see him; and how he contrived his death and would have had his cupbearer to have poisoned, who gave the king of Bohemia warning thereof and fled with him to Bohemia.

Remember also how he sent to the Oracle of Apollo, and the answer of Apollo, that she was guiltless and that the king was jealous, etc., and how except the child was found again that was lost, the king should die without issue; for the child was carried into Bohemia and there laid in a forest and brought up by a shepherd. And the king of Bohemia his son married that wench, and how they fled into Sicilia to Leontes; and the shepherd having showed the letter of the noble man by whom Leontes sent a was [away?] that child and the jewels found about her, she was known to be Leontes' daughter, and was then sixteen years old.

Remember also the Rogue that came in all tattered like coll pixci [i.e. colt pixie],[2] and how he feigned him sick and to have been robbed of all that he had, and how he cozened the poor man of all his money, and after came to the sheep-shear with a peddler's pack and there cozened them again of all their money. And how he changed apparel with the king of Bohemia his son, and then how he turned courtier, etc. Beware of trusting feigned beggars or fawning fellows.

1 Forman's account is taken from his *Booke of Plaies and Notes thereof per formans for Common Pollicie*, Bodleian Ashmole MS 208 (reprinted in Chambers, *William Shakespeare*, ii. 340–1); spelling and punctuation have been modernized.

2 According to *OED*, a 'colt pixie' is 'a mischievous sprite or fairy, formerly believed in, in the south and south-west of England'. Its first recorded usage is found in 1542; its last in 1870. Two citations specify a fairy assuming the disguise of a ragged colt to lure men or horses into bogs, and then vanishing. Kermode calls the term 'a doubtful reading of doubtful significance' (179).

APPENDIX B SOME DOUBLING POSSIBILITIES IN *THE WINTER'S TALE*

The list of characters appended to *The Winter's Tale* text in the First Folio indicates sixteen speaking roles, along with generic lords, gentlemen, servants, shepherds, and shepherdesses. Unmentioned are Time, Mopsa, Dorcas, officers, the jailer, the mariner, the two ladies attending Hermione, and the satyrs. Four characters – Archidamus, Antigonus, Mamillius, and Emilia – are needed only for the first half of the play; Leontes, Hermione, Paulina, Dion, and Cleomenes leave the action by the end of 3.2 but reappear in Act 5. In the Bohemia phase (3.3–4.4), two familiar figures from Act 1, Polixenes and Camillo, are joined by a new set of characters: Shepherd, Clówn, Time, Autolycus, Perdita, Florizel, Mopsa, and Dorcas. With the exception of Mopsa, Dorcas, and Time, all of the new characters make the trip back to Sicilia for the final act. It would seem that with the long pastoral sequence, Shakespeare has constructed the play to be amenable to the widely accepted practice of doubling.

T. J. King posits that when the play was first performed 11 men could play 15 principal parts and 5 boys could play 8 principal boy parts for 97 per cent of the lines; the remaining lines could be assigned to 7 men playing 24 minor adult parts, and 6 boys playing 13 minor boy parts.[1] The total cast requirements for *The Winter's Tale* would be 18 men and 11 boys. The doubling options proposed by King are as follows:

For Adult Actors in Principal Roles:
Antigonus and 3rd Gentleman
Servant to Leontes, Time, Servant to (Old) Shepherd
Dion and 1st Gentleman

For Adult Actors in Minor Roles:
Archidamus, Shepherd, Satyr
Officer, Shepherd, Satyr
Gaoler, Cleomines, Shepherd, Satyr
Gentlemen, Shepherd, Satyr, 2nd Gentleman
Lord to Leontes, Mariner, Shepherd, Satyr
Lord to Leontes, Bear, Shepherd, Satyr
Shepherd and Satyr

For Boy Actors in Principal Roles:
Mamillius and Perdita
Emilia and Dorcas
Lady and Mopsa

Five of the six boy parts for minor characters are given as 'Shepherdess and satyr', the remaining boy playing the 2nd lady, a shepherdess, and a satyr. According to King's conjectured cast assignments, seven men can play six small speaking parts and 18 mutes; six boys can play one small speaking part and 12 mutes.

In their work on Shakespeare's vast romance, critics and directors have implemented an almost infinite variety of doubling choices, most of them more liberal and provocative than

[1] T. J. King, *Casting in Shakespeare's Plays*, 1992, esp. 92–3, 244–5, and 255.

King's speculations. A chart of some of these doublings is included in Table 1, p. 268.[2] Some observations on selected choices[3] – illustrating practical, thematic, and/or virtuoso doubling[4] – follow.

Mopsa and Dorcas

The two named shepherdesses who appear only at the sheep-shearing feast in 4.4 could logistically have appeared earlier as the two ladies-in-waiting to Hermione (2.1) – with one specifically playing Emilia in 2.2 – or as Dion and Cleomenes. Not only would the latter arrangement juxtapose the rustic characters' natural abandon with the 'stuffed sufficiency' of the emissaries to Apollo's temple, it would also recognize each duo's openness to wonder, whether of gods (3.1) or of ballad-lore (4.4.248–68). More creative 'adjectival' doubling involves linking the shepherdesses to Paulina and Hermione,[5] thereby contrasting the decorum, loyalty, and rectitude of the two female pairs. In the case of Hermione, the pairing might also remind audiences of the spirited, witty woman who had demonstrated an attractive down-to-earth sexuality in her dialogue with both Polixenes and Leontes in 1.2. While the doubling of Mopsa with Hermione recalls the name of Perdita/Fawnia's mother in Greene's *Pandosto*, the doubling of Dorcas with the queen carries symbolic meaning since the shepherdess shares the name of the holy woman Tabitha/Dorcas who is reported to be raised from the dead by St Peter in Acts 9 (see List of Characters, p. 81). A Dorcas/Hermione pairing would thus hint at the 'resurrection' to come.

Hermione

Besides the roles of Mopsa and Dorcas, Hermione's long absence from the stage yields other intriguing possibilities. Although comparatively minor, the doubling of the queen and the Mariner (as in Cohen) provides a way of having '"Mom" watch over Perdita';[6] it also visually

[2] Each horizontal row presents a doubling scenario for the actor playing the principal speaking part listed on the left in a single performance; it assumes the physical availability of an actor to take on other roles as a result of his initial character's exits and entrances. The table makes no claim to comprehensive inclusiveness; it is simply intended to provide a sampling of choices and, perhaps, to spark further creative options in the reader's mind. The cast lists supplied in Mullin-Muriello, the annual *SQ* bibliographies, and *ShakB* reviews have been invaluable in documenting choices actually realized in performance. Where performance citations are provided, these should likewise not be taken as all inclusive.

[3] Doublings of the bear and Time are addressed in the Introduction on pp. 32 and 34–8, respectively.

[4] Practical refers to the most efficient and logistical allocation of roles in companies with limited personnel. Thematic – or what Stephen Booth calls 'adjectival' – serves to 'inform, comment on, and perhaps, augment the events enacted' ('Speculations on Doubling in Shakespeare's plays', in *King Lear, Macbeth, Indefinition, and Tragedy*, 1983, 134); Booth cites as an example the four adult actors who played Flute, Snout, Starveling and Snug as Peaseblossom, Cobweb, Moth, and Mustardseed. Related to thematic doubling is the 'generic' or 'parallel' pairing of characters with similar functions and qualities (e.g. Benvolio and Balthasar in *Romeo and Juliet*, and John of Gaunt and the Gardener in *Richard II*). 'Generic' is Mahood's term (13); 'parallel' is Giorgio Melchior's ('Peter, Balthasar, and Shakespeare's Art of Doubling', *MLR* 78 [1983], 789). 'Virtuoso doubling' (see Arthur Colby Sprague, *The Doubling of Parts in Shakespeare's Plays*, 1966, 14–22) allows an actor playing a character who appears at the beginning and end of a play or who disappears midway through to tackle a role that is completely different from the earlier one in order to demonstrate his or her acting skills (e.g. the Ghost and the Gravedigger in *Hamlet*, Henry IV and Justice Shallow in *2 Henry IV*).

[5] Examples include Bell Shakespeare Company, Canberra, Australia, 1997; Shakespeare and Company, Lenox, MA, 1997; Staatstheater, Braunschweig, 1997; Brave New World, London, 1998; Washington Shakespeare Company, Arlington, VA, 1998; Hudson Valley Shakespeare, NY, 1998; and Southwark Playhouse, London, 2000.

[6] Correspondence with the director.

connects the woman who trusts in Apollo to be her judge and the sailor who 'recognises in the storm Apollo's anger at the act of abandoning the infant Perdita [3.3.2–6]' (Mahood, 209). The more significant doubling, one that augments character and theme while also showcasing the actor's versatility, is the pairing of Hermione and Perdita, first essayed by Mary Anderson at the Lyceum in 1887. (Other actors taking on the same challenge include Viola Allen [New York, Knickerbocker Theatre, 1904], Judy Dench [in Nunn], Maria Tucci [in Kahn, 1975/76], and Pamela Nyberg [in Kahn, 1987].) This doubling plays up Perdita's innate royalty and underscores the resemblance between mother and daughter noted in the text (5.1.224–27; 5.2.31–2, 45); the downside is that the generational rhythm at the heart of the play which allows the old to be renewed by the young – Leontes in 5.1 and Hermione in 5.3 – is perhaps adversely affected. In addition, such doubling likely necessitates a speechless Perdita in 5.3 (a mute having her back to the audience tends to take her place)[7] as well as the cutting of the reference to Hermione's 'wrinkles' (5.3.27–9) – Shakespeare's pointed reminder of the irrevocable ravages of Time.[8]

Leontes

In Cohen, Leontes (and Paulina) doubled as two of the lead players in a band of minstrels, singing and playing guitars to accompany the shepherds' dance. Gone, of course, was Leontes' harsh rigidity; in its place was a musical joie de vivre that suggested the heretofore not seen 'waggish' side to his character to which Hermione approvingly alludes in 1.2.64–5. As a substitute for the satyrs' dance, the tango that he performed with the actor doubling Hermione and one of the denizens of Bohemia 'had enough of violence, love, and lust in it' to intimate something about the marital relationship that existed both prior to the opening scene (perhaps suggesting a full and healthy sexual bond) and during the first half of the play (when violent degradation becomes the norm).[9] Another possible doubling is that of Leontes and the Shepherd (a choice that requires the absence of the latter from the final scene – see 5.3.0 SD n.).[10] This casting illustrates Melchiori's parallel doubling: two characters who are fathers to Perdita turn against her and lose her, each in different ways.

7 A last-minute substitution in Nunn let Perdita speak her lines but the 'trick seemed obvious and technically distracting', the stagy mechanics of a quick-change by way of a glittering, mirrored box undermining the emotion of the moment and countering any gain sought from the mother–daughter resemblance and the opportunity for Judi Dench to demonstrate her thespian range (Bartholomeusz, 122, 220–1).

8 Other doubling choices have included Hermione and the Clown (Shakespeare Institute Players at the Shakespeare Institute, Stratford-upon-Avon, 1996) and Hermione and a 'mad shepherdess' in a German production (Hamburg, 1978). At a 'meet the cast' evening following a performance of Kahn's 2002 *WT*, Dawn McAndrews (Director of Education, The Shakespeare Theatre, Washington, D.C.) recalled a university production in California in the 1990s in which Hermione and Autolycus were doubled. The idea was to demonstrate a witty answer to questions about what Hermione was doing during her sixteen-year absence from the play. An example of virtuoso doubling, this pairing was also intended to underscore the contrast between Apollonian order and Dionysian abandon. The etymological connection between the name Hermione and the god Hermes arguably lends support to doubling the part with Autolycus, linked by name and by larcenous behaviour with Hermes' Roman counterpart, Mercury.

9 Cohen (correspondence).

10 That the Shepherd's exit at the end of 5.2 immediately precedes Leontes' entrance in the final scene might argue against this pairing, but the two parts were successfully doubled in a production by Shakespeare and Company, Lenox, Mass., 1997. If the Shepherd is excluded from 5.3 and Leontes enters last, there would be a limited window of opportunity to make the switch; momentary special effects of music and lighting to create the reverential atmosphere of 5.3 might also add extra time. The proximity of a similar exit and entrance at the end of 4.4 and beginning of 5.1 does not pose as much of a problem given the buffer of Autolycus' closing speech in the former scene.

Antigonus

Doubling Antigonus and Camillo is a choice favoured by critics and directors alike.[11] As Paulina's lament for her lost husband (5.3.130–5) shows, Antigonus may be dead but he is not forgotten. To an audience that saw the same actor in the parts of Camillo (Acts 1, 4, and 5) and Antigonus (Acts 2 and 3), Leontes' proposal that Paulina marry Camillo 'would have seemed less arbitrary, less an act of mere authorial tidiness' (Booth, 147): to conclude 'the story line of this winter's tale, this old wives' tale, . . . with Leontes getting his old wife back and the theatrical event . . . with Paulina getting her old husband back' further augments the 'great restitution' that marks the play's final scene (Booth, 149).

An Antigonus/Shepherd doubling underscores the paternal affection both men show Perdita: one reluctantly abandons her as a baby and the other happily discovers her soon after.[12] Both men – Antigonus rather unexpectedly at the last minute – assume that the baby is born out of wedlock (3.3.41–5, 68–72) and both, in close proximity, talk about the will of the gods (3.3.7, 65–6). Doubling these two parts might also be suggested by the Shepherd's surprising inside knowledge of Antigonus as 'old', something he would have no personal knowledge of and a point never mentioned by the Clown who had met Antigonus (see 3.3.104 n.).

Richard Proudfoot's proposal of an Antigonus/Autolycus doubling adds 'another layer to the already lacquered artifice of [5.2], in which Autolycus serves as a slightly unexpected auditor of the third Gentleman's narration of the death of Antigonus'.[13] Although essentially a doubling of contrast rather than symmetry, Proudfoot points to several similarities: each suffers a shoulder injury (3.3.86–7; 4.3.67–8); each invokes the image of a wolf (see Antigonus's prayer at 2.3.185–8, and the etymology of Autolycus in the List of Characters, p. 81); and each becomes an instrument of Apollo, Antigonus by depositing the baby on the shores of Bohemia, and Autolycus by aiding Florizel's escape with Perdita back to Sicilia (4.4.648–52). Finally, like Autolycus, a court rogue 'rusticated', Antigonus brings into Leontes' court 'the language of the countryside, or at least the stable and the hunting-field' (2.1.134–5).

Mamillius

The character most frequently recommended by critics and chosen by directors as a doubling partner for Mamillius is Perdita, a pairing that may have occurred in the original staging of the play; then it would have been a boy actor in the two parts, whereas today it tends to be a female.[14] A petite young actress, appropriately disguised and acting 'young' in the early acts, can credibly (as demonstrated in Cohen) suggest a boy around eleven or twelve and make the shift to a sixteen-year-old girl in Act 4. Such doubling – along with the Antigonus/Camillo pairing – graphically illustrates the motif of renewal, rebirth, and resurrection. For Meagher (19), who thinks that Shakespeare winks at the audience's recognitions, the dead prince

[11] Booth, 145–7; John C. Meagher, 'Economy and Recognition: Thirteen Shakespearean Puzzles', *SQ* 35 (1984), 7–21, esp. 18–19. Cohen, who was inspired by Booth's observations to double the two parts (along with those of Mamillius and Perdita), thought that 'the choice did wonders for our sense of forgiveness at the end' (correspondence with director).

[12] Performance examples include Royalty Theatre, London, 1903; Old Globe Theatre, San Diego, 1998; Tygres Heart Shakespeare Company, Portland, OR, 1999; and Southwark Playhouse, London 2000. Bartholomeusz reports a student production that he directed (xiii).

[13] R. Proudfoot, 'Verbal Reminiscence and the Two-part Structure of *The Winter's Tale*', in Hunt, 288–9.

[14] Booth, 145–6; Meagher, 19; Proudfoot, in Hunt, 288, 289; and Mahood, 14. In addition to Freeman, Doran, and Cohen, performance examples include Montana Shakespeare in the Parks (1998), Brave New World, London (1998), and Shakespeare and Company, Lenox, MA (2000).

re-embodied in the young princess in 5.1 proleptically allows the audience to recognize 'an aspect of what Leontes was in the process of recovering', his family. Critics who advance the Mamillius/Perdita doubling argue for its palliative effect in easing an audience's grief over the loss of the young prince, particularly when played by the same boy actor (Booth, 146; Mahood, 14).[15]

For all the resonance of the Antigonus/Camillo and Mamillius/Perdita doublings, however, there may be a potential problem with this theatrical choice, perhaps best phrased as a question: Are we intended to have our grief palliated? Is the loss of Mamillius from the characters' collective memory in the final scene meant to be more 'palatable' (to use Booth's word)? The fact that Shakespeare seems to go out of his way in the final act to remind both the on-and offstage audiences of those permanently lost – an innocent child and a decent though flawed man – makes the ending of *The Winter's Tale* unique among the other final plays, more bittersweet and poignant. Some losses are irrevocable no matter the fervour of our wishes to the contrary. That may be the underlying point behind Hermione's wrinkles.

In offering his answer to the 'Camillo-Paulina marriage' puzzle in 5.3, Meagher writes: '[P]ractical economy imposed doubling, and doubling both imposed conditioning restraints and offered the chance for Shakespeare to play around with opportunities afforded by his audience's recognition that doubling was in fact taking place'.[16] *The Winter's Tale* offers a convincing case that Shakespeare continued to 'play around' with doubling opportunities to the end of his career; its performance history demonstrates how directors and actors have intriguingly done the same to prove that 'the doubleness of the benefit defends the deceit' (*Measure for Measure* 3.1.257).

[15] See Booth's explication of the 'intercourse between fictional and theatrical reality' in 5.1.175–7 when the same boy player takes on both roles (146). Mahood (225 n.30) reports that a boy, Trilby James, 'beautifully played both parts' in a 1990 revival by the English Shakespeare Company. In a review of E. Hall's all-male *WT*, Patrick O'Connor describes an effective portrayal by Tam Williams, especially noteworthy because the actor was not a boy but a tall and robust adult (*TLS*, 8 July 2005, 18).

[16] Meagher, 10.

Table 1 *Doubling Possibilities in The Winter's Tale**

ROLE	ACT 1	ACT 2	ACT 3	ACT 4	ACT 5
Leontes	LEONTES	LEONTES	LEONTES/BEAR	TIME	LEONTES
	LEONTES	LEONTES	LEONTES/SHEPHERD	SHEPHERD	SHEPHERD/LEONTES**
Camillo	CAMILLO	ANTIGONUS	ANTIGONUS	CAMILLO	CAMILLO
	CAMILLO		CLEOMENES	CAMILLO	CLEOMENES/CAMILLO
	CAMILLO		DION	CAMILLO	DION/CAMILLO
	CAMILLO	JAILER	MARINER or BEAR	CAMILLO	CAMILLO
Polixenes	POLIXENES	JAILER	CLEOMENES	POLIXENES	CLEOMENES/POLIXENES
	POLIXENES		DION	POLIXENES	DION/POLIXENES
	POLIXENES	ANTIGONUS	ANTIGONUS	POLIXENES	POLIXENES
Autolycus	ARCHIDAMUS	ANTIGONUS	ANTIGONUS	AUTOLYCUS	AUTOLYCUS
	ARCHIDAMUS	JAILER	MARINER or BEAR	TIME/AUTOLYCUS	AUTOLYCUS
Florizel	ARCHIDAMUS	JAILER	MARINER	FLORIZEL	FLORIZEL
Clown	HERMIONE	HERMIONE	HERMIONE/CLOWN	CLOWN	CLOWN/HERMIONE***
	ARCHIDAMUS	JAILER	MARINER or BEAR	TIME/CLOWN	CLOWN
Shepherd	ARCHIDAMUS	JAILER	SHEPHERD	SHEPHERD	SHEPHERD
	LEONTES	LEONTES	SHEPHERD	SHEPHERD	SHEPHERD/LEONTES
	ARCHIDAMUS	ANTIGONUS	ANTIGONUS/SHEPHERD	SHEPHERD	SHEPHERD
Antigonus	CAMILLO	ANTIGONUS	ANTIGONUS	CAMILLO	CAMILLO
		ANTIGONUS	ANTIGONUS	AUTOLYCUS	AUTOLYCUS
		ANTIGONUS	ANTIGONUS/SHEPHERD	SHEPHERD	SHEPHERD
Archidamus	ARCHIDAMUS		SHEPHERD	SHEPHERD	SHEPHERD
	ARCHIDAMUS	ANTIGONUS	ANTIGONUS	AUTOLYCUS	AUTOLYCUS
	ARCHIDAMUS		CLOWN	CLOWN	CLOWN
	ARCHIDAMUS	JAILER	MARINER or BEAR	TIME	
Paulina		PAULINA	PAULINA	MOPSA	PAULINA
		PAULINA	PAULINA	DORCAS	PAULINA
Hermione	HERMIONE	HERMIONE	HERMIONE	DORCAS	HERMIONE
	HERMIONE	HERMIONE	HERMIONE	MOPSA	HERMIONE
	HERMIONE	HERMIONE	HERMIONE	PERDITA	PERDITA/HERMIONE

ROLE	ACT 1	ACT 2	ACT 3	ACT 4	ACT 5
	HERMIONE	HERMIONE	HERMIONE/CLOWN	CLOWN	CLOWN/HERMIONE
	HERMIONE	HERMIONE	HERMIONE/MARINER		HERMIONE
Mamillius	MAMILLIUS	MAMILLIUS		PERDITA	PERDITA
	MAMILLIUS	MAMILLIUS		TIME	
Perdita		EMILIA		PERDITA	PERDITA
	HERMIONE	HERMIONE	HERMIONE	PERDITA	PERDITA/HERMIONE
	MAMILLIUS	MAMILLIUS		PERDITA	PERDITA
Dorcas	HERMIONE	HERMIONE	HERMIONE	DORCAS	HERMIONE
		PAULINA	PAULINA	DORCAS	PAULINA
			DION or CLEOMENES	DORCAS	DION or CLEOMENES
		EMILIA	EMILIA (as one of the ladies)	DORCAS	
Mopsa	HERMIONE	HERMIONE	HERMIONE	MOPSA	HERMIONE
		PAULINA	PAULINA	MOPSA	PAULINA
			DION or CLEOMENES	MOPSA	DION or CLEOMENES
		EMILIA	EMILIA (as one of the ladies)	MOPSA	
Emilia		EMILIA	EMILIA	PERDITA	PERDITA
		EMILIA	EMILIA	DORCAS	
		EMILIA	EMILIA	MOPSA	
		EMILIA	EMILIA/MARINER	TIME	
Time	ARCHIDAMUS	ANTIGONUS	ANTIGONUS	TIME	
	ARCHIDAMUS	JAILER	MARINER/CLOWN	TIME/CLOWN	CLOWN
	MAMILLIUS	MAMILLIUS	BEAR	TIME	
Dion	ARCHIDAMUS	JAILER	DION	TIME	DION
Cleomenes	ARCHIDAMUS	JAILER	CLEOMENES	TIME	CLEOMENES

[*] Alternate doubling scenarios are shown. A slash (/) indicates that the doubling will occur within the same act. The chart focuses for the most part on specifically named speaking parts in the List of Characters and does not address other doubling possibilities (e.g. anonymous lords and ladies, gentlemen, shepherds, shepherdesses, satyrs, etc.).

[**] Would require absence of Shepherd from 5.3 (see 5.3.0 SD n.)

[***] Would require absence of Clown from 5.3 (see 5.3.0 SD n.)

APPENDIX C *THE WINTER'S TALE* IN PERFORMANCE: SELECTED ISSUES, SCENES, AND PASSAGES

With four excellent book-length examinations of the play's performance history available[1] – and because the present edition incorporates numerous examples from performance in the introduction, glosses, and supplementary notes – what follows is a sampling of theatrical choices relevant to selected issues, scenes, and passages.

Choices of temporal setting

Because the temporal setting seems so fluid, encompassing classical, medieval, and early modern frames of reference,[2] it is difficult to pinpoint the fictional time of the story. Expanding Bethell's view (*Study*, 32–5) that the Bohemian coastline is intended to reinforce the play's non-realistic mode, Orgel concludes (37) that the strange bit of topography should be seen as 'one of the elements stamping the play as a moral fable – like the title itself, it removes the action from the world of literal geographical space as it is removed from historical time'. Charles Kean in 1856, however, took the references to Apollo seriously enough to set his production in the Greek world of fourth-century BCE, a decision that influenced most subsequent nineteenth-century productions. Modern stagings emphasize the marvels associated with romance and winter's tales by placing Apollo's oracle in such improbable worlds as Caroline (Hall), Regency (Hands), Victorian (Syer), and Edwardian (Noble) England; Civil-War America (Bohnen); and Romanov Russia (Phillips) to name only a few theatrical choices. Writing on the 1976 Nunn-Barton revival, M. L. Greenwald notes that critics caught hints of ethnic groups such as Finnish, Eskimo, Slavic, Norse, American Indian, Cossack, Serbo-Croatian, and Antarctican and deduced a 'purposefully ambiguous milieu . . . a timeless, primitive culture in which the play's improbable events would appear naturally as elaborate folk rituals celebrating the cycle of life' (*Directions by Indirections: John Barton of the RSC*, 1985, 178).

Bohemia as contrasted with Sicilia

While there is a degree of sameness to the Sicilia setting no matter the period selected – palaces, ballrooms, aristocratic manor houses, and penthouse suites all possess a generic formal elegance and sophistication – a vast array of differences characterizes the interpretation of Bohemia: e.g. an intimation of Botticelli's 'Primavera' (H. Williams), a gypsy motif suggestive of southeast Europe (Phillips), an image of Warwickshire (Hall), a 'Watteauesque miniature' (Bohnen), a Glastonbury or Grateful Dead concert and camp-out (Hytner), an Alpine village (Kahn), a Caribbean island (Cohen), and Appalachia (Warchus).[3] Whatever

[1] In addition to Bartholomeusz, Draper, and Warren, see Patricia Tatspaugh, *The Winter's Tale: Shakespeare at Stratford*, 2002.

[2] Examples include Apollo and his oracle, satyrs, a queen who is the daughter of the emperor of Russia, a country scene that seems right out of Shakespeare's own native Warwickshire, Puritans who sing 'psalms to hornpipes', a statue supposedly created by the sixteenth-century Italian artist Guilio Romano, medieval allusions to trial by combat and Dame Partlet, contemporary mention of European courts, and Christian references to Judas, the Prodigal Son parable, and Whitsuntide.

[3] Some of these productions I have seen myself; for others I am indebted to theatre histories and reviews: for Harcourt Williams, Bartholomeusz, 181; for Hytner, Michael Billington, *The Guardian*, 25 May

the choice, the goal is to create a world markedly different from Sicilia, the contrast usually set in terms of vitality and natural simplicity.[4] Noble's use of balloons rigidly attached to neatly arranged chairs in the opening sequence became a tree-like parachute of bright colours by which Autolycus was lowered into Bohemia in 4.3 (see illustration 10, p. 14), 'a bold gesture', according to Richard McCabe who played the rogue, 'that told the audience we were now entering a different world, and not to be influenced by what had gone before'; McCabe remembers an '[almost palpable] feeling of release in the audience' when he made that descent as though they sensed a movement 'from darkness into light' (in Smallwood, *Players*, 63). Besides songs and dances,[5] a virtual explosion of colour often marks the move to Bohemia. Even when directors react against the 'arctic whiteness [of Sicilia] which has become a cliché' in revivals since Nunn,[6] the effect, at least by comparison with what follows, is dark and muted, the palette consisting of black and gray mixed with shades of amber, russet, brown, burgundy, forest green, and midnight blue (e.g. Hall, Bergman, and Kahn).

2.3.0 SD

Seemingly guided by the question 'Who's there?' (2.3.9), many editors (beginning with Capell) and most directors (following Kemble, 1802) prefer to have Leontes enter or be discovered 'alone', thus suggesting a movement from the literal prison of the previous scene to the figurative one of Leontes' own mind. Bergman, for example, not surprisingly, opted for the cinematic effect of a disembodied Leontes, lighting only the king's head on a darkened stage during the opening lines;[7] and in Bedford, upon completion of the opening speech, a solitary Leontes threw himself across a chaise, where light from a window cast a shadow resembling jail bars (Ward, 'Bedford', 39). Even in Noble, where courtiers watched the king through a gauze box – almost as though Leontes 'were a psychiatric patient under observation, . . . struggl[ing] with his insecurity and despair' (Smallwood, 'Shakespeare 1992', 349) – the effect remained one of aloneness. A radical break from this tradition was M. Davis' choice to show Leontes and his lords sitting around a table, playing cards, drinking, and looking exhausted – the efforts to distract the king from his mental anguish in vain (Ward, 'Davis', 28).

2001, 27, and Byron Nelson, *ShakB* 20.1 (2002), 15; for Warchus, Russell Jackson, *SQ* 54 (2003), 175, and correspondence with Ralph Cohen (who opined a bayou setting); for Phillips, Ralph Berry, *SQ 30*, 1979, 169; and for Bohnen, Lori Newcomb, *ShakB* 18.4 (2000), 28.

4 Kean's choice of oriental opulence for Bithynia (his substitution for Bohemia), while different from the classical Greek design he had for Sicilia, is an obvious exception to the norm of simplicity, but as a scene drawing from the promptbook at the Folger Shakespeare Library shows, the costumes seem simpler and more rustic than those found in the first half of the play.

5 Although not textually required in Sicilia, directors have often introduced music into the first act. Kean called for an elaborate Pyrrhic dance, vestiges of which lingered through the rest of the nineteenth century. The typical choice of modern directors is the stylized formality of a stately ballroom dance (e.g. Phillips, Bergman, Bohnen, and Kulick); Kahn, however, preferred a classically inspired piano-violin duet performed by Leontes and Mamillius. The music of Bohemia, more fluid and vigorous, spans such types as calypso (in Cohen), the square dancing of 'country lasses and young dudes . . . tromping' (in Wentworth; see Timpane, 18), and the raucous sound of a boom-box blaring rock and roll (see Ward, 'Bedford', 40).

6 Warren, *Staging*, 95; examples include Nunn-Barton, Howell, Eyre, and Hands. Breaking with the 'arctic white' look for Sicilia, Kulick, having opted for black formal wear in the first scene – the dresses shimmering with touches of green and blue – costumed everyone in Bohemia in white, even Autolycus. The colour change encouraged a view of Bohemia as a pristine world of innocence, especially since the erotic panels constantly reconfigured in the first half of the play were no longer visible.

7 Similarly, in Howell, a headshot of Leontes sitting all alone at a table lit by a single candle fills the screen.

3.1

In the first half of the nineteenth century, Kemble (followed by Phelps and, on occasion, Macready) relocated the scene between 2.2 and 2.3, thus allowing the action to move directly from Leontes' call for a judicial session to the trial (3.2). Kean (1856) made the scene's excision a regular practice for the rest of the century. Although Granville-Barker (1912) restored the episode to its Folio place, many modern directors choose to cut it (e.g. Brook, Bergman, Bedford, Kulick, and Lewis). When not omitted, the scene's treatment often mirrors the wonder expressed by Cleomenes and Dion, whose joint account 'lends whatever credence is necessary to the oracle before its words are read' (Bennett, 84), 'so that Leontes' rejection of [Apollo's message] is felt . . . as an actual blasphemy which draws [the god's] wrath down upon him' (Mahood, *Bit Parts*, 80).[8] Examples of such stagings include the miming of an elaborate Greek Orthodox ceremony (in William) (see Warren, *Staging*, 118); the disembodied voices of two men carrying torches on a darkened stage (in Lapine); and the use of a mirrored scrim through which the two emissaries could be seen descending an ethereally lit stairway, their lines spoken in heavily miked voices (in Kahn).

3.2

(1) Hermione's blocking: From Kemble on, many directors have had the actress, with all eyes trained on her, remain confined to one spot for most, if not all, of Hermione's defence, thus foreshadowing her appearance as a statue in 5.3. Mrs. Siddons occupied a chair and Mrs. Kean a litter (see Bartholomeusz, 53–4, 90–1, 93); Becky Peters (in Cohen) remained on a stool until the moment of her collapse; and Anastasia Hille (in Warchus) was chained to a microphone. Sally Dexter's stillness on a central rostrum (in Hall) so impressed Stanley Wells that he described her as 'statue-like' (Wells, 143); similarly, Kate Trotter (in Bedford) stood enclosed in a prison dock, 'erect and proud, never touching the railing around her' (Ward, 'Bedford', 39). The effect of isolated stillness was perhaps most shocking in Kretzu's revival where a shackled Hermione sat motionless under a single glaring light bulb, a staging that recalled the brutal interrogation scenes in Orwell's *1984* and Koestler's *Darkness at Noon* (Shurgot, 'Kretzu', 27).

(2) The delivery of Hermione's defence: Although contemporary accounts indicate that Mrs. Kean moved from despair and weakness to indignation and energy in her speeches at Hermione's trial, the usual delivery has been one of consistent stoic resolve, e.g. the 'rich quiet' and 'excessive restraint' of Lillah McCarthy (in Granville-Barker) and the 'ideal serenity' of Diana Wynyard in Brook (see Bartholomeusz, 155, 173). (For an easily available representation of this traditional approach, see Anna Calder-Marshall's performance in Howell [1980].) The final decades of the twentieth century, however, began to see a delivery often punctuated with copious weeping and/or vigorous defiance, possibly signalling a new performance norm. As an example of a fiery Hermione, Penny Downie (in Hands), 'still in elegant white', shouted her defence at Leontes, a choice which led Roger Warren to lament the degeneration of 'one of the most intensely moving and powerful scenes in Shakespeare . . . into a nagging domestic row' ('Shakespeare at Stratford-upon-Avon, 1986', *SQ* 38 [1987], 86).[9] The novel approach of Jana Tyrrell (in Whitney) had deconstructionist implications:

[8] Contrary to Felperin's claim ('Tongue-tied our Queen', 8) that the 'reported awe' of Cleomines and Dion, as the only validation of Apollo's presence in the play, militates against considering the oracle as speaking with 'unquestionable divine authority'.

[9] A similar response greeted Suzanne Burden's Hermione in Noble's 1992 production when it went on tour in 1994. Replacing Samantha Bond who had projected 'a calm, steely pride' (Smallwood, 349), Burden gave 'a more bravura emotional performance than the dignified one we have been taught to expect' (Ranald, 13); the picture accompanying the review shows a weeping Hermione, with her head down, and her hands on the chest of a clearly unmoved Leontes.

with Leontes circling her as 'an interrogator might a bound political prisoner', this queen was so stunned 'that her only defence was desperate, ironic laughter, an incredulity that reduced her husband's words and actions to comic nonsense' (Shurgot, 'Whitney', 36.)[10]

4.4.322 SD (Dance of the Satyrs)

Few productions have rivalled Kean's (1856) satyrs' dance with at least 300 individuals in 'wild disguises', all engaged in a boisterous Dionysian 'revel of organized confusion' (Cole, *Life of Charles Kean*, 173, as cited in Bartholomeusz, 93). Nunn's staging for the RSC in 1969, while not given to Kean's supernumerary excesses, nevertheless provided a 'most original, and controversial, treatment': a 'wild, whooping dance' of a 'crew of hirsute hippies in beads and skins' that seemed like an 'interlude imported from *Hair*' (the notorious, taboo-breaking musical of the late 1960s) (Draper, 66). Sometimes performed by rowdy young men given to 'foot stomping, thigh womping, and floor banging' (Ward, 'Bedford', 40), the dance is often staged with a prominent display of phallic symbols and horns (e.g. Hall and Doran). The 'testicular red balloons of gloriously discrepant dimensions' and 'phallic broomsticks' adorning Noble's yokels (Smallwood, 'Shakespeare 1992', 351) were a far cry from the 'mythical and ancient' look of Granville-Barker's horned and classically masked satyrs (Bartholomeusz, 140, 152). Perhaps, in recognition of the production challenges posed by a theatrical tradition foreign to modern audiences, the entire sequence is frequently either cut (e.g. Brook, Howell, Bergman, Kulick, and Kahn) or radically refigured to convey its sensual tenor: e.g., a tango by the actors whose main roles were those of Leontes and Hermione (Cohen); a ritualistic, primal African dance by a single male actor (Lewis, see illustration 12, p. 15); and a dumb show depicting the sexual tensions of a royal love triangle (Lapine).

4.4.609, 618 SD (The exchange of garments)

As a way of resolving this textual crux (see Supplementary note), Garrick, in his eighteenth-century adaptation *Florizel and Perdita*, omitted the entire exchange of clothing and had Autolycus attribute his later courtier-like appearance to garments stolen from a silken gamester whom he found in a drunken stupor under a hawthorn tree – an interpolation borrowed by Kemble (1802) and Phelps (1845) but dropped by Kean (1856), never to be heard again in a London theatre (Bartholomeusz, 32, 42–3, 83–4). In New York, two months before Kean's revival, the producer and comic actor William Burton, rather than ignoring the problem 'as so many producers have done and still do, . . . almost solved it with a neat piece of business suggested by' Camillo's advice to Perdita to take Florizel's hat and to 'dismantle' herself. According to a note in the promptbook, Burton called for a hat and red cloak trimmed in gold to be placed on a bench (both items presumably being part of the royal garb Florizel had removed before donning his 'swain's wearing'). Perdita took the hat, and Autolycus seized the cloak, 'which made it easy for him to assume courtly airs before the Shepherd and Clown' (Bartholomeusz, 103).[11] The Folger editors (247) offer as 'one possible expedient' having Florizel wear his rustic costume 'over his royal attire and then strip

[10] When she first essayed the role in Syer, Lise Bruneau was 'beseechingly piteous toward Leontes . . . not giving up the attempt to reach the man she loves until "Therefore proceed" [3.2.106], only then sinking into stoic resolution' (Armstrong, 31). Reprising the part six years later in Kahn, Bruneau gradually moved from pity to fury. In a post-performance discussion, she commented that the one opportunity Hermione has 'to let Leontes have it' is the trial scene; this time she held nothing back, allowing her emotions to build until she collapsed in the arms of her women, her energy spent.

[11] Perhaps in a nod to Burton's ingenuity, Lewis (2002) had Florizel hand Autolycus a gray cape that was conveniently lying on a chair; ceremoniously draping himself in the cape (with only boxer shorts underneath since he couldn't fit into the prince's tight-fitting pants) and with Florizel's wreath on his head, Autolycus then proceeded to wear his new attire with great affectation.

off the disguise once Polixenes has left, so that the garments Florizel gives Autolycus are a prince's suit'. Gentleman (1774) had implied something similar in his note to 'What I was, I am' (4.4.444): '[Florizel] throws open his shepherd's vest, and discovers his rich garment'. Whatever the interpretation by editors and directors, this seeming costume inconsistency is the type of problem that causes little or no difficulty in watching a performance, audiences getting caught up in an exchange often staged with the manic pace and slapstick of farce (e.g., Nunn/Barton, where the action was 'uproarious . . . as the other characters on stage virtually pulled [Autolycus's] trousers off him' [Draper, 67]).

5.2

'When the theatre wasted its time with elaborate place changes, one passage [5.2] used to be cut. Today we can hardly do without it' (Trewin, 266).[12] The play's penultimate scene, often faulted for narrating rather than dramatizing the reunion of Leontes and Perdita, was restored to the stage in its entirety by Granville-Barker in 1912, something not repeated until Brook's 1951 revival (Bartholomeusz, 178). Barker appreciated the preparatory function of the scene in whetting the audience's appetite for the wondrous revelation that was soon to follow, the poetry of 5.3 being heightened by its contrast with the 'fantastic prose and fun' of what Draper (40) would later call the 'courtly extravaganza' of the first half of 5.2 and the 'burlesque anti-masque' of the second half. Barker's success with the scene was largely the result of the celebrated comic talent of Nigel Playfair, who, 'having been killed off in the middle of another London play, stepped nightly across to the Savoy to play the Third Gentleman' (Mahood, *Bit Parts*, 11).

The efforts of later directors to make the expository first part of the scene lively owe much to Barker's recognition of its comic potential. Bergman, for instance, with only two gentlemen, showed the first desperately needing to relieve himself while the second, oblivious to his companion's situation, continued with his seemingly never-ending narrative. Others (e.g. Lapine, Wentworth, Bedford, Kulick, and Warchus) increase the number of speakers in order to energize the interaction with a sense of bustling movement. Lapine, in fact, filled the stage with individuals from different social ranks, each picking up part of the narrative so as to suggest a communal response to the reported wonders[13] – all while Autolycus, uttering sighs and 'Ahs', picked the pockets of unsuspecting narrators. Warchus portrayed the gentlemen as reporters positioned at pay phones on opposite sides of the proscenium arch, all frantically phoning in the news to their respective papers.[14] Although most modern directors play the gentlemen's sequence for comedy, both Brook (see 5.2.74–5n.) and Nunn revealed 'a serious edge to it', the latter by designating two of the gentlemen as Cleomenes and Dion: the result was a moment of 'delicate and moving solemnity' that recalled the reverence of 3.1, the reactions of Autolycus providing comic counterpoint (Bartholomeusz, 205, 218).

[12] Nine years earlier, however, Robert Speaight observed that the scene leaves 'more than one of us . . . long[ing] for [the gentlemen] to get to the end of their story' ('Shakespeare in Britain', *SQ* 20 [1969], 435).

[13] In 1980, Howell had attempted something equally public in her decision to show citizens hurrying along a promenade in the background and buzzing what was in the air as the Gentlemen and Autolycus occupied the foreground.

[14] I am grateful to Ralph Cohen for this example.

APPENDIX D *THE WINTER'S TALE:* A SELECT PERFORMANCE CHRONOLOGY

(See list of Abbreviations and Conventions on pp. xv–xxviii for full theatre company names)

Date	*Director, Company, Theatre, City*
1611	(15 May) The King's Men, The Globe, London
1611	(5 November) The King's Men, First Banqueting House, Whitehall
1612/13	(December-February) The King's Men, First Banqueting House, Whitehall
1618	(7 April) The King's Men, First Banqueting House, Whitehall
1623/4	(18 January) The King's Men, Second Banqueting House, Whitehall
1633/4	(16 January) The King's Men, Second Banqueting House, Whitehall
1741	Henry Giffard, Goodman's Fields, London
1756	David Garrick, *Florizel and Perdita, a Dramatic Pastoral* (an adaptation), Drury Lane, London (revived frequently until 1795)
1802	John Philip Kemble, Drury Lane, London; revived 1807 and 1811 at Covent Garden
1823	William Macready, Drury Lane, London; revived 1837, Covent Garden, and 1843, Drury Lane
1845	Samuel Phelps, Sadler's Wells, London; revived 1848, 1855, 1858, 1860
1856	William Burton, Burton's Theatre, New York
	Charles Kean, The Princess's Theatre, London
1887	Mary Anderson, Lyceum Theatre, London
1906	Max Reinhardt, Deutsches Theatre, Berlin
	Herbert Beerbohm Tree, His Majesty's Theatre, London
1910	Winthrop Ames, New Theatre, New York
1912	Harley Granville-Barker, Savoy Theatre, London
1929	Henry Jewett, Repertory Theatre, Boston, MA
1933	Harcourt Williams, Old Vic, London
1937	Ben Iden Payne, Shakespeare Memorial Theatre, Stratford-upon-Avon
1948	Anthony Quayle, Shakespeare Memorial Theatre, Stratford-upon-Avon
1951	Peter Brook, Phoenix Theatre, London
1958	Douglas Campbell, Stratford Festival of Canada, Ontario
1960	Peter Wood, Shakespeare Memorial Theatre, Stratford-upon-Avon
1965	Hugh Evans, OSF, Ashland, OR
1968	Frank Dunlop, Cressida Productions/Warner Bros., film
1969	Trevor Nunn, RSC, Stratford-upon-Avon
1975	Michael Kahn, American Shakespeare Festival, Stratford, CT (revived 1976)
	Audrey Stanley, OSF, Ashland, OR
1976	Trevor Nunn/John Barton, RSC, Stratford-upon-Avon
1978	Robin Phillips and Peter Moss, Stratford Festival of Canada, Ontario
1980	Jane Howell, BBC-Time Life, television film
1981	Ronald Eyre, RSC, Stratford-upon-Avon
1986	Terry Hands, RSC, Stratford-upon-Avon
	David William, Stratford Festival of Canada, Ontario
1987	Michael Kahn, The Shakespeare Theatre, Washington, DC
1988	Peter Hall, Royal National Theatre, London

1989	James Lapine, NYSF, Public Theatre, New York
1992	Adrian Noble, RSC, Stratford-upon-Avon (on tour in US, 1994)
1994	Ingmar Bergman, Royal Dramatic Theatre of Sweden, Stockholm (on tour in US at BAM, 1995)
	Stanislav Sokolov, Animated Shakespeare series, *WT* broadcast BBC2, 7 December 1994
1996	Fontaine Syer, OSF, Ashland, OR
	Scott Wentworth, NJSF, Madison, NJ
1997	Mike Alfreds, Lyric Theatre, Hammersmith, England
	Montgomery Davis, WSF, Platteville, WI
	Declan Donnellan, Maly Drama Theatre, St Petersburg (on tour in Plymouth, England, 1999)
	David Freeman, New Globe, London
1998	Brian Bedford, Stratford Festival of Canada, Ontario
1999	Gregory Doran, RSC, Stratford-upon-Avon
	Jon Kretzu, Tygres Heart Shakspeare Company, Portland, OR
2000	James Bohen, APT, Spring Green, WI
	Brian Kulick, NYSF, Central Park, New York
2001	Nicholas Hytner, Royal National Theatre, London
	Scott Whitney, Harlequin Productions, Olympia, WA
2002	Ralph Alan Cohen, Shenandoah Shakespeare's American Shakespeare Center, Blackfriars Theater, Staunton, VA
	Michael Kahn, The Shakespeare Theatre, Washington, DC
	Irene Lewis, Center Stage, Baltimore, MD
	Tom Rowan, Theater Ten Ten at Theater Ten Ten, New York
	Matthew Warchus, RSC, Stratford-upon-Avon
2003	Barry Edelstein, Classic Stage Co., New York
2005	Edward Hall, Propeller Company, Watermill (UK) and on tour in the United States

READING LIST

This list is a selection of some of the critical works (many of them cited in the Introduction and Commentary) which may prove helpful in further study of the play. Anthologies of criticism providing useful starting-points are those of Bloom, Hunt, and Muir.

Janet Adelman. 'Masculine Authority and the Maternal Body: The Return to Origins in the Romances', in *Suffocating Mothers: Fantasies of Maternal Origin in Shakespeare's Plays, Hamlet to the Tempest*, 1991, pp. 193–238, esp. 219–38

Paul Alpers. 'Pastoral Speakers', in *What is Pastoral*, 1996, pp. 185–222, esp. 204–22

Dennis Bartholomeusz. *The Winter's Tale in Performance in England and America, 1611–1976*, 1982

C. L. Barber. '"Thou that beget'st him that did thee beget": Transformations in *Pericles* and *The Winter's Tale*', *S.Sur.* 22 (1969), 59–67

Leonard Barkan. '"Living Sculptures": Ovid, Michelangelo, and *The Winter's Tale*', *ELH*, 48 (1981), 639–67

Anne Barton. 'Leontes and the Spider: Language and Speaker in Shakespeare's Last Plays' [1980], in *Essays, Mainly Shakespearean*, 1994, pp. 161–81

Catherine Belsey. *Shakespeare and the Loss of Eden: The Construction of Family Values in Early Modern Culture*, 1999, chap. 4

Samuel L. Bethell. *The Winter's Tale: A Study*, 1947

David Bergeron. 'Shakespeare's Romances: *The Winter's Tale*', in *Shakespeare's Romances and the Royal Family*, 1985, pp. 157–78

Harold Bloom, ed. *The Winter's Tale: Modern Critical Interpretations*, 1987

Michael D. Bristol. 'In Search of the Bear: Spatiotemporal Form and the Heterogeneity of Economies in *The Winter's Tale*', *SQ* 42 (1991), 145–67. [Revised as 'Social time in *The Winter's Tale*', in *Big-time Shakespeare*, 1996, pp. 147–74.]

Stanley Cavell. 'Recounting Gains, Showing Losses (A Reading of *The Winter's Tale*)', in *Disowning Knowledge in Six Plays of Shakespeare*, 1987, pp. 196–206

Louise Clubb. 'The Tragicomic Bear', *Comparative Literature Studies* 9 (1972), 17–30

Nevill Coghill. 'Six Points of Stage-Craft in *The Winter's Tale*', *S.Sur.* 11 (1958), 31–42

R. P. Draper. *The Winter's Tale: Text and Performance*, 1985

Katherine Eggert. *Showing Like a Queen: Female Authority and Literary Experiment in Spenser, Shakespeare, and Milton*, 2000, chap 5.

Lynn Enterline. '"You speak a language that I understand not": The Rhetoric of Animation in *The Winter's Tale*', *SQ* 48 (1997), 17–44. [Incorporated in *The Rhetoric of the Body from Ovid to Shakespeare*, 2000]

Inga-Stina Ewbank. 'The Triumph of Time in *The Winter's Tale*', *Review of English Literature* 5 (1964), 83–100. [Rpt. in Hunt, pp. 139–55]

'From Narrative to Dramatic Language: *The Winter's Tale* and its Source', in *Shakespeare and the Sense of Performance: Essays in the Tradition of Performance Criticism in Honor of Bernard Beckerman*, ed. Marvin Thompson and Ruth Thompson, 1989, pp. 29–47

Howard Felperin. 'Our Carver's Excellence: *The Winter's Tale*', in *Shakespearean Romance*, 1972, pp. 211–45

Charles Forker. 'Perdita's Distribution of Flowers and the Function of Lyricism in *The Winter's Tale*', in *Fancy's Images: Contexts, Settings, and Perspectives in Shakespeare and His Contemporaries*, 1990, pp. 113–25

Charles Frey. *Shakespeare's Vast Romance: A Study of 'The Winter's Tale'*, 1980

Harold Goddard. *The Meaning of Shakespeare*, 2 vols., 1951, 2. 262–76

Patricia Southard Gourlay. '"O My Most Sacred Lady": Female Metaphor in *The Winter's Tale*', *ELR* 5 (1975), 375–95. [Rpt. in Hunt, pp. 258–79]

Joan Hartwig. '*The Winter's Tale*: "The Pleasure of that Madness"', in *Shakespeare's Tragicomic Vision*, 1972, pp. 105–25

R. G. Hunter. *Shakespeare and the Comedy of Forgiveness*, 1965, chap. 8

Maurice Hunt, ed. *The Winter's Tale: Critical Essays*, 1995

M. Lindsay Kaplan and Katherine Eggert. '"Good queen, my lord, good queen": Sexual Slander and The Trials of Female Authority in *The Winter's Tale*', *RD* ns 25 (1994):89–118

Knapp, James A. 'Visual and Ethical Truth in *The Winter's Tale*', *SQ* 55 (2004), 253–78

Mary Ellen Lamb. 'Engendering the Narrative Act: Old Wives' Tales in *The Winter's Tale, Macbeth*, and *The Tempest*', *Criticism* 40 (1998), 529–53.

Louis L. Martz. 'Shakespeare's Humanist Enterprise: *The Winter's Tale*', *English Renaissance Studies: Presented to Dame Helen Gardner in Honour of Her Seventieth Birthday*, ed. John Carey, 1980, pp. 114–31

William Matchett. 'Some Dramatic Techniques in *The Winter's Tale*', *S.Sur.* 22 (1969), 93–108

Russ McDonald, 'Poetry and Plot in *The Winter's Tale*', *SQ* 36 (1985), 315–29. [Rpt. in Hunt, 298–318]

John Mebane, ed. *Cymbeline, The Winter's Tale, and The Tempest: An Annotated Bibliography of Shakespeare Studies, 1864–2000* (Pegasus Shakespeare Bibliographies), 2002

William R. Morse. 'Metacriticism and Materiality: The Case of Shakespeare's *The Winter's Tale*', *English Literary History* 58 (1991), 283–304

Barbara A. Mowat. 'Rogues, Shepherds, and the Counterfeit Distressed: Texts and Infracontexts in *The Winter's Tale*', *S.St.* 22 (1994), 58–76

The Dramaturgy of Shakespeare's Romances, 1976

Kenneth Muir. *Shakespeare: 'The Winter's Tale', A Casebook*, 1969

Carol Thomas Neely. 'Women and Issue in *The Winter's Tale*' (1978), in *Broken Nuptials in Shakespeare's Plays*, 1985, 191–209.

Stephen Orgel. 'The Poetics of Incomprehensibility', *SQ* 42 (1991), 431–7
Bill Overton. *The Winter's Tale* (The Critics Debate), 1989
Patricia Parker. 'Temporal Gestation, Legal Contracts, and the Promissory Economies of *The Winter's Tale*', in *Women, Property, and the Letters of the Law in Early Modern England*, ed. Nancy E. Wright, Margaret W. Ferguson, and A. R. Buck, 2004, 26–49.
'Sound Government, Polymorphic Bears: *The Winter's Tale* and Other Metamorphoses of Eye and Ear', in *The Wordsworthian Enlightenment: Romantic Poetry and the Ecology of Reading*, ed. Helen Regueiro Elam and Frances Ferguson, 2005, pp. 172–90.
Gail Kern Paster. *The Body Embarrassed: Drama and the Disciplines of Shame in Early Modern England*, 1993, chap. 5
Richard Proudfoot. 'Verbal Reminiscence and the Two-part Structure of *The Winter's Tale*', *S.Sur.* 29 (1976), pp. 67–78. [Rpt. in Hunt, pp. 280–97]
Fitzroy Pyle. '*The Winter's Tale*': *A Commentary on the Structure*, 1969
Wilbur Sanders. *The Winter's Tale* (Twayne's New Critical Introductions to Shakespeare), 1987
David Schalkwyk. '"A Lady's 'Verily' Is as Potent as a Lord's": Women, Word, and Witchcraft in *The Winter's Tale*', *ELR* 22 (1992), 242–72
James Edward Siemon. '"But It Appears She Lives": Iteration in *The Winter's Tale*', *PMLA* 89 (1974), 10–16. [Rpt. in Bloom, 47–58]
Susan Snyder. 'Mamillius and Gender Polarization in *The Winter's Tale*', *SQ* 50 (1999), 1–8 [See next entry.]
'Memorial Art in *The Winter's Tale* and Elsewhere: "I will kill thee / And love thee after"'(pp. 197–209) and '*The Winter's Tale* Before and After' (pp. 221–33), in *Shakespeare: A Wayward Journey*, 2002. [Rpt. 'Mamillius and Gender Polarization', pp. 210–20]
B. J. Sokol. *Art and Illusion in The Winter's Tale*, 1994
Patricia E. Tatspaugh. *The Winter's Tale* (Shakespeare at Stratford), 2002
Valerie Traub. 'Jewels, Statues, and Corpses: Containment of Female Erotic Power' [1988], in *Desire and Anxiety: Circulations of Sexuality in Shakespearean Drama*, 1992, pp. 25–49, esp. 42–9

Printed in Great Britain
by Amazon

84545474R00181